Shipley Proposal Guide™

Larry Newman, CPP APMP Fellow

Shipley Associates
532 North 900 West
Kaysville, UT 84037
888.772.WINS (9467)

www.shipleywins.com

4.1 Edition
2016

ISBN: 978-0-9714244-9-4

This *Proposal Guide* has three aims: 1) Help individuals and organizations win competitive business more effectively, efficiently, and consistently; 2) Offer clear guidance to business development professionals that is practical and easy to find and; 3) Record best-practice guidelines.

Help individuals and organizations win competitive business more effectively, efficiently, and consistently.

Guidelines in each entry are based upon the fundamental principles of our consulting practice:

- Align your proposal with the customer's evaluation process.
- Use a disciplined business development process that emphasizes up-front planning.
- Schedule to the process and maintain schedule discipline.
- Base your strategy on the customer's perspective.
- Focus your effort early and throughout with an early executive summary.
- Apply proven project management principles to proposal development.
- Use a disciplined, customer-focused writing approach.
- Use reviews to both control and add value to the process.

Organizations implementing these principles, supported by the guidelines in this *Proposal Guide,* will capture more business at a lower cost.

Offer clear guidance to business development professionals that is practical and easy to find.

The concept for the *Proposal Guide* originated when individuals in client organizations repeatedly asked similar questions:

Is this written down anywhere? Now it is.

Most training for sales professionals focuses on enhancing sales skills and explaining the features and advantages of their organization's products and services, but not on how to direct, prepare, or contribute to proposals. This is the first easy-to-use reference for business development professionals who are seeking practical, clear guidance on how to win competitive business in all markets, large or small, domestic or international, private sector or public. In addition, the *Proposal Guide* was selected in 2005 as the primary reference for the Association of Proposal Management Professionals (APMP) Foundation Level certification exam.

Record best-practice guidelines.

At Shipley Associates, we have observed and recommended industry best practices in business development training, consulting, and process reengineering since 1972. We endeavor to follow these principles in our consulting practice, teach them in our training practice, and share them in this *Proposal Guide.*

This *Proposal Guide,* like the companion *Capture Guide* and *Business Development Lifecycle Guide,* offers guidelines, not rules. Reality encompasses more shades of gray than can be covered in a guide intended to be concise. When in doubt, do what the customer says and be consistent.

Are the guidelines unique? Not usually.

Can you find all of these guidelines in any other reference? No.

What's New In the Fourth Edition

To reflect primarily changes in technology, 4 topic sections were updated: Electronic Submittal, Production, Proposal Management Plan, and Proposal Preparation Tools.

The following 6 topic sections were shortened and refocused on the proposal manager's role: Bid Decisions, Capture Planning, Executive Summary, Process, Proposal Strategy, and Reviews. Bid Decisions are addressed more specifically in the *Capture Guide* in Decision Gate Reviews.

The following topic sections were moved to the *Capture Guide* because they are most directly relevant to the capture manager's role: BD-CMM, Performance Based Acquisition, Persuasion, Presentations to Customers, Pricing to Win, Teaming, and Value Proposition. Pricing was refocused and re-named Costing and also moved to the *Capture Guide.*

The 5 model documents focused on various types of sales letters were also moved to the *Capture Guide* as most relevant to the capture manager or sales role. The 3 executive summary model documents are included in both *Guides,* as both the capture manager and proposal manager have key development roles. A fourth model document illustrating how a value proposition is incorporated in an executive summary was added to both *Proposal* and *Capture Guides.*

The Shipley *Proposal Guide, Capture Guide,* and *Lifecycle Guide* are now extensively cross-referenced and integrated. We hope you will find this refocused and updated Fourth Edition to be an even more valuable tool that helps you and your organization win competitive business more effectively, efficiently, and consistently.

Proposal Guidelines are designed and written to help business development professionals answer routine questions about how to win competitive business more effectively, efficiently, and consistently.

Readers seeking a broad overview of the business development process should review the *Shipley Business Development Lifecycle Guide* and additional process books.

Many of the guidelines involve the preparation of written documents, especially sales proposals. The alphabetical arrangement of the entries allows business development professionals to answer questions easily and rapidly. Numerous examples and suggestions gleaned from industry best practices make the guidelines practical and applicable to real-world competitions.

For new users of the *Proposal Guide*, consider the following time-saving suggestions:

- Use the alphabetical arrangement to find a specific topic. You may have to try several titles before you find the information you want. If you cannot find a topic, refer to the Index.

- After you have found the relevant entry, review the short summary and the numbered guidelines in the shaded box at the beginning of the entry. Then turn to the guideline that appears to answer your question.

- Read the guideline and following text. Be sure to review the examples to help clarify the guideline. Because individual prospects and competitions are unique, the guidelines are only suggestions rather than rules or legal requirements.

- Consider the context of the guideline and accompanying examples. Check to see if any notes, beginning with the word **NOTE**, add additional information about options or exceptions to the guideline.

- Turn to the cross-referenced entries if you still have questions. Cross-references have this format: *See* ACTION CAPTIONS. Entries in other *guides* include the name of the guide.

- Refer to the *Lifecycle Guide* to clarify how topics integrate with the *Shipley 96-step Business Development Process*.

- If your question involves preparing a document, check the MODEL DOCUMENTS section of the *Proposal Guide* for additional applications of the guideline.

The model documents illustrate best practices in business development and current American business English. All documents follow the guidelines as closely as possible, subject to unique aspects of the specific competition.

Different individuals, organizations, market sectors, and countries use similar and potentially confusing terms. The following terms are used in this *Guide*:

- Bid request vs. RFP, RFT, RFQ, ITT, or solicitation

- Commercial vs. nongovernment or private sector (Not meaning cost or terms and conditions).

- Customer vs. prospect, prospective customer, buyer, prospective buyer, or client.

- Graphics vs. visuals.

- *Evaluators* applies to people who read any part of a proposal. *Readers* applies to people who read non-proposal documents.

No reference book can answer every question. To help answer difficult, more specialized, or more obscure questions, refer to one of the numerous excellent books, references, or online resources available.

Acknowledgments

My thanks to the many people who generously gave advice, assistance, and support:

- The hundreds of clients from nearly 30 countries who taught me so much while I was trying to help and teach them.
- My fellow consultants who patiently reviewed multiple drafts and suggested improvements. I apologize for not being able to name all of you.
- My partners at Shipley Associates, who supported the preparation of the *Proposal Guide.*

Several people must be both thanked and named:

- Dr. Larry Freeman, for the inspiration in the original *Shipley Style Guide* (now *Franklin Covey Style Guide*), for setting standards for clarity and economy of writing that I strive to meet.
- Sonya Ellis, for graphics, page, and document design, and production management of the integrated, three-*Guide* series. Lynn Allen, Lisa Davis, Kathy Rettenberger, and Patti Ferrin for their design and editing support on this or prior editions.
- Nancy Rosen, my wife, for understanding and encouragement while I worked on all Editions.

About the author

Larry Newman is Vice President and a founding partner of Shipley Associates. He joined Shipley Associates in 1986 as a consultant and training facilitator, helping clients win competitive business in 30 countries and varied selling environments.

Mr. Newman authored all three Shipley Associates *Guides*: *Proposal Guide, Capture Guide,* and *Business Development Lifecycle Guide.* The *Shipley Proposal Guide* was awarded the Society for Technical Communication's Award of Excellence in 2008. With approximately 50,000 copies in print since 1999, the *Shipley Proposal Guide* was selected as the basis for APMP proposal management professional certification. In 2010, he authored the *Shipley Capture Guide,* 2nd Edition. Like the *Proposal Guide,* several organizations have selected it as the basis for professional capture management certification.

He has developed and facilitated numerous Shipley Associates workshops in capture planning, proposal writing and management, executive summary writing, sales writing, and costing. He is an Association of Proposal Management Professionals (APMP) Fellow, is APMP accredited at the Professional level, and has presented at more than 20 professional association conferences. He also developed the *Proposal Guide* podcast series in 2008, downloadable on iTunes.

Alphabetical Listing

Topical Listing

Proposal Writing

Sales and Capture Management

Model Documents

Abbreviations are shortened forms of words or phrases used to avoid cumbersome, lengthy phrases. Use abbreviations only when you are sure your readers will understand them.

When space is limited, abbreviations are appropriate in proposals, particularly in lists, tables, graphics, and charts. Familiar abbreviations, such as Mr., Mrs., Dr., and A.M., would be jarring if spelled out.

Abbreviations help you avoid repeating long words and phrases, but your meaning must be clear to every potential reader and evaluator.

These guidelines are limited to aspects common to sales documents. Consult a style guide for further guidance, especially when preparing scientific and technical documents.

Abbreviations

1. Use abbreviations only when you are sure your readers will understand them.

2. Define acronyms, initialisms, and other potentially unfamiliar abbreviations the first time you use them in each major section of your document.

3. Insert a list of acronyms with definitions in proposals exceeding 25 pages.

4. Develop a list of acceptable abbreviations before the kickoff meeting, and keep it current.

5. Use standard abbreviations for titles immediately before and after proper names.

6. Limit Latin abbreviations.

7. Avoid inappropriate abbreviations.

8. Use a single period when an abbreviation ends a sentence.

In general, if the word would be capitalized, then the abbreviation would be capitalized. Exceptions to this rule include DoD, written with a lowercase *o*, as used by the U.S. Department of Defense and laser and radar, which have been accepted as words. Companies and organizations may deviate from the capitalization rule when abbreviating their own name or products. Follow the convention set by the originator of the abbreviation.

Words, phrases, and units of measurement are commonly abbreviated.

Abbreviated Words

Ave.	Avenue
Bldg.	building
Mr.	Mister
Lat.	Latitude

Abbreviated Phrases

GNP	Gross National Product
R&D	Research & Development
IQ	Intelligence Quotient
PA	Public Address [System]

Abbreviated Units of Measurement

Btu	British thermal unit
km	kilometer
oz	ounce
rpm	revolutions per minute

Abbreviations include acronyms and initialisms. Acronyms are abbreviations pronounced as words:

Acronyms

BAFO	Best And Final Offer
BASIC	Beginners' All-purpose Symbolic Instruction Code
CAD	Computer-Aided Design
CDRL	Contract Data Requirements List
ESOP	Employee Stock Ownership Plan
FAR	Federal Acquisition Regulation

laser	Light Amplification [by] Stimulated Emission [of] Radiation
NAFTA	North American Free Trade Agreement
NASA	National Aeronautics and Space Administration
NATO	North Atlantic Treaty Organization
radar	RAdio Detecting And Ranging
SOW	Statement Of Work

Initialisms are acronyms formed from the initial letter or letters and pronounced as letters:

Initialisms

BP	British Petroleum
CIA	Central Intelligence Agency
DoD	Department of Defense
IBM	International Business Machines
IDIQ	Indefinite Delivery Indefinite Quantity
FBI	Federal Bureau of Investigation
MOD	Ministry Of Defence (UK)
RFP	Request For Proposal
RFQ	Request For Quote
RFT	Request For Tender
SSA	Source Selection Authority
WBS	Work Breakdown Structure

Familiar abbreviations are perfectly acceptable in sales documents. Avoid overusing unfamiliar acronyms and initialisms in sales documents. Unfamiliar, unnecessary, and over-used abbreviations can obscure meaning and project an arrogant tone.

1 Use abbreviations only when you are sure your readers will understand them.

Familiar abbreviations, often written without periods, are acceptable.

CD-ROM	CIA
ESPN	FBI
IBM	NASA
NATO	UK
UPS	USA

NASA is soliciting proposals for new and innovative propulsion systems.

Abbreviations are often used out of context in proposals due to the different education, work experience, and cultures of writers and readers.

Acronyms can be misunderstood:

ATM = Asynchronous Transfer Mode
              Automatic Teller Machine
              Air Traffic Management

Define potentially unfamiliar abbreviations.

2 Define acronyms, initialisms, and other potentially unfamiliar abbreviations the first time you use them in each major section of your document.

Style guides offer conflicting advice. Select one style and follow it consistently.

Define unfamiliar abbreviations in each major section that might be read separately. Proposal evaluators seldom read an entire proposal front-to-back. Instead, they read portions, seeking answers to specific questions.

If an abbreviation might be unfamiliar to any reader, define it. Proposal evaluators are multiple and varied. Your proposal must be clear to everyone, not almost everyone.

Select and consistently follow one of two naming conventions:

1. Write the full name followed by the abbreviation in parentheses at the first mention in each major section.

   The Royal Navy (RN) solicited proposals for two fleet oilers.

2. Write the abbreviation followed by the full name in parentheses at the first mention in each major section.

   The RN (Royal Navy) solicited proposals for two fleet oilers.

3 Insert a list of acronyms with definitions in proposals exceeding 25 pages.

Place a list defining potentially unfamiliar acronyms in larger proposals, even if most readers will not bother to consult the list.

The 25-page limit is arbitrary. The helpful tone implied is often more important than the usefulness of the list.

4 Develop a list of acceptable abbreviations before the kickoff meeting, and keep it current.

Cut editing time by developing a list of acceptable abbreviations, jargon, and other naming conventions before the initial kickoff meeting, pass it out at the kickoff meeting, and keep it current.

Consider these questions:
- How will you refer to the customer?
- What will you call your bidding team?
- Will you use U.S.A. or USA?
- What terms or words do you want to encourage or discourage using?

Contributors often conceive more unique naming conventions than you can find and fix with the *search and replace* tool in your software package. Creating and publishing a group-approved abbreviation list can reduce the amount of editing required to remove unapproved, conflicting, or potentially embarrassing items before submission.

5

Customarily, titles are placed before the name and positions are placed after the name, e.g., *Mr. Frank Nestor, Account Manager.*

Use standard abbreviations for titles immediately before and after proper names.

Titles Before Proper Names
Mr. Stephen Shipley
Dr. Jonas Salk
Prof. Edward Dean
Dr. Martin Luther King, Jr.

Titles After Proper Names
Cathy Allen, M.D.
Francis Wilkins, C.P.A.

Do not abbreviate a title that is not used with a proper name:

Not this

Several Drs. protested additional malpractice insurance increases.

This

Several doctors protested additional malpractice insurance increases.

Avoid redundant titles such as *Dr. Evan Luce, Ph.D.* Choose one title or the other: *Dr. Evan Luce* or *Evan Luce, Ph.D.*

6

Avoid a potentially arrogant tone by eliminating foreign language phrases unless addressing a customer's phrase, such as *force majeure* in a contracts clause.

Limit Latin abbreviations.

Latin abbreviations are inappropriate in most sales proposals because they suggest a stuffy, arrogant, or academic tone. Latin abbreviations are appropriate in bibliographic citations, literary, academic, and informal writing.

Use the appropriate English phrase in formal writing.

Not this

Our senior proposal consultant, Mr. Benjamin Carter, has helped numerous organizations capture new business, e.g., EADS, Lotus, BT, and BAE.

This

Our senior proposal consultant, Mr. Benjamin Carter, has helped numerous organizations capture new business, for example, EADS, Lotus, BT, and BAE.

Here are some common Latin abbreviations with definitions:

e.g. (Latin *exempli gratia*) . . . . .for example
et al. (Latin *et alibi*) . . . . and others; and elsewhere
etc. (Latin *et cetera*) . . . . . .and so on; and the rest
i.e. (Latin *id est*) . . . . that is; namely; in other words
P.S. (Latin *postscriptum*) . . . . to write after

7

In formal writing, including proposals, avoid the following abbreviations in body text: personal names, holidays, units of measurement, days, months, divisions of written works, cities, states, countries, and parts of business names unless they are part of the official name.

Avoid inappropriate abbreviations.

Personal name
Charles (not Chas)

Holidays
Christmas (not Xmas)

Units of measurement
pound (not lb.)

Days and months
Monday, December (not Mon., Dec.)

Divisions of written work
chapter, section, page (not ch., sec., p.)

States and countries
Montana (not Mont., or MT)

Parts of Business name
Shipley Associates (not SA or Shipley Assoc.)

Use B.C., A.D., A.M., P.M., No., and $ only with specific dates, times, numbers, and amounts.

400 B.C. (or B.C.E.)
10:30 A.M. (or a.m.)
3:00 P.M. (or p.m.)
A.D. 40 (or C.E.)
No. 12 (or no. 12)
$1000

8

Use a single period when an abbreviation ends a sentence.

The final decision maker is Kevin Keats, Ph.D.

However, if the sentence or clause ends with punctuation other than a period, then the other punctuation mark follows the period at the end of the abbreviation.

Will the final purchase decision be made by Kevin Keats, Ph.D.?

If your proposal arrives before 3 p.m., it will be evaluated.

Eliminate periods and spaces within most abbreviations unless convention dictates otherwise. Refer to a current dictionary, as conventions evolve.

Action Captions suggest action. Readers of an action caption should accept your ideas and begin to accept your proposal as the best solution to their needs.

While the graphic catches the reader's eye, the caption must deliver the persuasive message. Good captions interpret, inform, and persuade.

A graphic and its action caption enable the evaluator to grasp your key message without having to search the text for an explanation. Many evaluators, especially key decision makers, have little time and will skim your proposal. If the point of a graphic is not obvious, they will simply turn the page.

Place an action caption beside every graphic in your proposal, including photos, drawings, charts, graphs, tables, and even spread sheets. While not universally done in all business documents, labeling all types of graphics as *figures* makes it easier for the evaluators and will simplify proposal production.

Both evaluators and writers welcome this simplification because many graphics are combinations of photos, illustrations, tables, and charts. The alternative is to sort through identically numbered figures, tables, exhibits, and charts within the same proposal chapter.

Remember the *10-second Rule.* If readers don't get the point within 10 seconds, they will turn the page.

Labeling all types of graphics as *figures* differs from traditional technical writing practice but is increasingly accepted.

Action Captions

1. Use interpretative action captions with every graphic in your proposal.

2. Draft each action caption with three parts: the figure number, the title, and the caption.

3. Use informative titles rather than horse titles that often ambiguously label features.

4. Connect a customer benefit to the feature depicted in the graphic.

5. Quantify the benefit if possible.

6. Place action captions below the graphic.

7. Reference all graphics by figure number in preceding text.

8. Use a different typeface or style for the figure title, the caption, and the body text of the proposal.

---

1 Use interpretative action captions with every graphic in your proposal.

Graphics attract the evaluator's eye. Action captions add your *spin* or interpretation. If you do not interpret a graphic, evaluators are left to draw their own conclusion.

Good captions interpret the visual and suggest the benefit to the evaluators' organization:

Figure 1. Flexible Voice Messaging System. *You can end lost orders through dropped customer calls with our graphic operator interface and advanced networking software. Our modular design makes it easy to change or expand, improving your flexibility.*

Evaluators read proposals with much skepticism. Why risk unfavorable interpretations when you can offer a clear, supportable interpretation and explanation?

Note how the action caption in figure 1 increases the believability of the writer's claim by repeating *flexible* in the caption.

One insightful evaluator stated:

We went to the graphics and captions for the answer to our questions. If we found the answer, we didn't bother to read the text.

Many proposal professionals disagree over the proper length of an action caption. One view is to limit captions to a phrase or a single sentence. Unfortunately, short captions may omit important data or force evaluators to search the body text.

Do not worry too much about longer captions. Two to four sentences, while longer than normal, are acceptable and effective if they convey important information to the evaluator and are clear.

Captions are far more likely to be read than body text. Once a point is made in the caption, you do not have to repeat it in the body text. However, key points should be repeated for emphasis in slightly different words.

The following are additional examples of good action captions:

Figure 2. Cost of Computer Ownership Is Surprisingly High. *According to the Gartner Group, the total cost of PC ownership to the average business is approximately $5,000 per year. While the hardware capital cost has decreased, major costs associated with administration, technical* support,and end-user operations can be cut up to 30 percent when outsourced to PC Management, Inc.

Figure 3. Proven Technology for the Bishah Plant. *A few of our most significant design improvements are shown, all proven in production. You achieve a competitive market advantage while reducing operating cost and risk.*

Figure 4. Low-Risk, Six-Phase Implementation. *We have identified the key milestones and deliverables for each phase. The plan, as outlined, is flexible to permit us to incorporate changes based on our mutual review of the prior phase.*

Figure 5. Easy to Use with Minimum Training. *Queries are constructed by simply pointing and clicking on objects representing data tables and raw elements. Graphical Query Language (GQL) allows users to ask questions and receive valid answers after only 8 hours of training.*

Figure 6. Military Design Standards Increase Cost. *While military design standards for ruggedization appear to increase operational life, the low production quantity and added weight both triple acquisition cost and double operational cost versus commercial-off-the-shelf (COTS) alternatives. The minimal increase in operational life does not justify the large cost increase.*

2 Draft each action caption with three parts: the figure number, the title, and the caption.

Figure numbers are used to reference graphics in body text. Number figures sequentially in your proposal. On large proposals, number figures sequentially throughout major sections, as illustrated in this *Proposal Guide*.

When your proposal has numbered chapters or sections, insert the chapter or section number followed by the sequential figure number:

Figure 3-1.
Figure 3-2.
Figure 3-3.

Using detailed section numbers is a good idea during proposal development to facilitate coordinating text and graphics from multiple writers. The author of proposal section 3.4.5.1 would number the first graphic as:

Figure 3.4.5.1-1. *Flexible Voice Messaging System.*

However, this long figure number in the final proposal is cumbersome for the evaluator, so limit figure numbers in final proposal production to numbering within the major section. The previous example might change to:

Figure 3–12. *Flexible Voice Messaging System.*

Standard business writing convention is to discriminate figures, tables, charts, exhibits, etc. This practice can be both confusing in the normal proposal evaluation process and more difficult for proposal management and production.

For example, what do you call a spreadsheet with an inset graph or a graph with an inset table? At the risk of upsetting the writing experts, label all graphics as figures or exhibits to make it easier for both evaluators and proposal writers.

Because a proposal is a sales document, follow the figure number with an informative or interpretative title, as discussed in guideline 3.

Follow the title with an action caption that contains features and benefits and links the customer benefit to the relevant features shown in the graphic.

Connecting features and benefits is easier when a full sentence is used, or even several sentences. Phrases often contain only a benefit or only a feature:

Benefit only
Figure 3–12. Flexible Voice Messaging System. *Low cost solution.*

Feature only
Figure 3–12. Flexible Voice Messaging System. *Features graphic operator interface and advanced networking software.*

Benefit and Feature
Figure 8–12. Flexible Voice Messaging System. *Our low-cost solution is due to the graphic operator interface and advanced networking software.*

Some proposal writers and editors prefer to use the detailed section number throughout the final proposal. A compromise is to limit figure numbers to third-order section numbers in final production.

See FEATURES, ADVANTAGES, AND BENEFITS.

3 Use informative titles rather than *horse titles* that often ambiguously label features.

Labels are often ambiguous. Envision a picture of a horse in your proposal with the following caption:

Figure 7. *Horse.*

While most people laugh at this title, search your own proposals for similar examples:

Figure 8. *Organization Chart*

Figure 9. *PBX*

Figure 10. *Schedule*

See HEADINGS.

While slightly more interpretative, the generic caption for figure 8 is not much better:

> **Figure 8. Project Team.** *Our project teams are generally structured as shown.*

The following example is marginally better:

> **Figure 9. Project Team.** *Our project team is headed by a project manager. Five people report to the project manager.*

Avoid restating the obvious. Interpret the information in the graphic. Tell the evaluator *Why*, as shown in the following example:

Figure 10. Proven Team Organization. *Our project team will be structured as shown, based on the lessons learned from numerous similar previous projects. Our team is managed by a single, on-site, project manager with five direct reports. A larger span of control reduces effectiveness; fewer direct reports increases cost and lengthens response time.*

Figure 1 below shows a *horse title* as the *original* and a model action caption in the *revised* version.

Original	Revised

Figure 3-4. Buffalo.	**Figure 3-4. Buffalo No Longer Endangered.** *Cattle ranchers in Wyoming and Montana are angry at overgrazing caused by the expansion of buffalo herds leaving Yellowstone and Teton National Parks. Even elk and deer are feeling the effects of overgrazing.*

Figure 1. Avoid "Horse Titles." *The original has a horse title, stating the obvious: these are buffalo. The revised version has an informative title that is both reinforced and explained in the caption.*

4   Connect a customer benefit to the feature depicted in the graphic.

Following a basic principle of good organization, begin with the most important point to the evaluator. Captions that lead with the benefit are more customer focused than captions that lead with the feature. Benefits attract the customer's attention. Features support how the benefit is delivered. However, do not get overly concerned if the feature precedes the benefit. Captions comprising a few sentences are short enough that the evaluator will likely see the connection.

If you are struggling to identify the customer benefit, you have two possibilities:

1. You offer no customer benefit. Remove the graphic and caption from your proposal.
2. You do not know what benefits the customer is seeking. Perhaps you should not waste your time and resources bidding.

A caption should contain benefits and features and make a clear, plausible connection:

> **Figure 13. Cost-Effective Switch.** *Our in-house design makes the Bogen 480 a low-cost switch.*

Nothing in the caption makes a plausible connection. An in-house design could just as easily increase the cost. Improve the caption by specifying what feature of the in-house design leads to the lower cost. Review the captions in guideline 1 for better examples.

During proposal preparation, ask writers to draft and retain full action captions in their section text files. If writers prepare their own graphics to any degree, ask them to keep all graphics in a separate file, labeled with the detailed section number and the graphic numbered sequentially within the section. The person or persons assigned to produce the proposal are better equipped to insert graphics and captions consistently and efficiently into the final document.

The best way to develop a library of graphics and captions is to collect them from each proposal. Place them on a server that can be accessed by proposal writers and graphics support. A best practice is to develop an indexing and retrieval system that is searchable by key words and an identifying number. Maintain a link between each graphic and potential captions.

Action captions are similar to theme statements in structure. Both link benefits and features. Both are stronger when the benefit precedes the feature.

See GRAPHICS *and* THEME STATEMENTS.

Organizations that produce numerous proposals for similar products or services often maintain a library file of graphics and action captions. Retrieval is easier, but captions filed as part of the graphic are less likely to be tailored to the opportunity by proposal writers.

If graphics might be reused, place and retain a unique identifying number with each proposal graphic to facilitate retrieval. Assign a revision number whenever the graphic is modified. To avoid distracting readers, orient the identifying number vertically to the graphic in approximately 6-point type in the same position relative to each graphic.

Here is another tip to evaluate the captions in a proposal. Extract and print all captions in

the proposal. If the captions do not summarize your proposal and tell a persuasive story, they need more words and usually more benefits.

Standard graphics can often be used effectively to make a selling point if the action caption is tailored to each proposal opportunity. When boilerplate or stock graphics are kept with their action caption in the same file, writers seldom tailor them to the opportunity and seldom read them before placing them in the proposal.

5   Quantify the benefit if possible.

Captions, like theme statements, are more credible when the benefit is quantified and substantiated. Compare the following examples:

See THEME STATEMENTS.

Weaker, unquantified action caption

Figure 8-12. Flexible Voice Messaging System. *Our low-cost solution is due to the graphic operator interface and advanced networking software.*

Stronger, quantified action caption

See VALUE PROPOSITIONS.

Figure 8-12. Flexible Voice Messaging System. *Users have documented average operating cost reductions of 17 percent due to the graphic operator interface and advanced networking software.*

The second example is also more specific, citing the *average operating cost reductions* versus the more general *low-cost solution.*

Much like a value proposition, quantified benefits are more credible when the substantiation, usually supplied in supporting text, includes more of the following elements:

- **Specific.** States what is to be purchased.
- **Measurable.** Tells how much will be purchased.
- **Timed.** Cites the timing of the purchase and the savings or benefits.
- **Results Oriented.** States the result quantitatively, if possible.

Quantify benefits only when you can support your claim. Better to have a benefit unquantified than to lose credibility with customers.

6   Place action captions below the graphic.

In Western society, most readers read from top-to-bottom, left-to-right. An evaluator who spots a graphic will tend to first look below the graphic for the explanation. Normal practice for most newspapers is to place the caption below the graphic.

See GRAPHICS.

In the more sophisticated designs found in some magazines, journals, and books, the caption may be placed above or to one side of the graphic. However, the designer will still usually follow the principle of graphic

association: The caption is placed closer to the edge of the graphic than to any other item on the page, causing the reader to associate them. The principle of graphic association is illustrated in figure 2, applied to captions.

In the rapid-response mode typical of most proposal efforts, keep things consistent and simple. Place the caption in the same location relative to the graphic, preferably below, unless you are severely page limited.

7   Reference all graphics by figure number in preceding text.

All graphics, with their action captions, should stand alone. The evaluator must be able to get the point that you intended without having to read the body text.

Yet always refer to the graphic in the body text before it appears in the proposal. The approaches shown below are equally acceptable.

Some of the reasons our voice messaging system is so flexible are shown in figure 3-12.

Figure 3-12 shows why our voice messaging system is so flexible.

Place the graphic on the same or facing page to enable the evaluator to see the graphic without having to turn the page.

Change the section organization if necessary rather than force the evaluator to search for the graphic. Often evaluators do not search, and your point is lost.

8

Use a different typeface or style for the figure title, the caption, and the body text of the proposal.

See PAGE AND DOCUMENT DESIGN.

Action captions are the theme statements for the graphics. Use a different typeface or style to emphasize and differentiate the caption from body text. Because captions contain key selling points, the change of style increases the chance they will be read and remembered. Captions include the figure number, the figure title, and the explanatory text.

Different caption styles are acceptable for different proposals. Select a style for each proposal and be consistent. Most organizations adopt a consistent style for all proposals unless the style is specified in the bid request.

Using **bold** for the figure number and figure title draws the reader to the beginning of the caption. Informative titles create interest, enticing the reader to read the text in the caption. This convention is illustrated in this *Proposal Guide*.

While action caption styles may vary, consistently follow these guidelines:

1. In captions, the word *figure* should be capitalized. However, when referring to graphics in the text, even if you refer to a specific figure, do not capitalize *figure* unless it begins a sentence:

   As shown in figure 12, . . .

   Our project team organization is shown in figure 3–4.

   However

   Figure 3–4 shows our project team organization.

2. Use periods following captions that are complete sentences but not after captions that are incomplete sentences. If your captions mix complete and incomplete sentences, end all captions with periods.

3. The style of punctuation between the figure number, figure title, and caption text may vary. While all the examples shown below are acceptable, the first is cleanest while the last example is the least preferred.

Figure 3–12. Flexible Voice Messaging System.
Our low cost solution is due to the graphic operator interface and advanced networking software.

Figure 3–12: Flexible Voice Messaging System.
Our low cost solution is due to the graphic operator interface and advanced networking software.

Figure 3–12.—Flexible Voice Messaging System.
Our low cost solution is due to the graphic operator interface and advanced networking software.

Figure 3–12 Flexible Voice Messaging System
Our low cost solution is due to the graphic operator interface and advanced networking software.

INITIAL PLACEMENT

IMPROVED PLACEMENT

Figure #-#. Informative Title.
Action caption text, action caption text, action text.

Figure #-#. Informative Title.
Action caption text, action caption text, action text.

HEADING

Body text_____

HEADING

Body text_____

INITIAL PLACEMENT

Figure #-#.
Informative Title.
Action caption text, action caption text, action text.

IMPROVED PLACEMENT

Figure #-#.
Informative Title.
Action caption text, action caption text, action text.

Figure #-#.
Informative Title.
Action caption text, action caption text, action text.

When placing captions beside graphics, match line justification to the adjacent edge of the graphic.

NOTE: While the lower-right caption is easier to read, a designer wanting to lead with the caption title selected an upper-right placement with right-justified text against the graphic.

Figure 2. Visually Associate Graphics and Action Captions. *Place action captions closer to the relevant graphic than to any other page element. Placement below the graphic is recommended, but other locations are acceptable in special circumstances.*

Active and Passive Voice sentences both convey action, but active voice sentences are more persuasive, decisive, and confident. Use active voice unless you have a good reason to choose passive voice.

See FALSE SUBJECTS.

Proposals written in strong, clear language are more effective. Active sentences are usually shorter, more dynamic, and more forceful. Passive voice tends to create longer sentences. Decreasing unnecessary passive voice will shorten proposal sections.

Active voice is emphatic, decisive, and accepts responsibility for action. Passive voice weakens your message by evading responsibility and distancing you from your customer. The differences in form of active and passive voices are fairly easy to see.

Active sentences generally have three elements, usually in this familiar order:

1. An actor doing an action
2. A verb describing the action
3. A recipient being acted upon or receiving the action

Simply stated, **A** *does something or acts upon* **B**. Consider the following active sentence:

Our project manager (**A**) e-mails *(does)* a project status report (**B**).

In passive sentences, however:

1. The recipient takes the actor's place
2. The verb changes form and needs an additional helping verb
3. The actor is introduced in a *by* phrase or is omitted

Simply stated, **B** *is acted upon by* **A**. The example sentence stated passively becomes:

The project status report (**B**) is e-mailed *(is acted upon)* by our project manager (**A**).

The weakest passive sentences omit the actor. Simply stated, **B** *is acted upon*. The example sentence then reads:

The project status report (**B**) is e-mailed *(is acted upon)*.

This passive structure places the report first, leaves the project manager out completely, and thus evades responsibility. The active voice construction places the project manager first and accepts responsibility, giving the sentence greater clarity, emphasis, and credibility.

Active/Passive

1. Use active sentences unless you have a good reason to choose passive.

2. Use a passive sentence when you do not know or do not want to mention the actor.

3. Use a passive sentence when the receiver is more important than the actor.

4. Use a passive construction to clearly link two sentences.

5. Use personal pronouns and active voice to convey responsibility and clarity.

6. Convert passive sentences to active by rethinking, reordering, or rewording the sentence.

---

1   Use active sentences unless you have a good reason to choose passive.

Remember that:

- In active voice, the sentence *subject acts*.
- In passive voice, the *subject is acted upon*.

The most important reason to use active voice in sales documents is to be more convincing and persuasive. Customers are less interested in awarding a contract to an organization or person that seems weak-willed, evasive, or indecisive. Customers want the bidder to accept responsibility, make things happen, appear confident, meet requirements, and solve their problems.

Public figures often use passive voice:

The brief was filed yesterday.

Mistakes were made.

No one is responsible, least of all the speaker. The speaker appears to be an innocent bystander.

PASSIVE	ACTIVE
The baseline assessment data will be solicited in a telephone survey.	Assessors will solicit baseline data by telephone.
Monthly progress reports, key milestone reports, and a comprehensive final report will be submitted.	Our project manager will submit monthly progress reports, key milestone reports, and a comprehensive final report.
BD-CMM® can be used to determine how to extend the organization's current business development capabilities.	Management can use BD-CMM® to determine how to extend current business development capabilities.
Breathalyzer tests determine drivers' blood alcohol levels.	Police officers use breathalyzer tests to determine drivers' blood alcohol levels.
After the contract is signed, excavation will begin.	We will begin excavation after we sign the contract.

Figure 1. Examples of Passive and Active Sentences. *The active sentences are clearer and more persuasive.*

See STYLE AND TONE.

Compare the passive and revised examples in figure 1. In the first example, the active sentence names the actor and is more concise. The writing is clearer and more confident.

In the second active example, the project manager takes responsibility for the reports. In the third example we know who will use the BD-CMM. The fourth example states just exactly who you do not want to see if you drink and drive.

Writers sometimes inadvertently give life or action to inanimate objects, as in example four in figure 1. The sentence is concise but inaccurate. The test does not act, the police officer does.

Use active voice when you want to emphasize the actor. If you need to emphasize the recipient or omit the actor, then use passive voice. Passive sentences can be useful in proposals, depending upon your situation and strategy, as discussed in guidelines 2 through 4.

2 Use a passive sentence when you do not know or do not want to mention the actor.

Individuals make errors; organizations own errors. Avoid naming the actor to avoid blaming an individual. Avoid naming your organization as causing a problem if you want to emphasize the lessons learned from the experience.

No individual or organization named
The monthly status report did not arrive, but it could not be determined whether it had been misaddressed, misdirected, or misplaced.

Avoids naming responsible individual(s)
The network was deactivated for three hours.

The organization avoids responsibility
The distribution center construction was not completed on time because four weeks of unseasonably severe weather were not anticipated.

3 Use a passive sentence when the receiver is more important than the actor.

The opening or beginning of a sentence gets the most emphasis. Use a passive construction if you want to emphasize the customer benefits over the person or organization that delivers those benefits. In this instance, passive voice can improve the customer focus of the sentence.

Active voice, placing the feature before the benefit
Jenair securely attaches non-destructible assembly instructions and tools to the aircraft beneath the instrument panel to simplify fast and accurate field assembly of the aircraft.

Passive voice, placing the benefit before the feature
To simplify fast and accurate field assembly, non-destructible assembly instructions and tools are securely attached to the aircraft beneath the instrument panel at the Jenair factory.

However, passive construction is not the only option. The sentence could be reworded to emphasize the person doing the field assembly instead of the factory assembly.

Active voice, changing the actor and placing the benefit first
Soldiers can rapidly and accurately field-assemble the aircraft using the non-destructible assembly instructions and tools that are permanently attached to the aircraft beneath the instrument panel.

Who attaches the instructions (Jenair) and *where* (at the Jenair factory) are implicit and relatively less important than the benefits to the soldier.

4   Use a passive construction to clearly link two sentences.

Occasionally two sentences are linked so that key words are easily connected. In the following example, the second sentence is passive. The words *work packages* are deliberately repeated and placed close together to clarify the connection.

> Our Integrated Master Plan is composed of individual work packages. Each work package is linked to the Integrated Master Schedule and monitored by the program manager.

The active version is harder to comprehend.

> Our Integrated Master Plan is comprised of individual work packages. The program manager monitors each work package that is linked to the Integrated Master Schedule.

Making the second sentence passive smoothes the transition and improves clarity.

5   Use personal pronouns and active voice to convey responsibility and clarity.

Personal pronouns establish a personal, human tone. Personal pronouns commonly replace names of individuals or objects.

> I, we . . . . first-person
> you . . . . .second-person
> he, she, it, they . . . . third-person

See FALSE SUBJECTS.

Personal pronouns are preferred in proposals, as long as the identity of the person, team, or object is clear to the reader. Repeat the name if you think readers might not grasp the specific noun.

We and *our* are acceptable and preferred alternatives to slavishly repeating the name of your organization throughout your proposal.

We and *our* are equally acceptable and preferred when referring to teams. If you must refer to a team member, name the member. Use the same approach for teams comprising multiple divisions of a single organization or different organizations.

POOR *(Unclear Actor)*	IMPROVED
It is recommended by the lead engineer that a feed-forward sensor be added to the control system.	The lead engineer recommends adding a feed-forward sensor to the control system.
Design changes are observed to be beneficial based on the specific program selected, input from the TCO, and results of the literature review.	We have observed that design changes based upon evolving program requirements, TCO input, and our literature review would be beneficial.
Basic processes are established to track cost, schedule, and functionality, and the necessary discipline is in place to repeat earlier successes in business development opportunities with similar applications.	We have established processes to track costs, schedule, and functionality and have instituted disciplines to repeat earlier successes in business development opportunities with similar applications.
The organization is instructed to follow specific steps, involve specific personnel or departments, and adhere to a notional sequence of events in the process.	Our CEO instructed personnel and departments to follow a defined process.

Figure 2. Combine Personal Pronouns and Active Voice. *The active voice improved versions are both clearer and more concise. Additional editing, including eliminating false subjects, further clarifies the meaning.*

6   Convert passive sentences to active by rethinking, reordering, or rewording the sentence.

After converting passive sentences to active, you may need to further rethink the sentence to clarify meaning and shorten the sentence.

Passive

> Risk is assumed when implementing practices without the proper foundation being developed beneath them.

Active

> You assume risk when implementing practices without proper foundation.

> **With more editing:** Implementing practices without proper foundation is risky.

Passive

> A rigorous data evaluation program to be conducted by Smoke Busters, Inc., will yield the data needed to guide policy and the legislative changes required.

Active

> Smoke Busters will conduct a rigorous data evaluation program to guide policy and the legislative changes required.

> **With more editing:** Smoke Busters will rigorously evaluate the data to guide potential policy and legislative changes.

Passive

> Providing for improved training is the next step that will be taken in our process.

Active

> Providing improved training is the next step we will take in our process.

> **With more editing:** Next, we will deliver improved training.

Appendices, attachments, and annexes are seen as essentially similar by casual business readers but might have quite specific and different meanings to evaluators. Because each customer's meaning prevails, confirm that your understanding matches the customer's.

Webster's Dictionary, 14th ed., defines the following words as shown:

Annex: section added to a document addendum.

Appendix: additional or supplemental material added at the end of a document.

Attachment: anything added or attached.

Streamline your proposals and make them easier to evaluate by using appendices, attachments, and annexes.

1. Place content of interest to most evaluators in the body of the proposal.

2. Place content of interest to few evaluators in an appendix, attachment, or annex.

An **appendix** tends to be a self-contained document on a defined topic, attached to the main proposal but containing additional or supporting information.

An **attachment** tends to be data additions to a proposal, such as company annual reports, marketing brochures, installation lists, parts lists, test reports, requested plans and procedures, past performance testimonials, and resumes.

Annex tends to have a specific meaning to some customers. For example, the British Ministry Of Defense often uses *annex* instead of *appendix* for similar types of material.

Appendices

1. Use appendices, attachments, and annexes to streamline your proposal.

2. Limit appended material specifically to the information requested by the customer.

3. Treat requests for additional material as a sales opportunity.

4. Number or letter appendices sequentially.

5. Refer to all appendices, attachments, and annexes in the main body of your proposal.

---

1 Use appendices, attachments, and annexes to streamline your proposal.

In a proposal, assess whether the information is of interest to evaluators with differing backgrounds. Because most proposals consist of responses to a customer's questions, provide a summary answer to each question followed by support. If the support is extensive yet needed in the proposal, then consider relegating it to an appendix.

See QUESTION/RESPONSE PROPOSALS.

Short proposals are much more likely to be read, especially by senior influencers and decision makers. Government evaluators do not have to evaluate unsolicited material.

---

2 Limit appended material specifically to the information requested by the customer.

If the customer did not ask for the information, leave it out. Account executives and proposal writers often take the supermarket approach to proposal writing. That is, *"They might not know we offer a super widget, so let's tell them all about it. We might get lucky."*

Instead, include a statement like the following:

To make your evaluation easier, we have limited our response to the specific items that you requested. Should you need additional information on these or any other services, please contact . . .

List the additional information that you have available and who to contact to obtain the information. Intentionally limiting appended material eliminates the cost of gathering, preparing, and producing material that is seldom read.

If additional material is requested as a result of the evaluation, you can prepare it outside the submittal deadline, leaving more time to devote to the parts of your proposal that are more important.

3 Treat requests for additional material as a sales opportunity.

In many competitions, seller-customer contact is prohibited. If not, treat customer questions and requests for additional material as a sales opportunity while competitors are locked out.

When additional material is requested, make sure you understand the request, prepare it quickly and concisely, then present it personally, if possible. Exploit any opportunity to relate to the customer.

4 Number or letter appendices sequentially.

If your proposal sections begin with a number, letter the appendices. The reverse applies.

5 Refer to all appendices, attachments, and annexes in the main body of your proposal.

See ORGANIZATION *for a better understanding of the importance of providing a summary of appendices.*

Include short, informative summaries of the content of each appendix to tell evaluators what they contain:

> Attachment A contains our last three annual reports, as requested in your RFP.

If the appendix is extensive, draft a paragraph that summarizes the key points and previews the content. Most readers will accept your summary and will not read any part of the attachment.

The prior example could be strengthened if necessary to support a key selling point:

> Attachment A contains our last three annual reports, as requested in your RFP. The 50 percent annual increase in sales over the past 3 years demonstrates the increased demand for our services. Please note the stability of our management and financial performance, further supporting our low-risk approach.

Bid Decisions

Bid Decisions are aimed at eliminating opportunities or sales leads that you have a low probability of winning, permitting greater focus on opportunities that can be won. Consider splitting the bid decision into three distinct milestones: pursuit, bid, and bid validation.

For a better perspective on business development process milestones, *see* PROCESS *and* DECISION GATE REVIEWS, *Capture Guide*.

Decision Gate reviews are milestones Proposal managers are primarily focused on bid decisions, but capture managers.

Bid decisions are Decision Gate reviews triggered by customer actions at which senior management determines whether to advance, defer, or end the pursuit.

Bid decisions hinge on whether you have the capability or can obtain the resources to pursue and subsequently capture an opportunity.

Three distinct bid decision milestones include **pursuit**, **bid**, and **bid validation**.

A positive **pursuit** decision initiates preparation of the capture plan. A positive **bid** decision initiates preparation of the proposal plan. A positive **bid validation** decision initiates the final proposal kickoff meeting and the full proposal preparation process.

Improving your bid decision gate discipline is one of the most effective ways to improve win rates. Improved bid/no-bid discipline can double or triple win rates, while extensive training and coaching to improve proposal quality might lead to 15 to 20 percent improvements.

Explain no bid decisions to customers in a manner that enhances your future or immediate position. Enhance your future position by citing why your organization is unable to meet the requirements, quality standards, or expectations of either the customer's or your organization. In this

example, the seller does not offer the requested service:

> Wee Barks Doggie Daycare designed our facilities and services to meet the needs of dogs under 10 kilos. Until we can offer identical quality boarding services to larger dogs, we recommend you consider Wolf Works, a facility with similar quality standards.

In these examples, the seller seeks to modify the bid requirements:

> We are unable to prepare the quality solution and proposal that you expect by April 1, but we can prepare a quality bid if you extend the proposal due date to April 15.

> We cannot manufacture and deliver 10 systems within 6 months due to prior customer commitments. If you can accept delivery of 3 systems per month, commencing in month 4, we can submit a competitive bid.

Individual's bid recommendations are often influenced by job function. Proposal professionals focus on the immediate proposal—not bidding *losers* eliminates futile work, and winning offers limited monetary reward. Sales professionals see proposals prepared by someone else as free, the win rate on no-bids is zero, the win rate on the worst submittal is greater than zero, so what's to lose? Only senior management can balance the benefits, probability of winning, risks, direct bid costs, opportunity costs, and differing recommendations.

Bid Decisions

1. Use the pursuit decision to verify the lead fits your strategic direction and capability and to initiate capture planning.

2. Use the bid decision to verify you are positioned to win before committing to an expensive proposal effort.

3. Use the bid validation decision to ensure *show stoppers* are addressed.

4. Establish clear inputs, outputs, and responsibilities for each decision milestone.

5. Make all bid decisions promptly.

6. Tailor the process to your organization and the value of the opportunity.

---

1   Use the pursuit decision to verify the lead fits your strategic direction and capability and to initiate capture planning.

Use compatibility grids, checklists, weighted matrices, and decision trees to improve bid decisions. While tools will not make your decision, they often highlight what you do not know.

A positive pursuit decision initiates capture planning and preparation of the capture plan.

A generic compatibility grid is shown in figure 1. Plot leads on a grid according to their relative match with existing products and services on one axis and existing markets and customers on the other axis.

The plot highlights leads outside your core business that often carry higher risk. Typical questions for a pursuit decision checklist include the following:

- Is the lead within our business area?

- Does the lead fit within our strategic plan?

- To what extent are we known to the customer?

- Has the customer budgeted for the purchase?

- Do we have local representation?

- Who created the customer's vision for potential solutions?

- Do we understand who has the decision power and influence?

See CAPTURE PLANNING.

- Do we have any current or potential *coaches* or sponsors in the customer's organization?

- Is there an incumbent? Are the incumbent or others already favored?

- Do we have any competitive advantage, discriminators, or value-added aspects?

- How will the lead affect our existing business, positively or negatively?

- What resources are required for capture and are they available?

- What are the risks of bidding? Or not bidding?

- Can we win? How or why could we lose?

- Is the lead potentially profitable short-term or long-term?

Spending prior to the pursuit decision is relatively small. Because industry averages show that 20 percent of bid and proposal (B&P) funds are spent from pursuit to the bid milestone, a positive pursuit decision is essentially authorizing 20 percent of the opportunity's B&P funds for capture activities.

MARKET AND CUSTOMER MATCH

Sector	Match	Pursuit Indication	Probable Action
1	Similar product/ Similar market	Strong	Know product, market, and customer. Focus on competition.
2	Similar product/ New market	Caution	Learn the market. Establish your company in the market before focusing on the competition.
3	New product/ Similar market	Caution	Make sure you have a product to meet the need of your customer base, then focus on the competition.
4	New product/ New market	Weak/ Success unlikely	Drop. If you pursue, it will require a detailed plan and far more resources than leads in sectors 1, 2, and 3.

Figure 1. Lead Compatibility Grid. *Subjectively gauge and plot each lead relative to recently delivered orders. Beware of the customer who says, "I want another just like the last one, except . . . "*

2

Use the bid decision to verify you are positioned to win before committing to an expensive proposal effort.

Many of the questions asked at the bid milestone are similar to those listed under the pursuit milestone, except decision makers expect a more detailed response.

See PROPOSAL MANAGEMENT PLAN.

A positive bid decision initiates preparation of the proposal management plan.

After spending capture money on positioning activities, how successful were you? Consider adding these questions to the earlier list:

- To what extent have we influenced the customer's requirements?

- Does the customer rely on us for input and help?

- Do we know the competitors and their likely approach?

- Are there any surprises in the draft requirements? Do we know why?

Another approach is to use a bid decision tree like the one shown in figure 2. The usual problem with decision trees is what to do when the answer is not a clear *Yes* or *No*.

Many people remember a competition that was won despite negative indicators that suggested a no-bid decision. We conveniently forget the losses. Ignoring no-bid indicators increases the risk of losing. If you must proceed, compensate with additional, quality resources.

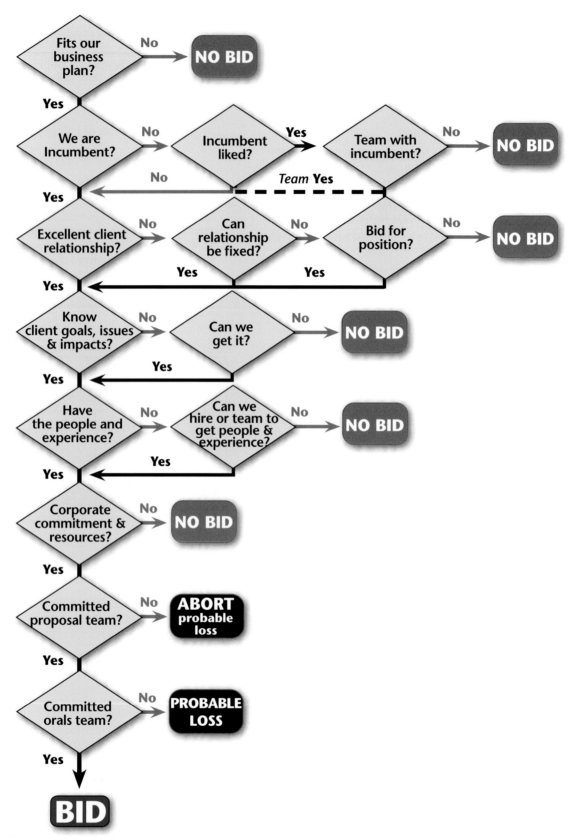

Figure 2. Bid Decision Tree. *Decision trees add discipline to the decision process. Tailor the tree to your organization. Be careful that you do not devolve into adapting the facts to fit the decision you want.*

3

See KICKOFF MEETINGS.

Use the Bid Validation decision to ensure *show stoppers* are addressed.

Show stoppers include changes in requirements that you cannot meet, unacceptable terms and conditions, unreasonable schedule, unacceptable performance warranties or penalties, or reliable information that the selection is wired. A positive bid validation decision initiates the final proposal kickoff meeting.

4

Establish clear inputs, outputs, and responsibilities for each decision milestone.

The inputs and outputs for the pursuit decision, bid decision, and bid validation decision are summarized in figure 3. All are generic and must be refined for each organization and for the size and value of the opportunity to the organization.

Clearly establish the level of authority required for each decision and who will make the decision.

PURSUIT DECISION

Inputs
Strategic plan
Annual business plan
Customer's strategic direction
Identified leads/opportunities

Outputs
Strategic fit agreed
Capture manager assigned
Capture plan to be prepared
Initial budget set
Tracking and review process set

BID DECISION

Inputs
Customer's strategic direction
Customer's needs and wants
Draft bid request
Current capture plan
Competitive assessment
Win strategy
Positioning effectiveness report

Outputs
Strategic fit confirmed
Proposal manager assigned
Proposal plan to be prepared
Proposal strategy to be prepared
Initial proposal budget set
First draft executive summary assigned
Solution overview assigned
Boilerplate and proof to be assembled
Tracking and review process set
Risk assessment assigned

BID VALIDATION DECISION

Inputs
Final bid request
Current capture plan
Current proposal plan
Draft executive summary
Solution overview
Boilerplate and proof examples
Risk assessment

Outputs
Approved capture plan
Approved proposal plan
Draft executive summary
Writers' packages (assignments) set
Proposal kickoff set
Tracking and review process set

Figure 3. Pursuit, Bid, and Bid Validation Decision Inputs and Outputs. *Customize each list for your organization. Revisit any of these decisions if inputs change significantly.*

5

Make all bid decisions promptly.

Establish clear guidelines for time limits and decision authority. Establishing a set time to consider all bid decisions lets everyone know what is required to get a prompt decision. Bid decisions tentatively conveyed to the proposal team lead to halfhearted efforts.

In one competition, a major systems company had delayed the bid decision. They had assigned 20 book bosses, giving them desks in a large bid preparation room. Seldom were more than 4 desks occupied. None of the book bosses thought they would really submit a bid.

6

Tailor the process to your organization and the value of the opportunity.

Commercial organizations with a short sales cycle usually consolidate the bid and bid validation into one milestone. When the sales cycle is 5 to 10 days, compensate by establishing and managing to explicit pursuit and bid parameters.

Organizations lacking clear bid parameters and management oversight exhibit excessive, unproductive proposal activity.

Business capture effectiveness improves when decision authority is clear and proportional to the value of the opportunity. Value is a function of the size, profitability, and follow-on potential of the opportunity.

Capture Planning is the process of identifying opportunities, assessing the environment, and implementing winning strategies oriented toward capturing a specific business opportunity. Consistently successful capture planning requires a written, action-oriented capture plan.

See Bid Decisions *and* Process.

This topic is written from the perspective of a proposal manager who is NOT concurrently assigned to the capture manager role. For an in-depth understanding of capture planning, refer to the *Shipley Capture Guide*.

See Model Documents 1-5,11,12, *Capture Guide.*

The aim of capture planning is to position the customer to prefer your organization and your solution to the exclusion of all competitors or to at least prefer you prior to any proposals being submitted.

Some commercial organizations use the terms capture plan and account plan interchangeably. However, many account plans are not opportunity specific and may be merely an allocation of the organization's revenue objective.

Capture planning is an opportunity-specific process following the pursuit decision gate milestone that continues in parallel with proposal planning and preparation until the opportunity is awarded.

Assign an individual to the capture manager role with the responsibility to win the opportunity, manage the capture planning process, and manage the capture team triumvirate. This triumvirate comprises the capture manager, program manager, and proposal manager. Note that roles are not necessarily positions, and an individual might assume multiple roles and support multiple opportunities.

Envision a capture plan as a framework, a series of folders or *buckets* where the capture manager assembles and organizes opportunity-specific data by topic. While the original capture plan medium was a written document, many organizations have evolved to presentation formats to facilitate collaborative reviews and updates and web-browser formats to facilitate collaborative development and sharing among virtual teams.

Capture Planning

1. Advocate a capture planning discipline to capture new business more efficiently.
2. Use the capture plan to jump-start the proposal planning process.

1 Advocate a capture planning discipline to capture new business more efficiently.

Capture planning offers benefits to everyone involved:

- **Sales and business development professionals** who orchestrate organizational resources use the capture plan to specify the needed positioning actions.
- **Senior managers** have a mechanism to leverage limited business development resources to most efficiently win business.
- **Proposal managers** slash proposal planning time, improve proposal quality and efficiency, and increase win rates.
- **Participants** stay committed, knowing their efforts are not being wasted.

Capture planning nests efficiently within the typical business development and planning process, as illustrated in figure 1. Business capture efficiency and effectiveness are improved when all employees have consistent information and communicate consistent messages to customers. Much of the information in one plan can be reused in subsequent plans.

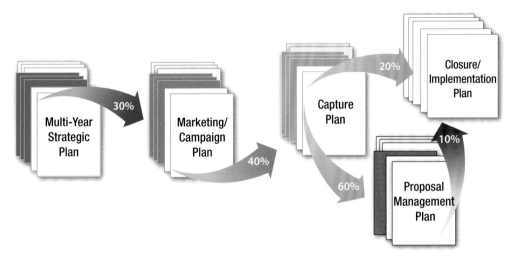

Figure 1. Capture Planning Improves Capture Efficiency. *Much of the data in each plan can be reused; it transfers or flows into the next plan. While the estimates vary, approximately 60 percent of the capture plan data is needed and resued in the proposal management plan.*

2

See STRATEGY, *Capture Guide.*

Use the capture plan to jump-start the proposal planning process.

Relying on the capture plan to quickly prepare the initial proposal management plan both saves time and presents a consistent message to the customer. In the absence of a capture plan, the newly assigned proposal manager starts from scratch, often with little help and under severe time constraints.

Capture plans and proposal management plans have the common elements illustrated in figure 2. Information on the customer, the requirements, and competitors transfers directly. The capture strategy needs to be extended or converted into a proposal strategy. Only the proposal outline, proposal preparation schedule, and the writer's packages need to be created.

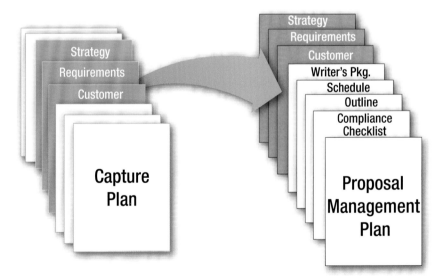

Figure 2. Base Proposal Management Plan on the Capture Plan. *A current capture plan effectively front-loads the proposal management plan. With approximately 60 percent of the information transferring from the capture plan, convert the capture strategy to a proposal strategy and add proposal-specific material from the bid request. Because the proposal submittal date is set by the customer, a shorter planning interval prior to kickoff leaves more time to develop a winning proposal.*

Choosing Correct Words makes sales documents more persuasive, effective, and easier to read. Common word problems include wordy phrases, incorrect words, and words with more than one meaning.

Good writers are always looking for resources to improve their writing and word usage. Participants in proposal training workshops often ask, "Can you give me some good words I can use in my proposals?"

No magic formula will turn your sales documents into models of effective persuasion. However, the following guidelines, derived from principles of good writing, extensive proposal writing experience, and recommendations of professional writers, will help you improve your ability to write persuasively.

Choosing correct words is important. Selecting the wrong word has several negative impacts in sales documents:

- Readers question your literacy. If you seem illiterate, then your facts might also be questionable.

- Readers question the possible working relationships. If you cannot communicate clearly in your proposal, perhaps you cannot communicate clearly on the proposed project.

- You increase your project risk when using incorrect or imprecise words in legal documents. Courts tend to support the word on the page, not what the author claims to have intended.

A broad range of word problems is discussed in this section. Choosing incorrect words reduces the persuasiveness of your sales documents. Worse yet, incorrect words can increase your risk, turning a profitable opportunity into a loss and a customer into a competitor's customer. Writers and editors must recognize and choose correct words.

Choosing Correct Words

1. Simplify or replace long words and wordy phrases.

2. Use the correct word in context.

3. Use the same words in the same context.

4. Revise words or phrases that could have more than one meaning.

5. Replace nominals with verbs or adjectives to make sentences more direct, concise, and easier to read.

6. Use precise, powerful, descriptive verbs.

7. Use *grabbers, transitions,* and *clinchers* effectively and appropriately in your proposals and presentations.

8. Avoid words and phrases that increase contract risk.

1

See CLICHES, JARGON, GOBBLEDYGOOK, *and* REDUNDANT WORDS.

Simplify or replace long words and wordy phrases.

Use small words. Simplicity counts. Long words tend to raise suspicions. The more simply an idea is presented, the more understandable and credible to more people.

Replace long words with shorter words if they have the same meaning. Just because *utilize* has more letters than *use* does not mean you are smarter. Use *use.* Wordy phrases use too many words to express an idea. Wordy phrases are similar to redundant words, gobbledygook, and cliches. Wordy phrases can be understood while gobbledygook is unintelligible. Overuse often turns a wordy phrase into a cliche.

Confirming our conversation . . .

Please do not hesitate to call.

We are pleased to present our proposal for . . .

Thank you for the opportunity to present our proposal for . . .

At best, wordy phrases are clumsy and obscure meaning. At worst, wordy phrases deemphasize or hide key ideas and prompt customers to tune out and select another bidder.

Common wordy phrases and recommended replacements are listed in figure 1.

WORDY PHRASES *with Simplifications*		
a large proportion of. . . . . many	in spite of the fact that . . . . .although	period of time. . . . . interval/period
along the lines of . . . . like	in (with) reference to . . . . . . .about/concerning	preowned airplane . . . . .used airplane
as a general rule. . . . . .usually/generally	in the event that . . . . if	prior to. . . . . before
as a result of. . . . . because	in the final analysis . . . . finally	put in an appearance. . . . . .appear
assuming that . . . . .if	in the nature of . . . . like	range all the way from . . . . range
at a later date in time. . . . . later	incendiary device . . . . bomb	reduced to basic essentials
at all times. . . . . .always	is comprised of . . . . comprises	(fundamentals) . . . . . essentials/fundamentals
at this moment in time . . . . now	is now employed . . . . works	reported to the effect . . . . reported/said
at this time. . . . . now	it is clear that. clearly	revenue enhancers. . . . . taxes
at which time. then	it is often the case that. . . . . often	selected out . . . . fired
be cognizant of . . . . know	kept an eye on. . . . . watched	subsequent to . . . . after
beyond a shadow of a doubt. . . . . . . doubtless	leaves much to be desired. . . . . poor	take appropriate measures . . . . .act
by virtue of the fact that . . . . because	make contact with . . . . meet	there is no doubt that. . . . . doubtless/no doubt
called attention to the	negative savings. . . . . .debts	to summarize the above. . . . . .in summary
fact that . . . . .noted/reminded	notwithstanding the fact that. . . . . . .although	until such time .until
come to a decision as to . . . . .decide	of considerable magnitude . . . . . big/large/great	was of the opinion that . . . . .thought
come to an end .end	on a few occasions . . . . .occasionally	went on to say. added
correctional facility . . . . prison	on account of the fact that. . . . . .because	with full approval. . . . . approved
detailed information . . . . .details	on the grounds that. . . . . because	with reference to . . . . about
economically deprived. . . . . poor	on the part of. by/for	with regard to . . . . .about/regarding
few in number . . . . few	on two different (separate) occasions . . . . .twice	with the exception of . . . . .except
for the reason that . . . . .because/since	owing to the fact that . . . . .since/because	with the object of. to
from time to time . . . . occasionally	in consideration of the fact . . . . because	with the result that. . . . . .so that
have the ability to . . . . can/be able	in light of the fact that . . . . .because	without variation . . . . .constant/stable
in conjunction with. . . . . .and		

Figure 1. Some Wordy Phrases with Simplifications. *Use the shortest word or phrase possible without changing the meaning.*

2

Assure, ensure, and *insure* (as shown in figure 2) mean to make certain or guarantee. However, in this *Proposal Guide,* the definitions given for these words are the ones typically used in proposals. The definition of these words also changes by country. Use each word consistently in your proposal and define your meaning if necessary.

Will and *shall* (as shown in figure 2) are often controversial and used interchangeably. Understand each customer's meaning.

See INTERNATIONAL PROPOSALS.

Use the correct word in context.

English is filled with deceptive word-pairs that are nearly identical but refer to unrelated concepts. A few, but not all, of the word-pairs commonly misused in proposals are listed in figure 2. Please refer to a good style guide for additional examples, preferably one prepared for business writers.

Words are often out of context in proposals due to the different education, work experiences, and the cultural differences of writers and readers. Education and work experience affect our understanding of words.

Acronyms can be misunderstood:

ATM = Asynchronous Transfer Mode
     Automated Teller Machine
     Air Traffic Management

Jargon can be used out of context:

Consideration: After due consideration, we will complete the project.

A layman might interpret consideration as meaning *careful thought.* A lawyer might interpret consideration as meaning *payment.*

Cultural differences lead to the phrase referring to the United Kingdom and the United States as, *"Two countries divided by a common language."* Native speakers from France and Canada use French differently. Spanish varies greatly among Spain and numerous Central and South American countries. The same applies to Portuguese spoken in Portugal and Brazil.

Confusion may result from English speakers who adopt words from other languages. The original meaning in either language may change over time. Further confusion results from words that sound and may even be spelled identically but have radically different meanings.

3

Use the same words in the same context.

Consistency matters. Use the same word repeatedly—you will be less confusing and more likely to be remembered.

However, the correct word for a context might be new. People like novelty. So seek to use words that gain attention and then use them consistently.

Discriminators are memorable if the word prompts a new take on an old idea. The combination of surprise and intrigue creates a compelling message. *Maximum maintainability* is less compelling than *easy to fix.*

Educators emphasize repetition because it is effective. Advertisers emphasize repetition because it is effective. Emulate them.

Changing the word, introducing a synonym for variety, frequently confuses the reader or listener. Readers skim, and listeners tune out. You might be sick of the word or phrase, especially if you have multiple revisions and rehearsals, but your audience might be hearing it for the first time.

See STYLE AND TONE.

Using different words with the same meaning is a style choice that might demonstrate your intelligence. However, readers and listeners might perceive it as an arrogant and off-putting tone.

4 Revise words or phrases that could have more than one meaning.

Words or phrases can have different meanings due to context or honest misunderstanding. The following examples illustrate confusing, multiple meanings.

1. Using a word out of context.

   Federal Bank can speed data transfer among branches with a modern ATM network.

Bank executives accustomed to ATM meaning *automated teller machines* might be confused about a telecommunications proposal referring to networks using asynchronous transfer mode protocol.

2. Using a word correctly that may be misunderstood by the reader.

All work will be billed bimonthly.

All work will be billed semimonthly.

The ambiguous *bi-* can mean either twice within a time period or every other time period. Semimonthly has always meant twice a month but suffers from confusion associated with bimonthly. Avoid the confusion by saying twice a month or every other month.

Figure 2 lists frequently confused words. If you suspect that your customer could misunderstand the meaning, use a word or phrase that cannot be misunderstood. Being clear can keep you in the competition and out of court.

CHOOSE CORRECT WORDS

accede .... agree to	infer ....to draw a conclusion
exceed ....to surpass	irregardless ....(do not use)
accept .... to receive	regardless.....................................(adj) heedless; (adv) despite everything
except ....excluding	it's .... contraction for *it is*
adapt...to adjust to	its ....possessive
adopt ....to accept formally or to take as one's own	loose ....unattached
affect .... (v) to produce an effect upon	lose .... to suffer loss
effect............................... (v) to bring about, (n) result	momentarily..for a moment (*not* in a moment)
among ....more than two involved	precede... to go before
between.. two involved	proceed... to begin or continue
appraise ....to give or estimate value	presently .... soon
apprise .... to tell or notify	at present...now
assure .... give confidence to	principal .... main, chief, money
ensure ....to make certain	principle... rule, belief
insure ....financial guarantee	refute ....to prove wrong (*not* deny, disagree, or contradict)
beside .... alongside	shall...obligatory in RFPs
besides .... also	will ....best efforts in RFPs
biannually *(avoid)*.................................... twice per year	cite ....to call; to appear; to quote;
biennially *(avoid)*.................................every other year	*or* to name, praise, or call attention to
bimonthly *(avoid)*...............twice a month or every other month	sight...vision
semimonthly *(avoid)* ....twice a month	site ....a location/place
can ....ability, permission, theoretical possibility	stationary ....fixed
may.. permission, possibility	stationery ....writing supplies
complement .... completing or supplementing	superlatives ....(for example: very, extremely)
compliment ....expression of praise	*Remove superlative adverbs and replace with strong words like* **excellent** *or*
continual...repeated	**outstanding.** *Superlatives are often perceived as presumptive and arrogant.*
continuous..uninterrupted	than.. comparison
council ....(n) a group	then .... at that time
counsel...................................(n) advice, (v) to advise	that *(defining or restrictive)* ....**example:** The computer
	that is broken is on the desk.

CHOOSE CORRECT WORDS	
credible ....believable	which *(nondefining or nonrestrictive)* .... **example**: The computer, which is broken, is on the desk
creditable .... praiseworthy	
credulous ....gullible	their..possessive
discreet ....tactful or prudent	there .... *(adv)* showing location
discrete ....separate or individual	they're..contraction of *they are*
disinterested..impartial	toward/towards ....Different form of the same word: *toward* usually American usage, *towards* usually British usage
uninterested ....not interested	
eminent ....prominent	unique..only one (*Nothing is almost unique.*)
imminent .... in the immediate future	who's..contraction for *who is*
fewer ....numbers	whose ....possessive
less ....amount	would..certain, 100 percent
flammable.. able to burn	probably would...very high, 80 percent
inflammable *(avoid)* .... able to burn *and* not able to burn	could...reasonably high, 50 percent
forward ....at or near the front	might .... moderate, 30 percent
foreword ....introduction to a book	you're.. contraction for *you are*
impact. *(n)* collision , force of collision, effect or impression made	your..possessive
impact .... *(v)* to pack together, strike forcefully	
(Questionable usage: to have an effect or impact)	
imply..to suggest	

Figure 2. Choose the Correct Word. *While far from complete, many of the words misused in sales documents are listed above. Please refer to a quality style guide or dictionary for a more exhaustive list and more extensive guidance. Note: Rather than listing in alphabetical order, words with similar meanings are grouped.*

5   Replace nominals with verbs or adjectives to make sentences more direct, concise, and easier to read.

A nominal is a word or group of words that function as a noun. Many proposal writers turn verbs into nouns, making the sentence more distant from the reader. For example, We had a proposal team meeting, is less direct and concise than, Our proposal team met.

Verbs are the most powerful and direct part of speech. Make your proposal writing more powerful, efficient, and easier to read by using verbs or adjectives to make your point, rather than nominals.

Converting prepositional phrases to adjectives is another way to make your sentences more direct and concise. Position the adjective in front of the noun and eliminate the preposition.

The examples in figure 3 show how statements become more powerful when nouns are replaced by adjectives, and when adjectives are replaced by verbs.

POOR EXAMPLE	BETTER/BEST EXAMPLE
Our project manager is the point of contact for new task orders. *(noun phrase-nominal)*	**Better:** Our project manager is the contact point for new task orders. *(adjective & noun)* **Best:** Contact our project manager for new task orders. *(verb)*
Completing the bottling plant after December 4, 20XX, would be in violation of the contract. *(nominal)*	**Better:** Completing the bottling plant after December 4, 20XX, would violate the contract. *(verb)*
The Shipley 96-Step Process has wide applicability for a variety of organizations. *(nominal)*	**Better:** The Shipley 96-step process applies to a variety of organizations. *(verb)*
Team HAWK fully supports the separate use of appropriate performance metrics for assessing performance of Third Level Maintenance tasks.	**Better:** Team HAWK fully supports using performance metrics to assess Third Level Maintenance tasks. *(eliminating the prepositions)* **Best examples:** *(State item warranting emphasis first, either using metrics or assessing performance)* Team HAWK supports using metrics to assess Third Level Maintenance task performance. Team HAWK will assess Third Level Maintenance task performance using metrics.

Figure 3. Simplify Sentence Construction. *Convert nominals to verbs or adjectives. Convert prepositional phrases to adjectives or adverbs. Nominals are words or groups of words that function as nouns. Shifting to a verb, adverb, or adjective construction is more emphatic and easier to comprehend. In figure 3, note how changing the verb* connected *to increase is truer to the intended meaning.*

6   Use precise, powerful, descriptive verbs.

Proposal writers often use general, imprecise, and even wimpy verbs that obscure meaning and increase sentence length. Search your proposals for verbs like allow, allow for, permit, provide, provide for, perform, and ensure.

Literally, do you mean to give the customer or yourself permission to do something? Reword the phrase using the more powerful and precise word that is often hiding in the sentence.

Figure 4 demonstrates improved constructions.

POOR	BETTER
Consideration is being given for . . .	We are considering. . . ; We considered . . . or, Consider . . .
We will provide opportunities for training.	We will train . . .; We train . . . or, Training is offered . . .
Bid/no-bid milestone reviews provide for improved decision making.	Bid/no-bid reviews improve bid decisions.
Our project manager performs task reviews.	Our project manager reviews tasks.
Our project management process, which is ISO-certified, allows for improved management decisions.	Our ISO-certified project management process improves management decisions.
The e-Entry system allows for the accurate entry of new orders by customer service representatives.	Customer representatives can accurately enter new orders using the e-Entry system.

Figure 4. Use Powerful, Accurate Verbs. *Replace imprecise verbs like* allow, provide, permit, perform, *and* ensure, *with a stronger, more accurate verb.*

The best proposals describe what the customer wants to hear, speaking directly to their issues, fears, hopes, and dreams. People forget what you say but remember how you made them feel. Are you perceived as the *safe choice*, or the *trusted team of colleagues* working with *reliable, familiar, proven products?*

Some of the most effective verbs prompt powerful, emotional, visual images that are more effective than a proposal graphic. *Imagine . . .* might be the most powerful verb in the English language, unless used inappropriately. Novels can be more powerful than films because the reader's imagination is more specific, visceral, and vivid than the screen image. Dr. Martin Luther King's *I have a dream . . .* speech phrasing connected with millions of individual's dreams without the need to precisely describe those dreams.

While not correct grammatically, consider using the future tense (*will train*) the first time you mention an event, then shift to the present tense (*train*).

Grammatically incorrect but stronger

To reduce transition risk, we will train all employees. Employees are trained to use the new workstations, get Help Desk assistance, and report network outages.

Grammatically correct but weaker

To reduce transition risk, we will train all employees. Employees will be trained to use the new workstations, get Help Desk assistance, and report network outages.

The grammatically correct version is weaker and longer.

7   Use *grabbers*, *transitions*, and *clinchers* effectively and appropriately in your proposals and presentations.

Grabbers are designed to capture a customer's attention without offending. Grabbers include headings, slogans, salutations, opening challenges, and theme statements.

Written and spoken language has a rhythm and texture. A string of words that have the same first letter, ending letters, sound, or cadence is more memorable. Alliteration and rhyme make a phrase memorable, within reason.

However, rare but deliberate violation of language rules is also memorable. Apple Computer's *Think Different*, was memorable. Often effective proposal grabbers are subtle

variations of popular advertising catch phrases. A proposal for a signal operator training simulator used a variant of the Memorex recording tape slogan: *Is it real or is it Unisys?*

Transitions signal a change of topic, link or relate topics, and regain the customer's attention. Traditional documents place transitions at the end of a topic or section, implicitly assuming the document is read in order. Because proposals are often scanned, transitions in proposals are more effective when placed at the beginning of a section to recapture the evaluator's attention.

Clinchers are closing statements in sales documents that prompt the customer to take the action you have requested. Effective clinchers prompt the customer to act.

Examples of grabbers, transitions, and clinchers are listed in figure 5.

GRABBERS	TRANSITIONS	CLINCHERS
Headings and Slogans	After careful study, . . .	Click on ____ to . . .
Can you afford to . . .	As you requested, . . .	For the fastest response, . . .
Proven . . .	As you witnessed at . . .	Go to our website to . . .
Compare the difference . . .	At less than the cost of . . .	If you agree that _____, then . . .
Switch to . . .	Best of all . . .	If you can't wait, call . . .
Easy to use.	But if you are more concerned with . . .	I'll call you at 2:00 p.m. Tuesday to . . .
The right choice.	Considering your recent service record, . . .	See for yourself by . . .
Salutations (other than *"Dear . . . "*)	Fortunately . . .	See what others are saying . . .
Welcome to . . .	If your managers are experiencing . . .	To ensure you get the first selection . . .
A special invitation . . .	In summary, . . .	Waiting could push you into the next . . .
Please attend . . .	More importantly, . . .	With current costs of ____ per day, can you afford to wait?
Join us . . .	Simply stated, . . .	
Proposal to . . .	So far, so good.	
Question	So what's the typical result?	
Are your managers . . .	To illustrate our approach, . . .	
Are you spending . . .		
Can you afford to . . .		
Can you . . .		
Statement		
In the 10 seconds it took you to read . . .		
Most sales managers . . .		
Challenge		
Capture more ____ by . . .		
Enjoy the . . .		
See how . . .		

Figure 5. Use Grabbers, Transitions, and Clinchers Carefully. *Most of these examples are found in advertising copy. Avoid empty claims. Be specific. Like poetry, every word counts in these key persuasive phrases.*

---

8   Avoid words and phrases that increase contract risk.

Choosing to avoid certain words can be as important as choosing correct words. Avoid the following categories of words and phrases:

- Unsupportable claims
- Superlatives
- Overly inclusive
- Unnecessarily negative
- Firm guarantees not required in the terms and conditions

Several categories overlap.

In figure 5, blanks (____) or ellipses (. . .) indicate where you would insert appropriate words or phrases for your products and services.

Unsupportable claims are not backed by evidence in the following text or graphics. Evaluators not only doubt unsupported claims, but they subsequently question the accuracy of the seller's other oral and written statements. For example, saying that you offer *quality laboratory testing services* does not discriminate your offer. No one says that they offer *poor quality service* in their proposal.

See JARGON.

Lack of specificity implies that you have no data to support your claim. Many unsupported claims are jargon, such as *world class, leading edge,* and *best-in-class.*

Superlatives often end in *est,* such as *greatest, best, fastest, lowest cost,* and *safest.* Superlatives are both hard to support and risky.

Advise writers and presenters to convert *est*-phrases to *er*-phrases. Use the *er*-phrase to explain, support, or justify *why.*

Poor est-phrases

Our PC hard drive is the fastest in the world.

Our order tracking software is the easiest to operate.

Better er-phrases

Our PC hard drive is faster than prior versions because it has a larger buffer.

The graphical user interface makes our order tracking software easier to operate.

Overly inclusive words can often be eliminated without changing the meaning. Elimination reduces contract risk. *All* and *every* are often overly inclusive. *Customary* and *as may be required* are vague and potentially overly inclusive.

Poor examples

All service calls are answered within 1 minute.

Every project manager is PMI certified.

We follow customary procedures when relocating staff.

Better examples

Service calls are answered within 1 minute.

Our project managers are PMI certified.

Staff relocation procedures are defined in our HR Policies & Procedures Manual.

Unnecessarily negative words and phrases are off-putting. State the positive side or implication. *Win rate* and *accuracy rate* are better than *loss rate* and *error rate.*

Poor example

Customer claims are never rejected without valid justification.

Better example

Customers are given an EOB (Explanation Of Benefits) stating how the claim was handled, who received reimbursement, and what portion of the claim, if any, was not covered by the plan.

Avoid **firm guarantees** that are not required in the terms and conditions. As performance-based acquisitions increase, firm guarantees are increasingly required. Most organizations' contracts or legal departments have established guidelines for their organizations.

Figure 6 lists words and phrases that should be avoided or used cautiously.

WORDS AND PHRASES TO AVOID

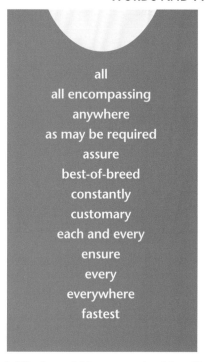

all
all encompassing
anywhere
as may be required
assure
best-of-breed
constantly
customary
each and every
ensure
every
everywhere
fastest

fully
greatest
guarantee
insure
lowest
most
never
no
reasonable and customary
safest
total
world-wide

Figure 6. Words and Phrases to Avoid or Use With Caution. *Start with this list and add your own words and phrases. Search your proposal for these words and consider whether changes are needed.*

Cliches are worn-out phrases or words that are no longer effective. Avoid cliches. Regular use usually indicates lack of thought and effort.

Cliches are a form of shorthand and difficult to avoid entirely. Cliches are tempting when the writer is struggling to express an idea. However, cliches reduce the persuasiveness of sales documents. If the cliche is noticeable, reword the phrase.

The word *cliché* comes from French. While the accent mark can be used, the word has been Anglicized and the accent is commonly omitted. Make your choice and **be consistent.**

Metaphors use a word or phrase to suggest likeness or similarity. These may become cliches over time if overused.

Many metaphors make inappropriate comparisons:

> Our engineers have a *long row to hoe* to complete the data warehouse design by July 1.

Mixed metaphors can be laughable:

> Our program manager is a *tower of strength*, who will forge ahead with this program. *(Towers do not move.)*

Other cliches are alliterations, such as *labor of love* and *feel free to.*

Cliche examples often overlap with redundant words, such as *final analysis*, and wordy phrases, such as *thanking you in advance* and *confirming our conversation.*

Cliches

1. Eliminate noticeable cliches from your proposals.

---

1 Eliminate noticeable cliches from your proposals.

Cliches are worn-out words or phrases that have lost meaning or effectiveness. Writers use cliches habitually. Sales and sales support professionals use cliches to open or close sales documents out of habit, convenience, or to avoid serious thought:

> Confirming our conversation . . .

> Enclosed please find . . .

> We are pleased to present . . .

Remember two key principles of organization to reduce opening cliches:

1. Begin with the most important point to the reader.

2. Avoid unnecessary or long setups.

Many proposals open with seller-focused cliches.

> Global Corporation is pleased to have the opportunity to present this proposal for Super Widgets.

> Thank you for allowing us to submit our proposal for Super Widgets.

Is your gratitude the most important concern of the customer?

Cliched openings evoke images of begging.

Professional sellers offering valuable products and services in a complex sale should interact as professionals. Begging debases the professional image you are seeking to foster.

Closing with cliches wastes the opportunity to close with power. Readers remember the first thing they read, the last thing they read, and repeated points.

Cut thoughtless, cliched closes.

> Please don't hesitate to call.

Instead of using cliches, prompt action. Suggest the next step. Enable action.

To prompt those who read your executive summary to read your proposal, close with an introduction or preview to your proposal.

> Our proposal mirrors the issues discussed in our meetings. Should your requirements change, we welcome the opportunity to discuss further enhancements.

Many sales documents seek extensions or additions to existing contracts. If the next realistically achievable step is action, suggest the action.

> I will call you June 6 at 2:00 P.M. to answer any questions and to schedule a follow-up meeting. Please call me at 800-777-0077 for additional information.

While possibly seeming aggressive, this proactive close is more realistic. Most sales professionals know that customers invited to call seldom do.

Noticeable cliches distract the customer from your message. Others delay the reader from getting to the message, wasting the reader's time.

Writers often make return calls difficult by omitting a phone number and the name of the contact. Make sure the action suggested is possible:

> Please call Kevin Newman, our proposed Acme Project Manager, at 800-777-0077 for additional information.

Here are a few favorite (poor) sales and proposal cliches:

> Global Corporation is grateful for the opportunity to be a participant in this switching proposal.

> We take much pleasure in enclosing our proposal for . . .

> The XYZ Team is a force in being.

Additional cliches are listed below in figure 1.

CLICHES

A can of worms
A-1
acid test
a slam dunk
as a matter of fact
at the end of the day
at this point in time
attached hereto
avoid it like the plague
awaiting further orders

Back to the drawing board
bang for the buck
banner week
benefit of the doubt
beside the point
best-of-breed
better late than never
bite the bullet
block out
built-in safeguards

Circumstances beyond our control
city fathers
clean slate
come full circle
confirming our conversation
considered opinion
conspicuous by its absence
cream of the crop
crying need
customer intimacy
cut to the chase

Dark horse
dead meat
discreet silence
dog-and-pony show
drastic action
driving down costs

Each and every
easier said than done
existing conditions

Feel free to
few and far between
final analysis
food for thought
foregone conclusion

Get everyone on the same page
give the green light to
goes without saying
golden boy
good team player
grave concern
grind to a halt

Had me stumped
hammer out a deal
hard and fast
hat in hand
have a field day
heard it through the grapevine
hew and cry
horns of a dilemma
hot pursuit

Ill-fated
in close proximity
in no uncertain terms
in the loop
in the pipeline
in this day and age
innocent bystander
iron out the problem
inside track
involve all our/your stakeholders

Keep options open

Last analysis
last but not least
last-ditch effort
leaves much to be desired
level playing field
line of least resistance

Make sure we're pulling in the same direction
make the case for
man of the hour
marked contrast
moment of truth
moot point
more or less
moving the goalposts

Narrow escape
needless to say
needs no introduction

One and the same
ongoing dialog
open and shut
out of the loop

Paradigm shift
point blank range
point in time
point with pride
pushing the envelope

Quick and dirty

Raising the bar
reading from the same page
reinventing the wheel
research-proven and field-tested
runnning against the wind/tide
run of the mill

Sacred cow
said and done
seamless infrastructure
seamless transition
second to none
seeing the big picture
select few
serious money
seat of the pants
smoke and mirrors
spending a bundle
substantive and sustained change

Take it off-line
thanking you in advance
the big picture
thinking outside the box
those present
tie-breaker
too numerous to mention
track record
turnkey operation

Unprecedented opportunity
unprecedented situation

Wear and tear
where the rubber meets the road
winning and inclusive culture
without further ado

Figure 1. Examples of Common Cliches Used in Sales Documents. *Replace noticeable cliches with the simplest, most direct word or words available.*

Color adds impact to documents and presentations. Depending on the industry, nearly all presentations and many proposals use color.

See GRAPHICS *and* PHOTOGRAPHS.

Without color, your documents (and, by reflection, your organization) may appear outdated.

However, a United States Federal Acquisition Regulation warns that, "overly elaborate proposals may indicate the offeror's lack of cost consciousness and are to be avoided." Many other governments have similar warnings.

The low cost of color printers dates the excessive cost argument when color is used appropriately. Many bidders use color on covers, executive summaries, and frequently throughout a proposal.

Color is effective when it draws attention to the main elements of the graphic. Keep colors the same hue if elements are of equal importance. Use tints to show greater amounts of the same element. Place warm colors (e.g., red, orange, or magenta) in front of cool colors (e.g., blue, green, or tan).

Full color printing on expensive stock for an entire proposal is excessive for some customers but acceptable or expected with others. Consider each customer and be consistent.

Color

1. Use color where it adds the most value.
2. Establish color standards as part of your normal style sheet.
3. Adjust your color scheme to the medium.
4. Follow the recommendations of graphics professionals.
5. Consider the emotions and associations evoked by color and possible sight limitations.
6. Balance the benefits of color with its increased production time and cost.

1 Use color where it adds the most value.

Color is a visual emphasis device. Spend your limited color budget to reinforce your strategy, connecting client benefits to key discriminators.

Nearly all proposals use color on the covers. Try to develop a color graphic that conveys the essence of the sale.

When numerous proposals are submitted to a customer with a largely undefined evaluation process, the engaging color proposal cover might cause it to be read.

Clever proposal covers, packaging, and presentation can have a powerful impact in the right situation, as in these examples:

A bidder to develop a software package for a large pizza chain submitted a proposal in the chain's box, creating a strong, positive impression.

An executive summary submitted to a national rental car chain was prepared to emulate the color rental folders at the customer's airport counters.

See RELEVANT EXPERIENCE/PAST PERFORMANCE.

A cover graphic, repeated on the first page of the executive summary, showed color pictures of the desired products superimposed on a declining cost curve. The proposal was to reduce the cost of a critical raw material used to manufacture the desired products.

A state competing to have a multinational's 2500-employee facility built in its state submitted copies of the proposal in replica Pony Express leather pouches, delivered on horseback in time for the evening news.

Use color in the executive summary, the most important pages in your proposal.

An executive summary to a frozen food trucking company for information technology (IT) outsourcing used small color photos of the customer's convenience stores. The executive summary demonstrated understanding of the customer's business and the added value of IT support in helping the trucking company meet client commitments and maintain product quality.

Color photos or graphics showing the benefits of the product or service are usually more effective than photos of the product or delivery of the services being quoted.

Use color in the rest of your proposal where it adds value. While color logos are OK, fairly standard, and recommended, they will not discriminate you from most competitors.

Use color graphics to support your claims of experience and offer proof of performance. Photos showing you performing similar work inspire confidence.

2 Establish color standards as part of your normal style sheet.

See PAGE AND DOCUMENT DESIGN.

Set color standards early to save time. Maintaining color standards is easier on larger proposals with professional graphics support.

If many different individuals produce their own proposals, establish one or two style sheets in the software of choice with colors defined. Two standards, one conservative and one more colorful, permit a better match with the customer's business style.

3 Adjust your color scheme to the medium.

On-screen colors often project differently. Either carry your own tested projector and laptop or try to test the borrowed projector before making your presentation.

See PRESENTATIONS TO CUSTOMERS, *Capture Guide.*

The high contrast of black print on white paper makes text easy to read. Most proposals are printed on white or near-white paper using dark or colored ink.

Careless use of color sometimes makes a proposal hard to read. Black or dark print on color or shaded backgrounds with little contrast makes reading difficult.

White or reverse print on dark background is also hard to read with extensive text, a common practice in marketing materials.

Presentations must be color adjusted to the medium. Laptop screens and TV monitors are more visible with dark backgrounds and light print. Because light print tends to be swallowed by dark backgrounds, select a bolder or wider version of your font to improve readability.

Direct computer projection systems permit use in rooms with full lighting. Use light backgrounds and dark text with a quality projector.

4 Follow the recommendations of graphics professionals.

While color selection and document design are usually improved when left to graphics professionals, many proposals and sales documents are created by individuals or small teams without assistance. A few principles will help you use color more effectively.

Begin with the style standards or guidelines of your organization. Follow them or refer to guidelines in published style guides, design books, or the desktop publishing documentation manuals that came with your software. Alternatively, imitate the style of similar documents that appeal to you and the customer.

A basic color wheel shows colors in different hues. A shade is a darkened hue, created on paper by adding black. Conversely, a tint is created on paper by adding white. The color wheel in figure 1 shows the relationship between hues, tints, and shades.

If the customer dictates color and styles, follow the customer's instructions.

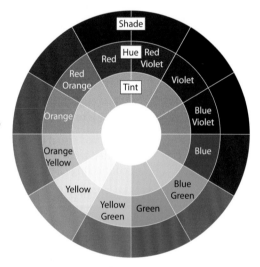

Figure 1. The Color Wheel. *Complementary colors are opposite on the color wheel. Their high contrast is used to grab attention and highlight differences. Harmonious colors are adjacent on the color wheel. Harmonious colors, shades, or tints are used to show subtle variations and to show associations, harmony, or consistency between elements.*

5

Consider the emotions and associations evoked by color and possible sight limitations.

See INTERNATIONAL PROPOSALS.

Consider your corporate image, the audience, and the objective of your presentation. Colors may cause the emotional responses summarized in figure 2.

Colors evoke different emotions in different cultures, impacting international proposals.

For example, in several Eastern countries, white is associated with death and mourning. In the United States, white is associated with purity and innocence. Certain color combinations may evoke unintended associations with holidays, such as orange/black (Halloween), and red/green (Christmas). Check with people from the local culture to prevent embarrassing mistakes.

Consider that 10 percent of the male and 5 percent of the female population are red/green color blind. Being color blind does not mean a person sees in black and white or blue mono-chrome but might confuse shades of red, green, and brown, or blue and purple. Whether colors are confused depends on the intensity of the hue and the brightness of the light conditions. Consider these guidelines on color design:

- Avoid similar saturations of red, green, brown, gray, or purple next to or on top of each other; do not use these colors together in a gradient blend.

Other cultures have entirely different emotions and references attached to colors. In many Eastern societies, red and black are associated with power and good. White is often the color of mourning and death. In Islamic societies, certain shades of green have religious significance.

Research color use when preparing proposals and documents targeting international customers.

- Create a strong, bright contrast between foreground and background colors for both page text and images. Even severely color-blind readers can differentiate similar colors when contrasted between light and dark.

- Add textures, patterns, or shading to set off special areas. Do not use colors alone in graphics such as bar charts, maps, and navigation bars.

- Use contrasting colors and contrasting saturations to differentiate between important items when you must use color alone.

Use two cool colors for text and graphics on a slide or page. Cool colors are calm and relaxing for most people. Cool colors include:

Use hot colors sparingly: one or two key words, bullets, arrow points, or special effects. Hot colors are stimulating; never use them for text. Hot colors include:

COLOR	EMOTIONAL ASSOCIATION	BEST USE
Blue	Peaceful, soothing, cool Authority, power (sometimes)	Backgrounds (90 percent of all business presentations) Dark shades often used for printed headings
White	Neutral, purity, wisdom	Font color choice for dark background
Yellow	Warm, cheerful	Bullets, subheads on dark background
Red	Losses, danger, action Excitement, energy	Bullets and highlights, seldom as a background
Green	Money, growth, assertive Warmth, comfort (sometimes)	Highlights, occasionally as a background

Figure 2. Making the Best Use of Color. *In Western cultures, colors tend to have the emotional associations indicated. Remember that persuasion is 50 percent emotion and 50 percent logic. The specific emotional association will vary with the type of audience, individual, and culture.*

6

Balance the benefits of color with its increased production time and cost.

See PRODUCTION.

Preparing graphics and printing in color may double time estimates and cost.

Color graphics increase file sizes. Many organizations send final color printing to an outside vendor, which impacts production time.

Consider color-matching problems. Different monitors, printers, and projection systems use different color systems. Often the graphic that looks great on screen will print or project with different colors depending on the printer, the projector, and the software.

Color matching can consume inordinate amounts of production time. Use color where it counts.

Compliance and Responsiveness are often confused. Both must be addressed.

Compliance means strict adherence to the customer's bid request, both the submittal instructions and the requirements.

Responsiveness means addressing the customer's underlying needs. Proposals can be responsive but not compliant, or compliant but non-responsive. Confusion reigns.

Compliance with instructions means that you have followed the requested format, answered all questions, completed all forms, and submitted your response to the right person and place on time. Compliance with requirements means that you have agreed to meet bid request requirements

See PROPOSAL STRATEGY.

Government buyers bound by law can use non-compliance as a reason to eliminate your bid. Whether they actually do eliminate your bid varies depending on the relative compliance of the other bidders and governing regulations.

Non-government buyers are free to ignore or use non-compliance as a reason to eliminate a bidder.

Assuming a responsive proposal addresses the customer's underlying needs, your approach might be compliant or non-compliant, depending on whether your approach or solution is specified in the bid request:

A customer needs the grass cut to a specified height. Their bid request specified a weekly cutting by push mower for the calendar year.

1. A compliant but arguably non-responsive bidder could agree to cut the grass weekly for 52 weeks, even though the grass might be dormant in winter.
2. A non-compliant but responsive bidder offers to use a robot mowing system that senses grass height and cuts as necessary, thus keeping the lawn at the desired level but reducing the number of mowings and perhaps the total cost.
3. Others could offer to cut the grass weekly with a riding mower versus the push mower, also noncompliant but responsive.

As the examples show, deciding whether to be fully compliant and responsive is an implicit question when determining your solution and strategy.

Compliance and Responsiveness

1. Do what the customer asks when you get to the proposal stage.
2. Prepare a compliance checklist for all formal bid requests.
3. Prepare a compliance checklist for all informally solicited bid requests.
4. Use compliance checklist shortcuts with caution and understanding.
5. Construct a response matrix early to help plan and track every response.
6. Submit a compliance response locator with your proposal to make evaluation easy.

1

Do what the customer asks when you get to the proposal stage.

If the customer asks you to turn in your proposal while standing on your head, practice standing on your head.

Do what the customer requests. Non-compliance is the easiest way to eliminate an unwanted bidder.

Many popular selling systems advocate non-compliant solutions. These systems suggest that offering a compliant solution puts all power into the customer's hands, enabling the customer to compete on price. They recommend offering an innovative, value-added solution that increases the seller's margins.

Non-compliant solutions can win, providing you are early in the sales process when you can influence the customer to make the specifications less proscriptive or to change the specifications.

After the final bid request is issued, non-compliant solutions are riskier. Your degree of risk depends on the restrictiveness of the buying rules and the relative power of the individuals influencing the buying decision.

2

Prepare a compliance checklist for all formal bid requests.

Compliance checklists are lists of bid request requirements and customer questions that must be answered in your proposal.

Compliance checklists have multiple, evolving uses:

- Clearly identify each requirement and sub-requirement during bid request analysis. Missed or poorly scoped requirements might impact bid decisions, risk analysis, and pricing.
- Show where each requirement will be addressed in the proposal. Each writer must be given clear writing assignments to reduce costly and time-wasting revisions.
- Help color team reviewers verify a compliant response. Reviewers will be more efficient, focused, and constructive.
- Form the basis of the response matrices that serve as roadmaps to the proposal for evaluators.
- Drive preparation of the program work plan at or before transition.

Proposal writers and managers may not prepare compliance checklists because, "They take too much time when we could be writing the proposal."

Preparing compliance checklists and outlines early in the proposal planning process saves more time than they take to prepare.

The procedure to prepare a compliance checklist is listed below. Compliance checklists are most important for large, multilayer bid requests.

For guidelines on handling multilayer bid requests, *see* OUTLINING.

The terms compliance checklist, requirements checklist, and compliance requirements checklist mean the same thing. A response checklist is different, however, because it includes the response to the compliance requirement.

Note how the following compliance checklist example clarifies precisely what the proposal must contain and places each requirement in a separate table row.

Bid Request Excerpt

4.2 System Diagnostic Tools

What diagnostic tools are built into your system? Indicate those that are available only to the network management personnel. Indicate those that are available only from the central switch site and those that are available from nodes, terminal locations, etc.

REFERENCE	COMPLIANCE REQUIREMENT
4.2	Specify the diagnostic tools built into our system.
4.2	Indicate the diagnostic tools available only to the network management personnel.
4.2	Indicate the diagnostic tools available only from the central switch site.
4.2	Indicate the diagnostic tools available from nodes, terminal locations, etc.

Compliance Checklist Methodology

1. Follow the order of topics and paragraphs in the bid request. Within paragraphs, follow the order of sentences.

2. List each requirement as a separate checklist item. If a sentence or paragraph contains two or more requirements, then list each requirement as a separate item.

3. Use the customer's words and phrases in the checklist. Do NOT paraphrase. Use the customer's language.

4. Begin each item with the action verb used in the bid request, such as *identify, list, discuss, show, indicate, demonstrate,* and *describe.* These verbs tell the proposal writer what the customer wants to see in the proposal.

5. Use the compliance checklist as a guide to write each section. Base your section outline on the checklist, and follow the order of topics exactly as it appears in the checklist.

6. Periodically check to see that every requirement has been met.

3   Prepare a compliance checklist for all informally solicited bid requests.

When you do not have a formal bid request, list the customer's requirements from meetings, phone calls, customer file notes, and intelligence resources.

By building the compliance checklist collaboratively with the customer, you offer a valuable service, you can potentially influence the requirements, and you can reduce surprise requirements and prevent elimination for noncompliance.

Prepare compliance checklists for informally solicited proposals as follows:

1. List the requirements as you understand them.

2. Verify your list and add requirements as you discover them in face-to-face meetings and phone calls.

3. Prioritize your list by categories.

4. Seek final customer buy-off via a read-through when possible.

5. Submit a copy of the final compliance checklist along with your proposal.

In some instances, this *checklist* may become the basis for a subsequent competitive bid analysis. If so, you have the advantages of more time and influence. For example:

A commercial property manager was sending an unsolicited letter proposal to prospective tenants. A table included in the letter, shown below, suggested features that should be required, what features were available in the offered property, and provided a place to compare competing properties. Based on the features listed, no competing property could be superior. No seller would list a feature that was not available unless the seller knew the customer did not want that feature.

Recommended features	Sunset Green	#1	#2
Covered parking	✓	___	___
24 x 7 security	✓	___	___
Motorway access < 1/4 mile	✓	___	___
Metro access < 2 blocks	✓	___	___

---

4   Use compliance checklist shortcuts with caution and understanding.

Many potentially time-saving short cuts are possible. Each carries risk, as summarized in figure 1.

METHOD	ADVANTAGES	DISADVANTAGES
Colored markers used to highlight all *shall's* indicating bidder requirements.	Fast.	• Not all requirements are preceded by a shall. More difficult and expensive to distribute to each writer.
Underline or circle, then number each requirement.	Fast, easily photocopied.	• Easy to separate imperative verb from the requirement.
Physically cut requirements from a copy of the bid request. Group by section for writer assignments.	Can be done anywhere, low-tech.	• Can separate imperative verb from the requirement. Lost pieces of paper.
Electronically cut and paste requirements into spreadsheet program. Assign section number and sort list for writers' assignments.	Reliable, available. Imperative verb can be duplicated down a column. No added cost.	• Can take more time than electronic stripping programs.
Proposal preparation software does the stripping electronically and prepares writer packages.	Appears to be easier, especially on large bid requests.	• Can be expensive and hard to operate. • Still requires careful review. • Items can be easily missed.

Stripping is the process of building the compliance checklist, described in guideline 3.

Figure 1. Comparing Bid Request Stripping Methods. *Your choice of stripping method will depend on the size and number of bid requests to be stripped and the risk of potential errors.*

5 Construct a response matrix early to help plan and track every response.

A response matrix, sometimes called a compliance matrix, is a road map for the evaluator that connects the customer's individual bid request requirements or questions to each specific response in your proposal.

Response matrices may also include summary responses and indications of compliance or noncompliance.

Prepare response matrices as a routine part of proposal planning prior to the kickoff meeting. Preparing them just before submittal is similar to preparing as-built drawings after the building is complete. Both are time consuming, often incomplete, and easily skipped.

The response matrix shown in figure 2 is the type prepared early in the proposal planning stage. Not all of this matrix would be submitted with the proposal.

An expanded bid request compliance matrix, shown in figure 3, is constructed by the proposal manager to help manage the preparation of individual proposal sections.

VOL II TECH PROPOSAL SEC/PARA	PROPOSAL OUTLINE TITLES	PARA. PAGES (SUB TOTAL)	SECTION PAGES (SUB TOTAL)	RESP. AUTHOR	MUST COMPLY WITH BID REQUEST REQUIREMENTS					
					PPI	EVAL CRIT	SOW PARA.	SPEC FNCTNL RQMTS	CDRL	OTHER BID REQUEST RQMTS
2	Technical Discussion		150	Lead	L043(D)	M.2.0	1			
2.1	TI-SNIPS Concept Selection	0.25	3.00	Arthur, D	L.043(D)	M.2.1	1.2		4	
2.1.1	Concept Review and Comp	0.25		Arthur, D	L.043(D)	M.2.1				
2.1.2	Concept Selection	2.50		Arthur, D	L.043(D	M.2.1				
2.2	Power System Concept	7.00	67.25	Arthur, D	L043(D)	M.2.2			4	WBS 2.04
2.2.1	System Description	0.25		Arthur, D	L043(D)	M.2.2a	1.3.1	2.3.3		WBS 2.1
2.2.2	Reactor Subsystem	8.00		Bradley, R	L043(D)	M.2.2a	1.3.1	2.3.3 1.3.4 1.3.5		WBS 2.2
2.2.3	Power Conversion Subsystem	8.50		Christian, J	L043(D)	M.2.2b	1.3.2	1.2.1, 2		WBS 2.3
2.2.4	Distribution Subsystem	10.50		Davidson, J	L043(D)	M.2.2c	1.3.3	1.3.4		WBS 2.4
2.2.4.1	Reaction Control	8.00		Davidson, J	L043(D)	M.2.2c	1.3.3.1	1.2.14		WBS 2.4.1
2.2.4.2	Power Distribution and Cond	4.00		Davidson, J	L043(D)	M.2.2c	1.3.3.2	1.2.14		
2.2.5	Heat Rejection Subsystem	7.50		Evans, G	L043(D)	M.2.2d	1.3.3.3	1.3.3		
2.2.6	Shielding Subsystem	7.00		Freeman, J	L043(D)	M.2.2e	1.3.3.4	1.2.10		
2.2.7	Power System-to-Spacecraft I/F	6.50	10	Grand, R	L043(D)	M.2.2f	1.3.3.5	1.2.5		
2.3	Design Maturity and Risk Mitigation	0.25		Jones, B	L043(D)	M.2.3	1.4	1.2.16		
2.3.1	Risk Identification and Red Team	2.75		Jones, B	L043(D)	M.2.3.1	1.5		2	
2.3.2	Key Technology	1.00		Jones, B	L043(D)		1.5			
2.3.3	Critical Components	4.00		Jones, B	L043(D)		1.6			
2.3.4	TI-SNPS Flight Demo Prog	2.00		Jones, B	L043(D)		1.7	1.2.3	7	
2.4	Projected Performance	0.25	10	Hanks, T	L043(D)	M.2.4	1.2	1.2	4	
2.4.1	Performance Requirements	0.25		Hanks, T	L043(D)		1.2	1.2	4	
2.4.1.1	Power Level	0.50		Hanks, T	L043(D)		1.2.1	1.2.1		
2.4.1.2	Power Density	0.50		Hanks, T	L043(D)		1.2.2	1.2.2		
	TOTAL	**81.75**	**90.25**							

Figure 2. Formal Bid Request Compliance Matrix. *A response matrix prepared early in the proposal planning cycle allocates pages to each section and assigns authors. Relevant sections are listed. Tasks are tied to relevant Statement of Work (SOW) sections and Contract Data Requirements List (CDRL).*

PROP SCTN/ PARA #	PROPOSAL OUTLINES TITLES	PARA PAGES (SUB TOTAL)	SEC PAGES (SUB TOTAL)	RESP AUTHOR	PPI L-2 PARA 3.2.X	PARA TITLE	REQUIREMENT	EVAL CRITERIA M.4	PARA TITLE	REQUIREMENT
II	Mgmt Proposal		25.0	Holloway, K	8.2	Management Proposal	• Describe mgmt structure and processes used to control prog • Describe procedures, methods, tools, and facilities you intend to use • Describe how mgmt methods are proactive and process oriented	3.0 4.0	• Gen Basis for award • Mgmt area	• Mgmt and Tech areas are equal; cost is third • Three items in Mgmt area: 1st Prog Mgmt. Resource Mgmt & Mgmt. Control are less important than 1st and are of equal importance to each other
1	Introduction		2.0		3.2.1	Introduction	• Incl. in matrix from the skills, experience, and qualifications of indiv's who will perform contract tasks, what portion of the work they will perform, and percent of time applied to efforts. Key people resumes req'd			
2	Program Mgmt Plan	0.25	11.0		3.2.2	Program Mgmt Plan	• Address orig. structure F&R assignmts, procedures, processes & rptng rqmnts for initiation, monitoring control completion, test & validation of tasks, projects, prgms. PMPs: be responsive to draft PCO TL	3.0 4.0	• Gen Basis for award • Mgmt area	• Mgmt and Tech areas are equal; cost is third • Three items in Mgmt area: 1st Prog Mgmt. Resource Mgmt & Mgmt. Control are less important than 1st and are of equal importance to each other
2.1	Mgmt Planning & Control				PTL 4.1	Task 1: Mgmt Planning & Control	• Establish a prog origin structure, policies, and procedures to ensure all program objectives are met			

Figure 3. Expanded Bid Request Compliance Matrix. *Expanded bid request compliance matrices are used on large, complex responses with multiple writers. Managers, writers, and reviewers find them useful to develop a coordinated, coherent response with minimum revision. Note that many of the words in the requirements column are abbreviated to reduce the size of the table.*

6

Submit a compliance response locator with your proposal to make evaluation easy.

The compliance response locator, shown in figure 4, is submitted as part of the proposal. This tool simplifies the evaluator's task of quickly finding where your proposal addresses each requirement specified in the bid request. Additional columns are often added that summarize whether the response is compliant. If you are worried about being capriciously eliminated for non-compliance, consider the hairsplitting, *Compliant with qualification*.

Another best practice is to place a *Why us?* summary on the first page of every volume or major section of a proposal. This summary is usually a table that relates the key customer requirements, your offering, and your unique discriminator(s). This table helps evaluators tie your offering to their needs and makes it easy for them to justify selecting your solution. If you cannot convince them in one page, you need to refine your solution.

BID REQUEST REQUIREMENT		PROPOSAL RESPONSE	BID REQUEST REQUIREMENT		PROPOSAL RESPONSE
SECTION	TITLE		SECTION	TITLE	
L.24(b)(3)(i)a.	Technical Approach	2.1	SOW 3.1	Task Completion Schedule	4.2
L.24(b)(3)(i)b.	Understanding of Goals/Objectives	2.2	SOW 3.2	Review Candidate GGSF Exper	2.1.1.1, 3.1.1
L.24(b)(3)(i)c.	Understanding of Configurational . . .	2.3	SOW 3.3	Analyses of Candidate GGSF Exper	2.1.1.1, 2.1.2.1, 3.1.1
L.24(b)(3)(i)d.	Understanding of Goals/Objectives	2.4	SOW 3.4	Identify Facility Subsystems	2.2, 2.3.2, 3.1.1
L.24(b)(3)(i)e.	Understanding of Goals/Objectives	2.1–2.5	SOW 3.5	Assess GGSF and MCPF Tech Area	3.1.1.3
L.24(b)(3)(ii)	Technical Approach/Methodology	3.1	SOW 3.6	Critical Supporting Areas	2.1.1.2, 2.2, 2.5.3, 3.1.1, 3.2
L.24(b)(3)(iii)	Innovation	3.2	SOW 3.7	Issues Requiring Further Study	3.1.1.2
L.24(b)(3)(iv)	Study Plan	4.1	SOW 3.8	Identify Freedom Subsystems	2.4
L.24(b)(3)(v)	Study Schedule	4.2	SOW 3.9	Rqmts for Use of A1 Expert Systems	2.3.2, 3.2
L.24(b)(3)(vi)	Key Personnel	App.	SOW 3.10	Assess Facility Mission Rqmts	2.2, 3.1.1, 4.2
L.24(b)(3)(vii)	Study Manager	5.2, App.	SOW 3.11	Final Report	4.1

Figure 4. Compliance Response Locator. *Response locators enable the evaluator to easily find answers to the questions in the bid request. Notice that because page numbers are not included, this matrix can be prepared early. Waiting until page numbers are firm puts too much work at the end. Section numbers are sufficient.*

Cover Letters are a common part of most proposal submittals. While cover letters have relatively little influence on the evaluation team when compared to the executive summary, they are conspicuous by their absence.

Cover letters should reflect the key themes found on the first page of your executive summary but be far less comprehensive. The focus of the cover letter will depend on the reader.

For a large, multivolume proposal shipped in several boxes, include a letter of transmittal that serves as a packing list to tell the person who accepts delivery what is included.

See EXECUTIVE SUMMARY.

When the person receiving the shipment has a role in selecting the winner, the cover letter presents another opportunity to sell.

Three model cover letters are included in the MODEL DOCUMENTS section.

Use the four-box organizational structure, described in ORGANIZATION.

Cover Letters

1. Use your cover letter to cite your key discriminator, directly tied to a key customer need.

2. Have the cover letter signed by the highest ranking person in your organization who touched the customer during the capture planning phase.

3. In a single page, include two or three powerful reasons to select your offer.

4. Close with a short paragraph that points the reader to your proposal, includes the project name and RFP number, gives a contact person and number, and cites terms such as how long your offer is valid.

1

See CHOOSING CORRECT WORDS *and* CUSTOMER FOCUS.

Use your cover letter to cite your key discriminator, directly tied to a key customer need.

Open with a client-focused theme statement like the opening to your executive summary:

> ReadyMaids.com can continue to focus on the explosive growth in home cleaning services by selecting an information technology (IT) support vendor like Global Information Technology (GIT), with an entire division specializing in franchise support.

Avoid opening with the cliches:

> Thank you for the opportunity to submit our proposal for IT support.

Also avoid this seller-focused opener:

> Global Information Technology is pleased to present our proposal for IT support.

2

Have the cover letter signed by the highest ranking person in your organization who touched the customer during the capture planning phase.

Skeptical customers know that a cover letter signed by the CEO of a multibillion dollar organization simply means someone wrote a letter and got it signed.

Draft it early and have it signed by the highest ranking person in your organization that the customer knows. Reinforce this contact during the capture phase by arranging a meaningful interchange between the signer and a senior person in the customer's organization. Then reference the meeting in your cover letter:

> In our meeting on October 15, Superintendent Austin indicated that the Sunrise District was looking for a partner that understood the needs of metropolitan school districts.

3

In a single page, include two or three powerful reasons to select your offer.

Cite any value-added aspects of your offer that save time, save money, or reduce risk. Cite any special efforts you have taken to address key customer concerns. Reinforce any truly unique experience or outstanding performance with the customer's organization or a similar organization. Carefully avoid using a patronizing or arrogant tone.

4

Close with a short paragraph that points the reader to your proposal, includes the project name and RFP number, gives a contact person and number, and cites terms such as how long your offer is valid.

Avoid closing with a legal-sounding paragraph that essentially says you are not responsible for anything. Consider adding the following to a concise closing paragraph:

- Note what is included in your proposal.
- Include a contact name, address, and number.
- Indicate how long your offer is valid.
- Cite special terms or conditions.
- Cite the contract name and RFP number.
- Indicate the signing person is authorized to make this offer.

Customer Focus is a trait that everyone claims but few communicate. When someone in a business development role is asked, *"Are you customer focused?"* the usual answer is, *"Of course!"*

What features make one document more customer focused than another document? Do different individuals perceive customer focus differently? Do individuals with different cultural backgrounds or positions perceive customer focus differently?

To determine the answer, we asked individuals to rank the customer focus of five documents. The base document was a 2-page executive summary. For each of the five documents, appearance and content were fixed while writing and organization varied. Figure 1 lists the controlled and variable features of the five test documents. All five versions were by the same seller to the same customer for the same products and services.

To date, more than 5,000 people from 40 countries and 5 continents have completed this exercise in English, Korean, Japanese, Danish, Swedish, and French. The results have been consistent across cultures:

1. Seventy percent ranked the same document as most customer focused.

2. The composite ordinal ranking was consistent from group to group.

3. The least customer-focused version was ranked last by 70 percent of the participants.

4. About one-half of the participants could cite specific mechanical aspects of the writing that explained their ranking.

Eight guidelines indicate how to increase the perceived customer focus of a document. Readers rate a document's customer focus higher when more of the guidelines are followed and when the guidelines are followed more frequently.

These guidelines to improving the customer focus of sales documents are more relevant and important when applied to executive summaries and sales letters than to individual proposal sections.

See EXECUTIVE SUMMARY; *and* SALES LETTERS, *Capture Guide.*

CONTROLLED FEATURES	VARIABLE FEATURES
• Page layout • Fonts • Visuals • Action captions • Quotes from users	• Cites customer's organizational vision • Links customer's vision to the immediate purchase • Cites the customer's hot buttons • Makes ownership of the hot buttons explicit • Addresses each hot button in the order listed • Names the customer before the seller • Names the customer more often than the seller • Cites benefits before features

Figure 1. Customer Focus Research Experiment. *To determine which document features most affect the reader's perception of customer focus, five test documents were created with the same controlled features and different variable features. These findings are the basis for the following customer focus guidelines.*

Customer Focus

1. Cite the customer organization's vision.

2. Link the customer's vision directly to the immediate purchase.

3. Cite the customer's hot buttons.

4. Make customer ownership of the hot buttons explicit.

5. Address each hot button in the order listed.

6. Name the customer before the seller in paragraphs and sentences.

7. Name the customer as many or more times than the seller.

8. Cite benefits before features.

1

Cite the customer organization's vision.

Only the top-ranked version cited the customer organization's vision:

Cascadia Timber is ranked as the No. 1 company in the world by Forester's Monthly for low cost, innovative forest management. Cascadia Timber

Chairman Woody X. Pine set the following strategic direction:

We have to do everything better, more efficiently from a cost point of view, more effectively from an impact point of view.

Cascadia Timber Annual Report, 1996

For the document ranked as the most customer focused, *see* MODEL DOCUMENTS. Excerpts here are from that model executive summary.

Too many proposal writers demonstrate their understanding of the customer's needs by copying a few paragraphs from the bid request, demonstrating only that they can copy.

A significant minority of the participants felt that citing the customer's vision was pandering.

Yet numerous studies of buyers have found that while nearly all bidders are technically qualified, the organization selected was the one that *had the best understanding of the customer's business.*

---

2   Link the customer's vision directly to the immediate purchase.

Connecting the customer's vision to the immediate purchase demonstrates your perspective. After your offer is selected, the direct link to the organization's vision may help the project get funded over other, unrelated but competing projects.

Cascadia Timber's Forest Management Division helps improve efficiency and effectiveness by adopting innovative forest management practices.

Buyers sometimes get so close to the immediate project that they lose perspective.

---

3   Cite the customer's hot buttons.

Citing the customer's hot buttons immediately places the focus on what the customer needs instead of what you are selling. Hot buttons are an amalgam of issues, needs, requirements, and evaluation criteria. To develop a hot button list of two to four items, do the following:

1. List all the major hot buttons you can recall.
2. Group similar hot buttons to reduce the list to two to four items.
3. Restate the grouped hot buttons using the customer's words.

Note how the following example continues from the previous example connecting

the vision and the immediate need, then transitioning into the hot buttons:

> In support of Cascadia Timber's strategic direction, the Forest Management Division verbally requested proposals for 20 ultralight aircraft to be used as a forest management tool. In our meetings with Forest Management and purchasing, individuals cited four primary needs: *IMMEDIATE NEED*
>
> 1. Affordable, portable, and easily transportable
> 2. All-conditions observation and communication platform
> 3. Safe and easy to fly
> 4. Easy to assemble and maintain in the field *HOT BUTTONS*

---

4   Make customer ownership of the hot buttons explicit.

Make ownership of their hot buttons explicit by citing your source, preferably in the customer's organization.

The following statement lacks ownership:

> The ideal aircraft must meet four primary needs:
> . . .

The following makes ownership explicit:

> In our meetings with Forest Management and Purchasing, individuals cited four primary needs:
> . . .

Even if you have had no contact with the customer, you can soften the statement by broadening your source:

> In our experience with other, similar forest management organizations, most cited four primary needs: . . .

If your organization has been accused of technical arrogance, you may be making statements like this:

> Cascadia Timber needs to improve forest management by purchasing an aircraft with the following features: . . .

---

5   Address each hot button in the order listed.

See MODEL DOCUMENTS for the complete example.

You have announced your document's organization with your hot button list. Follow it, in exact order. Make your subheadings identical to your hot buttons. Use the same words.

Failing to follow your announced organization subtly suggests that you do not keep your word.

The following example shows how a hot-button list is reflected in subsequent subheadings.

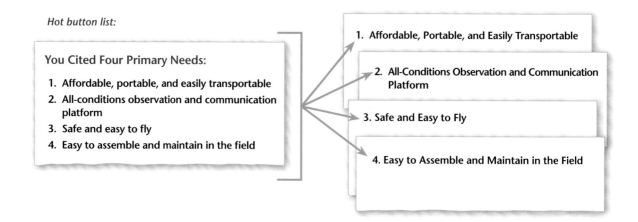

Hot button list:

You Cited Four Primary Needs:

1. Affordable, portable, and easily transportable
2. All-conditions observation and communication platform
3. Safe and easy to fly
4. Easy to assemble and maintain in the field

1. Affordable, Portable, and Easily Transportable
2. All-Conditions Observation and Communication Platform
3. Safe and Easy to Fly
4. Easy to Assemble and Maintain in the Field

6

Partner can have positive or negative connotations, depending on the customer. Avoid using jargon unless the customer requests *a partner*.

See Choosing Correct Words.

Name the customer before the seller in paragraphs and sentences.

Scan the opening sentences of each paragraph in your documents. Do they tend to open with the words *We*, *Our*, or your organization's or product's name?

Seller-focused example

Jenair Sports can reduce Cascadia Timber's cost of forest management in remote, roadless areas by supplying 20 versatile ultralight aircraft and proven Jenair long-term support.

Customer-focused example

Cascadia Timber can reduce the cost of forest management in remote, roadless areas by selecting a partner to supply 20 versatile ultralight aircraft that also offers proven long-term support.

The seller was not named in the second example. The words *a partner* could have been replaced with the seller's name *Jenair*. Because the reader clearly knows whose proposal it is, naming the seller again is not necessary. Both are correct. Using *a partner* softens the tone.

When discussing your organization, try to state what others say, not what you say about yourself. Contrast these two statements:

Seller-focused example

Colossal has 75 percent of the widget market.

Customer-focused example

Seventy-five percent of widget purchasers selected Colossal.

7

Name the customer as many or more times than the seller.

Strive to mention the customer as many or more times than you mention your organization. Include all pronouns in your count.

This measure is accurate in an executive summary; the ratio will drop in detailed proposal sections.

8

See Organization.

Cite benefits before features.

Following basic organizational principles, begin with items of greatest interest to the customer, the benefit rather than the feature.

Note the difference in these proposal excerpts:

Jenair Sports is offering 20 Endeavor ultralights for $9,500 each, less than one-half the cost of 3/4 ton 4-wheel drive trucks. This can reduce the cost of forest management. The Endeavor offers a unique combination of features:

- The wings, tail assembly, fuselage, and down tubes are oriented along a slim axis and secured in a rugged transport case for portability.
- Two people can carry the 196-lb. fuselage crate, one carries the 45-lb. engine crate for transportability.

Compare the preceding excerpt with a more customer-focused version:

Cascadia Timber can reduce the cost of forest management by purchasing 20 Endeavor ultralights from Jenair for $9,500 each, less than one-half the cost of 3/4 ton 4-wheel drive trucks. The Endeavor offers a unique combination of features:

- For portability, the wings, tail assembly, fuselage, and down tubes are oriented along a slim axis and secured in a rugged transport case.
- For transportability, two people carry the 196-lb. fuselage crate, another person carries the 45-lb. engine crate.

Rules 6 through 8 are complementary. Citing benefits first tends to pull in the customer's name first. Closing with a benefit tends to place the customer's name last.

Daily Team Management is focused on efficiently executing the proposal management plan. Detecting deviations from the plan early minimizes the cost of corrective action in a project with a fixed delivery date.

See PROPOSAL MANAGEMENT PLAN *and* STORYBOARDS.

The difficulties of managing a proposal team are compounded when the following conditions exist:

- Large team
- Dispersed team
- Part-time members
- Members from different organizations
- Untrained, inexperienced members

The proposal manager has three key tools to keep the team on schedule:

1. Detailed Proposal Management Plan (PMP)
2. Daily stand-up meeting
3. Proposal Development Worksheets (PDW) or storyboards

The proposal manager's primary objective is to prepare a winning document, on time. Any activity that adversely impacts this objective must be identified and eliminated or managed.

Daily team management activities must be tempered by team conditions, size of the proposal, and available budget and resources.

Daily Team Management

1. Prepare a Proposal Management Plan.

2. Define and document your solution first.

3. Confirm that all contributors understand their assignments.

4. Conduct daily stand-up meetings with the proposal team.

5. Focus team members on their next, immediate task.

6. Use storyboards to track the progress of individual writers.

7. Review a single aspect of all storyboards each day.

---

1 Prepare a Proposal Management Plan.

See PROPOSAL MANAGEMENT PLAN.

Good proposal plans are detailed, written, and available for review and reference. Poor plans are in the manager's head. The only evidence of a quality plan is one that is written and can be both reviewed and used as a daily management tool.

Select a medium that is compatible with your organization. Proposal management plans need not be in a single document. Increasingly, proposal management plans comprise multiple files that are browser-accessible to virtual proposal team members.

The shorter the response time, the greater the need to plan because you have no recovery time.

If you think the proposal plan does not need to be written, then the proposal should not be written. No bid.

For a response time under two weeks, use a quarter of the available time to plan, then execute your plan flawlessly, and you can win.

---

2 Define and document your solution first.

Good proposals are possible with a clear, documented solution. Good proposals are impossible with an unclear, undocumented solution.

Take the time to define your baseline solution first. If you begin writing the proposal before the solution is defined, the result will be a loser full of generic descriptions, boilerplate, and *Trust me* statements, all totally lacking in customer focus.

---

3 Confirm that all contributors understand their assignments.

See KICKOFF MEETINGS.

The kickoff meeting is where contributors to a proposal must receive answers to four basic questions:

1. What is my task?
2. How do you want it done?
3. When is it due?
4. How do I charge my time?

Too many organizations mistakenly use the kickoff meeting as a planning meeting rather than to establish clear task assignments.

After giving assignments, immediately follow up with contributors to confirm they understand their assignment in the context of the entire proposal.

A responsibility matrix shown in figure 1 is closely related to the bid request compliance matrix. Use a responsibility matrix to track the status of each writing assignment by author and due date.

The complexity of the matrix varies with the complexity of the proposal.

PROPOSAL PAR #	PROPOSAL SECTION	RELEVANT BID REQ'ST PAR #	AUTHOR	PAGE LIMIT TARGET	STORYBOARD ASSIGNED	FIRST REVIEW	FINAL DATE	MOCKUP REVIEW DATE	PINK TEAM	GRAPHICS DUE DATE	FIRST DRAFT	RED TEAM DATE
None	Exec Sum	M	S. Ross	4	19 Mar	25 Mar	28 Mar	31 Mar	02 Apr	10 Apr	15 Apr	
1.0	Tech Ov	L.2.1	W. Lou	2	21 Mar	26 Mar	28 Mar	31 Mar	02 Apr	10 Apr	15 Apr	

Figure 1. Proposal Responsibility Matrix. *Sometimes called a program control matrix, proposal managers use the proposal responsibility matrix to assign and monitor the status of each section assigned to each writer. Using spreadsheet software, add a row for each task and a column for each milestone. Keep a current version prominently displayed in the proposal room and review progress in the daily stand-up meeting.*

---

4 Conduct daily stand-up meetings with the proposal team.

The term "stand-up" comes from the idea that forcing participants to stand would keep the meeting brief.

See TEAM SELECTION AND MANAGEMENT.

See VIRTUAL TEAM MANAGEMENT.

Keep the focus on the status of the proposal and, specifically, what tasks must be completed near-term.

Hold your 15-minute stand-up meeting at the same time each day, usually the first thing each morning. Take problem-solving discussions outside the stand-up meeting. When issues surface that need discussion, determine who needs to participate, set a time to meet, then move to the next item. Record all actions assigned.

The proposal manager conducts the meeting, supported by the program or solution lead if they are different people. Potential topics include the following:

- Upcoming milestones
- Action items
- Procedural changes

- New customer information
- Teaming or subcontract considerations
- Solution refinements
- Solution milestones or schedules
- Strategy refinements
- Changes in the bid request, proposal outline, or response assignments
- Graphics, editing, or publication support issues

When managing a dispersed team, compensate for the lack of co-location by daily web conference, teleconference, and/or e-mail.

Proposal managers who assume that everything is on track because *"I have not heard about any problems from contributors"* are in trouble.

---

5 Focus team members on their next, immediate task.

See SCHEDULING.

Writers do better with smaller tasks and shorter deadlines than with a few large tasks and longer deadlines. If task deadlines are set by day, authors interpret the deadline to be *close of business* on the due date, burdening management or production support.

Present a high-level milestone schedule showing major events at the kickoff meeting or the next subsequent meeting with the proposal team. Within a few days, turn the milestone schedule into an *inch-stone* schedule. The inch-stone schedule divides major tasks into smaller, clearly defined subtasks. Give

everyone a due date and time for each assigned task. Stagger due dates and times to smooth production.

Use the stand-up meeting to reinforce progress, commend excellent work, and remind contributors what needs to be done that day. Make contributors responsible to meet the schedule to the hour. If they cannot meet it, they must reschedule with management and/or trade due times with another contributor. Inch-stones help keep contributors focused on immediate tasks, giving a sense of immediacy and completion.

6

See STORYBOARDS AND MOCKUPS.

Use storyboards to track the progress of individual writers.

While storyboards are primarily a writer's tool, helping writers plan their sections before writing, storyboards are also powerful management tools.

Keep the most current version of each storyboard posted on the proposal room walls and on a web-accessible server. You will quickly spot authors who are falling behind task. Their storyboards are often missing, empty, or do not change from day to day.

7

See PROPOSAL STRATEGY.

Review a single aspect of all storyboards each day.

Proposal managers need a method to achieve consistency, coherency, and compatibility across all proposal sections.

Trying to read all the storyboards daily becomes overwhelming. Instead focus on reviewing a single aspect of all storyboards each day.

Select a member of your core team to review storyboards with you, choose one of the following topics, establish your review standards, and review the same topic on each storyboard.

Storyboard topics include:

- Theme statements
- Graphics
- Action captions
- Summaries
- Introductions
- Benefit/Feature table
- Risk management
- Relevant experience and past performance
- Compliance
- Content compatibility with other storyboards
- Ghosting

Discriminators are features of your offer or solution that (1) differ from a competitor's offer and (2) are acknowledged by the customer as important. Both conditions must be met.

Differentiators meet only the first condition. They are the features of your offer that differ from the features of a competitor's offer. Differentiators are often called unique selling points (USPs).

However, if the difference does not matter to the customer, it is not important. Hence, discriminators are differentiators that are acknowledged by the customer as important.

The strongest discriminators are true for you and not true for any of your competitors. The weakest discriminators are true for you and not true for at least one of your competitors.

The strength of a discriminator also depends on its importance to the customer. The CEO of a large defense contractor once said, "We must identify at least one truly unique discriminator to justify bidding."

If the customer cannot identify discriminators among the various offers, then low price becomes the remaining discriminator. However, most buyers say that relatively small differences among offers become the discriminators among the winner and the losers.

If you are not certain if your features are discriminators, see FEATURES, ADVANTAGES, AND BENEFITS.

Discriminators

1. Identify discriminators by understanding your customer, your competitors, and yourself.

2. Identify both positive and negative discriminators and position them as positively as possible.

3. Continuously reexamine whether a discriminator still discriminates.

4. Develop discriminators by continuing to define them more specifically.

5. Emphasize discriminators that focus on people, experience, performance, and understanding of the customer's business. They are usually the most powerful discriminators.

---

1   Identify discriminators by understanding your customer, your competitors, and yourself.

When you rent a car, do you ask about the color of the car? No?

When you purchase a car, do you ask about the color of the car? Yes?

If so, paint color is a discriminator when you buy but not when you rent.

Many sellers have either not seen what their competitors offer or rely on obsolete data about their competitors. When you claim to have a unique approach but do not, then you lose credibility with your customer.

Even worse, many writers know so little about what they offer that they describe it generically:

We offer an experienced network technician.

This claim doesn't explain the experience of the technician or how the customer will benefit.

Customers, often not experts in what they are buying, need help to determine the importance of your discriminators. When you

do not know specifically what your competitor offers, discriminate your features against other criteria, like national averages, independent study results, or to other approaches that you considered but rejected as inferior.

Consider these good examples:

Our job site safety record shows that we experience 50 percent fewer lost-time accidents than the national average for comparable construction activity.

While not all outsourced employees will choose to transition to a new support vendor, independent studies by the Acme Group show that our job offer acceptance rate is 14 percent above the industry average and that our retention rate long-term is equal to the retention rate of new employees.

We considered using a fast-track construction approach, which initially appeared to cut four weeks from the construction schedule. However, after studying the local permitting review and approval process, we decided it might offend state regulatory officials and actually increase the risk of expensive schedule delays.

2   Identify both positive and negative discriminators and position them as positively as possible.

Many proposal writers focus exclusively on their positive discriminators. Also identify and deal with your negative ones:

Negative discriminator

Our company manufactures the only seals ever used on submarines that operate below 2000 meters. Recently a seal failed, endangering the crew. Our client then spent $250 million to determine the cause, with our assistance.

Clearly, the seal failure is a major negative discriminator. A possible reply:

As the only designer and manufacturer of seals for submarines operating below 2000 meters, and after spending $250 million learning how to improve seal design, can you afford to teach another supplier how to make them?

While possibly too direct for some in a written proposal, the example illustrates how you can emphasize the positive side of your negative discriminators.

3   Continuously reexamine whether a discriminator still discriminates.

The power of the discriminator to an individual may vary over time.

Many procurements have been lost because the seller assumed the reason they won the last contract still applied.

Consider these examples:

Decaffeinated coffee is far more popular in the evening than in the morning.

Here, the power of discriminators to an individual is cyclical over a day.

A major engine manufacturer won a large order by selling a replacement engine that offered greater thrust. In the next competition, they followed the same strategy, offering increased thrust as their key discriminator. They lost when the customer calculated the life-cycle cost of the additional fuel and judged it more important than increased thrust.

Here the customer's perceived needs changed. Also, the factions with power may have changed from users to the economic buyer.

4   Develop discriminators by continuing to define them more specifically.

Note the progression from generic to specific:

Experienced manager.

Experienced project manager.

All project managers have a minimum of 10 years of experience.

Fred Jones, our proposed manager, has 10 years of project management experience.

Fred Jones, our proposed project manager, also managed the similar North Cove project to an on-time delivery and within budget.

A writer in a national proposal publication coined the phrase "generic specific," words that sound specific but are really generic. Discriminate by being specific and offering proof.

Generic Specific Language

The program manager will regularly review the risk log with the program team and pursue mitigation actions as needed.

Specific Language Revision

Dave Lee, Program Manager, will review the risk log every Friday and publish corrections on the program website by close of business on the following Monday.

What is the real meaning of a discriminator like the following:

200 years of experience on our team

Does the team include 20 people with 10 years of experience each or 200 people with 1 year of experience each? Be specific by quantifying, if possible.

Consider another example:

Improved fuel economy

We may fail to quantify because we do not know how much fuel economy will improve, we are too lazy to find out, or we do not want to be held accountable.

Be as specific as possible. Oddly enough, the claim of a 14.5 percent improvement is more credible than a 15 percent claim, appearing to be more precise.

5

Emphasize discriminators that focus on people, experience, performance, and understanding of the customer's business. They are usually the most powerful discriminators.

See RELEVANT
EXPERIENCE/PAST
PERFORMANCE.

See EXECUTIVE SUMMARY,
and FEATURES,
ADVANTAGES, AND
BENEFITS.

Each person is unique; even identical twins are not truly identical. If the customer values the differences in the abilities of the individuals you propose, use these differences as discriminators.

Frequently, sellers throw away the opportunity to use individuals as their discriminators by stating:

All our people are good; it does not matter who you get.

By the time the contract is awarded, we do not know who will actually be available.

We do not have a Big Name like our competitors, so we will not name anyone. We do not play bait-and-switch.

Maximize the customer's interest in the individuals you propose by building a rapport between the customer and these key individuals before the bid request is issued.

Consider your own purchase of skilled services, such as selecting the person or company to remodel your home. Nearly everyone in this situation wants to know, *"Who will actually be in my home doing the work while I am away?"*

No two companies have been awarded the same jobs, so your specific experience is different. If you can persuade the customer to care about the difference, you have a discriminator.

Extend your discussions of experience and performance beyond the *appendix, experience,* or *past performance* sections of the proposal. Cite experience and performance throughout your proposal to substantiate all claims. Use a Success Story Template such as the one found in guideline 4 of RELEVANT EXPERIENCE/PAST PERFORMANCE, to present your experience and performance in a customer-focused manner.

Most customers for complex systems and services can readily identify several organizations with sufficient talent, expertise, and resources.

The critical discriminator is often an understanding of the customer's business, vision, and immediate needs. The winner is often the selling organization that best shows how it can help the customer achieve its strategic vision.

Discriminate yourself by demonstrating your understanding of the customer's business throughout your entire proposal. Do not limit integrating discriminators to the executive summary and finals briefing.

Electronic Submittal of proposals is increasing, but no common approach has emerged. Electronic submittal for new competitive procurements is often a backup to paper submittal.

Because the technology of electronic submittal will continue to evolve rapidly, this entry may be obsolete after publishing.

Good sources of current information are various federal agency websites and the Association of Proposal Management Professionals (APMP) at www.apmp.org.

See PAGE AND DOCUMENT DESIGN.

The specified electronic submission format usually does not conform with the format bidders typically use to prepare proposals. Many customers request text and graphics in combinations of software that do not work well together.

The appropriate submittal format depends on how the electronic submittal will be used. If you can influence the customer, recommend the following formats based on the customer's objectives:

- To archive, the seller's format should be sufficient, providing it is prepared with a widely available package.

- To support the paper-version evaluation, Adobe® Acrobat® PDF format seems to be the best choice. The free viewer lets evaluators search text, copy, paste, print, and view the entire page with integrated graphics and text.

- To enable paperless evaluation, most available commercial packages will generate Acrobat PDF files with the above capabilities.

Submission delivery refers to how the customer wants the electronic version delivered, usually CD-ROM or up-load to a server. Submittal via the web raises concerns about file size, security, time stamping, return receipts, file corruption, or simply whether potentially printed and/or viewed copies will appear as intended.

Often purchasers from U.S. government agencies impose page limits to reduce the evaluation effort required and the time and cost to prepare the proposal.

Increasingly, file size matters. Many quick-turn task order bids under Indefinite Delivery Indefinite Quantity (IDIQ) contracts require only electronic submittals. The bid request might impose file size limits or the customer's e-mail server might have a file size limit. A 5 mega byte (MB) file size or a 10 MB server limit is common, which significantly impacts embedded graphics.

Unfortunately, file-size limitations often bear little relationship to the printed size of a proposal. Different software requires different file sizes, and later versions of the same software are usually larger.

Graphics file sizes vary depending on whether they are pixel or raster based. Scanned images can be monsters, depending on the resolution. The graphics inserted into print files often get even larger.

About the only meaningful limitation that is relevant to the individual evaluator is the number of pages, whether physical or viewed on-screen.

Electronic Submittals

1. Follow each customer's instructions exactly or do not bid.
2. Use the Adobe® Acrobat® PDF file format whenever possible.
3. Check and recheck for viruses.
4. Use forced page breaks to control pagination.
5. Use graphic files that offer adequate resolution for printing or viewing.
6. Learn and test all systems early in the preparation process.
7. Furnish at least one hard copy, if allowed by the customer.
8. Consider a landscape, three-column, or PDF format for proposals that will be reviewed on-screen.

1 Follow each customer's instructions exactly or do not bid.

Following the rules is not optional. Buy the hardware or software required to conform or do not bid. Use the software packages, versions, or releases specified. If none are specified and you do not know what the customer uses, ask. Use the same hardware platform the customer uses to reduce problems.

2 Use the Adobe® Acrobat® PDF file format whenever possible.

Files prepared in most common word-processing packages, as well as all leading desktop publishing software, can be converted to PDF (portable document format) files. The viewed version is identical on any platform and prints reliably on all printers, including offset press when properly packaged.

3 Check and recheck for viruses.

The last thing you need is to infect the customer's system with a computer virus. The chances of passing on a virus increase proportionally to the following factors:

- More contributors
- Greater use of boilerplate
- More geographically dispersed teams
- More contributors in multiple countries
- Greater use of web resources

Check for viruses early, often, and just prior to shipping after all reviews are complete.

4 Use forced page breaks to control pagination.

Following this guideline will help evaluators see the material as you intended. However, no solution is fool proof.

Pages viewed on-screen may look different on different screens, depending on the screen size and display settings. Even with identical computer hardware and software, different printers with different print drivers

or fonts might make a page print and/or display differently. Even worse, the different print drivers and font sources can change pagination, making your table of contents and index incorrect.

5 Use graphic files that offer adequate resolution for printing or viewing.

The goal is to submit graphic files that require as little memory as possible without producing a *grainy* or *pixelated* appearance. Smaller files load and print faster. Unless producing the proposal for offset printing, 150 dpi (dots per inch) is generally adequate for most laser or inkjet printers. For on-line viewing, a 72 dpi resolution is adequate.

Graphics programs offer multiple formats when saving files. Consider how the graphic will be used, whether printed, viewed on-screen, or inserted in a presentation. If you anticipate future edits, save the graphic in the

native file creation format, and save in a more compact format that is compatible with your anticipated use and software.

Here are some general guidelines:

- If images are for print, use TIF/TIFF. If you need an editable version, use your software's native file format.

The optimal file format also depends upon the type of graphic, whether photograph or solid-color line art, as summarized in figure 1. Common graphics file formats, definitions, and features are summarized in figure 2.

TYPE	PROPERTIES	BEST QUALITY	SMALLEST SIZE	MAXIMUM COMPATIBILITY (PC, MAC, UNIX)	POOREST QUALITY
Photograph	Continuous tones, no text, few edges	TIF or PNG	JPG	TIF or JPG	GIF
Line art	Solid colors, text or lines, sharp edges	PNG or TIF	TIF, GIF, or PNG	TIF, GIF, PNG	JPG

Figure 1. Match the Image to the File Format. *The optimal graphics file format depends upon the type of graphic, customer requirement, and end use(s).*

FORMAT	DEFINITION	FEATURES
BMP	Windows Bitmap	Not compressed, quite large
GIF	Graphics Interchange Format	Limited to 256 colors
JPG	Or JPEG (Joint Photographic Experts Group)	Smallest, loses detail when edited and saved
PNG	Portable Network Graphics	Supports 16 million colors
TIF	Or TIFF (Tagged Image File Format)	Standard for printing but not for web browsers
WMF	Windows Metafile	Used in Windows applications for line art
EMF	Enhanced Metafile	Successor to WMF, for Office applications, compatible with print drivers

Figure 2. File Formats and Features. *While the software evolves rapidly, these are the most frequently encountered graphics file formats in electronic and printed proposals.*

6 Learn and test all systems early in the preparation process.

Only the naive fail to test production systems, including the electronic ones.

An *expert* always assures that there will be no problems. Do not bet your job on an expert's reassurances.

7 Furnish at least one hard copy, if allowed by the customer.

Just in case something does go wrong, a hard copy will ensure you meet submittal instructions. Despite requesting electronic proposals, customer evaluation teams with multiple members will often have a few who do not like to evaluate on-screen. These evaluators will appreciate having a choice of evaluation media.

8 Consider a landscape, 3-column, PDF format for proposals that will be reviewed on-screen.

Some evaluators also evaluate on-screen. With a single monitor, on-screen evaluators may prefer a narrower portrait presentation. Alternatively, they may use an additional monitor or may place the evaluation window above or below the proposal window. If so, the wider page would be preferred.

The best page design for A4 (a metric standard of 210mm x 297mm, or 8.268" x 11.693") or 8.5" x 11" paper may not be the best design for a computer screen. For support, consider the evolution of web pages. Early web pages often were taken directly from paper documents with little modification and were ineffective.

Proposal page designs tend to be portrait, meaning a larger height than width. Computer screens tend to have a larger width than height. Consider going to a two- or three-column format to make your proposal easier to read on-screen. Use PDF format to ensure the viewer sees the content exactly as you intended, regardless of computer platform.

Another option is to send a hyperlinked file, but only if you have the necessary tools and skills. A hyperlinked file contains embedded links to additional files or screens that may contain graphics, supporting data, more detailed explanations, and full-motion video with sound.

Keep the following in mind when preparing electronic submittals:

- Be specific in your requests to customers to avoid being surprised by their answers.
- Always collaborate with the customers to understand what will work best for both of your organizations.
- Explicitly follow each customer's final instructions. Surprises are almost always negative. The best time for constructive collaboration is early in the sales cycle.

Executive Summaries are the most important pages in a proposal. They set the tone for individual evaluators and are often the only pages read by the decision makers.

Three executive summaries are included in MODEL DOCUMENTS.

Because the executive summary is owned by the capture manager but often written by the proposal manager, this topic section is also included in the *Capture Guide*.

The draft executive summary should be developed early during capture planning. The capture manager should prepare the first draft and present it at the Preliminary Bid Decision Gate review to demonstrate understanding of the customer's hot button issues, vision, and the seller's baseline solution.

The initial draft is often only an outline with place-holders for the seller's solution. While the capture manager maintains executive summary ownership, the proposal manager often transforms the outline, mockup, or first draft into a draft acceptable for the proposal kickoff.

Readers of your executive summary must clearly understand your solution and its unique benefits and be able to justify recommending your solution over competing solutions.

Effective executive summaries meet the following criteria:

- Connect your solution to the customer's business vision
- Identify the customer's needs and make ownership of those needs explicit
- Connect your solution directly to the customer's needs
- Offer clear proof of your claims
- Show how you offer greater value than the competition
- Be brief but comprehensive by eliminating confusing technical details that are better explained in the body of the proposal
- Indicate the next step, usually by previewing how your proposal is organized

Executive summaries are also powerful internal tools:

- Help refine your bidding strategy
- Become a vehicle to gain senior management endorsement
- Communicate your strategy in-house to all contributors
- Drive proposal development
- Become a model for the complete proposal

Executive Summary

1. Always include an executive summary.

2. Maintain a customer focus throughout.

3. Build on your existing sales process and strategy.

4. Organize the content to be clear and persuasive.

5. Expand the Four-Box Template into a single- or multiple-page draft.

6. Develop your executive summary based on proven best-in-class practices.

7. Follow sound writing guidelines.

8. Follow a defined process when preparing on short notice.

1

See ORGANIZATION.

Always include an executive summary.

If the customer asks for an executive summary, submit one. If not, do so anyway.

Call it whatever the customer calls it. Common alternatives are management summary and management overview.

Independent of what the customer calls it, understand the difference between a summary and an introduction. A summary summarizes the essential content of your proposal. An introduction indicates how your proposal is organized. Other terms for introduction are preview, road map, and informal table of contents.

To include an executive summary when the proposal outline is strictly defined in the bid request, you have several compliant alternatives. One is to include a separately bound executive summary. Place a copy in every volume submitted, either in a pocket in the front or in the binder. Note that in page-limited proposals, the executive summary is considered part of your technical proposal.

An alternative is to make the executive summary the first part of your volume summary in each volume of the proposal.

Summarize at all levels: proposal, volume, section, and question.

2

See Customer Focus.

Maintain a customer focus throughout.

Check the focus of your executive summaries against the following criteria:

- States the customer's vision
- Connects the vision to the immediate purchase
- Cites the customer's hot buttons in order of importance or the order listed in the bid request

- Makes the customer's ownership of the hot buttons explicit
- Addresses each hot button in the order introduced
- Names the customer more than the seller
- Names the customer before the seller in the document, paragraphs, and sentences
- Cites benefits before features

3

See Capture Planning *and* Proposal Management Plan.

Build on your existing sales process and strategy.

To maintain a consistent message with your customer and to save time, exploit your existing internal information sources as much as possible.

Many organizations have embraced a strategic and/or tactical sales process. Exploit it to develop your executive summary rather than starting over. With a little effort, you can map the information from existing sales templates into your executive summary.

When business development people are asked to draft the executive summary, too many still pull the last one they prepared, do a *search and replace* for customer and product names, add one or two sentences, and submit. They continue to tailor their last executive summary for subsequent opportunities until the executive summary completely unravels.

Most of the information needed to prepare the executive summary is contained in the capture plan and proposal management plan. The

three key worksheets summarized in figures 1, 2, and 3 are recommended to help assemble and organize the information needed for an executive summary. One example issue is completed to illustrate each worksheet.

The most frequently overlooked portion of strategy statements is how the strategy will be implemented. Note the *how* in the following example:

> We will emphasize our ability to test full-scale components by including a photo of our Manchester test facility.

Using the information in the three worksheets shown as a source, prepare the Executive Summary Solution Worksheet shown in figure 4 with the same hot buttons/issues consolidated from the other three worksheets.

You now have the information needed to begin drafting your executive summary.

*Shipley*Associates **Integrated Solution Worksheet**								
Item No.	Customer Issues	Customer Requirements	Available Solution	Gap	Competitor Solution	Discriminators	Strategy	Action Required Enter Opportunity Name Here
1	System must be available.	8 hr. response time.	2 hr. response time	1 hr	3 hr. response time	Faster response but more expensive?	Emphasize no additional cost with cellular.	Show current response time. Show photo- service with cell phone.

Figure 1. Integrated Solution Worksheet. *The primary focus of this template is to arrive at a competitive solution that is aligned with the customer's issues and requirements. The strategic messages communicated in sales calls must also be communicated in the executive summary.*

For additional uses of the *Integrated Customer Solution Worksheet* and *Bidder Comparison Matrix, see* CAPTURE PLANNING, PROPOSAL STRATEGY; *and* TEAMING, *Capture Guide.*

ISSUES	WEIGHT	US (SCORE)	COMPANY A	COMPANY B
Seller's service quality	30	25	20	15
TOTAL SCORE	100			

Figure 2. Bidder Comparison Matrix. *The primary focus of this template is to discern how the customer organization perceives your team's solution versus your competitors' as it relates to the customer's issues. In this example, service quality is seen by the customer as a strength.*

STRATEGY STATEMENT WORKSHEET

- We will emphasize our strengths in: *delivering 2-hr. response*
  by: *including summaries of our actual service response in the prospect's area.*

- We will mitigate our weaknesses in: _____

  by: _____

- We will highlight our competitors' weaknesses in: _____

  by: _____

- We will downplay our competitors' strengths in: _____

  by: _____

Figure 3. Proposal Strategy Statements. *The primary focus of proposal strategy statements is to identify ways you can implement or convey your strategy on paper in a written executive summary and proposal.*

To use all features of form, enable macros. See Word Help for instructions.
For context-specific help, press F1 (Windows) or Help (Mac OS).
If there are more than 4 hot buttons, use additional worksheets.

ShipleyAssociates®

**Executive Summary
Solution Worksheet**

Plan Using the Solution Worksheet

Hot Buttons			
#1	#2	#3	#4
Improve system availability			

Solution

2-hr. response

Alternative(s) Considered

3-hr. response

Discriminators

No additional cost. Greater availability

Proof

Experience

List area clients & equip #'s

Performance

Quote records - use XYZ quote

Copyright 2016 Shipley Associates.   1

Figure 4. Executive Summary Solution Worksheet. *Either complete this worksheet by extracting information from the previous three templates or simply begin with this one.*

4

Organize the content to be clear and persuasive.

See MODEL DOCUMENTS for examples of executive summaries in the four-box organizational style.

See ORGANIZATION.

See MODEL DOCUMENT 3 for an example.

Transfer the content that you developed and summarized in the Executive Summary Solution Worksheet into the Four-Box Template, shown in figure 5.

The Four-Box Template is based on fundamental principles of how to organize a persuasive document.

This four-box organizational approach is nearly always more customer focused than the narrative or mirror approach. The mirror approach is a mini-version of your proposal, most often used when the proposal is formally solicited, and the structure is rigidly defined in the bid request.

The Four-Box Template includes four primary *boxes*, organized around your customer's hot button issues:

Box 1

Summary: Align with the customer's vision, summarize needs, preview your solution, and indicate compliance.

Box 2

Introduction: Introduce the customer's hot buttons.

Box 3

Body: Present your solution aligned with the customer's hot buttons, including substantiating detail as proof of your claims.

Box 4

Review: Much like Box 1, summarize the needs and your solution, and state the next step.

Use the Four-Box Template to draft an executive summary in an organized, expandable structure. Also, use it to prepare other sales documents and presentations.

If you have developed a quantified value proposition, consider organizing your executive summary around components of the value proposition rather than hot button issues. State your quantified value proposition as the theme statement in Box 1. Introduce quantified components in Box 2, and then expand on each component in Box 3. Restate your value proposition in Box 4, and introduce the proposal.

CONTENT

Box 1–SUMMARY: Recognize customer's vision, challenges, and objectives, and introduce your solution.

Box 2–INTRODUCTION: Establish and prioritize customer's needs (current needs and desired status). This is a preview of what's to come—key points, customer issues, challenges, etc.

Box 3–BODY: Present solutions to the customer's needs, emphasizing benefits and results. Identify your proof. Maintain the same organizational scheme introduced in Box 2.

Box 4–REVIEW: State why the customer should select you. Summarize the unique contribution your solution makes to your customer's success. Indicate the next step.

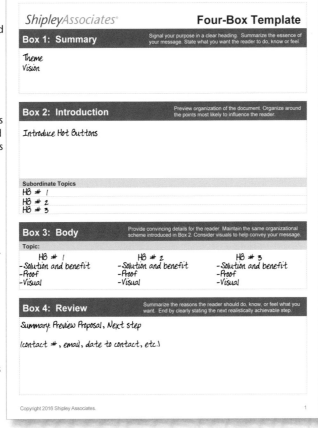

PROCESS

1. Brainstorm a high-level strategic theme that encompasses the customer's strategic direction, this specific opportunity, and your overall strategy to address needs. Write the theme and introduction to the executive summary in Box 1.

2. Copy the customer's top hot buttons from the Executive Summary Solution Worksheet into Box 2. These customer hot buttons will be the basis for the bullet points.

3. Copy the hot buttons from Box 2 into Box 3 as subtitles.

4. Under each subtitle in Box 3, list the paragraphs that you plan to write to communicate your organization's solution, including:
   - The benefits and features of the solution, emphasizing any applicable discriminators.
   - The visuals of any type that will be included. Think of visuals before text.
   - Proof of claims to be included. Most should be visual.
   - Alternatives and justification of your approach.

5. Restate your overall strategy and summarize your solution and discriminators in Box 4. Suggest the next step as appropriate.

Figure 5. Using a Four-Box Template. *The content of each "box" is summarized on the left. Follow the process steps on the right to map your winning sales strategy into your executive summary.*

5

See Value Proposition, *Capture Guide.*

Expand the Four-Box Template into a single- or multiple-page draft.

The Four-Box Template helps you identify key selling points within a customer-focused, clear framework. Expand the framework into a first draft:

- Develop the visuals.
- Draft action captions for the visuals.
- Draft text directing evaluators to the graphics.
- Draft text describing your solutions.
- Draft text describing your experience and proof of performance.
- Summarize your costs/pricing if permitted by purchasing rules.
- Draft text summarizing how your proposal is organized.

Figure 6 illustrates how the Four-Box Template is expanded into a 5-page executive summary. Allocate pages in the executive summary according to the relative importance of the topic to the customer, tempered somewhat by the relative competitive strength of this feature or aspect of your offer. Determining the total length of your executive summary is discussed in guideline 6.

If you develop value propositions as an integral part of your sales approach, summarize them in your executive summary. Present your summary value proposition in Box 1. Introduce individual value propositions in Box 2. Discuss each value proposition against your solution in Box 3. Summarize in Box 4.

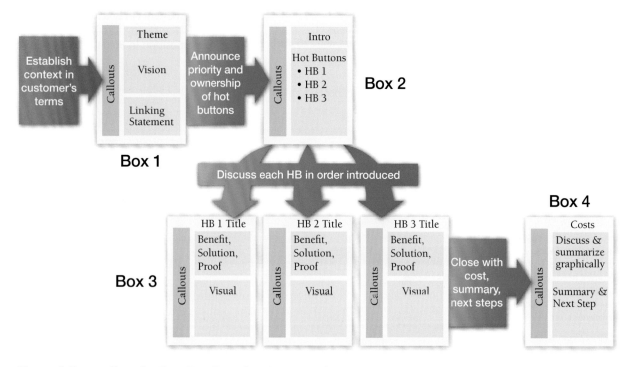

Figure 6. Expanding the Four-Box Template into a Multi-Page Executive Summary. *In this example, Boxes 1 and 2 occupy the first page. Each of the three hot buttons is discussed on a single page, in the order introduced. Visuals are included if appropriate. The last page includes the costs and a brief summary before pointing the evaluator to the rest of the proposal.*

6 Develop your executive summary based on proven best-in-class practices.

See PRESENTATIONS TO CUSTOMERS, *Capture Guide.*

The following guidelines are based on years of consulting and observation of best practices in organizations with a proven ability to cost effectively win business.

- Sales should complete the first draft of the executive summary prior to the proposal kickoff meeting.
- The proposal manager or sales support should review the draft, add detail on the solution, and complete it early enough to permit review by sales and management.
- Review your draft executive summary with your customer-coach if possible.

- Limit the total length to 5 to 10 percent of the page length of your proposal, tempered by how much you think this particular customer's managers will read.
- Make it more visual than the rest of the proposal.
- Use your executive summary as the basis for your finals briefing. Update it if needed and distribute copies to the customer at the end.
- Maintain your customer focus from start to finish.

7 Follow sound writing guidelines.

See RELEVANT EXPERIENCE/PAST PERFORMANCE.

Follow these writing guidelines to consistently write effective executive summaries. As a manager, use it as a review checklist.

- Except in small proposals (under 20 pages), write the executive summary as a stand-alone document.
- Write executive summaries for upper-level, non-technical decision makers.
- Make the executive summary brief but comprehensive.
- Include visuals throughout the executive summary.

- Do not assume that readers of the executive summary have been privy to information given during earlier sales calls.
- Organize the executive summary using a customer-focused framework.
- Clearly state what you are offering and how it benefits the customer.
- Offer clear proof of your claims.
- Tie major discriminators prominently and explicitly to a customer issue.

8 Follow a defined process when preparing on short notice.

See PRESENTATIONS TO CUSTOMERS, *Capture Guide.*

Use this abbreviated procedure when you are out of time or called on to draft an executive summary on short notice.

1. Define the customer's hot buttons, for Box 2. (Two to five hot buttons.)
2. Allocate all major requirements, high-level aspects of your solution, and your discriminators to at least one hot button, for Box 3. If you have help, assign the drafting of one or more of the hot button portions of Box 3 after completing this step.
3. Draft a paragraph connecting the customer's vision, the customer's immediate need, and the most unique aspect of your solution, for Box 1.

4. Summarize the price, your solution, *why you*, and indicate the next step, for Box 4.
5. Review the content as a team, then edit carefully. Be especially careful if you have multiple contributors.
6. Spend the rest of the time available polishing. Resist changing your solution.

If you have the opportunity to present your proposal to the customer, use your executive summary as the basis for the presentation. Prepare the slides using your graphics and text, presented in the same order, and leave a copy of the executive summary with your customer as a written summary of your presentation.

False Subjects are words like *it* and *there* that refer to nothing. Eliminate false subjects.

False subjects displace the true subject of a sentence, waste readers' time, and obscure meaning. Eliminating false subjects shortens the sentence.

False subjects are typically placed at the beginning or middle of sentences.

> It is this step that must be correct.

It seems to stand for step, but replacing the pronoun is terrible.

> Step is this step that must be correct.

Begin with the true subject.

> This step must be correct.

Unfortunately, *this* is an indefinite pronoun. Which step must be correct? Using indefinite pronouns forces busy evaluators to search prior text to determine which step. Name the step.

> Step three must be correct.
>
> *or*
>
> The field-demonstration step must be correct.

False Subjects

1. Eliminate false subjects.

1

Also *see* ACTIVE/PASSIVE VOICE, CHOOSING CORRECT WORDS, GOBBLEDYGOOK, JARGON, REDUNDANT WORDS, *and* STYLE AND TONE.

Eliminate false subjects.

Eliminate false subjects whenever possible to make your writing clearer and more concise. Occasionally, false subjects are necessary, as in the following examples.

> It is raining.
>
> It is 8:00 a.m.

Examples of false subjects are shown in figure 1. Note how the revisions are simpler, more direct, shorter, and easier to comprehend. False subjects are at either the beginning or middle of each example sentence. Using simpler, concise words further clarifies and shortens the sentence.

BEFORE *With False Subject*	AFTER *Eliminate False Subject*	BETTER *Eliminate False Subject and Simplify Further*
In recent years, there have been significant declines in the prevalence of tobacco use among active duty personnel. (18 words)	In recent years, tobacco use among active duty personnel has declined significantly. (12 words)	Recently, active duty personnel have used fewer tobacco products. (9 words)
There is some evidence of late completion of task orders. (10 words)	Some evidence shows late completion of task orders. (8 words)	Some task orders are being completed late. (7 words) OR: Some task orders are late. (5 words)
It is certain that changes will need to be made to this design based on the results of the pilot program. (21 words)	We need to change the design based on pilot program results. (11 words)	Design changes are needed based on pilot program results. (9 words)
It will also be possible and feasible, as the outsourcing project proceeds, to identify and definitize important opportunities to further improve the overall utilization of the application. (27 words)	As the outsourcing project proceeds, identifying opportunities to improve overall application utilization is possible. (14 words)	We can identify ways to improve application use during the outsourcing project. (12 words)

Figure 1. Eliminate False Subjects. *Eliminate false subjects and accompanying extraneous words. Use the shortest, simplest, and most correct word. Note how active-voice sentences further shorten sentences and appear more dynamic.*

Features, Advantages, and Benefits are needed to sell effectively in person and in a proposal.

Sales and proposal professionals with extensive training about features, advantages, and benefits, often omit benefits, fail to link features to benefits, or mention benefits only at the end of a presentation or **proposal section.**

Some sales systems stress features, advantages, and benefits while others dismiss them as obsolete. These different views about the importance of features, advantages, and benefits are mostly semantic, resulting from proponents trying to discriminate their sales systems.

Differentiators are features of your offering that differ from a competitor's offering—often called a "unique selling point." *Discriminators* are features of your offer that (1) differ from a competitor's offer (differentiator) and (2) are acknowledged by the customer as important.

See DISCRIMINATORS.

Features are separate aspects of the seller's product or service, such as speed, schedule, process, price, training, certification, capacity, weight, size, or color. For example: (features in italics):

The controller has *400MB of memory.*

This model offers *rack-and-pinion steering, 110 horsepower, and a 7-year/70,000 mile warranty.*

Advantages are how, in the seller's opinion, the product or service can help the customer.

Notice how the features link to advantages in the following examples (advantages in italics):

The controller's 400MB of memory allows you to *store more instructions than your current model.*

The rack-and-pinion steering provides a *fast, accurate steering response.*

Advantages are more powerful than features, and are, in fact, potential benefits.

Benefits are advantages that can solve a problem for the customer. They address the specific issues for which the customer is seeking a solution. Advantages become benefits only under two conditions:

1. They are linked to the customer's needs *(issues).*

2. The customer wants them.

Customer issues are the perceived impediments to successfully achieving an objective and are also referred to as worries, hurts, or pains. Benefits help the customer past these impediments to success. In this way, benefits become the converse of issues: if an issue represents a cost or pain, the benefit eliminates the cost and relieves the pain.

Generic examples of benefits that alleviate issues include reduced cost or risk and improved quality, reliability, profit, or safety. (Benefits in italics).

Our CNC controller with 780MB of memory can meet your need to *electronically download larger CAD instructions.*

Your interest in *avoiding Manhattan's numerous road hazards* is possible when you specify accurate, responsive, rack and pinion steering.

As selling points, features have the least impact on decision makers and can lead to price concerns if overused. Advantages are stronger than features. Convert advantages to benefits as the sale advances to minimize objections, especially in complex sales. Helping the customer see value is especially useful when the customer does not initially value the advantages, or even views them as negatives.

Collaborate with the customer to understand the customer's issues, concerns, and preferences. Collaboration builds rapport and educates both customers and sellers. Explicitly link your features to advantages and convert advantages to benefits. All are important. Customers must explicitly acknowledge or confirm the value of a feature to convert its advantage into a benefit

Benefits have the strongest and most lasting impact on the customer's decisions because they are explicitly linked to alleviating issues. In short, customers buy benefits.

Features, Advantages, and Benefits

1. Collaborate with the customer to develop a common vision of the customer's issues and needs.

2. Members of the selling team must have a common understanding of the customer's issues and needs before they discuss the features and benefits of their solution.

3. Convert advantages to benefits as the sale progresses.

4. Emphasize benefits over features in a complex sale.

5. Quantify benefits whenever possible.

1 Collaborate with the customer to develop a common vision of the customer's issues and needs.

Features linked to benefits become your potential discriminators.

See DISCRIMINATORS.

Benefits cannot be accurately addressed until the customer and the seller develop a common vision of the customer's issues and needs and of an acceptable solution. Experienced sellers routinely make educated guesses about what a customer needs. These guesses can be wrong if the customer's needs are latent or if this customer's needs are different from previous customers' needs.

Consider the following statement to an auto buyer:

> This auto's 4-cylinder engine, rated at 56 miles per gallon, will give you an economical way to commute.

Most proposal writers would cite the 4-cylinder engine as the feature and economical way to commute as the benefit. The economical way to commute is a benefit if the customer is purchasing the auto to commute. If the customer is interested in racing the auto, this feature is a negative benefit. If the customer is wealthy and unconcerned about fuel economy, the feature is merely an advantage. If the customer is reimbursed for operating expenses, the economical operation is neither positive nor negative.

Sellers that claim to know the benefits of their offerings before collaborating with the customer are guessing. When the customer and seller have a common vision of the solution, the seller can accurately address customer benefits.

2 Members of the selling team must have a common understanding of the customer's issues and needs before they discuss the features and benefits of their solution.

Sales systems that dismiss the importance of features and benefits are dismissing generic benefits. Generic benefits are often advantages at best and negative at worst. To understand this nuance, review the dialog in a commercial or the captions in an advertisement. Note the "benefits" that do not interest you.

Many sales professionals and their sales support staff misunderstand and misuse features, advantages, and benefits in their sales documents. Consider your proposals:

1. Are they feature rich and benefit poor? Customers buy benefits. They remember benefits well after most features are forgotten.

2. Do they lead with features and close with benefits? Readers often stop reading before they get to the benefits.

3. Are features linked to benefits? Customers with less expertise than the seller need to see the direct link between the feature and benefit to value the feature.

4. Are the benefits cited generic and only mildly appealing? Did this customer indicate a need or desire for these benefits?

Frequently sales people accurately identify the benefits but fail to communicate them to their proposal writers. With no direct knowledge of the customer's issues and needs, writers guess about benefits or ignore benefits. Alternatively, writers discuss what they know best, the features of their products and services. Writers with short deadlines often use previously written material and ignore benefits because it saves time. Consider this example:

> A seller touts a hair restoration product (feature) that promises to create "great hair" (advantage) and suggests an improved social life (benefit). The customer is a confident, happily married man with great hair.

> This seller fails because (1) the customer already believes he has "great hair," and (2) the customer does not require "great hair" to improve his social life because he is happily married.

3 Convert advantages to benefits as the sale progresses.

To review how features and benefits are incorporated into sales planning documents and proposals, *see* ACTION CAPTIONS, CAPTURE PLANNING, PROPOSAL MANAGEMENT PLAN, PROPOSAL STRATEGY, *and* THEME STATEMENTS.

Advantages are valuable early in a sale because customers will accept intelligent assumptions made by the seller. As the sale advances, the seller is expected to listen carefully and develop competence about specific customer needs. Continued reliance on early assumptions indicates a lack of seller competence, i.e., "This seller does not understand what I need."

The discipline of creating capture plans, sales plans, proposal plans, early executive summary drafts, strategy white papers, theme statements,

and action captions encourages the sales team to do three things:

- Identify issues
- Convert advantages to benefits
- Connect benefits to a specific feature of its offer

Organizations that rely extensively on previously written material usually submit ineffective proposals. Such proposals are full of features and advantages. Too few advantages are accepted as benefits by the customer.

4 Emphasize benefits over features in a complex sale.

Complex sales are characterized by multiple buyers, multiple sellers, high values, and long sales cycles. Simple sales have a single buyer and seller, low value, and a short sales cycle.

In complex sales, buyers purchase benefits, not features. For example:

> A major organization is purchasing a $5 million computer numerically controlled machine tool. A detailed analysis of the cost and benefits of available tools and options with each tool is made to determine the bottom-line impact. No one selects machine tools because, "We liked the color."

Features can positively impact simple sales. Personal examples of a simple sale might be a telephone, TV, stereo, or hand tool. Buyers of these items justify their purchase with reasons like the following:

- It looked good.
- I liked the color.
- It fit the available space.
- It had more features than the other model.

Features place emphasis on the seller and the seller's products and services. However, customer's care about themselves and their organizations. They want to know whether the benefits generated by specific features of the seller's solution will address their issues and deliver the benefits they seek.

Customers faced with mind-numbing lists of features that are not linked to benefits resort to looking for the lowest price.

The following example, common to many computer users and web surfers, illustrates what often happens when features are not linked to benefits.

We all hate to wait for our computer to complete a task. We feel the "pain" of wasted time, our issue. We talked to three experts who recommend three different solutions:

EXPERT	FEATURE	ADVANTAGE
1	Upgrade 400MHz processor to 2.0GHz	5x increase in processor speed
2	Upgrade memory from 512MB to 2GB	4x increase in memory
3	Upgrade 56K modem to DSL connection	10x increase in data transfer speed

All three experts assure us that their recommended solution will save us time. We are confused by the diverse recommendations, uncertain whether any of the recommendations will solve our problem, so we don't buy. We fail to see a valid link between the feature, the claimed advantage, and the benefit we seek.

In this example, the customer's issue is clear—wasted time. The cause, however, is not clear. When the cause is clear to the customer, the customer can approve the solution.

5 Quantify benefits whenever possible.

Many organizations involved in complex sales routinely train their sales teams to develop value propositions for the reasons just listed. While sales teams struggle to identify and quantify benefits, the process is beneficial. Collaboration is improved, their solutions are improved, and the purchase decisions are usually easier and quicker.

See VALUE PROPOSITION, *Capture Guide.*

The potential value of benefits ranges from tangible and quantifiable to intangible and perhaps non-quantifiable. Customers determine value and will not become customers until the value of the benefits being purchased exceeds the price.

Quantifying benefits helps the seller in at least three ways:

1. **Forces collaboration:** Because only customers can determine value, the customer and seller must collaborate to determine the value of a solution. After the customer has helped determine the value, the solution seems more acceptable.

2. **Sharpens vision:** Quantifying benefits improves the solution. The least beneficial features are dropped and more beneficial features might be added. Both the customer and the seller gain a clearer vision of the solution.

3. **Better justifies a price that is already quantified:** Customers often make a value judgment that the solution is worth the price. However, as sales become more complex, customers increasingly need quantitative support for their value judgment. Group purchase decisions are easier when the benefits clearly exceed the price.

Gobbledygook is pompous or abstract words and phrases that garble, obscure, or confuse meaning. Eliminate gobbledygook by using specific, concise words and phrases.

Gobbledygook is the result of using abstract or pompous words and long, convoluted sentences. The meaning is often unintelligible. Both bid requests and proposals contain gobbledygook, often termed "governmentese."

Not this

In order to bring the proposed uniform facility operational software update plan to final completion, each and every personal desktop computational unit must be inventoried as to its currently installed and operational software.

This

To complete the software update, we will need a list of installed software on each PC.

Gobbledygook, like cliché, jargon, redundant words, and wordy phrases, reduces the persuasiveness of sales documents. Eliminate gobbledygook.

Gobbledygook

1. Use specific words.

2. Avoid long, complex, and convoluted phrases.

---

1 Use specific words.

Being specific improves clarity and credibility. Are you selling a weapon system, an airplane, or an F-22?

When you plan to "interface" with the customers, do you plan to call, write, meet, teleconference, send an e-mail, or kiss them?

Many writers are vague because they either do not know how to be specific, or they want to avoid being wrong. While understandable, readers may sense the writer is being evasive and cannot be trusted.

Proposal writers often avoid being specific to reduce the risk to their organization. For example, if you say that you will report regularly, then you cannot be challenged or sued if you report daily, weekly, monthly, or annually. If you say that you will reduce the customer's costs, then you cannot be challenged by your contracts department or by the customer for insufficient cost reductions.

Generalized claims often suggest that you either do not understand the situation or are intentionally evasive. Neither is likely to convince the customer to select your offer.

Sellers must balance their desire to reduce their risk against the probability of winning the bid.

Figure 1 lists pompous and simple alternatives.

GOBBLEDYGOOK

Pompous	Simple	Pompous	Simple	Pompous	Simple	Pompous	Simple
Accordingly	so	Demonstrate	show	Locality	place	Ramification	result
additional	more	discontinue	stop	leverage	use	remunerate,	
ameliorate	improve	disseminate	distribute			remuneration	pay
ascertain	learn			Magnitude	size	request	ask
acquire, purchase	buy	Employ	hire or use	manifest	show	residence	home
activate	start	encounter	meet	manufacture	make		
apprehend	catch	evacuate	leave, empty, clear	methodology	method,	Scheme	plan, idea, project
apprise	tell	exceedingly	very		process, approach	sophisticated	complex
approximately	about	exhibit	show	modification	change	stonewalling	lying
assistance	help					subsequently	later
attempt	try	Fabricate	make	Necessity	need		
		function	work, act	numerous	many	Terminate	end
Cognizant	aware					transmit	send
commence	start	Heterogeneous	different	Paramount	main, chief		
completion	end			perspective	view	Utilization	use
configuration	shape, design	Interface with	call, meet, discuss	possesses	has	utilize	use
		inform	tell	proceed	go		

Figure 1. Examples of Gobbledygook. *Use the shortest, simplest, most specific word available.*

2 Avoid long, complex, and convoluted phrases.

Gobbledygook is common in opening sentences of proposals, especially executive summaries. Writers try to be so inclusive that meaning is lost.

Original version

As we enter the 21st century, the demographics of secondary school students, the attitudes of legislators at all levels of government and parents toward the accountability of schools that their children attend, the increasing demands on teachers and school administrators to improve their performance year-over-year, the discussions over sources of funding, and concerns about the potential for violence and other unhealthy conditions make this an auspicious time to examine a new cohort of high school students in the tradition of the Department of Education's longitudinal data-collection studies, which were first started with the National Longitudinal Study of 1972.

Improved version

National, state, and local policy makers and educators are striving to improve the effectiveness of America's educational system based on facts rather than perceptions. The growing debate about school quality, diversity, standards, and personal safety supports the need to both extend and update the available data.

Word count drops from 101 in the original to 46 in the revision.

Concerns about risk have prompted many writers to open with multiple qualifications before making their claim:

Original version

If no major issues arise, existing regulations remain fixed, the required skilled professionals are available, weather remains suitable for construction, war does not commence, all subcontractors and suppliers perform as promised, and all payments arrive as promised, we should complete the vaccine manufacturing facility on schedule.

Improved version

We will complete the vaccine manufacturing facility on time, unless one of the following unlikely events occurs: . . .

Grant Writing is a branch of proposal writing practiced largely by non-profit organizations seeking funds to maintain or expand their services. Grant writers can win more funding by following sales proposal guidelines and best practices.

A grant is a *monetary* award given by a *funder*. Funders are government agencies, foundations, corporations, or even private individuals. Most funders require a grant proposal that describes and justifies how the funds will be used.

Grant proposals are as varied as the activities they support—from aiding children with birth defects, to funding scientific research, to beautifying playgrounds. Similarly, grant proposal application requirements and evaluations process vary.

Funders require grant applications consisting of an application form, a proposal, or both. An application form is exactly that—a form that asks for the applicant's name, address, and other information, including the applicant's reasons for requesting the funding. Using application forms simplifies evaluation, fosters the appearance of fairness, and may reduce application time.

A grant proposal, as discussed in this *Proposal Guide*, is usually an original document with a logical structure and a clear argument for funding. For some grants, a full grant application requires both a completed form and a written grant proposal.

A primary difference between a grant proposal and a typical sales proposal is the number of competitors. Most sales proposals have fewer than ten competitors, while hundreds may vie for a single grant or a portion of the funds available.

Grant proposals share common elements with proposals for professional services, such as architectural, engineering, and research and development (R&D). Both have numerous competitors, and the evaluations often incorporate peer reviews.

Most professional services proposal guidelines apply to grant proposals. Both respond to well-defined criteria but operate under a similar "no single right answer" concept.

Superior grant applications are persuasive sales documents.

Grant Writing

1. Verify your eligibility.

2. Identify and address the funder's explicit, implicit, and hidden issues.

3. Consider how your proposal will be evaluated.

4. Carefully follow all submittal instructions.

5. Follow sound document organization principles.

6. Lead with a short, compelling executive summary.

7. State your goals as an attractive, positive vision, linked to quantitative objectives.

8. Describe the acute needs of your target population vividly and precisely. Use emotional appeal backed by the most credible facts available.

9. Address the program's goals in every section.

10. Directly link project objectives, activities, milestones, and costs.

11. Link all expenses to required activities and emphasize added value.

12. Support all claims.

13. Limit appendices to requested material.

14. Use emphasis devices to engage reviewers, simplify review, shorten the proposal, and raise your score.

1

Verify your eligibility.

See COMPLIANCE AND RESPONSIVENESS.

Everyone in your organization must understand eligibility guidelines and agree to comply with those guidelines.

Eligibility rules are complex, so verify your eligibility. Eligibility applies at several levels:

- Minimum standards to apply for the grant
- Preferences or extra points given to bidders with desired characteristics
- Acceptable service approaches

For example, government funders may set cost-effectiveness criteria. Programs exceeding the cost-per-participant criteria are ineligible.

All funders have award guidelines and funding priorities. Save time by scanning funders' profiles in the award guidelines for the following items:

- **Limitations** describe locations, applicants, or activities they will not fund.
- **Purpose and activities** should reflect your organization's values.
- **Fields of interest** should fit your program activities and target population. Funders might not use your terms or jargon.

- **Types of support** must match how you plan to use the funds. Funders may direct, limit, or exclude support for capital investments, overhead, operating activities, travel, paid staff, or consultants.
- **Previous grants or grantees** may be excluded. Conversely, funders might prefer to focus funding in a specific area or to direct funding to specific organizations.
- **Grant amounts** may be limited due to budget constraints or the desire to fund multiple programs. Some funders will not fund more than a set percentage of an applicant's total budget.

Determine the types and sizes of grant awards made by non-profits in the U.S. by reviewing their Internal Revenue Service Form 990, available online. Look for the *Grants and Contributions Paid* section. New applicants seldom get all the funds or even the largest single award. Consider the likely number of rewards and request an "average" amount.

2

Identify and address funders' explicit, implicit, and hidden issues.

See PROPOSAL STRATEGY.

Issues are funders' concerns, not yours. Concerns that the applicant has about a solution or approach are called *gaps*—the difference between what the funder wants and what the applicant can offer. Issues are owned by the funder, not the applicant. Avoid the confusion caused by mingling funder issues and applicant gaps.

All proposals should focus on funders' issues. The goals, objectives, proposed activities, experience, and performance of the applicant are relevant and interesting to evaluators only if they are linked to funders' issues. Your proposal is your opportunity to convince them that you are the best candidate to address their issues.

The first place to look for funders' issues is in their stated funding goals and objectives. Review funders' other public materials. Discuss funders' issues with individuals from their

organizations, when possible, without being intrusive or violating funders' guidelines.

You will find three types of issues—explicit, implicit, and hidden. Explicit issues are stated and owned by funders. When restating them, use the funders' terms. Do not paraphrase or switch to your own terms.

Implicit issues are implied, may or may not be understood, and are often not readily apparent to everyone. When restating implicit issues in your proposal, reword them to be explicit.

Hidden issues are either unknown or intentionally unstated. The most dangerous hidden issues are "unmentionable." For example, public figures may be reluctant to discuss some issues for fear of alienating an important constituency. Address hidden issues positively or avoid them.

3

Consider how your proposal will be evaluated.

Influence reviewer selection when possible. Recommend peer reviewers, when permitted, but be aware of potential conflicts of interest.

Winning proposals are consistently easy to evaluate at every step of the evaluation process and, as a result, receive higher scores. Typical evaluation steps are:

- Initial screening
- Independent, individual review and scoring
- Identification and resolution of scoring anomalies

- Recommendations and approval for funding
- Permission to proceed and disbursement of funds.

The **initial screening** eliminates proposals that do not meet the most basic submissions criteria:

- Are all forms included?
- Are all forms completed and signed?

- Are page limitations and format guidelines met?
- Are requested funding levels acceptable?
- Are all eligibility guidelines met?
- Are all required dates met (submittal, commencement, conclusion, reporting)?

When faced with hundreds of proposals, the incentive is high for screeners to quickly eliminate unqualified entries.

Initial screening also eliminates the entries that may not comply with legal requirements. Government funders must follow the law, or their decisions can be challenged. Non-government funders have more latitude, but they generally stay within the organizations' guidelines. Comply with all submission criteria to avoid initial rejection.

If your proposal passes the initial screening, it moves to **independent, individual review** and **scoring**. This detailed review compares proposal content with funding agency criteria.

Several experts may independently evaluate your proposal. Their evaluations will be based on how well you meet the established funding criteria. Reviewers score the proposal or assigned sections and provide comments justifying their score.

If **scoring anomalies** occur, reviewers typically identify and resolve them. Reviewers are

asked to discuss and defend their scores when high and low scores vary more than a predetermined amount.

After scores are tallied and differences resolved, **recommendations and approval** for funding follow.

However, even if you receive a recommendation for funding, do not assume you can proceed. Sufficient funds may not be available, or other situations may arise to prevent funding. When all conditions are met and you know **funds are or will be disbursed**, then proceed.

Evaluation processes range from formal to informal. Generally, the more detailed or formal the evaluation process, the larger the proposal will need to be. Guidelines include:

- Governments tend to use more formal evaluation procedures and request larger proposals.
- Corporations and private individuals tend to want proposals less then five pages long and have a less formal evaluation process. Engage them on the first page or risk rejection.
- Foundations have varying processes. Determine if they prefer a formal or informal process and submit a proposal to match that preference.

Not all grants are numerically scored. Other grading systems might be used.

4

See Customer Focus *and* Outlining.

Carefully follow all submittal instructions.

To get the highest possible score, read the grant proposal submittal instructions carefully and follow them exactly, even if they are illogical.

Proposal reviewers will expect to find your responses in the specified order. Any deviation from the order of instructions makes the reviewers' tasks more difficult and suggests that you might not follow through on grant requirements. The result would likely be a lower score.

When instructions are not clear, explain your approach in a positive, customer-focused manner.

Poor explanation

While you did not specifically request the background and history of our organization, we have included it in the "Overview" section to demonstrate our long commitment to improving the reading skills of elementary school students.

Better, customer-focused explanation

To simplify your evaluation, we have summarized our prior elementary school student reading skill enhancement activities in a short sidebar. All subsection topics are discussed in the order requested in your submittal guidelines.

5

Follow sound document organization principles.

While the principles of organization vary slightly from document to document, organizational guidelines for grant proposals and sales proposals are similar.

1. **Carefully follow all submittal instructions.**

2. **Organize information to simplify evaluation.** Use graphics, tables, informative headings, and callouts to help reviewers find information and relate it to their needs.

3. **Group similar ideas.** A scattered, disorganized response suggests you cannot organize and manage proposed activities.

The required contents for grant proposals vary by government agency and foundation. Figure 1 summarizes and contrasts the contents for both.

See CHOOSING CORRECT WORDS; *and* PERSUASION, *Capture Guide.*

State your most important points first. Place remaining points in decreasing order of importance to the reader. If reviewers cannot find answers they need right away or if they lose interest, they will stop reading.

Summarize at all levels. Begin each section with an introductory summary. If reviewers quit reading after the first sentence of each section, would they get your key point for that section? Preview supporting points in the same order you will present it. If reviewers quit reading after the first paragraph, would they understand your message? Will they be able to find the points in your text that were previewed in your introduction? big sentences, and big words.

After the introduction, include material that supports your point and presents your message. Follow the point order you presented in the introduction. Close with a section summary. Reviewers hear your message three times: In the introductory summary; in the supporting material; and in the closing summary. If your proposal is very short, you may only need a brief introduction and closing.

Adjust your writing style to the reviewers. Use the correct terms, but do not overuse jargon and acronyms. While reviewers may be familiar with certain jargon and acronyms, these terms are dull, less vibrant, and have less emotional appeal. Remember that persuasion requires both emotion and logic. Too many grant writers mistakenly assume that reviewers have similar backgrounds and embrace jargon,

GOVERNMENT AGENCY	FOUNDATION
1. Application cover form	1. Cover letter (Introduction, purpose, amount requested, closing)
2. Executive summary or abstract	2. Cover sheet (Requesting organization, key contact, mission statement, finances, summary of grant request)
3. Table of contents	
4. Program narrative	
5. Budget	3. Narrative (Executive summary, description of the program and proposed impacts)
6. Certifications, forms	
7. Attachments	4. Attachments (Limited to requested items)

Figure 1. Content Lists for Grant Proposals. *These are general lists, as required contents vary. Corporations tend to want shorter, simpler proposals than foundations. For example, target 30 pages for government agencies, 7-to-10 for foundations, and 3-to-5 for corporations, excluding required attachments.*

6

See EXECUTIVE SUMMARY, GRAPHICS, SERVICE PROPOSALS, *and* THEME STATEMENTS.

Lead with a short, compelling executive summary.

The executive summary is the most important page in a grant proposal. It provides a brief, but comprehensive, guide for individual reviewers and is often the only section the decision maker will read.

The executive summary is a synopsis of the entire proposal content, not an ordering of information as in an introduction. Executive summaries for grants are often called abstracts or previews. Name it using the funder's terminology. If the funder does not ask for an executive summary, provide a 1-page summary anyway.

Grant summaries should meet the following criteria, not necessarily in this order:

- Identify the funder's needs in explicit terms, using the funder's terminology.
- Identify the funder's goals and objectives, again using the funder's terminology.

- State your solutions, and connect them directly to the funder's needs.
- State your goals and measurable objectives, and connect them to the funder's goals and objectives.
- Summarize how your solution positively sets you apart from your competition.
- Summarize the beneficial impact (benefit), cost, timing, and funding amount requested.
- Incorporate visual and emotional support of your claims, where possible.
- Maintain a customer focus throughout.
- Use sound writing guidelines.

7 State your goals as an attractive, positive vision, linked to quantitative objectives.

Goals are outcomes or the state that you will attain. Goals are rooted in the vision of what you will attain when the grant is completed and are not measurable or timed. Funders also have goals. To win, you must connect your goals to the funders' goals.

Objectives are measurable, timed milestones. Each goal has a supporting series of measurable objectives or benchmarks that lead to the goal. The objectives in the grant announcement must be the objectives for your program. Address every objective in your needs or problem statement, and link every activity to an objective.

Draft either outcome or process objectives. Outcome objectives are stronger and more convincing because they imply a measurable improvement. Outcome objectives tend to begin with words like *expand, increase, reduce,* or *collect.*

Process objectives are not quantifiable or measurable; they are either complete or not complete. Process objectives tend to begin with words like *provide, establish, develop, initiate,* or *create* and link project deliverables/activities to outcome objectives.

Write process objectives only if required. Because funders will look for measurable outcomes rather than activities for their funding, outcome objectives are more powerful and persuasive.

State goals and objectives in a single sentence. If you cannot, simplify.

Outcome objectives are more powerful, persuasive, and ultimately more successful than process objectives.

*See **Guideline 10**.*

Superior objectives incorporate three parts

1. What quantified change will occur?
2. Who will be impacted?
3. How will they be impacted?

Review the following goal and sub-objectives:

Good example

Goal 1: Improve the reading skills of American children

Outcome objective 1a: Raise the reading ability of 25 grade 1-4 children in the Gallatin Valley by two grade levels.

Outcome objective 1b: Dedicate 100 Pet Partner® hours per week to practice reading with individual, grade 1-4 children in the Gallatin Valley at participating public libraries and elementary schools.

Notice how the following process objective is weaker and less persuasive than outcome objective 1b.

Less effective process objective

Process objective 1c: Provide the opportunity for grade 1-4 children in the Gallatin Valley to practice their reading skills by reading to Pet Partner teams at participating public libraries and elementary schools.

What if no children participate? How many libraries, schools, and children must participate for the program to be successful?

While the target group is clear, cite or identify the number of children, practice hours, and service locations.

8 Describe the acute needs of your target population vividly and precisely. Use emotional appeal backed by the most credible facts available.

Vividly emphasize the acute problem that you will address if your grant is funded. Funders want the greatest benefit for the money spent. They also want to fund where needs are greatest. Adopt a strategy that the needs you address are dire and immediate, and that their funding will relieve the suffering.

Write about all aspects of the problem very specifically. If you cite facts and statistics, use the most credible sources. Most-to-least credible types of statistical sources are:

- What this potential funder says
- What other, similar funders say
- What truly independent sources say
- What you say

Less successful proposals tend to emphasize the last of these—applicants' opinions about the

Federal grants must contribute to the benefit of the public as a whole, not just the benefit of an individual public agency.

Clearly differentiate public needs, the funder's needs, your target population's needs, and your own needs for funding.

needs, their services, and their organizations. All applicants stress their worthiness. Making identical assertions will not discriminate your request.

Keep all facts current, usually with nothing older than 5 years. Demonstrate your expertise but do not exaggerate. Precisely address every program objective in the grant application, describing each service lacking in your area.

Addressing the need as dire can be difficult when seeking a renewal, extension, or supplementary funding. Funders might question your effectiveness. Instead, emphasize the need to expand a proven but limited program. Show that the needs of people *outside* your program are still dire, or explain that the people being served have additional needs.

Poor example

Numerous politicians, educators, and media articles have bemoaned the poor reading skills of young children. A significant minority that begin their education with poor reading skills remain poor achievers in all areas. Those that begin behind stay behind. You can help Park City elementary and preschool children succeed by supporting the R.E.A.D.® Program.

Better example

In 2002, in our highest poverty schools, 68 percent of fourth graders could not read at the basic level, according to the U.S. Department of Education. Over the last 15 years, 15 million students have graduated from high school without the ability to read at the basic level. First Lady Laura Bush noted in her *Ready to Read/Ready to Learn* initiative:

We know that children who have poor beginning reading skills are less likely to develop better reading skills throughout their school careers. Children,

who start school behind, often stay behind. We can reverse that trend.

Your own report, Park City Education Statistics for 2002, cited 3000 students in this at-risk category. Your own statistics noted that in 2001, R.E.A.D. participants improved their reading skills two to four grade levels. At a cost of less than $200 per child, the Park City School District should not only renew the R.E.A.D. Program, but also support its expansion to serve 500 at-risk children during the 2003–2004 term.

Note how the poor example was based on the applicant's opinion and lacked statistics. In contrast, the better example cited facts from the U.S. Department of Education, the First Lady, and the potential funder's own study. Also note that the dire continuing need focuses on the population not yet being served.

9

See CUSTOMER FOCUS *and* THEME STATEMENTS.

Address the program's goals in every section.

The typical contents of a grant were listed in guideline 5. Address the program's goals in every section. Remember that the funder's goals in the grant application are your goals for this program.

Much like drafting customer-focused theme statements, begin the first sentence of each section by restating a funder's goal linked to the topic that you are discussing. Consider these examples:

Executive Summary Theme Statement

Your goal of reducing the auto traffic congestion in the Gotham City central business district by 10 percent can be met by funding the Loaner Bike Program at $5,000 per month.

Program Narrative Theme Statement

Gotham City's 10 percent auto traffic reduction goal can be met if 15 percent of the sub-one mile trips within the core area are via a maintained, free, convenient fleet of Golden Gotham loner bikes positioned in 80 convenient bike racks.

Budget Theme Statement

The 10 percent auto traffic reduction goal is achieved with a low initial cost because the bikes come from unclaimed property.

Note that all three theme statements link the auto traffic reduction goal to a specific feature of the applicant's program.

10

See RELEVANT EXPERIENCE/PAST PERFORMANCE, figure 4, for a related example matrix.

Directly link project objectives, activities, milestones, and costs.

Linking proposed activities to at least one objective suggests that the activity is necessary. Linking milestones to an objective suggests you know how to manage the activities and measure progress. Linking all costs to objectives suggests that all costs are necessary.

When grant writers fail to link objectives, activities, milestones, and costs, reviewers question their necessity. Linking them all suggests that you understand exactly what you will do when funded.

The best way to link objectives, activities, milestones, and costs is in a matrix. Constructing this matrix will test and improve your understanding of your program. Because few grant writers link objectives, activities, milestones, and costs, your program appears clearer, better managed, lower risk, and more cost effective.

11 Link all expenses to required activities and emphasize added value.

While many applicants use unpaid volunteers, quantifying the value of volunteer hours might give you an edge over other applicants.

See APPENDICES. All aspects apply to grant proposals.

Linking expenses to required activities is an extension of guideline 10. Presenting a total budget is easier for the writer than for reviewers, who cannot easily determine if all items are necessary.

Prepare your standard budget, but then allocate all items against the activities. Split categories among activities. Present your allocated budget, not the combined budget.

Emphasize added value in your budget. For example, an organization seeks $20,000 to train, supervise, and motivate 100 volunteers that each donate 2 hours weekly over 1 year (a total of 10,000 service hours following training). The grant writer could argue that volunteers' time at $15/hour is worth $150,000.

Thus, the value proposition for the funder is to spend $20,000 for $170,000 worth of services.

No one wants to pay for anything that appears unnecessary, especially the individuals charged with selecting programs to be funded and monitoring their performance. A program manager for a government agency, corporation, or foundation would feel pretty good about spending $20,000 for $170,000 worth of services.

Do not feel that what you are proposing to do is so deserving that you must be funded. Good grant writers present all programs as deserving. Give reviewers a quantitative as well as an emotional justification to fund your program.

12 Support all claims.

Emphasize your claims and support them. Preserve your credibility with reviewers by removing unsupported claims.

Note that support and proof differ. Support requires at least one example. Proof is much stronger and more difficult to substantiate.

For example, delivering a service one time is support that you can do it again. Proving that you can deliver a service every time requires a 100 percent successful track record.

13 Limit appendices to requested material.

See all sections listed under the *Document Design* heading in the topical table of contents for explanations and examples.

If the materials are not requested or required, do not include them. Do not place materials in an appendix because you think they are interesting, because you always include them, or because you think the grant application should have asked for them. Instead, focus your attention on the most important pages, the body of the proposal.

Appendices are used to streamline documents. Incorporate materials of interest to all reviewers in the proposal. Place materials of interest to only a few readers in an appendix.

Grant writers often append complimentary news clippings, citations, awards, thank-you letters, service photos, facility photos, and quotes from local officials and organizations. While well-received, the approach with the most impact is to incorporate excerpts in the proposal to directly support your claims. Do both when space and time permit.

Refer to all appended materials in the body of the proposal. Include short informative summaries of each appended item.

Place appendices in the following order:
- As requested in the grant application
- As referenced in the proposal

To clearly distinguish the proposal and the appendix, number proposal pages and letter appendix pages, A-1, A-2, . . ., B-1, etc.

Grant applicants often do not meet directly with funders. Instead of stuffing an appendix with additional and costly materials, list the materials, services, and presentations you provide as available upon request. If they bite, you get an audience that others might not get. This proven sales tactic can give you a significant advantage.

14 Use emphasis devices to engage reviewers, simplify review, shorten the proposal, and raise your score.

The best grant proposals are about the service, not the provider of the service. Use all of the emphasis devices discussed in this *Proposal Guide* to emphasize your services.

Photos and graphics may have many interpretations. Do not put in a photo just because it is a great photo. The photo must be directly relevant to the services proposed. Figure 2 shows six photographs and notes why they should or should not be used in a particular proposal.

This photo emphasizes a patient with a therapy dog, but this is not a R.E.A.D.® program service. Emphasize photos that show the proposed service, not other services of the organization, however worthy.

This photo is ideal. Both volunteers are focused on the reader. Reading is clearly the primary activity and the entire Pet Partner team is shown delivering the service.

It's hard to resist this photo, but the emphasis is on the dog. A reviewer primarily concerned with improving children's reading skills could easily question, "Why should I be funding someone's pet?" Even if the reviewer understands the concept, how might it appear to their employer? Emphasize the person receiving the service.

While this child is not reading, no one can miss his pleasure. The volunteer is appropriately present but de-emphasized in the background. Note how this actual caption made a powerful point: "Children who participate report that they know the dogs are listening to them. We all value good listeners; children are no exception."

The success of this photo depends on the "spin" in the caption. A careful reviewer might note that the adult is reading, not the child. The following caption makes the photo effective: "While children spend most therapy time reading in a relaxed, supportive environment, the adult partner will occasionally assist with difficult words or passages."

The emphasis is clearly on the service, but the volunteer is not shown. Could someone think the dog is unsupervised? While a good photo, it is not as effective as photos 2, 4, and 5.

Figure 2. Selecting Appropriate Photos. *A favorite, grant-worthy, and innovative program is Reading Education Assistance Dogs (R.E.A.D.), by Intermountain Therapy Animals (ITA). R.E.A.D. is just one of several ITA programs. The goal of the R.E.A.D. program is improving the literacy skills of children through the assistance of registered Pet Partner therapy teams. While the R.E.A.D. program has been featured in the Wall Street Journal, ABC World News with Peter Jennings (10/27/00), and NBC Nightly News with Tom Brokaw (04/19/02), the R.E.A.D. program could be confused with other ITA programs that a potential funder would not support. Do not lose funding by discussing worthy but unrelated programs. (Images and excerpts courtesy of Intermountain Therapy Animals, Salt Lake City, Utah.)*

Graphics

Graphics are one of the most effective ways to persuade the customer to select your solution. Graphics convey both facts and emotion, equally important aspects of effective persuasion.

Graphics have a multiplier effect on your message. Done well, your message is remembered vividly; done poorly, and your message is obliterated.

High-level readers of proposals, those either making or influencing the selection decision, often only skim proposals, looking at the graphics that stand out, then reading the captions, headings, highlight statements, and the executive summary. These readers must be able to see why you should be selected without reading body text.

Evaluators reviewing each question and requirement will often get together and ask two questions:

- "Did anyone find anything about . . . ?"
- "Which proposal is the best proposal?"

Effective graphics leave overall positive impressions and can make it easy for evaluators to find detailed answers to questions.

Studies of retention show that after a single reading, evaluators will remember twice as much of what they see in a graphic as what they read in text. In addition, when evaluators both see and read the same point, they recall six times as much. The key elements in retention were repetition and dual modes of acquisition.

Writers of winning proposals tend to both visualize and state why they should be selected.

Too many proposal writers still think that their customers are different, that their readers might be turned off by graphics. Such writers justify their lack of graphics with statements like, "Our evaluators are scientists, engineers, or accountants. They just want the facts."

Graphics done well are the facts. Poor, inappropriate graphics are an insult to the evaluator.

Today's readers see professional graphics in business documents, magazines, newspapers, TV, and movies. They expect similar quality graphics in professional proposals.

The wide availability of high-quality graphics, graphics generation software, and color printers make it feasible to create eye-catching, professional graphics and integrate them into proposal text.

The most successful sales people save time and stay on message by using similar graphics throughout the sales cycle. Reuse essentially the same graphics in sales presentations, white papers, executive summaries, proposals, and finals or short list briefings. Repetition increases retention. Just adapt graphics to the situation and medium.

Graphics

1. Select or create graphics that demonstrate your understanding, emphasize your strategy, and highlight your discriminators.
2. Conceive the graphics before you write the text.
3. Select graphics that best support your message.
4. Design or modify graphics until they are understandable by all evaluators.
5. Keep graphics simple, uncluttered, and easy to read, with one key idea per graphic.
6. Introduce graphics in the text before they appear in the proposal.
7. Integrate graphics into the text.
8. Orient graphics vertically.
9. Minimize cumbersome foldouts.
10. Minimize text in graphics. Concentrate text in an action caption.
11. Number graphics in order of appearance in major sections.
12. Include an interpretative action caption with every graphic.

1

Select or create graphics that demonstrate your understanding, emphasize your strategy, and highlight your discriminators.

One of the best ways to demonstrate your understanding of the customer's needs is to visualize what is possible if your solution is selected. People buy benefits, not features, so visualize the benefits—similar to the following good examples:

Laundry soap commercials show happy people going somewhere in clean clothes.

Restaurants show diners enjoying themselves.

Cell phone ads show people talking excitedly, with smiles on their faces, or a person getting help in an emergency.

A photo in an aircraft engine proposal showed a huge, complicated engine with a seven-piece tool kit in the foreground. An informative caption emphasized that the engine could be maintained with the seven tools.

When selling aircraft to the Army, a seller's photo showing battle-ready troops storming out of the aircraft is far more effective than a clean photo of the aircraft without troops.

When selling complex technologies and services, helping the customer visualize what will happen, as shown in figure 1, is usually more effective than describing your approach in dense text. Note the benefits in the caption.

Customers are usually purchasing an improvement in their current process. Show potential process improvements in graphs, charts, sketches, or photos. Even when competitors offer the same solution, the one presented graphically appears superior.

> Customers seek benefits and care relatively little about the process as long as you appear to have a method to deliver the benefits.

Visualize your discriminators to help evaluators remember your differences, while associating your discriminators with the benefits to their organization.

Side-by-side comparisons are particularly effective in highlighting discriminators:

- Current process/proposed process
- Complex process/simplified process
- Old product/new product
- Side-by-side graphs, bar, or pie charts
- Side-by-side scrap bins

Note the side-by-side comparison in figure 2 that compares the current and proposed alignment of a highway. Even the captions are separate to heighten the contrast.

Because graphics are highly emphatic, use them to convey important information. Do not insert graphics to *break up the text.*

The following examples represent poor ways graphics have been used:

A proposal graphic occupied an entire page showing a single finger pressing a single button on a phone set.

Proposals include clichéd clip art sketches of clasped hands to represent a proposed partnership (even when not requested), a light bulb to represent a good idea, or smiley faces to represent happy users.

Clip art can be used in graphics but must be used carefully. Note how relatively simple clip art is used effectively in figure 3 to depict how to brew at home.

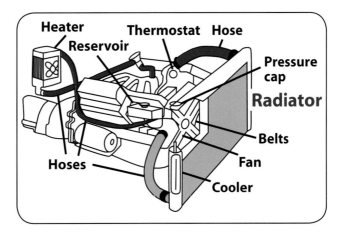

Figure 1. Inside Your Cooling System. *You achieve high reliability and minimal maintenance with modern auto cooling systems. As your engine reaches its optimal operating temperature, the thermostat opens, permitting hot coolant to flow out of the engine block and through the radiator. The relatively cool outside air lowers the coolant temperature before cycling it back to the engine. The heater is essentially another small radiator, which radiates heat to the air inside the car.*

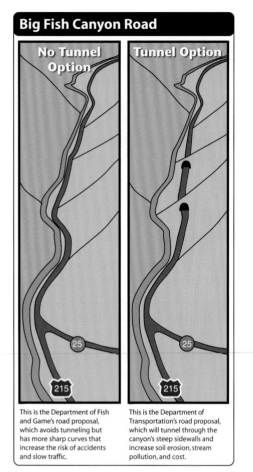

Figure 2. Side-by-Side Comparisons Emphasize Differences. *Graphics, like the one above, are effective to contrast the current versus proposed approach, alternative approaches, or your approach versus a competitor's approach.*

Figure 3. Use Clip Art Carefully. *Considering that many books have been written on home brewing, the relative simplicity of the graphics and text creates the impression that the task is both well understood by the writer and likely to be completed successfully. Note how the slight rotation of the recipe card heightens interest as do the mugs behind the step numbers.*

---

2 Conceive the graphics before you write the text.

See STORYBOARDS AND MOCKUPS.

Create graphics first. Write the text last. Do the things first that will have the greatest persuasive impact on the evaluator.

Preparing graphics first is a huge time saver, often cutting writing time by one-third. Everyone wants to wordsmith text. A graphic is either correct or not. After completing the graphics, writers often find they have much less text to write.

If text is drafted before the graphic is developed, most writers stubbornly resist deleting the now-redundant text.

Proposals often contain long descriptions of processes that would be better depicted in a graphic. Figure 4 shows how black ice forms on roadways. Text descriptions could take pages. The graphic uses a fraction of the page and is clear.

Figure 4. Depict Processes Graphically. *This four-part graphic explains a process much more easily, clearly, and briefly than could be done using only text. Prepare similar graphics to explain complex technical processes and eliminate the cumbersome and ineffective text descriptions that most sellers use.*

Many proposals are for technical services. The written descriptions of these services are frequently too complex to be understood, and the complexity suggests greater risk.

Instead, depict your service processes graphically as shown in figure 5. Often the only discriminator among contractors is the clarity of the explanations of their services.

Another bonus—you can reuse these graphics in every proposal for the same services and eliminate pages of boring text.

Evaluators often say, "We looked at the tables, charts, and graphics first. If we found the answers, we did not bother to read the text."

The entire storyboarding process used to create winning proposals is focused on designing proposal sections graphically in response to the bid request and then conceiving appropriate graphics.

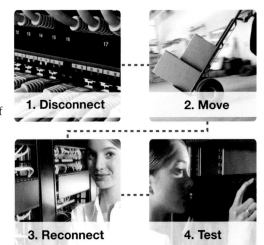

Reliable 4-step Equipment Move Process. Simple and proven processes are more reliable. Our technicians disconnect equipment, labeling cables as needed to simplify reconnection. During the move, all equipment is packed to prevent damage. Technicians reconnect each item and completely test the equipment to ensure operators can immediately resume productive work.

Figure 5. Use Graphics to Sell Your Processes. *This graphic shows an excellent way to eliminate tiresome prose or bullet points describing a process. Once developed, graphics like this can be used in multiple proposals. Clarity implies simplicity, which suggests low risk.*

---

3 Select graphics that best support your message.

The type of graphic you select should depend on the point you want to make with the evaluator. Figure 6 summarizes which types of graphics can be used to best support your message.

Do not select graphics simply because they are available. Keep the following selection guidelines in mind:

- Charts show relationships or the flow between items.

- Graphs show correlations, trends, or comparisons, depending on whether it is a line, bar, or pie graph.

- Photos show realism, that the item exists.

- Illustrations show specific features and eliminate extraneous detail that could be confusing in a photograph.

- Maps and drawings show relationships, often to scale.

- Tables emphasize actual numbers. When the absolute value of the number is most important, use a table. When a comparison or trend is most important, use a graph.

For example, when discussing your salary, do you want to see a graph (trends in salaries) or the amount you will be paid (table of comparable salaries)? For most, comparability is more important than the trend. If you start low enough, the trend looks great, but you are still underpaid.

TYPES OF GRAPHIC	Advantage Disadvantage [1]	Cause/ Effect	Chronology	Compare/ Contrast [1]	Costs Prices	Decisions Alternatives	Designs Components	Organizational Relationships	Processes	Policies Procedures	Trends
Bar Graph	✔		✔	✔	✔	✔					✔
Blueprint							✔				
Combination	✔	✔	✔	✔	✔ [3]	✔		✔	✔	✔	✔
Flow Chart		✔	✔			✔		✔	✔	✔	
Illustration	✔	✔	✔ [2]	✔		✔	✔		✔ [2]		✔
Line Graph		✔	✔	✔	✔						✔
Map/Site Plan						✔	✔				✔
Photograph	✔	✔	✔ [2]	✔			✔		✔ [2]		✔
Pie Graph	✔			✔	✔	✔					✔
Schematic Drawing							✔				
Table	✔	✔	✔	✔	✔	✔		✔		✔	✔
Tree Diagram						✔		✔	✔	✔	

[1] Almost any side-by-side comparison can show advantages/disadvantages.

[2] Photographs or illustrations can be presented in a series.

[3] Excellent cost combinations are tables with an inset graph, or a graph with an inset table.

Figure 6. Support Your Strategy with Appropriate Graphics. *Different types or styles of graphics will support your strategy, purpose, or intent better than others. Use this table to help you select more appropriate graphics. The footnotes offer further recommendations.*

4 Design or modify graphics until they are understandable by all evaluators.

See EXECUTIVE SUMMARY.

Choose graphics that are appropriate to the readers of that section of the proposal. Executive summary graphics must be understandable by all potential readers, including non-technical ones.

Within a proposal and within proposal sections, you can increase the technical complexity of both graphics and text. Begin with a succinct, clear summary that is broadly understandable. Then increase the complexity as needed to satisfy your more technical evaluators. The less technical evaluators will have quit reading and jumped to the next section. Apply this guideline to both graphics and text.

While highly technical proposal sections will have more complex, technical graphics, only include sufficient technical detail to make them correct. Proposals are not technical treatises, and readers often perceive overly technical graphics as technical arrogance.

Some of the most useful stock materials for a proposal writer are boilerplate graphics. But always tailor boilerplate graphics for the evaluators of each proposal.

5 Keep graphics simple, uncluttered, and easy to read, with one key idea per graphic.

Like good paragraphs, good graphics have one key point. If you realize that you have several points, divide them into several graphics.

When brainstorming graphics, ask yourself these questions:

- What is the overall point I am trying to make?
- What is the most important idea that I must communicate?
- What is the central concept?

- How are we different in this area?
- What is unique, desirable, or beneficial?

Many large organizations bidding government programs have prepared elaborate macro graphics that portray the entire program. These graphics are understandable after they have been explained for 30 minutes. They do not work well in a proposal with a single paragraph caption. Very few evaluators have the patience to figure them out.

Keep the 10-Second Rule in mind. If evaluators cannot get the point in 10 seconds, they will turn the page. Does the graphic in figure 7 pass the 10-Second Rule with you?

See CUSTOMER FOCUS.

Complex graphics become clearer over time—to the seller. Few customers give a complex graphic more than 10 seconds before turning the page or tuning out.

Figure 7. Use the 10-Second Rule to check Your Graphics. *All but your most technical graphics should pass the 10-Second Rule. Did the graphic capture your interest? Did you get the message within 10 seconds?*

A better approach is to explain complex concepts through a series of graphics that build to your point.

A proposal writer was assigned to explain the management structure for a 2,600-employee contractor-operated government facility. He developed a five-page foldout that extended from the company president to first-level supervisors and through all 12 business units. The draft caption title was, "Top Management Visibility."

See COLOR.

The complexity of the organization chart and the large number of levels between the president and the proposed organization contradicted the message in the caption.

The fix was one graphic showing the senior management link to the proposed facility manager, a second graphic showing the 12 operating departments, and a third graphic showing each department.

The final series of 14 charts told the management story simply and convincingly. Each graphic had an extended caption, some taking 1/4 to 1/3 of a page. No additional body text was needed beyond the section summary and introduction.

Some graphics cannot be saved; they must be reconceived and recreated, as shown in figures 8 and 9. In figure 8, the help desk process is outlined in the smallest type. The circle suggests a continuous cycle, and the graphic is cluttered with numerous department names.

The intent was to emphasize that a single call would lead to the resolution of a customer's problem. Figure 9 emphasizes the single call to the help desk while downplaying the source of help. Figure 8 is seller focused; figure 9 is customer focused.

To reduce rework, decide on the finished size of your graphic before it is drawn. Frequently, graphics are drawn in one size, then reduced to fit, making lettering hard to read or line width inappropriate.

When writers have graphics assistance, ask each writer to specify an approximate finished size, such as full-page, half-page, or quarter-page. Alternatively, specify column inches, depending on your page design.

Well-designed graphics have a foreground, middle-ground, and background. Foreground objects are centered or slightly off-center, appear in front, have greater line width, or are more visible through the use of color or size.

Middle-ground items show the overall object or concept. These items are usually sketched with medium-weight lines and are less brightly colored.

Background items are used to establish context, enhance realism, and add balance. Background items are behind or to the side of fore- and middle-ground objects and are sketched with lighter, narrower lines in more neutral colors.

Nothing stands out when graphics are drawn with the same line width and color throughout, as illustrated in the poor graphic in figure 10.

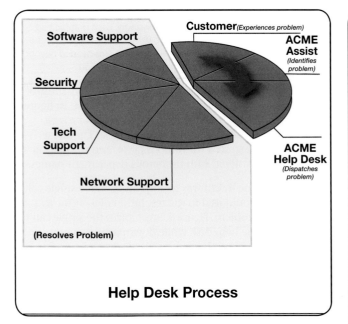

Help Desk Process

Figure 8. Seller-Focused Graphic with "Horse Caption."
If you bother to figure out this graphic, you might get the impression that calling the seller's help desk leads to a runaround response. While perhaps realistic, this was not the message intended.

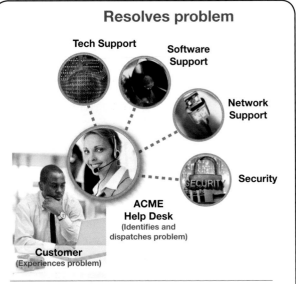

Responsive Help Desk Process. Any user experiencing a problem makes a single call to the ACME help desk. The ACME operator can identify and solve most problems. Some problems will require the assistance of other support experts, but all assistance is managed through the help desk to minimize the need to make callers *start over* with each new expert.

Figure 9. Customer-Focused Graphic with an Action Caption. *In contrast to figure 8, the title adds "responsive" to emphasize the benefit to the customer. The action caption explains the process, including features and benefits.*

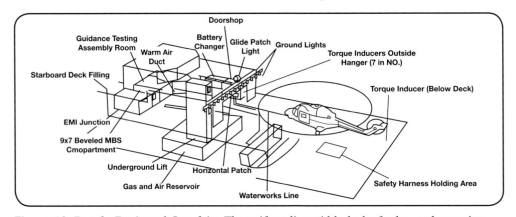

Figure 10. Poorly Designed Graphic. *The uniform line width, lack of color, and excessive labeling of irrelevant details ensure that nothing stands out. The complete lack of a caption in the original graphic ensured that the evaluator did not get the point intended.*

6   Introduce graphics in the text before they appear in the proposal.

Introduce every graphic in the text before it appears in the proposal. Readers encountering a graphic that has not been introduced may get confused.

Introduce the graphic by telling how it fits with or supports other proposal content. You do not have to repeat the content of the graphic in your text. For reinforcement, make the same point in different words.

Make your introduction informative and specific:

> Figure 3 indicates how we helped a major services company in Sweden raise its capture percentage to 68 percent.

> Our 24 x 7 national call center in Salt Lake City is shown in figure 4.

Avoid noninformative introductions like this:

> See figure 5.

> Our organization chart can be found in figure 6.

Like a good action caption, a good introduction puts the spin on the graphic that you want, helping the evaluator interpret its meaning. While we joke about political spin doctors, action captions put the spin on our graphics.

Recognize some exceptions where graphics may not be introduced in prior text. With careful page design, graphics can be so well integrated into the text that introductions can be omitted. A professional executive summary is the most likely part of a proposal to meet this criterion. Eliminating introductions of graphics in proposals is higher risk than in other business documents because the writing and production are done by different individuals under tight time constraints.

See Action Captions, Executive Summary, *and* Page and Document Design.

Another exception might be when a graphic appears at the top of a page in a new section or in the left-hand margin. Also avoid unnecessarily breaking columns of text to insert a graphic if the reader could be confused about where to read next. Such confusion is common in proposals with multiple column page designs, as illustrated in figure 11.

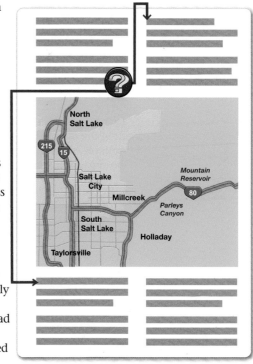

Figure 11. Where to Next? *Minimize evaluator confusion by placing the graphic at the top or bottom of the page. Placing graphics in the middle of text columns as shown may confuse your readers.*

---

7 Integrate graphics into the text.

To enable evaluators to refer to a graphic without turning the page, place graphics on the same or the facing page. Evaluators asked to turn to another page, or worse, an appendix, usually do not.

See Appendices.

Avoid referring to graphics as a group:

> Our approach to facility construction is shown in figures 1 through 14.

Technical and scientific writers traditionally place all graphics at the back for the convenience of the writer. Make your proposal easy to read for the evaluator by integrating your graphics into the text.

---

8 Orient graphics vertically.

Design your proposal to enable the evaluator to read it without rotating or steering the book. Avoid any action that interrupts the flow of ideas from the document to the reader.

If you have numerous graphics better suited to a horizontal or landscape page, consider orienting the entire volume in the same direction. Cost volumes full of spreadsheets are a common example.

---

9 Minimize cumbersome foldouts.

Foldouts have numerous drawbacks:

- Take extra time for the evaluator to unfold and refold
- Make your proposal look much thicker
- Lead to larger, complex graphics that are harder to understand
- Often get torn, removed, or lost from handling
- Require a separate production process followed by error prone insertion in each volume at the last minute

Use foldouts when needed, typically for the following types of graphics:

- Project schedules
- Staffing charts
- Cross-reference matrices
- Engineering drawings

10 Minimize text in graphics. Concentrate text in an action caption.

Concentrate the text with your primary message in the action caption where you can use word processing tools like spellcheck, search, and replace. Production costs are also reduced by letting word processing handle the text and letting the artists do graphics.

Excess text clutters the graphic and distracts from the message intended. Figure 10 is an example of text cluttering a graphic with the excessive numbers of labels.

Insert keys and legends that enable evaluators to understand the graphic, but try to group them to reduce clutter rather than inserting them wherever you have space.

When given the choice of using direct labels on items or a key, use direct labels unless the excessive number of labels clutters the graphic. Remove labels from items not being addressed.

By minimizing text in graphics, graphics are easier to tailor for subsequent proposals without embarrassing inclusions of the wrong client or product name.

Minimizing text in graphics is a guideline with many exceptions. The graphic in figure 12 has extensive text, however, the text is grouped and organized for maximum clarity. Note the simplicity of the graphics in figure 12.

While having skilled graphics support is a great aid to preparing winning proposals, you can use relatively simple graphics to attract a reader's attention, as shown in figure 12. Anyone can find a picture of a car. The car attracts the reader; the text conveys the message.

Another exception is shown in figure 3 where a visual page is inserted as a graphic. Consider the following similar examples, all used in proposals:

- Table of Contents—to show the contents of a plan
- Letter of Commendation—to show excellent, relevant experience
- Certificate—to show compliance with established standards
- Procedure—to show an approach or evidence of a proven approach
- Template/Form—to demonstrate the item already exists
- Sidebar—to label specialized content

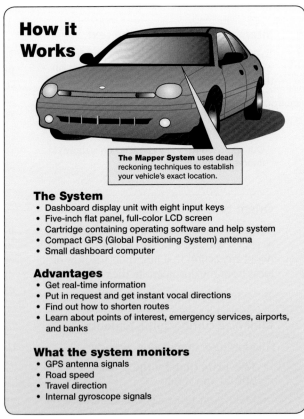

Figure 12. No Artist—Still No Excuse. *Some graphics just draw attention to the text message. In this example, any car graphic (including clip art) would have worked. Do not let the lack of a skilled artist stop you from using graphics in proposals.*

11

Number graphics in order of appearance in major sections.

To make evaluation easy, refer to all graphics as figures or exhibits and number them consecutively within major sections of your proposal.

Refer to both tables and figures as figures. With many forms of blended graphics, such as tables inserted within a figure, adopt a single naming convention to simplify the process for both the evaluator and yourself.

In a short proposal, label all graphics consecutively. In proposals with multiple sections, label them consecutively within sections. Use the section number, an en dash, then the figure number.

> Figure 3–2. Informative Title. Full sentence(s) action caption.

To facilitate matching graphics with section drafts, use the complete section number during proposal development. Then simplify section numbers when control of section drafts is transitioned to the production coordinator.

DURING PROPOSAL DEVELOPMENT	DURING PRODUCTION DEVELOPMENT
Figure 3.2.4-1	Figure 3–10
Figure 3.2.4-2	Figure 3–11
Figure 3.2.4-3	Figure 3–12

Place a complete list of all figures at the beginning of your proposal, immediately after the table of contents.

In multivolume proposals, place a list of figures in every separate binder. Include either the complete list of all figures in the proposal or just the figures contained in that volume. Place the list of figures immediately behind the table of contents for each volume.

12

Include an interpretative action caption with every graphic.

Action captions interpret the graphic for the evaluator. They impart your spin.

All action captions include three parts:

1. Figure number
2. Informative heading
3. Complete sentence(s) explaining the relevance of the graphic to the evaluator, including both benefits and features

See ACTION CAPTIONS *and* FEATURES, ADVANTAGES, AND BENEFITS.

Some graphics are simply inappropriate for the proposal. Figure 13 shows appropriate (on the left) and inappropriate (on the right) graphics for a project management process.

Sometimes a caption cannot save a graphic. The graphic in figure 8 has a *horse caption*. Even if the caption in figure 9 is used with the figure 8 graphic, the graphic is still not effective. The primary focus is on the seller and not the customer.

The message intended is redrawn and accompanied by a more effective caption in figure 9. When graphics just do not seem to work, even with a good action caption, reconceive the message intended.

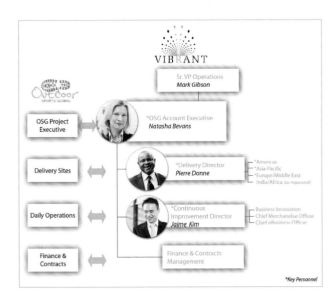
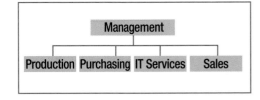

Figure 13. Select Appropriate Graphics. *In a proposal section for project management, the left graphic is more appropriate than the right graphic. The graphic on the right shows an elementary solution only and implies a lack of understanding of the need for personal interface with knowledgeable experts.*

Headings

Headings are essential features of a good proposal. They enable evaluators to quickly find answers to their questions.

Headings make a proposal easier to evaluate, and proposals that are easy to evaluate get higher scores.

Informative headings are one of the best ways to convey key selling points. Unlike formal theme statements, which are sometimes not read by evaluators, informative headings are nearly always read.

Headings enable formal evaluators, those looking for answers to specific evaluation questions on a score sheet, to rapidly locate answers. Informal evaluators, those skimming for content on specific topics, can also rapidly identify content of interest.

Like graphics and white space, headings help break up bleak masses of text, making your proposal more readable.

Headings

1. Use the exact heading dictated in the bid request.

2. Use telegraphic headings to label major sections.

3. Use informative headings in all other instances.

4. Limit numbered headings to three levels unless dictated by the bid request.

5. Use verb headings to convey action; use noun headings to signal your purpose.

6. Make the bulleted list of contents and section subheadings identical in proposal sections with an informal table of contents.

7. Signal the level of heading by placement on the page, size of type, type appearance, and section number.

---

1   Use the exact heading dictated in the bid request.

EXCEPTION: If the customer misspells *potatoe*, you should not repeat the misspelling in your document.

Headings may be directly dictated or implied in a bid request.

Directly dictated

Bid request excerpt:

2.0   Management Plan

1. Organization and Facilities. Include a current organization chart and a brief description of operational function. Describe your organization in terms of size and organizational stability. Identify relevant facility resources (e.g., word processing, graphics generation, DTP, and printing).

Proposal section headings:

2.0   Management Plan

    2.1   Organization and Facilities

If the bid request refers to *Project Management*, then do not change it to *Program Management*, even if that is your organization's usual term. Call it what the customer calls it. If the customer hyphenated the title, Integrated-Systems Engineering, then you hyphenate it, however unconventional.

---

2   Use telegraphic headings to label major sections.

See EXECUTIVE SUMMARY.

Recommended telegraphic headings in a proposal include major, expected, or standard sections. Telegraphic headings only label content:

Executive Summary

Management Summary

Technical Proposal

Cost Volume

Appendix

Most of these will also fall under the first guideline, headings dictated in the bid request.

Telegraphic headings are generally less desirable because they are not very interesting and are less likely than informative headings to capture the attention of busy readers.

3

Use informative headings in all other instances.

Informative, specific headings enable evaluators to immediately determine both the contents of a section and often the benefit to their organization.

Informative headings are like newspaper headlines. They convey the essence of the story and create interest before you read the story. Good informative headings make any document more user friendly, enabling the evaluators to make an informed choice about what and how much they read depending on their interests and needs.

Many proposal section headings are boring, general, and not informative:

Introduction

Organization

Design

Implementation

While these headings qualify as good telegraphic headings, use them primarily when dictated by the bid request instructions. More informative versions would be:

See Discriminators *and* Theme Statements.

How Our Proposal Is Organized to Ease Your Evaluation

Our Flat Organizational Structure Reduces Overhead Cost

T700 Bearing Design Based on Successful Demonstration Program

Continuous Support Through a Three-Phase Implementation

Make informative headings inclusive. Inclusive headings signal that only material mentioned in the heading will be covered in the section. Proposal writers using boilerplate often violate this recommendation.

Busy, skeptical evaluators are more likely to read an informative heading than a formal theme statement. Exploit this by giving your informative headings many of the features of good theme statements:

1. Link a benefit to a feature
2. Cite features that are discriminators

Emulate these examples of informative, inclusive headings that contain both features and benefits:

Cut Bearing Lubrication Downtime 20 Percent with Our Unobtanium, Tapered Design

Detecting Malignant Tissue in Real Time Using Biotec's Laser Probe

DOE Has Unlimited Access to All Proposed Sites to Speed the Phase II Permitting Process

Gain Comprehensive IT Expertise in the Financial Industry

Avoid Start-up Fees by Continuing the Current Contract

Maximize Business Capture Effectiveness by Selectively Outsourcing Proposal Management

Many proposal writers worry that their informative headings become too long when they follow these recommendations. While evaluators have made negative comments about long theme statements, they rarely complain about informative headings being too long.

4

Limit numbered headings to three levels unless dictated by the bid request.

See Compliance and Responsiveness.

Cross-reference matrices often do not contain page numbers because the page number is not known until the final document is published. Including page numbers in the cross-reference matrix is desirable but optional.

Proposals are accessed rather than read. Evaluators search for answers to questions, either formally or informally.

Two devices help evaluators find the information they want:

- Numbered or lettered headings
- Cross-reference matrix or compliance matrix

Use a numbering system with your headings on all but the shortest proposals, approximately five pages or less.

The cross-reference matrix links the specific question in the bid request to the proposal section number and heading where the question is answered.

If your cross-reference matrix does not contain page numbers, your subsection number should direct evaluators to within three pages of the answer. Then an informal table of contents at the beginning of the section and matching unnumbered, run-in subheadings should take the evaluator to the paragraph with the answer.

Using run-in subheadings is an effective way to facilitate evaluation by indicating content without adding more numbered headings.

A Run-in Heading. When you do not use punctuation, make the heading visually distinct from the rest of the text. Use boldface type or a larger typeface.

Always follow the client's bid request numbering and heading system, regardless of level. One such proposal required heading subsection levels 8, 9, and 10.

The levels of headings may be indicated by the numbering system, placement, size, or appearance of the heading. When given the choice, use numeric decimal numbering systems instead of alpha numeric systems to minimize potential reader confusion:

4.2.3.7   vs.   IV.B.3.g

Generally, the less technical your readers, the fewer levels you should use.

Large, formally solicited government proposals often need four to five numbered heading levels. If you cannot direct the evaluator to within a few pages of the answer, add another level. Ease of evaluation is more important than limiting heading levels.

5 — Use verb headings to convey action; use noun headings to signal your purpose.

See Lists.

When given a choice, keep headings parallel in structure. Parallel headings use the same grammatical structure. Parallel verb headings begin with a verb in the same tense. Verb headings tend to be more active and persuasive.

3.1   Cut Bearing Lubrication Downtime 20 Percent with Our Unobtanium Tapered Design

4.2.1   Detect Malignant Tissue in Real Time Using Biotec's Laser Probe

5.3   Gain Comprehensive Computer Expertise in the Financial Industry

8.7.4   Avoid Start-up Fees by Continuing the Current Contract

Noun headings begin with a noun or noun clause and tend to be more useful when answering the bid request question in the heading to avoid forcing evaluators to read the text.

7.2   DOE Has Unlimited Access to All Proposed Sites to Speed the Phase II Permitting Process

8.1   All Systems Operate on 220 Volt 50 Cycle Current

Limit or entirely avoid using question headings in proposals. Question headings may leave the impression with some evaluators that you do not know the answer.

2.0   Can Global Corporation Cut IT Costs?

2.3   How Does Titanium Hold Up in Space?

3.3   Is It Possible to Retrain Existing Personnel?

5.1.1   Can Enemy Missiles Be Detected in Time?

6 — Make the bulleted list of contents and section subheadings identical in proposal sections with an informal table of contents.

See Organization.

Writers that follow the fundamental principles of sound section organization often list topics in their section introduction, then draft informative headings for the subsequent subsections.

Introduction

In our meetings over the past 3 months, your medical technicians said the tumor diagnostic system must have the following characteristics:

- Accurate
- Available
- Cost effective

Subsection headings could be written as:

Test Accuracy Increased from 98 to 99.9 Percent

Availability Demonstrated at 95 Percent Over Two Years of Clinical Use

Beta Users Show Six-Month Payback

While all the headings reflect the same topic and convey important messages, skimming evaluators might not see the immediate connection. Either make the topics announced

in the introduction more informative and match them in the subheadings, or at least begin the subheadings with identical words:

Accurate to 99.9 Percent

Available 95 Percent of the Time During 2 Years of Clinical Use

Cost-Effectiveness Demonstrated by 6-Month Payback

Headings introduced in bulleted lists do not need to be numbered in the subsequent subheadings. However, if the subheading titles have section numbers, then use those same section numbers in the introductory list as illustrated below.

3.0 Introduction

In our meetings over the past 3 months, your medical technicians said the tumor diagnostic system must have the following characteristics:

3.1   Accurate

3.2   Available

3.3   Cost Effective

Subsection headings

3.1 Accurate to 99.9 Percent

3.2 Available 95 Percent of the Time During Two Years of Clinical Use

3.3 Cost-Effectiveness Demonstrated by Six-Month Payback

Be especially careful about making introductions and subheadings identical in the following situations:

- Extensive boilerplate is used to prepare the proposal.

- Multiple writers contribute to the proposal.

- Writers have limited training in or understanding of the basic principles of organization.

When extensive boilerplate is used, additional material is often inserted in section text but not introduced. Conversely, a writer eliminates material that is not relevant to the immediate proposal but forgets to change the introduction.

With multiple writers, a writer may decide to add or delete material without also realizing that the material is previewed in the introduction. A poor solution is to eliminate all introductions or previews. Unfortunately, this solution may be worse than the original lack of agreement between the introduction and the order of subsequent section content.

---

7 Signal the level of heading by placement on the page, size of type, type appearance, and section number.

Placement variations include centering, flush left, indented, and run-in.

A Centered Heading

A Flush-Left Heading

An Indented Heading

A Run-in Heading. The text begins following the period or colon and one or two spaces.

Size variations are possible by varying the point size of the lettering. Larger lettering indicates a higher level.

A 24-pt Heading
A 18-pt Heading
A 14-pt Heading
A 12-pt Heading

Make the size variation large enough to be obvious. Consider changing from **Bold** to Normal at about 24-point, depending on the font.

Appearance variations include the following, generally in the order listed:

1. Point Size
2. **Boldface**
3. Color
4. *Italics*
5. **Font change**
6. ALL CAPITALS
7. Underlining

See PAGE AND DOCUMENT DESIGN.

Generally, try to avoid using ALL CAPITALS and Underlining, as they are harder to read and are outdated, typewriter-like conventions.

Capitalize headings using the same conventions as for titles of books, articles, and other documents. An emerging trend is to capitalize only the first word in a heading, to make the heading more readable.

The most common font style for headings has been sans-serif with serif styles for body text. That convention has been followed in this *Proposal Guide;* however, designers may have sound reasons for other choices.

An emerging trend in many newspapers and magazines is to use serif fonts in headings *because they are easier to read.* In this instance, the designer may have chosen readability over emphasis. However, emphasis may be enhanced by increasing point size more significantly, using a different color, or using a noticeably different serif font.

Avoid using too many different types of fonts. For greater consistency, use the same font for all headings, and, perhaps, a different font for body text. Some designers choose to use the same font for both headings and body text to *make everything look like it is from the same document.* Often designers will choose a font created in both serif and sans-serif versions. For example, the fonts used in this *Proposal Guide* are both from the ITC Stone font family.

The decision of how to apply fonts is usually subjective. Set your style and be consistent.

International Proposals and international capture planning efforts need to be led by individuals who are familiar, and preferably native, to the culture of the customer. If you aim to win significant opportunities, develop the capabilities of your in-country management and support team.

Every country has different acquisition systems. International proposals take on many forms and variations. Bidders must be acutely tuned to specific business practices, customs, standards, and laws.

The trend is for international governments and business organizations to encourage more competitive bidding and more structured evaluation and decision making.

Political considerations, socioeconomic arrangements and investments, protectionism, and teaming with local organizations all play larger roles when acquisition rules are not tightly defined.

Winning bids integrate aspects of the solution, competitive situation, and price. In addition to the obvious differences in cultural customs and communication, consider how you will adapt your solution to the local business and

legal environment, management structures, management and reporting systems, tax structures, utilities, and infrastructure.

International business English is the most common language for commerce and often the only common language among diverse individuals in the customer's organization.

Numerous excellent references have been written about specific international differences in English usage. With the exception of the first two, the following guidelines are generic and limited largely to the writing and production of the proposal document.

International Proposals

1. Respect the customs of customers' countries.

2. Adapt your solution to the local business and legal environment, management structures, management and reporting systems, tax structures, infrastructure, and evaluation approach.

3. Use your normal capitalization, spelling, and punctuation when writing to a foreign contact in English.

4. Use customers' spelling conventions when replying to formal bid requests.

5. Keep your writing clear, short, and concise.

6. Use more graphics, but keep them simple.

7. When in doubt, over-punctuate.

8. Recognize that English usage varies significantly worldwide.

9. Prepare the proposal near the customer.

10. Use translation services cautiously.

11. Adjust your proposal preparation schedule.

12. Offer a *read-through*, oral presentation, and question-and-answer session to ensure your proposal is understood.

---

1   Respect the customs of customers' countries.

The conventions surrounding proposals and business development vary widely between countries, cultures, and organizations. Meticulously observe the usage and practices of each country.

Most business *guides* emphasize what you *should not* do:

- Do not criticize your contact or the person's country.

- Do not impose your pace or schedule on the customer.

What you *should do* is also significant. Find out what you can do to proactively create a positive impression. Local employees or representatives are vital and a formal mechanism should be put in place to evaluate and implement their recommendations for localization. Take into account the relative status of the local representative and the cultural norms that influence their ability to assert the importance of implementing their suggestions.

Locals will know the customs and can help you avoid awkwardness, embarrassment, or perhaps directly insulting the customer.

Consider this example:

A Scottish businessman working for a U.K. corporation was pursuing business in Hong Kong, China. After working closely with a local representative and the local office staff, he impulsively decided to buy a simple gift valued at £10 sterling for a Hong Kong staff person who had put in many hours of overtime on their proposal.

When presented with the gift, the staff person became extremely upset and immediately left the room.

This businessman later learned that in the Chinese culture, gifts of any value are *exchanged*, not given unilaterally. His gift had caused a loss of face because the staff person had no return gift immediately available.

2 Adapt your solution to the local business and legal environment, management structures, management and reporting systems, tax structures, infrastructure, and evaluation approach.

Customs can impact your solution as much as laws. For example, the age, sex, or religion of an individual might limit the ability of that individual to travel, meet, or interact with the customer. Presumed intellectual property protections and the interpretation and enforcement of your typical contract terms and conditions might be invalid or unenforceable.

Management structures, explicit and implicit individual roles, and variations in management and reporting systems often impact your customary project management, delivery, reporting, and billing processes. Tax structures differ and governance rules that evolved over decades might be totally unexpected from your viewpoint.

Presumptions about the availability and reliability of infrastructure vary. Securing local permits might prompt significant schedule changes and add unanticipated costs.

Evaluation approaches vary. Consider any document that you use to advance the sale to be a proposal. Understand how it will be used and what the customer expects; then design your document to exceed expectations.

Many international proposals are both directly compared among the evaluators and shared with other bidders. Understand each customer's confidentiality practices and regulations. Comply with the laws governing the sale.

Evaluators and decision makers are not only available but may expect to be contacted as an indication of your interest. **The only rule is that the customer rules.**

3 Use your normal capitalization, spelling, and punctuation when writing to a foreign contact in English.

With no other rules defined, customers expect you to be yourself. Use your normal approach for informally solicited proposals as well as the other business and sales documents that surround the proposal.

Follow the style customers use for their titles, name, company name, and address.

Be careful when mixing written material with American spelling and a U.K. English speaker, or conversely, U.K. English spelling and an American speaker.

An American presenting American materials in a foreign country is usually acceptable. However, an Englishman presenting the same American materials in the same country might not be equally accepted.

4 Use customers' spelling conventions when replying to formal bid requests.

Follow the rules of the dialect used by the customer. There are multiple dialects in many languages that affect spelling and word usage. American, British, Canadian, and Australian English, for example, use *s* and *z* differently.

While keeping sentences short, do not omit words for economy, as if sending a text message. Omitted words often confuse readers:

Not this

Will upload proposal p.m. to customer site.

This

We will upload our proposal this afternoon to Global Bank's web site.

While using the same spelling convention, you do not have to use the same format and font as was used in the bid request *unless directed to do so by the customer.*

The capitalization, punctuation, and spelling style you use is not as important as being consistent. Consistency both conveys professionalism and makes it easier for foreign readers to understand your message.

5

Also see CHOOSING CORRECT WORDS, GOBBLEDYGOOK, *and* JARGON.

Keep your writing clear, short, and concise.

Use short and simple words, sentences, and paragraphs. In international proposals, complexity can cause translation difficulties as well as confusion and misunderstanding.

Whenever possible, choose a short word over a long, complex, unfamiliar, or abstract word. While this guideline applies universally, it is even more critical in international proposals.

A fellow consultant noted: "English has a relatively simple structure, subject-verb-object. If you change the order, you have to understand punctuation."

Any sentence having more than 20 words is more difficult to understand. An easily readable newspaper, like *USA Today*, averages about 15 words per sentence and one or two sentences per paragraph. Too many short sentences tend to make the writing seem choppy, so writing instructors advise varying sentence length and using transition words. However, choppiness is not the primary concern in international proposals. If your proposal is translated, it will probably seem choppy, independent of how the original sentences were written.

Sentence fragments cause severe difficulties for international readers. Delete fragments or rewrite them as a complete sentence. Evaluators struggling to understand your meaning are unlikely to absorb content. Avoid sentences with subordinate clauses, which often appear as difficult to understand fragments to international readers.

Subordinate clauses are patterned like sentences, having subjects and verbs, but they function as adjectives, adverbs, or nouns. If this is confusing, consider an international reader. If a sentence or clause begins with one of the following words, consider making two sentences:

Because, since, although, even though, rather than, after, before, if, so that, while, when, who, whom, whose, which, that, whoever, whomever, unless, until

Avoid idioms, peculiar or specialized expressions which are used daily but are unfamiliar to members of the culture you are addressing. Idioms are cultural jargon and closely related to gobbledygook.

Here are a few examples:

IDIOM	SYNONYM
bear in mind	consider
workaround	temporary fix, alternate approach
be of one mind	agree
put up with	tolerate
put down	insult
input	enter (computer) or comment, suggestion

Evaluators repeatedly say that they favor proposals that are easy to read and evaluate. Clear, short, concise words, sentences, and paragraphs make international proposals easier to read.

6

See ACTION CAPTIONS, COLOR, *and* GRAPHICS.

Use more graphics, but keep them simple.

Graphics are more universally understood, summarize information and concepts quickly, and reduce the total size of a proposal.

However, foreign evaluators may not understand complex graphics without reading the supporting text that they are already challenged to understand. Simplify all graphics as much as possible and include complete action captions.

7

When in doubt, over-punctuate.

Punctuation is important in all types of writing, but it is mandatory in international documents. Without punctuation, the probability of the evaluator getting lost increases dramatically.

Over-punctuate international proposals, even though the trend is to under-punctuate in domestic correspondence. The intent of punctuation is to add clarity, so make sure your over punctuation is correct.

While usage will vary slightly, most common punctuation marks such as periods (.), quotation marks (""), and commas (,) are understood. Avoid or minimize exclamation points (!), ellipsis points (. . .), and virgules (/).

8

"In service" is jargon. Avoid unnecessary jargon, especially in international proposals.

See JARGON.

Recognize that English usage varies significantly worldwide.

Drop the notion that English is English everywhere in the world. Most are aware that U.S. and U.K. English vary, with many identical words having different and potentially embarrassing meanings.

Acronyms may have different connotations in different regions, even within the same industry. In rail operations, for example, TOC is used to mean Train Operating Company in the UK but in Australia refers to Train Operating Conditions.

Japanese English often does not distinguish between singular and plural words because Japanese speakers do not have singular and plural in their own language and may not be used to making such distinctions.

Egyptian English deviates from U.S. English by treating certain adjectives as nouns: *He is from the Egyptian* [delegation].

American English tends to turn verbs into nouns and nouns into verbs more frequently than U.K. English. Words such as author and euthanize are not commonly accepted as verbs in U.K. English. Yet finalize, editorialize, nationalize, publicize, and miniaturize are accepted. (Apologies to the U.K. English readers for the spelling.) Until commonly accepted, avoid using words that might divert or offend evaluators.

American English speakers and writers often add unnecessary prepositions to verbs. Many readers and listeners in both nations are distracted and irritated by these unnecessary prepositions. Eliminate them.

Consider the following replacement terms:

faced up to	faced
deliver on	deliver
head up	head
check out	check
check up, check up on	check
consult with	consult
free up	free
divide up	divide
cook up	cook
visit with	visit
skirt around	skirt
combine together	combine
join together	join
plan in advance	plan

Differences between U.S. English and U.K. English include different spellings of the same word, different meanings for the same word, and different words for the same meaning.

These examples in figure 1 illustrate how differences in understanding of the same language can lead to trouble or embarrassment. Be aware if you intend to propose successfully to people who are more fluent in U.K. English than in U.S. English.

U.S.	U.K.
bathroom	lavatory
biscuit	scone
center	centre
cookie	biscuit
defense	defence
dessert	pudding
elevator	lift
gas, gasoline	petrol
inventory	stocks
labor	labour
lucked out (lucky)	lucked out (NOT lucky)
parking lot	car park
pavement	road
pay raise or hike	pay rise
program	programme
realize	realise
sales	turnover
table (put aside)	table (act on now)

Figure 1. U.S. Versus U.K English. *Word definitions vary among English speakers.*

9 Prepare the proposal near the customer.

Prepare the proposal geographically near the customer when possible. Remotely-prepared proposals are inevitably less customer-focused and more inbred.

You need a staff that can write, present, and interpret customer's reactions. Even when English is the customer's primary business language, discussions, analysis, and evaluation are often in the native language.

Local preparation can increase your risk if you make unauthorized commitments. If you must prepare the proposal away from the customer, add a local representative to the team.

10 Use translation services cautiously.

If the customer requires translation or you decide to translate all or portions of your proposal, proceed cautiously. Be very particular about the translator's credentials.

In-country translators are a must. Even *good* U.S. translators seldom know local ways.

Language in other nations evolves just as English evolves. Your translator must be current and familiar with regional differences.

Due to the high risk of incorrect translation, use English unless delivering a translated proposal is part of your strategy. At best, an error can be embarrassing; at worst, it can kill the deal.

Review translated work carefully, especially names, numbers, and statistics. Consider having particularly sensitive portions back-translated to verify the translation has remained true to the original.

Computerized translation is improving rapidly but is not yet sufficiently reliable.

Design graphics and pages with translation in mind. Depending on the language, allow 20 to 30 percent more space for text expansion.

Expand your running glossary of acronyms and unique terms to aid the translator.

Translation requires time. Allow 2,000 English words per day per translator. To avoid problems in translation:

- Develop a list of key terms and agree with the translation team the words that will be used to replace them. Avoid using alternative terms that may confuse the reader. Keep the translation team as small as possible to reduce the potential for linguistic variations, inconsistencies or errors.

- Translate only from the base document to reduce the potential for lost meaning due to translations of translations.

Translation costs vary, depending on language and location:

Language	Cost per word (USD)
W. European/S. American	$ 0.22 – 0.34
Asian	$ 0.28 – 0.35
Scandinavian	$ 0.38 – 0.55
E. European	$ 0.28 – 0.41

Note that the absolute costs of translation vary, but the relative cost to translate different languages has remained consistent, though rising with inflation or adjusting with exchange rates.

11 Adjust your proposal preparation schedule.

See Scheduling.

Most countries outside the U.S. use A4-size paper, a metric standard that measures: 210 mm x 297 mm (8.268 in. x 11.693 in.)

Any customer can use missed deadlines as the reason to eliminate your proposal. Varying languages, time zones, cultures, technologies, and laws usually increase the time required to produce a winning proposal.

Translation often applies to many of the bid documents as well as the proposal. Discrepancies in the translated documents take more time to resolve.

Different time zones usually increase the time required. While many people have visions of writers in different time zones working around the clock, you still have the same number of writers available, and the communication time overlap might be narrow.

Many proposal managers who have managed writers in broadly different time zones say they would rather not do it again.

Each country has different utility standards, environmental requirements, and laws. Differences affect your solution and how your writers work.

Management reviews become more complex and reviewers are less likely to be co-located, thus leading to conflicting recommendations. Limits on technology transfer may require time for an outside Commerce Department or regulatory review.

Production time might increase with changes in paper size (A4) or the need to deliver electronic copy. Shipping takes longer and is subject to Customs problems.

12

Offer a *read-through*, oral presentation, and a question-and-answer session to ensure your proposal is understood.

Customers managing international competitions are acutely aware of and worried about the risks of misunderstanding sellers' proposals. Offering to make or even sponsor a *read-through* will both reduce customers' risk and potentially improve your position. Read-throughs give you the chance to observe customers' understanding and to clarify your offer.

An oral presentation followed by questions and answers is a good alternative to the read-through and takes less time. Note that all these options will raise proposal preparation costs, require more time, and require more resources.

If the competition is rigidly managed, all sellers will be given the same opportunity. If the competition is loosely managed, you may be the only seller allowed to present, giving you a significant advantage.

Jargon is specialized language used among members of a group or profession. Use jargon only when customers will be familiar with it and then only when plain English will not suffice.

Every technical discipline or profession needs a specialized vocabulary, but be aware that using jargon can obscure meaning for readers with different backgrounds.

Jargon often reduces the persuasiveness of documents, and excessive, unfamiliar jargon can even give them an arrogant tone. While intelligent, many proposal evaluators are not as expert as the writer, and using jargon may obscure meaning. Because both experts and non-experts evaluate proposals, be clear and concise, avoiding jargon where it might be misinterpreted.

Jargon can be 1) familiar language used in an unfamiliar way, 2) technical or specialized language unfamiliar to a particular reader, or 3) a mixture of both familiar and specialized language.

Consider the following examples:
You have to see our hot new radar.

Hot, a familiar word, can be misinterpreted in a variety of ways including: high temperature, trendy, or even stolen.

Operator efficiency is improved in monitors with a smaller dot-pitch.

Dot-pitch is a technical term that would have to be explained for many readers.

There are many key drivers to internal company change.

Drivers is a common word with specialized meanings, but it is used in this sentence in what could be an unfamiliar context for some readers.

Jargon

1. Minimize jargon. Define necessary jargon for non-expert readers.
2. Replace jargon with plain English when feasible.
3. Use the customer's jargon before using your organization's jargon.

1 Minimize jargon. Define necessary jargon for non-expert readers.

See ABBREVIATIONS.

See GOBBLEDYGOOK.

Minimize jargon in executive summaries, section summaries, and themes, which are more likely to be read by non-experts. Writers using unfamiliar jargon may confuse or alienate the customer.

While not strictly the same, abbreviations are a type of jargon. In proposals, treat jargon like abbreviations; define it the first time the word is used in each major section that is likely to have different evaluators or readers. Using too many abbreviations can make a proposal unreadable.

Jargon and gobbledygook are not the same. Good writing can include some jargon if the jargon is defined or understood in context. Good writing never includes gobbledygook.

Ultimately, customers determine whether jargon is acceptable. Hence, proposal writers must know their customers well. One customer may dislike common business jargon, while another may expect to see these terms used. Even if you see the word or phrase in a Scott Adam's *Dilbert*™ strip, consider replacing it with plain English.

Additional examples of common business and proposal jargon are listed in figure 1.

JARGON				
Acquisition streamlining action plan	Downsize	Headcount	Make redundant market driven mission-critical mission statement	Strategic alliance
Best-in-class best value	Empower enterprise	Industry-leading		Task force telecommute
Core business core competency cost effective cutting edge	Governance granularity	Joint venture	Paradigm partnering	Uncompensated overtime
		Knowledge management	Right-size	World class
		Leverage		

Figure 1. Examples of Common Business Jargon. *Use jargon cautiously, only when essential to express the correct meaning and if this customer will perceive it positively.*

2

Replace jargon with plain English when feasible.

Proposal writers often must choose whether to use customers' exact words or clear, impactful plain English. Plain English is more persuasive and the best choice.

For example, the bid request requires the system to be designed for *maximum maintainability*. Many proposal writers would repeatedly use the phrase *maximum maintainability* to describe their system.

Consider what phrase an advertising agency would use to describe the system. The agency would stress that the system was *easy to fix* or *easy to repair*. Which phrase is more memorable, concise, and clear?

Use or reflect the customer's language, but replace it with plain English when feasible.

3

See INTERNATIONAL PROPOSALS.

Use the customer's jargon before using your organization's jargon.

Jargon might be specific to an industry and an organization. Types of jargon are listed in order of acceptability:

- Customer's jargon
- Industry or business jargon
- Professional jargon
- Seller's jargon

The acceptability of jargon is in direct correlation to the number of individuals using that jargon in the customer's organization and the power of those individuals.

Minimize jargon in international proposals. Even when your jargon is defined, unfamiliar jargon is less likely to be persuasive and remembered.

Kickoff Meetings

Kickoff Meetings are critical milestones that require careful core team planning followed by professional execution. Good ones inspire teams; poor ones demoralize teams.

Kickoff meetings should be motivational, informative, and directive. Kickoff meetings have the following objectives:

- Initiate contributors' proposal efforts
- Answer questions about the opportunity
- Make writing assignments
- Coordinate upcoming activities
- Create a cohesive team

See Capture Planning *and* Proposal Management Plan; *and* Decision Gate Reviews, *Capture Guide.*

Kickoff meetings range from carefully planned and executed large-team efforts to loosely structured teleconference calls. Resist the urge to have a kickoff meeting as soon as you receive the bid request. Premature kickoff meetings offer the illusion of progress and lead to more rework and a less competitive proposal.

The proposal manager should lead kickoff meetings, supported by the capture manager.

Large-team proposals might have as many as four kickoff meetings:

1. The teaming or subcontractors' kickoff follows the formal commitment to team or subcontract. The purpose is to establish clear roles, responsibilities, and assignments.

2. The proposal kickoff follows two events: (1) bid decision and (2) subsequent planning that enables the core team to issue clear task assignments to each proposal contributor.

3. The proposal update kickoff follows the Bid Validation gate review, prompted by receipt of the customer's final bid request, and redirects each contributor's efforts based on changes in the customer's bid request.

4. The cost kickoff establishes estimating ground rules, procedures, guidelines, schedules, costing strategy, and task assignments.

Fewer than 10 percent of all proposals have multiple kickoff meetings.

Do not confuse your initial proposal planning meeting with a kickoff meeting. The event called the kickoff meeting for many organizations is actually an initial planning meeting, conducted in a conference call. These misnamed meetings loosely cover the following topics:

- Client requirements and perhaps motivators and hot buttons.
- Available solution, incorrectly termed *our strategy*.
- Broad area assignments, such as, "Fred has the technical, Mary takes the management, and Jim's group can do the production."
- Schedule, "We'll talk again next week. Your completed proposal section is due on . . . "

To make proposal team kickoff meetings more successful, these guidelines stress (1) planning before the kickoff meeting, (2) execution in a single setting, and (3) execution via teleconference.

Teleconference kickoff meetings are the only option for many organizations. If this is the case in your organization, carefully read guideline 7.

Nearly all materials distributed at the kickoff meeting are part of the Proposal Management Plan (PMP) or its appendices and attachments.

Kickoff Meetings

1. Allocate approximately 15 percent of the available preparation time to core team planning prior to the kickoff meeting.

2. Invite the right people.

3. Prepare a complete but concise agenda.

4. Prepare a comprehensive kickoff package in advance.

5. Review operational guidelines for proposal development.

6. Establish a tone of competent, professional proposal leadership and management.

7. Establish additional ground rules for teleconference kickoff meetings.

1

Allocate approximately 15 percent of the available preparation time to core team planning prior to the kickoff meeting.

A 10-day effort would allow 1 to 1.5 days to plan the meeting. A 45-day effort would allow approximately 1 week.

Preparation time will depend on draft bid request availability, your organization's willingness to commit to capture planning and core team planning, and your Proposal Management Plan completeness.

2

Invite the right people.

Invite the people whose work will be affected by the proposal, either by direct contribution, temporary loss of resources, or consequences:

- Senior managers who support and help motivate the team

- Program or product managers who own the solution

- Capture, sales, and/or marketing leads who represent the customer and align the proposal to sales efforts

- Proposal manager who is tasked to produce a winning proposal

- Volume managers or book bosses who manage portions of the team

- Writers and contributors who develop content

- Proposal specialists or coordinators who help the proposal manager coordinate section drafts and graphics

- Production or print shop supervisor who will format, publish, and copy the proposal

- Editors and graphic artists assigned to support the proposal

- Managers who are committing or losing resources to the proposal effort

- Teaming partners and subcontractors who provide text or pricing, providing they are exclusive to your bid and have signed teaming and nondisclosure agreements

Every proposal of any size requires a sponsor or owner—ranging from a management executive to the account executive. An executive sponsor for the proposal effort will help you get the right people for your proposal, from planning the kickoff meeting to submittal and negotiation. Major proposal efforts that cannot attract an executive sponsor should be stopped.

Executives in the most effective organizations view winning new business as a critical activity worthy of assigning their best employees. Executives in less-effective organizations tend to assign individuals they can spare or who are available. *Make the right people available* rather than rationalizing that the *available people are right.*

See SCHEDULING.

See TEAM SELECTION AND MANAGEMENT.

To comprehend the capture manager's role and perspective regarding proposal kickoff meetings, *see* ENGAGING PROPOSAL SUPPORT, *Capture Guide.*

3

Prepare a complete but concise agenda.

Target no more than 2 to 3 hours for a kickoff meeting with 10 to 30 contributors. Make the kickoff meeting informative and professional. Do not let it turn into a problem-solving event. Like daily stand-up meetings, when problems surface, limit discussion to who needs to be involved and when that group can meet.

A typical kickoff meeting agenda is shown in figure 1. Because everyone does not need to attend the entire meeting, arrange the agenda to permit the unneeded participants to leave after topics relevant to their roles are covered.

Establish a professional tone by distributing a copy of your agenda with the invitation to attend.

See DAILY TEAM MANAGEMENT.

TIME *(min)*	PERSON	TOPIC
5	Proposal Mgr	Welcome everyone and introduce participants
5	Senior Mgr	Deliver motivational remarks and indicate organizational commitment
10	Sales, Capture, or Marketing Lead	Give background on the customer and the opportunity
45	Proposal Mgr	Distribute and discuss the Proposal Management Plan (PMP), including outline, executive summary, out (WBS), writers' packages, and storyboards (when used)
10	Break	. . . .
5	Tech Vol Mgr	Outline technical approach
5	Mgmt Vol Mgr	Outline management approach
5	Cost Vol Mgr	Outline costing approach
15	Proposal Mgr	Discuss daily proposal operations and schedule
15	Proposal Mgr	Answer contributor's questions and dismiss meeting

Figure 1. Plan a Concise Kickoff Meeting. *Keep your kickoff meeting short, informative, and professional. Focus on being informative over being inspirational. Excuse people early who do not need to hear sensitive information or details about the solution, individual assignments, or daily team management. Teaming partners who have not yet signed a teaming agreement should usually be excluded.*

4

See PROPOSAL MANAGEMENT PLAN.

See PROPOSAL STRATEGY, SCHEDULING, *and* OUTLINING.

Prepare a comprehensive kickoff package in advance.

Determine exactly what material you need to distribute at the kickoff meeting. Start with the Proposal Management Plan (PMP).

Managers of smaller proposals in less structured markets and organizations should carefully review the recommended kickoff meeting materials listed in figure 2 and select those most relevant to your proposal.

REQUIRED ITEMS	CONTENT/FUNCTION
Proposal Project Summary	Information about the opportunity, contract type, value, official name, relevant dates, key contacts, scope, primary deliverables. All or relevant portions of the bid request.
Customer Profile	Customer needs, issues, hot buttons, evaluations process, and perception of your organization.
Proposal Strategy	Overall strategies, themes, and discriminators. Includes key messages and how they are to be implemented in the proposal.
Proposal Operations	Establishes approach, formats, protocol, resources, and approaches to review.
Proposal Schedule	Sets dates for key milestones.
Proposal Outline	Defines section numbers, headings, page allocation, responsible person, and incremental task deadlines.
Writers' Packages	First page of Proposal Development Worksheet (PDW) or storyboard, which includes the writer assigned, page limits or guidelines, information from the proposal outline relevant to each writer, along with the compliance checklist items assigned to that section.
Bid Request	Relevant parts or pointers to an electronic source.
DESIRABLE ITEMS	**CONTENT/FUNCTION**
Competitive Analysis	Competitor profiles, Integrated Customer Solution Worksheet, Bidder Comparison Matrix.
Roles and Responsibilities	Team members, location, contact info, role, expertise, cost center, and hours authorized.
Draft Executive Summary	Provide contributors with the overall perspective on customer's needs, proposed solution, and win strategy. Models good themes, graphics, action captions, and format.
WBS/WBS Dictionary	Breaks the proposal work into tasks, defining the hardware and data that will be delivered and services that will be performed.

Figure 2. Recommended Kickoff Meeting Materials. *To prevent serious misdirection of your proposal team, conduct the kickoff meeting after preparing most of these materials.*

5 Review operational guidelines for proposal development.

Establish clear operational guidelines at the kickoff meeting to minimize rework.

The simpler you can make it for contributors to follow your guidelines, the more likely they will actually follow them. For example:

See Storyboards and Mockups.

See Proposal Strategy.

See Executive Summary.

At a kickoff meeting for a major systems contractor, the production coordinator handed out a 12-page set of formatting instructions to each contributor, including different handwriting samples to help writers estimate the amount of finished text they would have when handwriting their drafts.

When asked, "Why so long?" the reply was, "The writers never seem to get it, so we have added more detail."

Writers ignored the handout. When asked why, one said, "I'm not a typist. I don't need it."

Give writers a word processing file template. Writers asked to read long instructions and correctly set up a file will usually ignore the instructions.

Clear operational guidelines will help achieve the following aims:

- Assess assigned task status
- Facilitate inputting, editing, developing and integrating graphics, and reviewing
- Coordinate writing tasks among writers
- Update and disseminate new information
- Develop and roll up cost data
- Verify consistent task descriptions and costs
- Increase senior management review and endorsement
- Identify and close gaps early to stay on schedule
- Verify drafts are compliant, responsive, and supportive of your strategy

6 Establish a tone of competent, professional proposal leadership and management.

Contributors enjoy working on a team that has senior management visibility and support, professional leadership, a clear win strategy, adequate resources, and a good chance of winning. You cannot fool your team into thinking you are competent when you have failed to plan before asking for their help.

7 Establish additional ground rules for teleconference kickoff meetings.

See Virtual Team Management.

Teleconference kickoff meetings often have these major business development weaknesses:

- No defined process to prepare proposals
- Unclear understanding of roles and responsibilities
- Little consequence for late task completion
- Rewards go primarily to the nonparticipants
- General view that proposals are not important
- Proposals are free—those deciding to bid do not pay for the proposal or do the work

Establish these practices:

- Separate the initial core team planning call from the proposal kickoff call. A small core team can resolve issues and make decisions faster without wasting contributors' time.
- Establish lines of authority. The ranking person on the call from each participating organization must make and stand by their decisions. Participants are not permitted to go back to their organizations for approval. Any organization that fails to participate must abide by the decisions of those who did.

- Establish a detailed, written agenda and distribute it early enough to permit participants to prepare.
- Take the time to poll participants for acceptance after each agenda item. Obtain closure on each item and summarize the decision.
- As tasks are assigned, ask the responsible individuals to restate their understanding and acceptance.
- Assign someone other than the person chairing the call to keep detailed minutes.
  E-mail a copy of the minutes to all participants and their managers a few hours after the call is completed. Ask them to confirm their acceptance in writing, usually by e-mail.
- Check progress of a dispersed team more frequently than when your team is co-located. No news is bad news when your team is dispersed.
- Test your submission process for hardware and software compatibility. Before drafts begin, ask each participant to submit sample text and one graphic in each of the file formats they plan to use.

Letter Proposals

Letter Proposals are short proposals, often not formally solicited, ranging from 1 to 20 pages. When acceptable to the customer, use letter proposals to minimize competition and to reduce or eliminate proposal preparation and evaluation costs.

See EXECUTIVE SUMMARY; *and* SALES LETTERS, *Capture Guide.*

Structure letter proposals, executive summaries, and sales letters similarly. Keep them customer focused and structured around the customer's hot buttons or key issues.

Too many letter proposals are deemed boilerplate documents that incorporate standard descriptions of the proposed products and services.

Instead, regard every document sent to a customer as a proposal. Each sales document must convince the customer's organization to agree to take the next step toward your overall sales objective.

Letter Proposals

1. Clarify the customer's expectations before preparing an unsolicited letter proposal.
2. Use the flexible Four-Box organization.
3. Use an informative subject line and incorporate a signal word.
4. In Box 1, connect your solution to the customer's organizational objectives, your prior work with the customer's organization, and the customer's immediate objectives for this purchase.
5. In Box 2, preview the proposal's organization, arranged according to the customer's hot buttons or key issues.
6. In Box 3, align your proposed solution to the customer's most relevant hot button or key issue.
7. In Box 4, close with a short summary and a clear indication of the next realistically achievable step.
8. Use graphics with captions to discriminate your letter proposal.
9. Include an executive summary comprising no more than 5 to 10 percent of the proposal.
10. Limit attached or appended materials to items specifically requested by the customer or essential to specialist readers.

1 Clarify the customer's expectations before preparing an unsolicited letter proposal.

Most sales professionals are trained to win the customer's business without submitting a proposal. In fact, many leading sales disciplines say having to submit a proposal is a sign of failure.

Explicitly discuss what information your customer will need in your proposal to make a decision. How can you meet your customer's expectations unless you know what they are?

Use language similar to one of the following examples to clarify customers' expectations:

Approach 1: You said that you will need a proposal before you can make a final decision. To make sure you get what you need, let's talk about what you would like to have included in our proposal.

Approach 2: You have used our products/services for years. To simplify your evaluation, shall we eliminate all the usual corporate background and history and focus specifically on what we plan to do on this project?

Approach 3: If we agree to limit the proposal to 20 pages on the specifics of this project, we can eliminate 100 pages of background, corporate history, and standard product descriptions and deliver the document that you expect in 4 days. Would this be acceptable to your evaluation group?

While getting the order without a proposal is ideal, remember that purchasing professionals are trained and purchasing processes are designed to require a proposal. Competition often both improves the quality of the solution and reduces the cost.

2 Use the flexible Four-Box organization.

Use the Four-Box organizational structure to prepare persuasive, clearly organized, and expandable letter proposals. The Four-Box organizational structure is based on fundamental principles of document organization.

The Four-Box structure for any type of sales document includes a heading and four distinct boxes. The heading is treated as a separate component and not included in Box 1.

Broadly viewed, the objective for each of the four boxes in a generic sales document is as follows:

- **Box 1:** Summarize the document.
- **Box 2:** Preview the document's organization, arranged according to the reader's hot buttons or issues.
- **Box 3:** Link the hot buttons to the writer's solution or key information. This is the body or main part of the document.
- **Box 4:** Summarize the document and suggest the next step.

See Executive Summary, Organization; *and* Sales Letters, *Capture Guide.*

While letter proposals, executive summaries, and sales letters should all follow the Four-Box organizational structure, each will vary depending on the seller's objective, the targeted evaluators or readers, and the complexity of the information.

The greatest differences among letter proposals, executive summaries, and sales letters are in the contents of Box 1. The suggested content for each of the four boxes for the three types of sales documents is compared in figure 1. Guidelines 4 through 7 discuss the content of each of the four boxes of a letter proposal.

Some of the listed elements will be excluded from some letter proposals depending on your history and relationship with the customer.

The Four-Box organizational approach is flexible in several ways. First, some of the suggested content might be either omitted, appear in a different order, or be placed in a different box. For example, the statement of compliance might be omitted because it is implied in other text, or it might be placed in Box 3 or 4 because it is relatively less important than other information.

Another type of flexibility with the Four-Box approach is that documents can be expanded or reduced to better match the importance of the information and the necessary level of detail. Figure 2 shows the Four-Box organizational approach applied to both 1- and 10-page letter proposals.

COMPONENT	TYPE OF SALES DOCUMENT		
HEADING TYPE	**LETTER PROPOSAL** *Informative* "Proposal to . . ."	**EXECUTIVE SUMMARY** *Telegraphic* "Executive Summary"	**SALES LETTER** *Informative* "Invitation, Request, etc."
BOX 1			
Theme Statement	Yes	Yes	Not needed
Vision Statement	Yes	Yes	Not needed
Linking Statement	Yes Vision-to-need	Yes Vision-to-need	Yes To previous event
Preview Solution	Yes "Solution"	Yes "Solution"	Yes "Request . . ."
Statement of Compliance	Desirable	Desirable	Not needed
BOX 2			
Introduce hot buttons	Yes	Yes	Yes
Explicit Ownership	Yes	Yes	Yes
BOX 3			
Ordered as in Box 2	Yes	Yes	Yes
Link hot button to content	Yes	Yes	Yes
Discuss Price	Mandatory	Desirable	Not applicable
BOX 4			
Summary	Yes	Yes	Yes
Suggest next step	Yes, to negotiate?	Yes, to read the proposal	Yes, to agree to seller's request

Figure 1. Comparing Letter Proposals, Executive Summaries, and Sales Letters. *All three types of sales documents should follow the Four-Box organization. The content of each box will vary depending on the specific sales objective, the targeted evaluators or readers, and the complexity of the information required to make or support the seller's point.*

One-Page Narrative Letter Proposal

> **BankTwo**
>
> Address　　　　　　　　　　　Date
>
> Informative Subject Line
>
> Opening vision statement
>
> Hot Button (HB)
> List　•HB#1
> 　　　•HB#2
> 　　　•HB#3
>
> Summary of offer aligned to HB: (HB—Solution, costs, benefits, added value
>
> Close with *Next Step*

Typical 10-Page Narrative Letter Proposal Outline

PAGE	CONTENT
1	Cover Page
2	Contents
3	Summary and Introduction
4	Introduce hot buttons
5	Hot button 1 discussion
6	Hot button 2 discussion
7	Hot button 3 discussion
8	Hot button 4 discussion
9	Summarize Offer, Schedule, and Cost Justification with Quantified Benefits
10	Closing Summary

Figure 2. Expandable, Flexible Four-Box Organizational Approach. *Expand or contract the same structure as appropriate. Allocate space according to the relative importance of the topic to your customer.*

3   Use an informative subject line and incorporate a signal word.

See HEADINGS.

Like a well-crafted headline, informative subject lines both summarize your key message and interest or engage the reader. Make the first word a *signal word* that immediately announces the purpose of your letter:

    Proposal
    Recommendation
    Request
    Invitation
    Contract
    Statement of Work
    Analysis
    Final Report

When you omit these elements, customers often stop reading.

Whether you want to label your proposal as a proposal depends on your sales strategy. If the customer requested a proposal, call it that. If you want to emphasize your consultative role, you might begin with one of the other signal words.

Informative subject lines include benefits when possible. Benefits immediately interest customers. Effective subject lines open with a signal word that defines the document's purpose for the reader:

Proposal to Supply Rail Cars at One-half of Current Cost

Recommendation to Immediately Contract for Legal Benefits to Enhance Executive Retention

Invitation to Contract for FY 2002 Desktop Support

Contract Provisions Approved August 1, 20XX

4   In Box 1, connect your solution to the customer's organizational objectives, your prior work with the customer's organization, and the customer's immediate objectives for this purchase.

Statements of compliance are somewhat controversial. Some professionals say they are required. Others say compliance is implied when a bid is submitted unless exceptions are stated in the bid. The correct answer is what the customer thinks.

See THEME STATEMENTS.

As listed in figure 1, Box 1 of a letter proposal may include a theme statement, vision statement, linking statement, preview of the solution, and a statement of compliance. Several of these items may be combined in a single sentence to be concise.

The theme statement summarizes everything you want to say in one sentence. Tie the benefit to your key discriminator. Vision statements demonstrate how well you understand the customer's overall direction and need. A customer will purchase from sellers who best demonstrate their understanding of the customer's business and immediate needs.

Linking statements that tie customer's immediate needs to the organization's objectives demonstrate your understanding and support funding this project versus competing projects.

The preview of your solution is often only a phrase. In the first Box 1 example shown below, the preview of the solution is in the theme statement, "... *supply 20 versatile ultralight aircraft [with] long-term support.*" In the second example, the solution is summarized in the first and last sentences, " ... *contracting with Able IT ...*" and " ... *an IT support partner ...*" Sales and sales support professionals often voice two objections:

1. Don't they already know their need?

2. What if I get it wrong?

First, of course they know. They need to be reassured that you know. Second, if you cannot get it right, you should not be bidding and do not deserve to win.

Note how the two examples link the customer's organizational objectives and immediate objectives to the offer and cite prior work.

CASCADIA TIMBER REPORT

THEME STATEMENT — Cascadia Timber can reduce the cost of forest management in remote roadless areas by selecting a partner to supply 20 versatile ultralight aircraft packaged with long-term support.

ORGANIZATIONAL VISION AND OBJECTIVES — Cascadia Timber is ranked as the No. 1 company in the world by Foresters' Monthly for low cost, innovative forest management. Cascadia Timber Chairman, Woody X. Pine, set the following strategic direction:

We have to do everything better, more efficiently from a cost point of view, and more effectively from an impact point of view.

LINKING STATEMENT TO THE IMMEDIATE OBJECTIVE — During our discussion over the past 6 weeks, you have indicated that Cascadia Timber's Forest Management Division helps improve efficiency and effectiveness by adopting innovative forest management practices.

THEME STATEMENT — Bank Two can cut IT support costs by 30 percent by contracting with Able IT, Ltd.

ORGANIZATIONAL VISION AND OBJECTIVE — Having emerged from the recent industry consolidation, Bank Two is now the second largest and fastest growing bank in the Northwest. Bank Two's board challenged management to increase ROI by 25 percent.

IMMEDIATE NEED — In our initial meeting 2 months ago, you stated that Bank Two's Operations Department would contribute to ROI improvement by seeking proposals for an IT support partner that can reliably deliver support at a 30 percent cost reduction.

5

In Box 2, preview the proposal's organization, arranged according to the customer's hot buttons or key issues.

Box 2 introduces the customer's hot buttons for the current purchase. Brainstorm an extensive list of needs, issues, hot buttons, key requirements, and evaluation criteria. Then consolidate or group them into three to five distinct items. Use the customer's words.

Prioritize them in one of two ways:

1. Order of importance to the customer
2. Order stated by the customer

Ideally, the customer states the hot buttons in order of importance. If you are not sure which hot buttons are more important, follow the order stated in the bid request, in other customer documents, or in discussions with the customer.

This becomes your hot button list. Now introduce the hot buttons, making customer ownership explicit:

Poor example *(No Customer Ownership)*

The ideal aircraft must meet four primary needs:

1. Affordable, portable, and easily transportable
2. All-conditions observation and communication platform
3. Safe and easy to fly
4. Easy to assemble and maintain in the field

Good example *(Explicit Customer Ownership)*

In our meetings with Forest Management and Purchasing, you cited four primary needs:

1. Affordable, portable, and easily transportable
2. All-conditions observation and communication platform
3. Safe and easy to fly
4. Easy to assemble and maintain in the field

All too frequently writers are asked to draft a letter proposal when they lack adequate customer contact or knowledge about the customer's needs. When this happens, set up the customer's hot buttons based on what you do know:

Good example

Our experience with customers in the forest products industry has indicated that most cite four primary needs:

1. Affordable, portable, and easily transportable
2. All-conditions observation and communication platform
3. Safe and easy to fly
4. Easy to assemble and maintain in the field

Note how the softer setup avoids being arrogant, gives you an out if you have the needs wrong, and validates your industry experience.

6

In Box 3, align your proposed solution to the customer's most relevant hot button or key issue.

If the hot button takes more than one page, insert a short introduction or preview between steps 1 and 2.

Occasionally you will have some additional content that must be included but that clearly does not fit against any of the hot buttons. First, verify that it is relevant, then introduce it between Boxes 3 and 4.

Link pricing and costing information to a relevant hot button or place it between Boxes 3 and 4. The following hot buttons are typically relevant to pricing:

— Reduce operating cost
— Increase market competitiveness
— Deliver operational plant within budget
— Payoff within 2 years

To keep your letter proposal brief but comprehensive, you must link all of your points to one of the customer's hot buttons, the ones listed in Box 2.

Make first-level subheadings in Box 3 identical in wording and order to the hot buttons introduced in Box 2. Customers are confused when either the wording or order changes.

Figure 3 illustrates how to identify and allocate your letter proposal content to a single section under one hot button. First, make lists of information you need to include in the proposal. Then, find a reasonable place for each item under one of the hot buttons.

Organize your response to each hot button in the following manner:

1. Succinctly state your solution to the requirement.
2. Provide supporting details, either graphically or in text.
3. Offer proof of experience and/or performance.

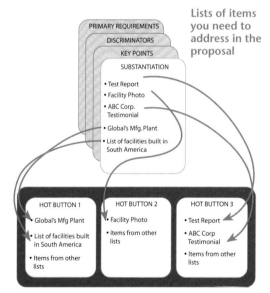

Lists of items you need to address in the proposal

Figure 3. Organizing Box 3. *First, list the primary customer requirements that you must address, your primary discriminators, key points, and relevant substantiation. Then allocate all items from each list in some reasonable manner under one of the hot buttons. As there is no single, correct allocation, try to group similar items and present them logically.*

7 In Box 4, close with a short summary and a clear indication of the next realistically achievable step.

Summarize the benefits the customer will enjoy from your solution. List them in the order presented, as concisely as possible.

Then proactively suggest the next step, usually a phone call or meeting to resolve any questions and to finalize the contract.

The following example summarizes the seller's offer in the first two paragraphs, then reinforces the seller's compliance and flexibility and suggests the next step in the last paragraph.

> Cascadia Timber has kept on the leading edge of innovative forest management techniques. Jenair

Sports welcomes the opportunity to supply 20 ultralight aircraft, flight and maintenance training, and long-term maintenance and inspection support to further Cascadia's leadership.

While many ultralights are used for recreation, the Endeavor's unique 10-year use by Special Forces personnel over similar terrain and more difficult conditions demonstrated its reliability in continuous operation.

Our proposal addresses all issues discussed in our meetings. Should your requirements change, we welcome the opportunity to discuss further enhancements. We will call you in 1 week to resolve any open items and to agree on the next step.

8 Use graphics with captions to discriminate your letter proposal.

See **Action Captions** *and* **Graphics**.

Few sellers use graphics in letter proposals. Emphasize the clarity of your thinking by using graphics with complete action captions in your letter proposal.

Consider using the following types of graphics in a letter proposal:

- Photos showing the product being used or the service being delivered
- Photos of reference sites
- Reference lists
- Organization chart of the delivery team
- Photos of the customer using or observing the product
- Brief schedule
- Pricing table

9 Include an executive summary comprising no more than 5 to 10 percent of the proposal.

The Four-Box organization is intentionally repetitive. As Jim Beverage noted in *The Anatomy of a Win,* "A good proposal is a summary of a summary of a summary."

Even with short letter proposals, include an executive summary.

Your executive summary need not be labeled. When using the Four-Box organization, the informative heading and Box 1 constitute the executive summary.

Executive summaries, previews, and closing summaries are intentionally repetitive because people remember the first items they see, the last items they see, and repeated items.

Few proposals, including letter proposals, are completely read from beginning to end. Repetition increases the probability that they will get your key points.

10 Limit attached or appended materials to items specifically requested by the customer or essential to specialist readers.

See **Appendices**.

Attaching extensive materials to a letter proposal dilutes your message and negates the primary objective of submitting a letter proposal—to reduce the time and cost of preparing and evaluating proposals.

If you must attach materials, follow the guidelines for appendices.

List the additional materials that are available but not included to ease their evaluation. Regard subsequent requests for materials as an opportunity to call on the customer when your competitors cannot.

Lists serve two important functions in proposals: (1) emphasize important points and (2) preview direction.

Readers are more likely to remember information presented in a list, especially a display list.

Evaluators searching proposals for answers to their questions use display lists to spot information and to point them to where the information is discussed in body text.

Guidelines for the optimal use of display lists in proposals are more specific and restrictive than in other business documents.

Proposals are read and accessed differently than most other business documents. Virtually no one reads them completely or continuously.

Evaluators are skeptical. They are trying to detect the spin in your message; what information has been slanted, omitted, or even deliberately misrepresented.

Unfortunately, many proposal writers use lists as a dumping ground for information. They put unrelated items in a list because the information is available and when they do not have a clear message in mind.

Lists

1. Make all items in lists parallel in structure. Begin each item with the same kind of word (noun, verb, adjective, or adverb).

2. Name each list.

3. Place the name of the list immediately in front of the list.

4. Limit list contents to the items named.

5. Limit your use of display lists to items deserving emphasis.

6. Minimize or eliminate confusing nested lists.

7. Begin display lists with numbers or letters if you are mimicking the bid request numbering system or if you refer to list items in subsequent text. Otherwise, use bullets or dashes.

8. Capitalize the first word in each item. End all items with a period only if at least one item is a complete sentence.

1

Make all items in lists parallel in structure. Begin each item with the same kind of word (noun, verb, adjective, or adverb).

Items listed must be consistent in form and structure. Each item begins with the same kind and type of word, e.g., verbs in the same tense.

Verb lists are the most effective type of lists in proposals because they convey a sense of action.

See FEATURES, ADVANTAGES, AND BENEFITS.

Verb list

The Party 2000 music system empowers DJ's to perform the following actions:

• Play any cut in random order
• Set play time for each cut
• Suppress voice tracks for Karaoke applications
• Adjust individual speaker volume

Adjective list

The Party 2000 music system includes the following features:

• Random play
• Variable play time for each cut
• Voice suppression for Karaoke use
• Adjustable volume for individual speakers

Noun list

The Party 2000 music system includes the following features:

• Amplifier with 200 watts
• Storage of 200 CDs
• Karaoke
• Speaker with individual volume adjustments

2

In addition to naming a list prior to the list, some writers name the list in the prior heading. Naming the list in the heading is not possible when the headings are dictated in the bid request.

See **Headings.**

Name each list.

Naming a list makes your proposal easier to understand when evaluators skim or search for answers to their questions. Naming a list also increases the probability that the list is parallel. In an unnamed list, the reader must read the list and determine what the items are.

Unnamed list

Our project manager will:

- Plan all work
- Set quality standards
- Report progress weekly

Unnamed lists often become a dumping ground, especially when boilerplate is used extensively and deadlines are short.

The following named list is easier to understand:

Named list

Our project manager will complete the following tasks:

- Plan all work
- Set quality standards
- Report progress weekly

3

Place the name of the list immediately in front of the list.

Sometimes the introduction to items in the list becomes so long that the reader forgets what was supposed to be in the list.

Named list with long setup (difficult to read)

When initiated by a call to the Help Desk, actions taken by our service technician will include the following unless the service call is initiated outside our normal business hours, 8:00 AM to 5:00 PM, EST:

- Review the service request.
- Determine probable cause using our proprietary Dr. Bug™ software.
- Schedule service call with the initiator.
- Make the call and fix the problem.

Named list with name before the list (easier to read)

When initiated by a call to the Help Desk, unless the service call is initiated outside our normal business hours, 8:00 AM to 5:00 PM, EST, our service technician will take the following actions:

- Review the service request
- Determine probable cause using our proprietary Dr. Bug™ software
- Schedule service call with the initiator
- Make the call and fix the problem

While the setup is too long in either case, the second is easier to understand because the named action precedes the list.

4

Limit list contents to the items named.

Many lists found in proposals are not the items named and not parallel in structure.

Our project manager will complete the following tasks:

- Plan all work.
- Set quality standards.
- Project managers cannot begin out-of-scope work unless approved by Purchasing in writing.

The third item is not a task. Such explanatory detail should be placed in a following sentence or omitted. Other lists are parallel in structure but do not contain the items named.

Our solution offers the following benefits:

- 24 x 7 service
- ISO 9000 certification
- Operational cost reductions
- 99.92 percent availability

The first two items are features, the third is clearly a benefit, the fourth is probably a benefit.

Calling a feature a benefit suggests you do not understand your customer's needs and that you may be trying to sell them something that they do not need, thus increasing the cost. Incorrectly confusing features and benefits is a major problem in many proposals.

5

See **Page and Document Design.**

Limit your use of display lists to items deserving emphasis.

Customers care about the benefits to them and their organization. In complex sales, features are relatively less important. Notice how features are emphasized over benefits:

The Endeavor is the ultimate in ultralight aircraft on the market today. Cascadia Timber can improve forest productivity and the efficiency of individual foresters with Jenair's comprehensive solution. In the attached proposal, you will see the following products detailed:

- Endeavor aircraft
- Pilot training
- Maintenance training
- Spare parts
- Radios
- Transportation and packing
- Disassembly/assembly approach
- Maintenance support
- Standard warranty
- Manuals

Notice how the benefit, *improve forest production and the efficiency of individual foresters*, is presented before the features (good) but buried in the middle of the second sentence (poor). The list of features gets the most emphasis by being surrounded by white space. Skim readers may only see the list of features. A more persuasive organization would begin with the second sentence, bullet list the benefits, then discuss the benefits in order. The features should be aligned with the appropriate benefit.

6 Minimize or eliminate confusing nested lists.

Nested lists are lists within lists. They are confusing, cumbersome, and sometimes border on the ridiculous.

Nested List (confusing)

All systems are shipped with these items:

- 27" flat-screen monitor
  – 27-inch (viewable)
  – LED-backlit glossy widescreen
  – TFT active-matrix LCD
  – IPS technology

- Apple Quad-Core CPU
  – ATI Radeon HD 5770 with 1GB GDDR5
  – Quad-Core Intel
  – 2.8 GHz processor
  – 1TB hard drive
  – 18x double-layer SuperDrive

- Coffee cup
  – Aluminum
  – Double insulated
  – Handle
    √ Black
    √ Plastic
    √ Detachable

7 Begin display lists with numbers or letters if you are mimicking the bid request numbering system or if you refer to list items in subsequent text. Otherwise, use bullets or dashes.

Readers assume that items in lists are placed in decreasing order of importance. Follow that convention.

Using bullets, dashes, or similar nonordered marks does not mean items are of equal importance. If you want the reader to know that all items are of equal importance, tell them.

8 Capitalize the first word in each item. End all items with a period only if at least one item is a complete sentence.

Many proposal writers incorrectly punctuate items in a display list like items in a paragraph list. Do not place commas at the end of display list items or a period at the end of the last item in the list.

Incorrectly punctuated display list (poor example)

Our project manager will complete the following tasks:

- Plan all work,
- Set quality standards, and
- Report progress weekly.

Correctly punctuated display list (good example)

Our project manager will complete the following tasks:

- Plan all work
- Set quality standards
- Report progress weekly

Punctuate a displayed list when the items in the list complete an introductory statement.

This style of punctuation in displayed lists is increasingly rare and outdated. Less than 10 percent of current editors retain this style.

Correctly punctuated display list (good example)

You may identify potential boilerplate material for your proposal by

1. Calling up the search screen,
2. Entering a word or topic, followed by striking the *return* key, and then
3. Reviewing the potential material that appears in the next window.

Traditional practice is to end all list items with a period only if at least one item is a complete sentence. This includes imperative commands when the first word is a verb and the noun is understood.

However, the current trend is to reduce unnecessary punctuation as much as possible. Some editors recommend making all list items either phrases or complete sentences. Make your choice and be consistent.

Many more punctuation variations are possible than have been discussed in this *Proposal Guide*. If you need further detail, refer to a writing style *guide* or manual of style.

Numbering Systems are used with the table of contents, cross-reference matrix, and headings to show the proposal's organization and allow evaluators to rapidly locate the answers to the questions asked in the bid request.

Ideally, your numbering system takes the evaluator directly to each answer. The compromise on large proposals is to balance the number of heading levels used with how closely the subsection number takes the evaluator to each answer.

The two basic numbering systems are the traditional or alphanumeric system and the decimal system.

Traditional System

Traditional outlines use the following numbering and lettering conventions:

    I.
        A.
            1.
                a.
                    (1)
                        (a)
                            1)
                                a)

Decimal System

In the decimal system, successive decimal points indicate levels of subordination:

1.0	2.0
1.1	2.1
1.1.1	2.2
1.1.2	2.2.1
1.1.3	2.2.2
1.1.3.1	
1.1.3.2	

Some bid requests simply skip numbers, reserving a section in case they need it later. Some place periods after the last number. Some drop in a letter when they want to use a single place and nine is not enough places.

For example, the author of a bid request wants bidders to discuss 11 items within section 3.2.4. Bidders may select any of the three following numbering options:

1	2	3
3.2.4.1	3.2.4.01	3.2.4.a
3.2.4.2	3.2.4.02	3.2.4.b
⋮	⋮	⋮
3.2.4.9	3.2.4.09	3.2.4.i
3.2.4.10	3.2.1.10	3.2.4.j
3.2.4.11	3.2.4.11	3.2.4.k

The concern with approaches 1 or 2 is that someone will insert a decimal point between the last two numbers. Assuming base-10 numbering, a single space permits 1 through 9. When a bidder uses letters, 26 places are possible—A through Z. Using a blend of numbers and letters may prevent the problem.

Numbering Systems

1. Mirror the numbering system of the bid request when possible.

2. If given a choice, select the decimal system over the traditional system.

3. Limit numbered subheadings to three levels plus an additional unnumbered sublevel, unless you are mirroring the bid request.

1

See OUTLINING.

See COMPLIANCE AND RESPONSIVENESS.

Mirror the numbering system of the bid request when possible.

No matter how poor the numbering system in the bid request, use it. Imagine how difficult evaluation is when each bidding company invents its own system. Often the evaluator did not prepare the bid request.

Place helpful notes in your proposal and your cross-reference matrix to make it easy for evaluators to correlate the bid request and your proposal.

Good Example

2.3 Intentionally blank. This section was skipped in our proposal to maintain identical section numbers between your RFP and our proposal.

Our proposal section numbers mirror the RFP section numbers except the L.21 prefix on every number was dropped for simplicity. For example:

RFP PARA. # . . . . .PROPOSAL PARS. #
L.21.1 . . . . 1.0
L.21.1.1 . . . . 1.1
L.21.3.3 . . . . 3.3
L.21.3.3.1 . . . . 3.3.1

2 If given a choice, select the decimal system over the traditional system.

The decimal system is instantly understandable. Three numbers means it is a third-level section. Additionally, the reader does not have to rebuild the real reference caused by an *a)* that goes with a *1* that goes to an *A* two pages previous, etc.

Assuming the traditional system, few readers instantly know "a" is a fourth-level heading—I.A.1.a.

Ever find yourself or see others saying the alphabet to determine which letter comes next? That seldom happens with numbers.

While the convention is established, many potential readers do not know the correct order for *a.*, *(a)*, or *a)*. Also, while increasing indentation at succeeding levels is most common for traditional systems, it can leave unusually wide left margins when combined with multi-column page designs.

3 Limit numbered subheadings to three levels plus an additional unnumbered sublevel, unless you are mirroring the bid request.

Guideline 1 always overrides guideline 3.

The greater the number of levels in the proposal, the harder it is to follow. If your numbering system can get the evaluator to within three pages or closer, your numbering system is probably adequate.

Use introductions and unnumbered or run-in subheadings to direct evaluators within subsections longer than one page. Either of the following examples is acceptable. The one on the left numbers all subsections. The one on the right uses unnumbered or run-in subheadings.

All Subsections Numbered

PROPOSAL OUTLINE

2.0 Management Plan

2.1 Organization Structure and Facility Resources

    2.1.1 Current Structure and Operation

        2.1.1.1 Project Team Structure

        2.1.1.2 Project Team Management

    2.1.2 Organizational Size and Stability

    2.1.3 Relevant Facility Resources

        2.1.3.1 Fire Protection Plan

        2.1.3.2 Seismic Protection Plan

Unnumbered Subsections

PROPOSAL OUTLINE

2.0 Management Plan

2.1 Organization Structure and Facility Resources

    2.1.1 Current Structure and Operation

        Project Team Structure

        Project Team Management

    2.1.2 Organizational Size and Stability

    2.1.3 Relevant Facility Resources

        Fire Protection Plan

        Seismic Protection Plan

Oral Proposals were approved in 1995 by the U.S. Office of Federal Procurement Policy (OFPP) as a substitute for information traditionally provided in written form under the cover of the offeror's proposal. Unlike most oral sales presentations, the oral proposal is not a direct restatement of information in the written proposal.

See PRESENTATIONS TO CUSTOMERS, *Capture Guide.*

A type of oral proposal has been used in non-federal competitions for years, often for professional services. Most entailed a written prequalification proposal, short-listing, then the winner was selected after a presentation that was specific to the customer's need.

OFPP believed that oral proposals would help achieve the following objectives:

- Reduce procurement time
- Improve information exchange to select the most advantageous offer
- Reduce buyer and seller costs
- Increase competition

The U.S. Navy released the following comparison of two procurements:

MEASURE	CONVENTIONAL	ORAL PROPOSAL
Time to award	30 mos.	3 mos.
Navy procurement head count	15-40	4
RFP length	1000 pages	3 pages
Cost to Navy	$6M USD	$NA

The twist with oral proposals is the unusually detailed written bid request instructions for the presentation that must be followed precisely.

Most government and many non-government organizations use oral proposals. While their original objectives remain, a key additional objective is to meet, interview, and assess the proposed delivery team. While the written proposal qualifies the selling organization, the oral proposal determines the winner.

Previously, when a presentation followed a written proposal, the team would focus first on the written document, then the presentation.

Now, the timing and extent of the oral proposal and the written proposal, if any, vary. Often both must be prepared in parallel, requiring a different and potentially more demanding preparation process. Bid requests normally specify the time, location, presentation facilities, length of presentation, visual aids, and who may present.

Note that while the intent was to replace the written proposal with an oral proposal, agencies frequently require both.

Oral proposals typically include the following sections:

- Sample tasks and other tests
- Requirements understanding
- Capabilities
- Approaches
- Experience
- Quality and transition plans

Oral proposals typically exclude the following sections:

- Cost information
- Representations and certifications
- Personnel resumes
- Performance history
- Contractual commitments

Oral Proposals

1. Prepare for an oral proposal by understanding the similarities and differences between written and oral proposals.
2. Develop a style that presents your nonverbal messages so they reinforce your verbal messages.
3. Plan your entire approach before preparing your presentation.
4. Organize your presentation by using the Oral Proposal Planner (OPP) to map content from the Proposal Development Worksheet (PDW) into the presentation.
5. Create effective visuals.
6. Rehearse early, realistically, and often.
7. Orchestrate the entire presentation.
8. Prepare a lessons-learned analysis to understand your win or loss and to improve subsequent proposals.

1 Prepare for an oral proposal by understanding the similarities and differences between written and oral proposals.

Oral and written proposals have similar requirements:

- Pre-positioning with the customer
- Making a good bid decision
- Understanding the audience
- Complying with bid request instructions
- Preparing a Proposal Management Plan
- Preparing and conducting the kickoff meeting
- Designing and implementing your strategy
- Adhering to schedule
- Storyboarding the proposal

Oral proposals have several fundamentally different requirements:

- Planning and developing written and oral proposals simultaneously
- Selecting, training, and rehearsing credible presenters
- Designing fewer but more critical graphics
- Rehearsing realistically
- Preparing to handle extemporaneous questions

Instructions for oral proposals vary by agency and procurement official:

- Delivery is at your site or theirs
- Delivery is taped or live
- Written proposals, submitted prior to or at the presentation, may or may not be required
- Media, handouts, and props may be specified and limited
- Presentation materials are often limited and must be submitted in advance with no subsequent modifications
- Presentation time is usually limited and structured
- Presenters and their roles are often specified, especially when teams are being tested

2 Develop a style that presents your nonverbal messages so they reinforce your verbal messages.

Nonverbal messages can reinforce, replace, or contradict the verbal message. Your goal should be to control your nonverbal messages so that they reinforce your verbal message. Reinforcing your verbal messages requires congruence of the verbal and nonverbal elements.

The verbal elements of a speaker's message are the words. The nonverbal elements include visual and vocal cues. Visual cues are the way the speaker appears, stands, moves, gestures, and looks at the audience. Vocal cues are the way the speaker says the words.

The nonverbal aspects of oral communication are vital to being clear, credible, and persuasive. Nonverbal elements affect clarity because approximately 70 percent of the information absorbed in oral communication stems from the nonverbal elements.

Your credibility is questioned when the verbal and nonverbal elements of your oral communication conflict. When this happens, audience members are more likely to trust the nonverbal elements when they determine the meaning of the message.

Effective persuasion is conservatively estimated to be 50 percent facts and 50 percent emotion. Emotion in a presentation is conveyed primarily by nonverbal elements, as shown in figure 1.

Presenters need to develop and display competent, acceptable nonverbal presentation skills. Evaluators do not expect stars. Assess the following nonverbal skills of your presenters and use rehearsals to minimize their negative impact.

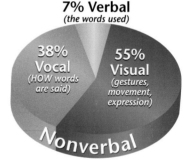

7% Verbal
(the words used)

38% Vocal *(HOW words are said)*

55% Visual *(gestures, movement, expression)*

Nonverbal

Figure 1. Importance of Nonverbal Communication to Persuade. *Research by Dr. Albert Mehrabian at UCLA demonstrated the importance of nonverbal communication to communicate emotion. He determined that 93 percent of the emotional content of a message is conveyed nonverbally by visual and vocal cues.*

Nonverbal Skills

1. Eye contact is one of the best ways to hold a listener's attention. Use specific drills to accustom presenters to hold eye contact for three seconds with individual audience members.

   Try this drill to improve a presenter's eye contact with the audience. Ask individuals in the audience to hold their hands up until the presenter has maintained continuous eye contact with them for three seconds. The presenter's objective is to get all hands down.

2. Facial expressions must naturally reflect your message. Smiling does not detract from a serious message. Use rehearsals to eliminate inappropriate facial expressions: frowns, sneers, smirks, etc.

3. Appearance should be appropriate, neat, and similar among presenters but not necessarily identical. Appropriate dress helps presenters feel confident.

Appropriate dress will depend on the country, culture, location, season, and industry. Try to dress slightly better than the audience. Groups of presenters should dress similarly, to look like a team, but not identically unless uniforms are normal dress. Discuss dress options during preparations, and preview all presenters' dress at a *dress* rehearsal.

4. Posture demonstrates confidence and self-esteem. Gestures between the waist and shoulders are strongest and project confidence. If using a podium, stand beside it, not behind it. Try to eliminate anything that blocks the audience's view of the speaker from the waist up.

5. Enter and exit confidently. Movement draws the eye of the audience and commands attention. Use movement to signal a change of topic. Move closer to the audience when emphasizing a point or addressing a question.

6. Gestures are an extension of movement. Practice gesturing, not gestures. Gestures that are studied look studied. Gestures will vary by presenter and will become more natural with rehearsal.

Audiences will accept a wide variety of speaking styles. Your primary objective should be to coach presenters to eliminate distractive mannerisms, not to turn them into robots. For example, if a presenter persists in placing a hand in a pocket, make sure there is nothing in the pocket that might rattle or jingle. If a presenter tends to bend pointers, click pens, or fiddle with markers, take those items away. Markers can be tied to charts. Laser pointers are nearly impossible to hold without a tremor. If used, point briefly, then switch off.

Seek solutions that minimally impact the presenter.

7. Voice delivery, not the words, carries 38 percent of the emotional impact. Vary voice volume, speed, and pitch. Pause for attention or emphasis. Enunciate carefully, especially when discussing complex points. Repeat key or complex points.

3

Common aspects to planning oral and written proposals are covered in greater detail in the Proposal Management Plan and are only briefly listed here:

- Analyze the bid request
- Create a compliance checklist
- Complete the PDW
- Develop an annotated outline

Plan your entire approach before preparing your presentation.

Both oral and written proposals require careful planning before preparing the presentation or drafting sections. A unique aspect of oral proposal planning is assessing the presentation situation.

Vital aspects of the presentation situation are the *time, setting,* and *occasion.*

Time aspects include the time allowed, the time of day, and the order of presenters.

Regarding the **setting**, determine the location and physical layout of the room, the number of evaluators present, and the resources available.

The **occasion** requires that you understand the situation in context; what outside events could affect your presentation?

4

The overall organization is similar to that recommended for executive summaries.

See Executive Summary *and* Storyboards and Mockups.

Organize your presentation by using the Oral Proposal Planner (OPP) to map content from the Proposal Development Worksheet (PDW) into the presentation.

Use the OPP, shown in figure 3, to build a presentation that is logical, responsive, consistent, and persuasive. Use the OPP to plan every major topic:

- Identify the time allotted to the topic
- Identify applicable evaluation criteria
- Show how strategy will be implemented
- Structure topic introductions
- Develop content point-by-point
- Summarize key benefits and features
- Close with power

When the customer requires a written and oral proposal, use the PDW to develop content. Then map the content from the PDW to the OPP to save time and maintain consistency. Data flows from the PDW, shown in figure 2, to the OPP, shown in figure 3.

If no written proposal is required, you could begin with the OPP. However, content planning is not as thorough, and important points are easily missed.

Order your main points in the same order as they were listed in the bid request. If no order is specified, order them in decreasing order of importance to the customer.

Use the Triple-S presentation formula to present each main point:

1. State

My first point is. . .

My second point is . . .

2. Support

Let's define . . .

What this means is . . .

For example, a previous client with. . .

The president of Acme said . . .

Imagine that . . .

Here is a picture of . . .

Independent testers found that . . .

3. Summarize

To summarize . . .

In essence . . .

What we are saying is . . .

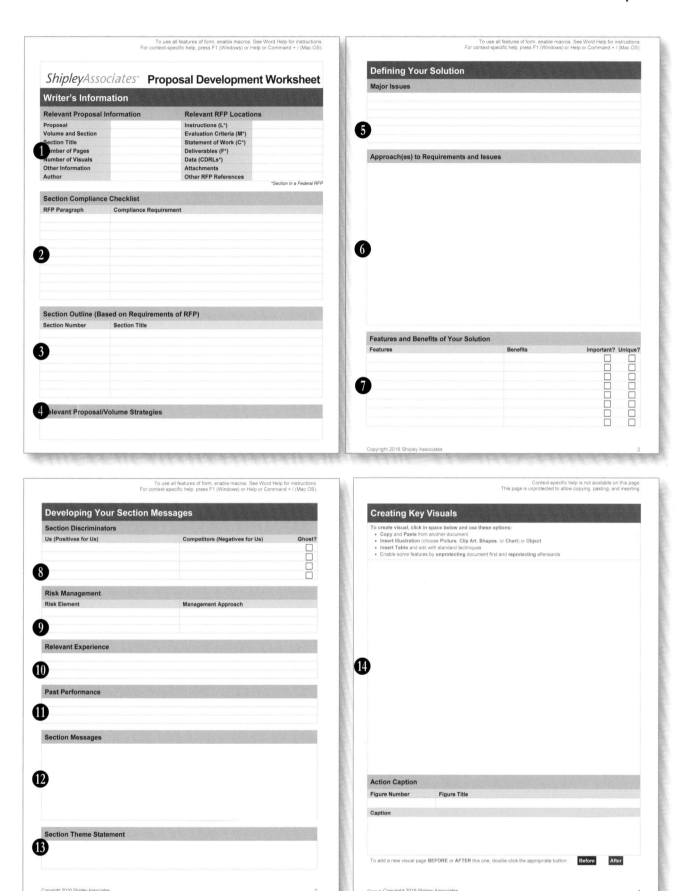

Figure 2. Flow of Data from PDW to OPP. *Note how the data developed in the PDW for responsiveness, customer focus, strategy, risk, past performance, and themes flows into the OPP shown in figure 3, indicated by the common numbering system.*

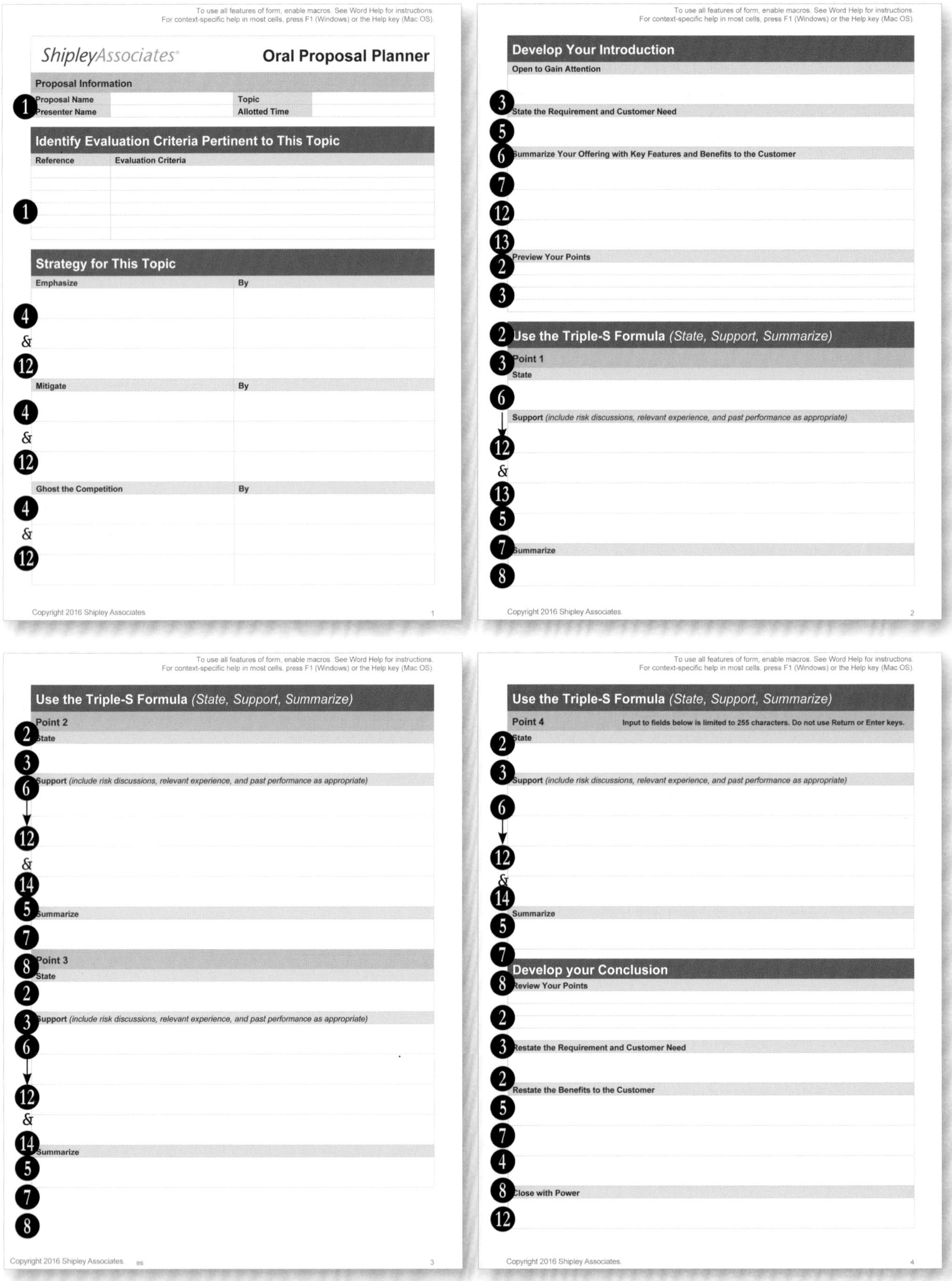
To use all features of form, enable macros. See Word Help for instructions.
For context-specific help in most cells, press F1 (Windows) or the Help key (Mac OS).

ShipleyAssociates

Oral Proposal Planner

Proposal Information

❶ Proposal Name		Topic	
Presenter Name		Allotted Time	

Identify Evaluation Criteria Pertinent to This Topic

Reference	Evaluation Criteria
❶	

Strategy for This Topic

Emphasize	By
❹ & ⓬	

Mitigate	By
❹ & ⓬	

Ghost the Competition	By
❹ & ⓬	

Copyright 2016 Shipley Associates 1

To use all features of form, enable macros. See Word Help for instructions.
For context-specific help in most cells, press F1 (Windows) or the Help key (Mac OS).

Develop Your Introduction

Open to Gain Attention ❸

State the Requirement and Customer Need ❺ ❻

Summarize Your Offering with Key Features and Benefits to the Customer ❼ ⓬ ⓭

Preview Your Points ❷ ❸

Use the Triple-S Formula *(State, Support, Summarize)* ❷

Point 1 ❸

State ❻

Support *(include risk discussions, relevant experience, and past performance as appropriate)* ⓬ & ⓭ ❺

Summarize ❼ ❽

Copyright 2016 Shipley Associates 2

To use all features of form, enable macros. See Word Help for instructions.
For context-specific help in most cells, press F1 (Windows) or the Help key (Mac OS).

Use the Triple-S Formula *(State, Support, Summarize)*

Point 2

State ❷ ❸

Support *(include risk discussions, relevant experience, and past performance as appropriate)* ❻ ⓬ & ⓮

Summarize ❺ ❼

Point 3 ❽

State ❷

Support *(include risk discussions, relevant experience, and past performance as appropriate)* ❸ ❻ ⓬ & ⓮

Summarize ❺ ❼ ❽

Copyright 2016 Shipley Associates 3

To use all features of form, enable macros. See Word Help for instructions.
For context-specific help in most cells, press F1 (Windows) or the Help key (Mac OS).

Use the Triple-S Formula *(State, Support, Summarize)*

Point 4 Input to fields below is limited to 255 characters. Do not use Return or Enter keys.

State ❷

Support *(include risk discussions, relevant experience, and past performance as appropriate)* ❸ ❻ ⓬ & ⓮

Summarize ❺ ❼

Develop your Conclusion

Review Your Points ❽ ❷

Restate the Requirement and Customer Need ❸

Restate the Benefits to the Customer ❷ ❺ ❼ ❹

Close with Power ❽ ⓬

Copyright 2016 Shipley Associates 4

Figure 3. Use the Oral Proposal Planner. *The planner lends structure and logic to develop powerful presentations that are easily followed and understood. The original content is developed in the Proposal Development Worksheet (PDW) or storyboard shown in figure 2. The numbers show the flow of data from the PDW to the OPP.*

With the core of the presentation complete, develop the introduction and summary.

Introductions have mandatory and optional functions:

Mandatory
- Gain attention
- State the requirement and customer need
- Summarize your offering/response and the associated benefit
- Preview your main points

Optional
- Establish credentials
- Define key terms
- Offer background
- Set the tone and establish rapport
- Introduce key program personnel
- Overview requirements

Gain attention in your introduction with a customer-focused statement of need, a shocking fact, challenge, quotation, illustration, story, or rhetorical question.

Like introductions, conclusions have mandatory and optional functions:

Mandatory
- Review main points
- Restate customer requirements/needs
- Close with power

Optional
- Transition to the next speaker
- Open to questions

Mirror your introduction in your conclusion. If you started with a challenge, quotation, or surprising fact, close with it.

5

For guidelines on creating proposal visuals, see COLOR *and* GRAPHICS.

Always test visuals on the actual delivery media, slides, transparencies, or projector. Colors may shift significantly in hue or intensity from computer monitor to projected image or printed transparency. Projectors also have variations in color and brightness depending on model and light or power output.

Create effective visuals.

Carefully selected visuals have a powerful effect on evaluators. Effective visuals help them remember your key messages, often after a series of presentations presented in one mind-numbing day or several days apart.

According to the Industrial Audio Visual Association, people remember what they see and hear better than if they learned in only one mode, as summarized in figure 4.

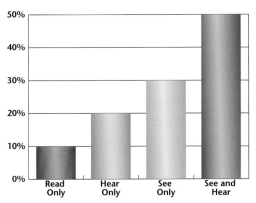

Figure 4. Memory Retention Based on Delivery. *The combination of repetition and multiple intake modes increases memory retention.*

The purpose of this guideline is to focus on and identify appropriate graphics for an oral proposal and how to present them effectively. For brevity, a discussion of the pros and cons of different media was eliminated.

With limited time and resources, use an organized process like the following to identify appropriate graphics:

1. Identify the number of visuals allowed. Two to three per minute is a maximum; add time if you need to comment on them.

2. Determine your key strategies and how you could depict each.

3. Review the evaluation criteria and major issues; then brainstorm what graphics tell compelling stories or offer proof of performance about each.

4. Review your PDWs for useful graphics.

5. Identify risks and visually depict risk mitigation approaches.

6. Visualize ways to portray added value.

7. Prioritize your visuals, one to three, low to high.

8. Retain the three's and as many two's as you have time to present.

9. Review the sequential logic of your visuals. Remove or add visuals as needed.

10. Do this quickly. Do not agonize. You will learn much more as you rehearse using the visuals.

Use the following guidelines to present effectively:

- Check sight lines to ensure everyone can see.

- Place the screen to one side of the room at a 45-degree angle, space permitting.

- Touch the screen, turn to the audience, then talk to the projected images. Pointers or light pencils poised in midair show every tremor and suggest nervousness.

- Rehearse with your visuals and always talk to the audience, not the visual.

- Use animation or progressive reveal to limit reading ahead.

- Summarize complex visuals; expand on simple visuals.

6 Rehearse early, realistically, and often.

Capitalize on your strengths and minimize your presentation weaknesses. Most of us are painfully aware of our weaknesses. Extensive practice with skilled coaching can make anyone much better.

Practice individual parts of your presentation. Then rehearse the entire presentation before a live audience while you time it.

Practice progressively. Initially, practice in nonthreatening situations; then add peers, videotaping, your boss, and final dress rehearsals.

While most oral proposals do not specify a question period, prepare for one anyway. Much of the real testing of a proposal team is during the question period.

Anticipate tough questions; prepare your answers, and rehearse answering them. Handled properly, the question period is an important opportunity to reinforce key ideas, clarify points, establish a rapport with individual evaluators, and generally discriminate your team and offer.

Learn a consistent method to address questions. Practice following these guidelines:

1. Respond to one question at a time.
2. Listen to the full question carefully.
3. Focus on the questioner:
   - Face the questioner.
   - Lean forward or move toward the questioner.
   - Establish eye contact.
   - Indicate active listening.

4. Do not interrupt.
5. Listen to the content (words) and for the intent (ultimate purpose) of the question.
6. If you do not know the answer, admit it or defer to someone else on your team.

Essentially similar to the *State, Support, Summarize* approach to present main points, follow these guidelines when answering questions:

1. Restate the question.
2. Concisely state your summary answer.
3. Support your answer.
4. Summarize or restate your original answer.
5. Ask if the questioner is satisfied.

For negative questions, do not restate the question. Agree with the questioner if possible. Try to address the positive side of what has been done.

As part of your preparation, develop two or three specific Very Important Points (VIPs). They usually flow from your strategy as expressed in your executive summary and are no more than 20 seconds long.

When you must deny an accusation, bridge or transition to one of your VIPs. When questions are hostile, restrict negative, nonverbal language, such as touching your head or face or shifting your weight.

7 Orchestrate the entire presentation.

Try to control as much of your presentation as possible. Appoint one person to be a facilitator, much like an MC.

Prepare backup materials and approaches. Anticipate what could go wrong and devise a solution.

Prepare handouts for distribution at the end, if permitted. Refer to them at the end, not the beginning. Offer electronic copies when appropriate.

8 Prepare a lessons-learned analysis to understand your win or loss and to improve subsequent proposals.

As with all proposal efforts, prepare a lessons-learned analysis after each oral proposal.

Ask each participant to submit a short self-assessment and team assessment. Collect and combine them into a formal report, and debrief the team so that everyone learns from the experience.

Request and attend a customer debrief as soon as the customer allows, win or lose. Summarize their comments in writing, add it to your formal report, and pass appropriate comments to presenters and contributors.

Organization

Organization is the key writing principle for most business documents, including proposals. A sound, well-conceived organization will make the actual writing easier, especially for writers with limited confidence in their writing skills. Nothing can save a poorly organized proposal.

Literature is typically ordered as a narrative flow that is read from beginning to end. Business and technical documents, newspapers, magazines, and professional journals are scanned, then referenced by readers searching for limited information at any one time. Readers' primary requirements are to:

- Immediately locate the information
- Immediately comprehend the information

Evaluators read proposals similarly. Few evaluators read the entire proposal, and virtually no one reads the proposal sequentially, start-to-finish, like a novel. Instead, they search for answers to a question, score the answer, justify their score, and then search for the answer to the next question.

Recall the last time you lost something. Why do you always find the item in the last place that you look? Because you stop looking after you find it. Why would evaluators keep reading after finding the answer?

Principles of organization for proposals, business documents, and technical documents differ slightly from document to document, depending on the type of document, the readers, the evaluation or referencing process, the intellectual content of the document, and the writer's purpose.

After you review these guidelines, you will see many similarities among proposals and national and regional newspapers and magazines. Most public media is designed to be rapidly and flexibly accessed and easily understood by diverse readers.

Well-organized proposals have common features:

- They announce their organization and follow it.
- Key points are clear and understandable for the intended evaluators.
- They are customer-focused, conforming to the evaluators' sense of what is important to them.
- They use multiple stylistic devices to enable evaluators to access the document virtually at random, quickly understand the organization and locate the information they need, and then comprehend that information.

Organization

1. Organize your proposal the way the customer tells you to organize it in the bid request.
2. Follow a consistent process to think clearly and then write quickly and effectively.
3. Organize information to make your proposal easy to evaluate.
4. Summarize at all levels.
5. Group similar ideas.
6. Keep set-ups short.
7. State your most important point first.
8. Adjust the writing style and graphics in each section of the proposal to the anticipated needs of the evaluator.
9. Use templates to help organize your messages before drafting text.

1

See OUTLINING.

See COMPLIANCE AND RESPONSIVENESS.

Organize your proposal the way the customer tells you to organize it in the bid request.

Mirroring the bid request's organization in your proposal might violate other recommendations in this *Proposal Guide*. However, your goal is to prepare an easily evaluated proposal, not necessarily a logical one.

Everyone's logic varies. Imagine how difficult multiple proposals are to evaluate when each proposal follows the offeror's unique logic.

Often evaluators do not prepare the bid request and are as frustrated with the imposed organization as you are. Not following the mandated organization only increases their frustration and potentially lowers your score.

Your top-level organization will vary depending on whether you have a bid request with specific organizational instructions, a bid request with no instructions, or an orally solicited proposal with no written bid request.

For casually or informally requested proposals, discuss the proposal contents, size, and organization with the customer. Use closed rather than open questions in this discussion. Suggest broad guidelines, and then seek agreement.

Poor questions

What do you want included in the proposal?

How big should the proposal be?

Better questions

Let's discuss what information you will need to make a thorough analysis and recommendation

for management approval. As a start, I suggest we include . . . Will that be sufficient?

To simplify your evaluation, I suggest we omit the typical corporate history and general technology descriptions and focus on the specific solution, our project team, and key milestone schedule. We could cover that in a relatively compact 35-page proposal. Would that meet your needs?

If a casually solicited proposal is competitive, your discussion gives you the edge over competitors that omit this step.

2 Follow a consistent process to think clearly and then write quickly and efficiently.

Use a step-by-step writing process to write both efficiently and effectively. Use the same approach each time you prepare any message, written or oral. You will spend less time figuring out what to do and have more time to prepare an effective message.

Most writers have experienced writer's block, when the ideas and words will not flow. Avoid or at least minimize writer's block by following this five-step POWeR™ writing process:

P *lanning*
O *rganizing*
W *riting*
e *xamining*
R *evising/Rehearsing*

The acronym POWeR has four uppercase letters and a lower case *e*. The uppercase letters represent stages or steps that the author controls. The lowercase *e* represents the examining stage where other people are asked to suggest improvements before the message is revised.

Apply these sequential steps when you prepare any kind of written or oral message. Substeps in each stage are summarized in figure 1.

The **POWeR** process applies equally well to writing and presenting. First prepare your presentation using the five-step process and add Rehearsing to the revising step.

PLANNING
• Determine your objective (to do, know, and/or feel)
• Analyze the prospective audience
• Analyze message content
• Select the optimal medium
• Develop content

ORGANIZING
• As instructed by the customer
• Summarize, then support
• Use Four-Box organizational approach
• Determine what will be emphasized

WRITING
• Draft
• Use emphasis techniques

eXAMINING
• Cool the draft
• Seek outside review (peers, managers, customer)

REVISING OR REHEARSING
• Make your message clear
• Make your message concise
• Make your message correct

Figure 1. Improve Communication Effectiveness and Efficiency by Using the POWeR™ Writing Process. *This five-step process is an effective and efficient way to develop written and oral messages. This approach is implicit within the business development process and tools discussed in this Proposal Guide.*

3 Organize information to make your proposal easy to evaluate.

Evaluators scan, locate, read, and then comprehend. Make it easy for evaluators to find the answers to their questions and easy for them to give you a maximum score.

Scanners are attracted by the following emphasis devices:

• Headings
• Graphics (photo, sketch, chart, table)
• Action captions attached to graphics
• Color

• White space
• Larger, bold, or colorful print
• Initial paragraphs
• Bullet lists
• Callouts
• Headers and footers

Use these emphasis devices alone or in combination. Here are a few examples:

• Group a series of answers in a table or matrix.

One U.S. Air Force evaluator said, *"We went to the tables and graphics first. If we found the answer, we didn't have to read the text."*

- Answer questions in informative headings.

Requirement

DOE must have unlimited rights of entry to all proposed sites during the site survey period.

Response

All Site Owners Agree to Unlimited Rights of Entry

We have obtained signed agreements from all twelve property owners within the proposed site indicating . . .

- Include a compliance matrix at the beginning of the proposal and perhaps at the beginning of proposal sections.

No one enjoys reading proposals. You should not care if they read every word of your proposal as long as they give you the highest score and select your solution. In fact, if evaluators have to read every word of your proposal, you will probably lose.

4

Summarize at all levels.

The first sentence, paragraph, and page of your proposal are the most important. The last sentence, paragraph, and page are potentially the second most important, but only if you assume evaluators will read them. When preparation time is limited, focus on the opening summary over the closing summary.

Inexperienced writers often confuse summaries and introductions. *Summaries* briefly restate your essential message. *Introductions* preview content and organization.

Opening any portion of a proposal with an introduction to yourself and your organization implies that you and the customer have not met. Perhaps worse, if they stop reading after the introduction, they will not get your key messages.

Instead, combine the summary and introduction, beginning with the summary. Place the introduction, preview, or an informal table of contents immediately after the summary. If the summary generates sufficient interest, the evaluator will keep reading. However, they might opt to jump to a specific topic. The introduction confirms that topic is included and tells them how to find it. Either way, you have met the evaluator's needs.

The executive summary should open with your overriding theme statement, stating the most important point you want every evaluator to remember. Follow the theme statement with a statement of the customer's vision, a link between the customer's vision and immediate need, an overview of your solution, and a statement of compliance, all within the first few paragraphs.

See EXECUTIVE SUMMARY.

See MODEL DOCUMENTS for examples of executive summaries.

Evaluators might quit reading at any time. Give evaluators your most important points before they quit reading by summarizing at all levels: the proposal, volume, section, subsection, and paragraph.

The executive summary should summarize your entire proposal, and volume summaries should summarize each volume. Open sections and subsections with a summary, and open individual paragraphs with summary sentences.

Finally, keep your word; maintain your credibility. If you introduce a series of topics, discuss those topics in the order introduced and name the topics identically, as shown in the following proposal excerpt:

INTRODUCTION

Our comprehensive solution incorporates a proven, COTS-based design; low risk implementation; and proven, dedicated project team.

Subheadings

Poor Examples
TECHNICAL SOLUTION
MANAGEMENT APPROACH

Better Examples
DESIGN
IMPLEMENTATION
PROJECT TEAM

Best Examples
PROVEN, COTS-BASED DESIGN
LOW RISK IMPLEMENTATION
PROVEN, DEDICATED PROJECT TEAM

5 Group similar ideas.

See STORYBOARDS AND MOCKUPS.

Separating similar ideas creates confusion and chaos. Grouping similar ideas in a proposal can be difficult:

- Bid requests scatter similar questions.
- Different questions require similar support.
- Multiple authors are unaware of the overlap.
- Authors draw answers from the same boilerplate (previously written materials).

See MODEL DOCUMENTS and QUESTION/RESPONSE PROPOSALS.

Use storyboards to help writers group similar ideas and to plan and review content before drafting.

Proposal managers have the primary duty to detect and resolve the inconsistencies and redundancies. Writers may also detect them by reviewing section drafts.

How you deal with redundancies depends on the size of the proposal, RFP page limits, and the relative importance of the materials. Do not insult the intelligence of the evaluator by inserting identical text without an explanation.

To eliminate cross-referencing among volumes, repeat the answer to the same question asked in different volumes. Tell them that you repeated your answer:

> We answered this question earlier in Volume 1, Section 1.2.3, and have repeated it here for your convenience.

Cross-referencing within the same volume is generally acceptable. Answer the question fully the first time it is asked. The next time the same question is asked, introduce your answer as shown:

> We answered this question earlier in Section 1.2.3 and have summarized our response here for your convenience. For detail, please refer to Section 1.2.3.

When bid request instructions force you to scatter information, exploit this opportunity to demonstrate your customer-focused approach:

- Insert a brief summary
- Insert a brief introduction

> While our flight test program will follow the low cost, low risk sequence of 1) laboratory tests, 2) ground tests, and then 3) flight tests, our response is ordered per your bid request instructions:
>
> 1. Flight tests
> 2. Laboratory tests
> 3. Ground tests

6 Keep set-ups short.

Some documents need a short set-up to help the reader place the document in the context of prior events. If so, keep your set-up short to get to your major ideas as rapidly as possible.

1. **Restate needs in your own words, while making the customer's ownership of the problem specific, for example:**

   > In our meetings with your key managers over the past 3 months and in your RFP, you said that you needed to . . .

   Avoid copying and pasting text from the bid request.

   Copying and pasting pages or paragraphs from the bid request demonstrates that you can copy-and-paste but not that you understand their problem.

2. **Begin with your value proposition or a benefit statement:**

   > Cascadia Timber can reduce annual forest management costs by $1,000,000 annually by purchasing . . .

   Avoid beginning with a cliche.

   > Thank you for the opportunity to present our proposal for . . .
   >
   > We are pleased to present our proposal for . . .

3. **Limit the set-up to a sentence or phrase:**

   > *In our meeting on April 15, you asked us to prepare a proposal summarizing how…*

   Avoid beginning by thoroughly summarizing prior events.

   > In 2001, we began by . . . Then we . . . Over the subsequent 3 years of the initial contract, we . . . Our extensive work culminated in your decision to request proposals from . . .

The first sentence links to the prior event. The second sentence begins with positive information, positively states a rationale, and then delivers the bad news. The final sentence closes with a positive statement to further soften the bad news and add perspective.

Good proposal writers use a similar approach when discussing poor performance. Stress lessons learned from poor performance and corrective actions taken. Carefully present, but do not ignore negative information.

7

State your most important point first.

See Lists.

In a fast-paced business environment, readers value the result over the support. Managers usually value results over process. A *Wall Street Journal* study found that 10 percent of their readers stopped reading after each column inch of copy. Six inches into a story, nearly one-half of the readers have quit reading.

Proposal evaluators have a similar reading pattern; they read until satisfied, score the question, then look for the answer to the next question.

Most writers write like the documents they read. Technical people tend to use a technical or scientific format. Scientists know that a result is useless unless the proper process was carefully documented so it can be followed by others to verify results. Hence, in the scientific format,

process is more important than the result and comes first in the document.

Proposal writers with technical backgrounds tend to lead to, rather than from, major ideas. Such writers build their case logically, fearing skeptical evaluators will not believe them unless they build their case.

Most newspapers, magazines, and professional business documents use managerial, or top-down, organization. They state their conclusion or result, and then support it.

When writing any proposal or business document, ask yourself, "If the evaluator or reader stopped reading at any time, have I placed my ideas or points in decreasing order of importance to the reader?" If not, reorder them.

8

Adjust the writing style and graphics in each section of the proposal to the anticipated needs of the evaluator.

When incorporating boilerplate or reuse material in your proposal, update summaries, introductions, and subheadings. First, tailor the summary to this competition. Next, if you add or delete topics, reflect those changes in the introduction. Then, order the topics in decreasing order of importance to this customer on this opportunity.

Choose graphics and a style of writing appropriate to the evaluators of each section of the proposal. For example, all evaluators, including nontechnical ones, must understand executive summary graphics. Highly technical proposal sections can contain more complex, technical graphics, but only include sufficient technical detail to make them correct.

Adjust your style of writing similarly. Larger paragraphs, sentences, and words are acceptable in more technical proposal sections. However, proposals are not technical treatises. Evaluators often perceive overly technical writing and graphics as technical arrogance.

Within a proposal and within proposal sections, you can increase the technical complexity. Begin sections with succinct, clear summaries that are broadly understandable. Then increase the complexity as needed to satisfy the more technical evaluators. The less technical evaluators will have quit reading and jumped to the next section.

Apply this guideline to both graphics and text.

9

Use templates to help organize your messages before drafting text.

See Executive Summary, figure 5, and Sales Letters, *Capture Guide*, figure 4, for specific adaptations of the Four-Box template.

Use templates customized for the type of document being written to encourage writers to follow a process approach.

When asked to write, most people think about drafting text. You will produce more successful documents if you follow a consistent writing process like POWeR™ and use customized templates.

When confronted with different templates, remember that following the process is more important than the exact content, form, or format of the template.

This *Proposal Guide* companion *Capture Guide* contain examples of the templates listed in figure 2.

The Four-Box template shown in figure 3 is the fundamental document organizer. The Four-Box organizational structure is incorporated in every model document. At the most fundamental level, the Four-Box template is shown in figure 3. The four elements or boxes are:

1. Summary
2. Introduction
3. Body
4. Review

Each box is then adapted to best achieve the writer's purpose by meeting reader(s)' needs.

TEMPLATE	FINAL DOCUMENT	TOPIC	GUIDE
Four-Box Template	Cover Letter Executive Summary Finals Presentations Letter Proposals Sales Letters	Cover Letter	*Proposal Guide*
		Executive Summary	*Proposal Guide*
		Presentation to Customers	*Capture Guide*
		Letter Proposals	*Proposal Guide*
		Sales Letters	*Capture Guide*
Proposal Development Worksheet (PDW); Storyboard	Proposal Section	Storyboards and Mockups	*Proposal Guide*
Oral Proposal Planner	Oral Proposal	Oral Proposals	*Proposal Guide*
Proposal Management Plan	Proposal Management Plan	Proposal Management Plan	*Proposal Guide*
Capture Planner	Capture Plan	Capture Planning	*Capture Guide*
Integrated Customer Solution Worksheet	Capture or Proposal Section	Strategy	*Proposal Guide/Capture Guide*
		Capture Planning	*Proposal Guide/Capture Guide*
		Executive Summary	*Proposal Guide/Capture Guide*
Bidder Comparison Matrix	Capture or Proposal Section	Strategy	*Proposal Guide/Capture Guide*
		Capture Planning	*Proposal Guide/Capture Guide*
		Executive Summary	*Proposal Guide/Capture Guide*
Success Story Template	Proposal Section	Relevant Experience/Past Performance	*Proposal Guide*

Figure 2. Use Templates to Organize Your Messages. *Using a template to develop and review content before writing saves time and improves the effectiveness of the final document. Remember that following the process is more important than the exact content, form, or format of the template.*

Box 1-SUMMARY: Summarize the essence of your message. State what you want the reader to do, know, and/or feel. Ask yourself: Would I achieve my objective if the reader stopped reading at the end of Box 1?

Box 2-INTRODUCTION: Preview or announce the organization of the document. Readers will not accept your ideas if they do not know where you are going. Organize around the issues or points most interesting to the reader.

Box 3-BODY: Follow the organization announced in Box 2. Align the customer's issues with the details needed to convince the reader to accept your ideas. Eliminate extraneous details that are interesting to you but do not support your purpose.

Box 4-REVIEW: Review or summarize the Do and Know portions first stated in Box 1. End by clearly stating the next realistically achievable step. In a memo or e-mail, this might be what you will proactively commit to do next. In an executive summary, this might direct them to the proposal. In a proposal section, Box 4 is optional, since many evaluators will stop reading as soon as they find the answer to their question.

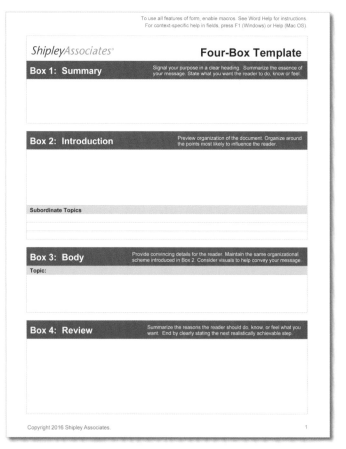

Figure 3. Four-Box Organizational Structure. *Apply this organizational structure to virtually any type of business document.*

Outlining is a crucial proposal management activity. All subsequent work is based on the initial outline.

See COMPLIANCE
AND RESPONSIVENESS,
CUSTOMER FOCUS,
HEADINGS, NUMBERING
SYSTEMS, ORGANIZATION,
PROPOSAL MANAGEMENT
PLAN, *and* STORYBOARDS
AND MOCKUPS.

Outlines are important in individual proposal writing efforts and essential in team writing efforts. The outline establishes the table of contents, serves as a proposal management tool, and helps writers see their task as it relates to the entire proposal.

Guidelines for developing sound proposal outlines are based on the principles of customer focus and organization. By following customers' instructions and organization, no matter how illogical, you demonstrate that you listen to your customers and give them exactly what they request. By following sound document organizational guidelines, you demonstrate your ability to meet the customer's needs in an easy to understand and convincing fashion.

Developing a compliant outline is often difficult. Nearly every bid request is confusing on the first reading. The difficulty increases with complex and poorly written bid requests, management pressures to start writing immediately, and individual pressure to use another organization because it is more logical or better matches something already written.

Outlining

1. Develop your proposal outline as the customer suggests, either in the bid request or verbally.

2. Prepare a top-level, topical outline that follows the customer's organizational priority. Mimic the numbering system, naming conventions, and order listed in the bid request.

3. Assign or allocate all other response requirements within the topical outline.

4. Use informative headings at section levels below those specified by the customer.

5. Allocate pages according to the relative importance of the topic to the customer.

6. Develop outlines for unsolicited proposals (1) collaboratively with your customer, (2) based on discussion with your customer, or (3) logically.

7. Annotate outlines as needed to guide writers.

8. Extend your outline into a Proposal Responsibility Matrix to help manage the proposal.

9. When you have to deviate from the bid request, always explain your deviation to the evaluator.

1

Develop your proposal outline as the customer suggests, either in the bid request or verbally.

First, follow the customer's proposal organization instructions precisely, even if they seem illogical. Then, apply sound organizational principles at succeeding levels.

Customers frequently direct or at least suggest how offerors' proposals should be organized. A common organization helps evaluators assess competing proposals.

See COMPLIANCE AND
RESPONSIVENESS.

Detailed proposal preparation instructions are required for U.S. federal bid requests issued under the federal Acquisition Regulations, FAR Part 15. The FAR requires the bid request structure shown in figure 1, with Instructions to Offerors in section *L*.

Acquisitions under other parts of the FAR are not as prescriptive, but most bid requests will have some type of preparation instructions.

International central, regional, and local government agencies of all types often include a relatively less detailed set of instructions on how to organize your proposal. Large companies that routinely compete in these market sectors tend to follow similar proposal solicitation procedures.

The complete lack of organizational instructions usually reflects a lack of established purchasing procedures or experience on the part of the people requesting the proposal. Treat this as an opportunity to favorably influence the bid request by collaboratively developing the proposal requirements and outline with the customer.

RFP	DESCRIPTION	TYPICAL CONTENT
A	Solicitation/Contract form	RFP table of contents, contact information, due date, submittal location; serves as contract when signed by offeror and government
B	Supplies or services and prices	Contract Line Items (CLINs) listing what is to be priced and how
C	Statement of work	Describes work required, i.e., specification
D	Packaging and markings	Product packaging and markings required
E	Inspection and acceptance	Product/service inspection and acceptance criteria
F	Deliveries or performance	When products or services are required
G	Contract administration data	Contract requirements not on solicitation form
H	Special contract requirements	Items not in Section I or other sections of the contract
I	Contract clauses	Clauses required by law or included in contract
J	List of attachments	Data requirements and organization, anything that did not fit elsewhere, and occasionally organizational instructions not included in Section L to permit using an otherwise standard RFP
K	Representations, certifications	Acknowledgment forms that must be signed and submitted with the proposal
L	Instructions to offerors	Instructions for proposal preparation, format, organization, content, length
M	Evaluation factors for award	Process, evaluation factors, and relative importance of the factors used to evaluate offers

Figure 1. How U.S. Federal Bid Requests Are Organized. *FAR Part 15, Contracting by Negotiation, prescribes this bid request structure for major competitive and negotiated procurements to simplify proposal preparation for offerors and to improve proposal evaluation by government source selection teams.*

If you have a bid request with no instructions on how to organize your proposal, mirror the organization of the bid request as closely as possible. Number, order, and name sections as was done in the bid request. When all else fails, make an assumption, state it clearly, and get on with proposal development.

State your assumptions explaining how your proposal is organized in your compliance matrix, table of contents, and introductions at relevant levels. This style choice conveys a helpful, reader-friendly tone.

The following two examples show how organizational assumptions can be stated in both formal and question-and-response bid requests:

See NUMBERING SYSTEMS *and* STYLE AND TONE.

Assumption stated in the contents and/or response matrix

All proposal instructions were followed explicitly. Our numbering system is identical to bid request Section L. Other requirements were inserted within the *L* dictated outline where they were most relevant. All responses to bid request requirements can be located in the Response Matrix.

Assumption for a non-Federal question and response style

All sections of the federal bid request, and all questions with multiple parts were answered in the order asked. Short summaries at the beginning of major sections establish perspective.

Many leading sales trainers recommend never accepting customers' initial vision of the solution or requirements. Instead, they recommend reengineering customers' visions or redefining their requirements. This recommendation is based on the premise that reshaping a customer's vision puts you in the leading position and makes a uniform, low-price selection more difficult.

Reengineering a customer's vision is valid earlier in the sales process but usually not after a final bid request is issued. If you find that to win you must reshape the customer's vision after the final bid request is released, look for another opportunity.

2

Prepare a top-level, topical outline that follows the customer's organizational priority. Mimic the numbering system, naming conventions, and order listed in the bid request.

Many bid requests are written by different people, with different knowledge and interests, over months or years. Follow the organizational priority set by those who manage the evaluation process.

For a U.S. federal bid request, develop your outline based on the following organizational priority:

1. Section L: Instructions, conditions, notices
2. Section M: Evaluation factors
3. Section C: Statement of Work
4. Section B: Supplies or services and prices
5. All other sections

On a large proposal effort or on a complex proposal, prepare a second-level outline first and get consensus among management and key team members. Then create a third- or fourth-level outline and try to keep it there. Avoid further substantial changes.

For all other written bid requests, look for similar instructions:

- Organizational instructions
- Evaluation criteria or hot buttons
- Statement of Work tasks
- Separately priced items or tasks

These recommendations are consistent among proposal professionals and based on who has control of the evaluation process. Different sections are often written by different types of people. *L* is prepared by the people running the procurement. *M* is prepared by the group making the selection decision. *C* is written by the people who understand the services or products or by their consultants, as much as 3 to 5 years earlier. They may or may not be users of the services or products. *B* is prepared by an accounting or financial person.

To emphasize compliance, retain and extend the numbering system used in the bid request.

Keep identical naming conventions. Capitalize the same words, hyphenate the same words, and spell them the same unless the word is misspelled.

Maintain the same order as listed in the bid request, even if the order is not logical to you.

Figure 2 shows how a top-level, topical outline is prepared from a bid request excerpt typical of any market sector. The bid request directly indicates the numbered, second-level topics, e.g., 2.1 Organization Structure and Facility Resources.

Adding the third- and fourth-level subsections depends on their page length. Generally, use a subsection number if the length exceeds two pages. Note the lower-level topics are included as unnumbered items but would not be listed in the table of contents.

If you are lucky, these sections are similar. When they are different, look to guideline 3.

RFP Excerpt

2.0 Management Plan

1. Organization Structure and Facility Resources. Include a current organizational chart and a brief description of operational function. Describe your firm's organization in terms of size and organizational stability. Identify facility resources (e.g., word processing, ADPE, etc.), which may be used for this project.

2. Relevant Corporate Experience. Relate two recent (within the last 3 years) successful corporate experiences in Software Development and Implementation Engineering, Data Base Management and Integration, User and System Integration, and Network Operation. For each completed project cited, provide the following information: project name, hardware and operating systems involved, user, description of work performed, experience in data communications and packet-switching, period of contract, contact point, subcontractors with contact name and phone number, description of subcontractor's involvement . . . .

Proposal Outline

2.0 MANAGEMENT PLAN
2.1 Organization Structure and Facility Resources
  2.1.1 Current Organizational Chart
  2.1.2 Size and Organizational Stability
  2.1.3 Relevant Facility Resources
2.2 Relevant Corporate Experience
  2.2.1 Software Development and Implementation Engineering Projects
    2.2.1.1 ABC Project
      —Project name
      —Hardware and operating systems
      —User
      —Description of work performed
      —Experience in data communications and packet-switching
      —Period of contract
      —Contact point
      —Subcontractors with contact name and phone number
      —Description of subcontractor's involvement
    2.2.1.2 DEF Project
  2.2.2 Data Base Management and Integration
    2.2.2.1 GHI Project
    2.2.2.2 JKL Project
  2.2.3 User and System Integration
    2.2.3.1 MNO Project
    2.2.3.2 PQR Project
  2.2.4 Network Operation
    2.2.4.1 STU Project
    2.2.4.2 VWX Project

Figure 2. Developing a Top-Level, Topical Outline. *Mimic the numbering system, naming conventions, and order of the topics listed in the bid request. Use the exact wording and naming conventions to simplify the evaluator's search for wording or topics in your proposal. The items listed under 2.2.1.1 are shown to illustrate subsection content under each project description but would not be included in the topical outline or table of contents.*

3   Assign or allocate all other response requirements within the topical outline.

After placing all response requirements embedded within the proposal instructions in your outline, you must assign or allocate all other requirements within the same topical outline. Augmenting the original topical outline with additional subsections and requirements is more difficult when different bid request sections have different structures.

A single-level bid request, like the example in figure 2, is relatively simple to outline. Multilevel bid requests are more complex.

Multilevel bid requests have the organization and requirements established at the top level plus additional overlapping requirements at one or more lower levels.

Multilevel bid requests are similar to a couple purchasing a house. Each partner establishes his or her own requirements; some are the same, some are unique, and some conflict.

Figure 3 illustrates how additional bid request sections other than the proposal instructions are incorporated into the proposal outline. Because there is no single correct answer, your compliance or response matrix becomes even more important.

When you extend the topical outline, aim for balance. For example, if you go only to 2.1 in one section, try to avoid going to 2.2.X.X in another section. Such differences imply an unbalanced response.

A disturbingly common approach is to develop the topical outline, and then instruct all contributors to "Read the bid request, identify the additional requirements relevant to your section, and address each one in your draft." The results are orphans that no one addresses and redundancies that several people address differently. Making the problem worse, redundant items may be double costed.

Bid Request Excerpt: Statement of Work

5.2 Management Reporting. Contractor shall maintain a current organizational structure for the assigned project team indicating all people assigned, a description of their duties, and how they are to be contacted. All proposed changes must be reviewed and approved by the Contract Administrator.

5.3 Facility Compliance. All facilities proposed must comply with all federal, state, and municipal zoning and building requirements, including continuing licensing and permitting standards. Contractor will maintain proof of compliance on site.

ZONING REGULATION

Fire alarms must be tested weekly, and evacuation procedures practiced monthly.

All buildings must meet applicable seismic codes, including a posting of compliance displayed prominently in the primary entrance area.

Proposal Outline

2.0 MANAGEMENT PLAN
- 2.1 Organization Structure and Facility Resources
    - 2.1.1 Current Organizational Chart
        - 2.1.1.1 Management Reporting
            - — Project Team Structure
            - — Project Team Management
    - 2.1.2 Size and Organizational Stability
    - 2.1.3 Facility Resources
        - 2.1.3.1 Facility Compliance
            - — Fire Protection Plan
            - — Seismic Protection Plan
- 2.2 Relevant Corporate Experience

Proposal Outline

2.0 MANAGEMENT PLAN
- 2.1 Organization Structure and Facility Resources
    - 2.1.1 Current Organizational Chart
        - 2.1.1.1 Project Team Structure
        - 2.1.1.2 Project Team Management
    - 2.1.2 Size and Organizational Stability
    - 2.1.3 Facility Resources
        - 2.1.3.1 Fire Protection Plan
        - 2.1.3.2 Seismic Protection Plan
- 2.2 Relevant Corporate Experience

Figure 3. Extending a Topical Outline for Multilevel Bid Requests. *Adding to the example shown in figure 2, a lower-level Statement of Work (SOW) section shown in blue lists requirements relevant to the Management Plan. The SOW further references zoning regulation in paragraph 5.3, which are excerpted in red type. The colored text shows how the additional requirements are folded into the proposal outline. The alternate approaches show two acceptable ways the outline could be prepared, depending on the length of each subsection.*

4

See HEADINGS.

Use informative headings at section levels below those specified by the customer.

Informative headings can impart a positive message. In the example shown in figures 2 and 3, the headings in black are all telegraphic and identical to the bid request. Some of the headings in blue and red can be improved by making them informative:

Telegraphic heading

Project Team Structure

Project Team Management

Fire Protection Plan

Seismic Protection Plan

Informative Heading

Proven Team Structure Reduces Risk

Responsive Team Management Improves Service

Proactive Fire Risk Management Cuts Loss

Earthquake Preparedness Is a Priority

Avoid combining theme statements and informative headings. These combinations are cumbersome and repetitive.

5

Allocate pages according to the relative importance of the topic to the customer.

Allocate pages based on the page limitations or recommendations in the bid request or suggestions from the customer. If none are given, attempt to discover the customer's expectations through a collaborative discussion. Attempt to reduce page-length expectations to optimize preparation time and cost unless a shorter proposal conflicts with your proposal strategy.

After determining or estimating the total page count, allocate pages according to the relative importance to the customer, tempered by your proposal strategy.

Determine relative importance based on the following indicators, in the order listed:

1. Evaluation criteria
2. Discussion with the customer
3. Judgment

Often evaluation criteria are both broadly stated and stated in order of relative importance. Use your judgment to allocate the page count among the first-level topical outline, then extend your allocation to subsections until all contributors have a clear page limit or guideline for their assigned sections. The approach is shown in figure 4.

RFP INSTRUCTIONS TO OFFERORS

All proposals are limited to 100 pages, excluding preface pages. Attachments are not included nor are they encouraged.

All proposals should contain the following sections:

1. System Hardware—Describe all hardware that will be supplied and how it connects with existing hardware. Include appropriate system diagrams.
2. System and Network Software—Indicate the software to be supplied, its capabilities, upgradability, and warranty.
3. Project Management—Indicate how the project will be managed, naming all proposed personnel judged *key* to this project's success. Include a first- and second-tier schedule that links to your proposed WBS and SOW. For all personnel, indicate the percentage of their time devoted to this project.
4. Training—Include a training plan for all operators and maintenance technicians. Indicate the additional support available and its cost.
5. Pricing—Include a complete pricing breakdown of all hardware, software, and services identified in the SOW.

EVALUATION CRITERIA

Proposals that fail to respond fully to all requirements as listed may be rejected without further consideration. Selection will be based on the evaluation team's judgment of the offer that affords the best value. The following evaluation factors are listed in decreasing order of importance: (1) Technical, (2) Management, (3) Cost.

In the Technical area, hardware is one-half as important as software but twice as important as training.

Figure 4. Establishing Page Count Guidelines. *Allocate pages according to their relative importance to the evaluator. Make the initial page allocation based on the evaluation criteria.*

ESTIMATED WEIGHTS AND PAGE ALLOCATION

Criterion	Category	Weight	Proposal Section	1st Cut Page Allocation	
1	Technical	50			50
			1. System Hardware	14	
			2. System and Network Software	28	
			4. Training	8	
2	Management	30	3. Project Management		30
3	Cost	20	5. Cost		20
				Total	100

ADJUSTED PROPOSAL OUTLINE

#	Section	Pages	Comments
	Executive Summary	6	Approximately 5 to 10 percent of total
1	System Hardware	12	Reduced, not a discriminator
2	System and Network Software	27	Equal to weight less executive summary
3	Project Management	32	Increased; discriminator for us
4	Training	10	Increased; hot button of key evaluator
5	Cost	8	Decreased; use tables extensively
	Total	95	
	Contingency	5	
	Page Limit per RFP	100	

Figure 5. Establishing Page Count Guidelines *(continued from previous page). Allocate pages according to their relative importance to the evaluator. After your initial page allocation, adjust it based on the number required and your strategy. Allocate 5 to 10 percent for the executive summary and 5 to 10 percent for the contingency that someone might exceed the limit.*

---

6 Develop outlines for unsolicited proposals (1) collaboratively with your customer, (2) based on discussion with your customer, or (3) logically.

When you do not have a formal bid request, discern the customer's requirements collaboratively in meetings or phone calls. Refer to previous proposals deemed acceptable by the customer, customer file notes, and intelligence resources.

Prepare a response checklist.

In some instances, this *checklist* may become the basis for a competitive bid. If so, you have influenced the requirements, giving yourself an advantage.

Follow these steps:

1. List the requirements as you understand them.

2. Verify your list and add requirements as you discover them in face-to-face meetings and phone calls.

3. Prioritize your list by categories.

4. Seek final customer buy-off via a read-through when possible.

5. Submit a copy of the final requirements checklist along with your proposal.

---

7 Annotate outlines as needed to guide writers.

If you want writers to include certain information, use a specific example, follow a set strategy, or tell them by annotating the proposal outline. Too frequently proposal managers ask writers, "Why didn't you discuss the ABC Project?" The usual answer, "You didn't tell me to," or, "I didn't know about it."

Avoid rework by annotating your proposal outlines.

8

Extend your outline into a Proposal Responsibility Matrix to help manage the proposal.

Extend your proposal outline into a Proposal Responsibility Matrix. Most proposal managers use a spreadsheet program, enabling them to add columns to track additional tasks associated with the development of each proposal section in the outline.

*Shipley*Associates	**Proposal Status Tracker**								Enter Proposal Name
Section Number	Section Heading (Title)	Page Alloc.	Author	Storyboard Due	Mockup Due	Pink Team Date	Red Team Date	Final Approval	Remarks
M	Executive Summary	4.	S. Ross	03/19/11	03/31/11	04/02/11	04/18/11	04/24/11	
L.2.1	Technical Overview	2.	W. Lou	03/21/11	03/31/11	04/04/11	04/18/11	04/24/11	

Figure 6. Proposal Responsibility Matrix. *Sometimes called a Program Control Matrix, proposal managers use it to manage and monitor the status of each section assigned to each writer. Using spreadsheet software, add a row for each task and a column for each milestone. Keep a version prominently displayed in the proposal room and review progress in the daily stand-up meeting.*

9

When you have to deviate from the bid request, always explain your deviation to the evaluator.

The Proposal Responsibility Matrix, shown in figure 5, is also discussed in DAILY TEAM MANAGEMENT.

Explanatory comments are in addition to always including a compliance or response matrix in every proposal. For unsolicited proposals, consider adding a topic index, directing evaluators to all significant topics.

When you are deviating from the bid request or you do not understand their intent, insert explanatory comments, like those in figure 6. This stylistic choice signals your desire to make things easier for the evaluator and suggests that your organization will be easier to work with if you win the contract.

At a proposal debriefing, the buyer said, "It was like you were reading our mind. We found 80 percent of the answers where we expected to find them." If 80 percent is mind reading, imagine what evaluators normally face.

At the beginning of compliance matrix

Our proposal mirrors your bid request organization and numbering system. The L.21 prefix was dropped for all proposal section numbers.

In a cost or price volume

All items costed correspond with tasks described in our technical volume.

This page is intentionally blank.

Section number x.x.x was intentionally skipped to maintain agreement with the bid request.

Figure 7. Explain Any Deviation from Bid Request Instructions. *Help evaluators understand how your proposal is organized by inserting short explanations. Insert explanations at the beginning of major sections, on the compliance matrix, or any other place where your organization might be unclear.*

Page and Document Design

Page and Document Design impact whether your proposal is read, how it is read, and whether it is remembered. The physical design of your proposal pages emphasizes or de-emphasizes your messages much like body language, word dynamics, and facial expressions in conversation.

The proposal might be the first deliverable that your Customer receives from your customer.

Resist excessive emphasis devices that make your proposal busy, cluttered, confusing, or unprofessional. The *ransom note* look is not professional.

The reading process is identical for technical documentation or a proposal. However, the motivation of the reader differs. The more interesting the subject to the reader, the more the reader wants the information, the less you have to entice the reader to read your document. How interested and motivated are evaluators in reading your proposal?

People are *lookers* first, then readers. A good page and document design entices readers, then facilitates understanding, even though evaluators may not be conscious of the design techniques used. A well-organized, visually appealing design helps evaluators find what they need to know rapidly and easily while reflecting your organization's professionalism.

Never underestimate the importance of the proposal's appearance. When competitors' offers differ minimally, the appearance and organization of the proposal can make the difference. Consider these comments from an evaluator:

Every answer was where we expected to find it. After we read it, we found that you did not fully comply with our requirements. But it was too late; everyone liked it too much.

See your proposal in its totality. The best proposals are a sequence of integrated impressions that are planned, coherent, and repeated to produce the strongest impact on evaluators. A well-designed proposal eases the evaluator's job. Visual elements entice readers, the organization is easy to follow, answers are easy to find, key points stand out, graphics are clear and conveniently placed, and the text is easy to read.

Your document and page design should consider the following elements:

- Page format
- Type size and font
- Color
- Covers and binding system
- Graphics type, size, style, and quantity
- Production requirements

Many proposal professionals cite the bid request warning, "Overly elaborate proposals may indicate the offerors lack of cost consciousness," as a justification for dull, plain proposals. With the cost of a computer, software, and color printer under $1,000, intelligent, attractive page and document design is not expensive.

The greater danger is to use a page and document design that suggests your organization is out-of-date. Claims of leading-edge technology and world-class products and services cannot counter a visually outdated proposal. However, artificial variety and inconsistent devices can be distracting, confusing, and off-putting.

Page and Document Design

1. Follow the customer's page and document design instructions.
2. Use a style sheet for every proposal.
3. Select a document and page style appropriate to your customer's organization, your industry, and your organization.
4. Adapt your layout to the structure of the writing.
5. Use white space to guide the evaluator and to emphasize key points.
6. Use headers and footers to help evaluators navigate your proposal while maintaining customer focus.
7. Select a page-column design that balances page limits, production requirements, readability, and graphics size flexibility.
8. Select complementary font styles, sizes, and leading.
9. Establish a consistent system for headings, themes, action captions, lists, and other page design features.
10. Choose and place graphics for maximum impact and readability.
11. Avoid overusing emphasis devices.
12. Use left-justified text.

1

"Point" is a measure of letter height, with 72 points per inch; 72-point text is 1-inch high.

Follow the customer's page and document design instructions.

Some bidders ignore instructions because they disagree with the instructions, the instructions do not fit their process, or they feel their approach is better. Consider the following examples.

A major computer company, highly regarded for its sales training, had training materials that said, "Our proposals should include these sections: . . ." and included a fixed list of topics. No mention was made to first follow each customer's proposal instructions. How could they claim to be customer focused while ignoring the customer's proposal instructions?

Bidders trying to get around page limitations used foldout pages. Subsequent bid request instructions were amended to count any page larger than 8.5" x 11" as two pages.

Follow preparation instructions precisely. Ask for clarification if needed. Bid request preparation is often rushed, and mistakes are common. Customers are not trying to trick bidders.

Consider submitting a sample page for approval. The worst possible result is that the customer refuses to answer.

2

Use a style sheet for every proposal.

Style sheets are essential, and they reduce preparation time. Whether you have single or multiple contributors, using a style sheet will give the proposal a consistent appearance, making it easier to evaluate.

A good style sheet both shows and tells writers the page layout; font choice, point size, and line spacing for body text and graphics text; and the colors to use. Figure 1 shows a style sheet for an asymmetrical two-column page design (also called one-third/two-third layout) with the narrower left column reserved for themes, callouts, and small graphics.

Establish an electronic template style sheet in the software of choice, and limit the physical style sheet, like the one in figure 1, to a single page. Many writers tend to ignore longer style sheets.

A frequent practice on proposals with multiple writers and a production support group is to give each writer a simplified style sheet

or template, either at the kickoff meeting, via e-mail, or over your intranet site. This simplified style sheet is easier for writers to use and cuts the time spent on formatting.

Style sheets reduce production time and enhance production flexibility. For example, if all body text carries the same, defined style, then a single style sheet change flows consistently through the entire document.

Production people generally strip out formatting before imposing their more complex style sheet, to prevent importing extraneous or conflicting styles. You can eliminate this step if you have a good style sheet and template and if contributors know how to use the template.

Regardless of deliverable format, some veteran proposal managers prefer to complete the proposal using their preferred layout software, then convert it to the customer's required format at the end. If you adopt this approach, test the conversion to verify it works.

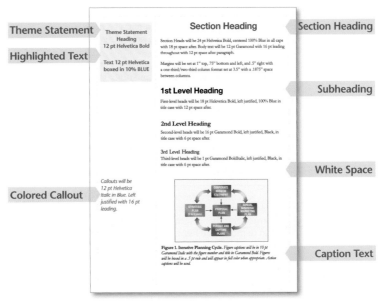

Figure 1. Establish a Style Sheet for Every Proposal. *Good style sheets both show and tell writers how proposal pages will look. They define the fonts, point size, color, and spacing for all text and graphics. Simple visual style sheets, like the one shown, help writers visualize the appearance of their draft.*

3

Select a document and page style appropriate to your customer's organization, your industry, and your organization.

The person in the production management role should build a list to document all style decisions. Most are common to all proposals, but some are unique to each proposal.

Creative proposal packaging and submittal activities might appear to be "cute" or artificial. However, customers are usually more receptive to creative packaging than some conservative members of the bid team. Carefully consider the customer's likely reaction. Use sound judgement. Slick packaging with weak content will reduce your win probability.

See Graphics *and* Resumes.

Document style refers to the overall look and binding, or packaging, of the proposal. Page style refers to the size and orientation of the elements on individual proposal pages.

Design tools will not make most of us designers. Good design is context-specific. Often, balanced order is simply boring while asymmetrical designs are dynamic, active, and expressive.

Have a professional develop one or two quality, standard proposal designs. Reassess those designs every 2 or 3 years. Then use the specific design most appropriate to each competition.

Proposal managers often think that competitors' proposals look much like their own proposals. Package your proposal to make it easy to identify, and design it to make it easy to evaluate while supporting your overall strategy.

Consider these examples to broaden your perspective:

The executive summary for a proposal to a rental car company was prepared to mimic the customer's folders used at pickup counters.

A cost volume, full of large spreadsheets, was presented in landscape format to better fit the typical spreadsheet layout.

A bid to a company whose current public advertising image was a western express rider on horseback was packaged in replica Pony Express leather pouches. To capture media attention, one set of the proposal was delivered on horseback, timed to hit local evening TV news.

A company competing to supply business software development services to a pizza chain delivered its proposals in the same boxes the customer used to deliver pizzas.

A mobile radio manufacturer had an audio voice-chip device, similar to ones used in greeting cards. The recording began in a voice filled with background static, then switched to a clear, CD-quality voice to emphasize the difference between analog and digital radio systems. Embedding the chip in the cover tempted evaluators to push the button until the battery died, repeatedly reinforcing a key discriminator

A woman was applying for a position as editor of the employee newsletter for a large, health care chain. Structuring her resume in a newsletter format to demonstrate her capability got her an interview.

Get the page size correct. North America uses a page standard of 8.5" x 11," often packaged in three-ring binders. Europe and much of the rest of the world use the A4 size, (a metric standard of 210mm x 297mm, or 8.268" x 11.693"), packaged in four-ring binders. Getting the size wrong tends to emphasize a foreign origin and a potential lack of compatibility.

Different packaging systems afford different cover art options. Ring binders offer a spine that can display titles, art, and text—features not possible with other types of binding systems. However, ring binders are difficult to store in filing cabinets, and pages can be removed or shuffled.

Ring binders are one of the easiest systems for rapid page changes during production. Conversely, one contractor noted that they did not use ring binders because they could be changed by customers.

Your packaging should be inviting and attractive to prompt the customer to read your proposal. Consider how proposals will be handled. Some packaging systems will look better than others after extensive handling.

One non-government evaluator described how packaging influenced the selection decision for a $50,000 branch store computer system:

I had 15 proposals and little time to evaluate. One cover caught my attention, and I remembered that the account representative for that organization was competent. I opened their executive summary and found the price was within my budget. I gave them the contract. I had no requirement to open the other 14 proposals.

Unless your proposal has fewer than 20 pages, use double-sided printing. Thinner proposals are less daunting to evaluate, and graphics are easier to integrate on the same page or a facing page.

Minimize foldouts unless they are required for larger graphics or response matrices, like the one shown in figure 2. Large graphics requiring foldouts include wiring diagrams, schedules, and some personnel charts.

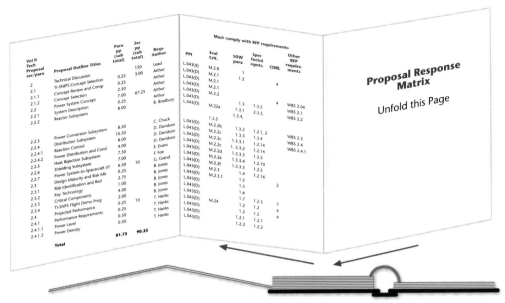

Figure 2. Using Foldouts for a Response Matrix. *The response matrix shown, placed at the front of a binder, has the matrix on the back side of the foldout that extends beyond the normal page. Evaluators can turn proposal pages without obscuring the response matrix. Similar response matrices can be placed in the back of the binder, but some evaluators miss them, even when referenced.*

4 Adapt your layout to the structure of the writing.

The need to make your proposal easy to evaluate and understand overrides other demands. Your design must both help and encourage the evaluator to enthusiastically score your proposal higher than other proposals. Consider adapting your layout to mirror the intellectual structure of your writing, as summarized in figure 3.

Nearly all of the Model Documents in this *Proposal Guide* reflect the Four-Box, intellectual organizational model presented in a complementary page design. Review MODEL DOCUMENTS for further examples of how to adapt page layout to the intellectual structure of the writing.

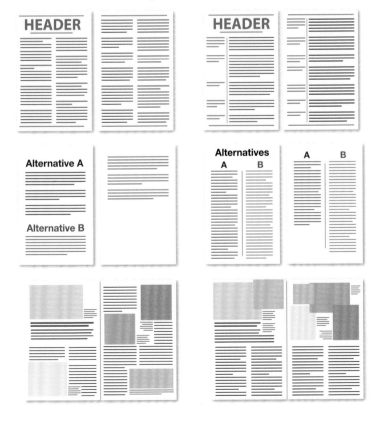

Question and Answer

Avoid the running text-look (left). Present it as discrete, paired twins (right). Place questions on the left, paired with answers on the right. Vary column width to reflect size. Use italic to reflect quoting the bid request. Consider smaller print for the bid request question because its readability is less critical. Place the summary answer in the first sentence in bold or larger type.

Pro/Con

Instead of discussing alternatives sequentially (left), place them side-by-side in contrasting type, color, or shading (right). Use the same approach in contrasting graphics.

Text-and-Graphics

Serially stringing text and graphics together often lends a crowded, dense appearance (left). Instead, group the graphics into a rich, visual composition (right).

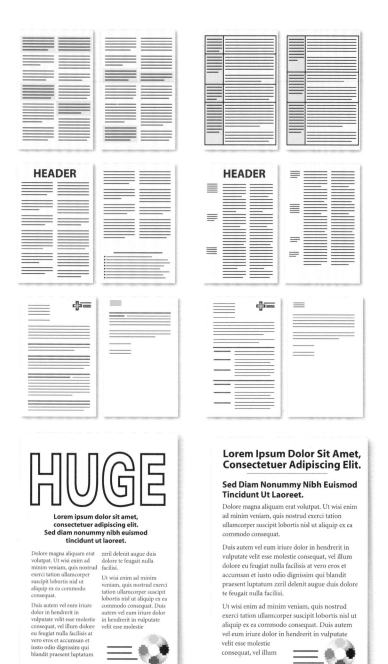

Tabularize requirements

Instead of answering relatively straightforward requirements in paragraphs of body text (left), place them in a table (right). Eliminate potential confusion by announcing your approach before the table.

Text with comments

Explanatory comments or notes are often placed at the bottom of the page (left) or the end of a section. If they are important, place them beside the text (right), in the left or right margin.

Asking questions about bid requests (As in Model Document 5)

Bidders' questions about a bid request are often submitted sequentially (left). Similar to the above question and answer example, group your questions in four elements:

- Your recommendation
- Current bid request provision
- Rationale for your recommendation
- Suggested bid request provision

Big ideas

You can shout at the reader by using huge headlines (left). While prominent, you cannot convey much in a headline of this size. Consider using larger, single-column text with a series of headings in decreasingly smaller point size.

Figure 3. Adapt Page Layout to the Structure of Your Proposal. *Help evaluators 1) immediately find information, and then, 2) quickly comprehend that information by adapting your layout to the intellectual structure of the writing.*

5   Use white space to guide the evaluator and to emphasize key points.

White space attracts and guides readers. Using white space to emphasize and link points is like using a spotlight to highlight a performer on stage. Two principles are involved

1. Emphasis—The more white space around a page element, the greater the emphasis.
2. Association—Readers visually link page elements that are grouped together.

Page elements include text, paragraphs, headings, bullet lists, tables, graphics, and even the edge of the page. Using white space for emphasis in lists is illustrated in figure 4.

Let in some air. Cramming as much as possible onto every page repels readers. Lighten your pages and attract readers by framing page elements in white space. A narrow 1/8" frame can make a huge difference. The wider the frame, the greater the emphasis.

Leaving open space at the top, bottom, or side of a page helps attract readers. Once you have attracted the reader, use as much text as needed. The most valuable parts of the page are the top and left side. Use them to first attract readers, and then to convey key points.

Figure 5 illustrates the visual association of page elements applied to both headings with text and graphics with captions.

Many of the decisions about how different page elements relate are implicit in the style sheet and are not evident to proposal writers. Even with a good style sheet, use desktop publishing assistance to produce a professional proposal that reflects your professional capabilities.

Version A

In the attached proposal, you will see the following products detailed: Endeavor aircraft, pilot training, maintenance training, spare parts, radios.

Version B

In the attached proposal, you will see the following products detailed:
- Endeavor aircraft
- Pilot training
- Maintenance training
- Spare parts
- Radios

Version C

In the attached proposal, you will see the following products detailed:
- Endeavor aircraft
- Pilot training
- Maintenance training
- Spare parts
- Radios

Version D

In the attached proposal, you will see the following products detailed:
- Endeavor aircraft
- Pilot training
- Maintenance training
- Spare parts
- Radios

Figure 4. Using White Space for Emphasis. *White space is used to emphasize a graphical element. This series of examples shows how increasing white space around the bullet list increases emphasis and thus, memorability. All versions are acceptable.*

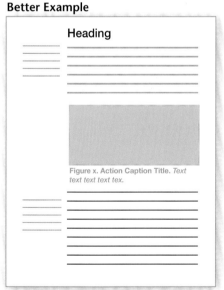

Poor Example   **Better Example**

Figure 5. Using White Space to Associate Page Elements. *Readers can more easily track through a document when related elements are visually associated. Heading should be closer to the following text than any other visual element. Captions should be closer to the related graphic than any other visual element. In the poor example, the heading is closer to the top edge of the page than the relevant text, and the caption is equidistant between the graphic and the text.*

6 Use headers and footers to help evaluators navigate your proposal while maintaining customer focus.

Nondisclosure and proprietary statements are typically placed at the beginning of the proposal, then referred to in the footer.

Check your printer to be sure your pages print fully. Many printers clasp the paper at the top or bottom, potentially cutting off page numbers placed too near the edge.

Evaluators would like to be able to open a proposal at random, page backward or forward to a major section heading, and readily understand where they are in the document. For maximum focus on the customer, place the following information in the header:

- Customer name and logo (left)
- Procurement name and number (right)

Place the following information in the footer:

- Offeror's name and logo
- Volume and page number
- Nondisclosure and proprietary statement references
- Win theme, slogan, or tag line
- Section name and number
- Date submitted
- Draft or final

With this much potential information, headers and footers can become cluttered. Group information, leaving more of the margins empty. Keep information in the same place, especially the parts that change, like page numbers and section names and numbers.

Use color, font style, and size to emphasize the most important information, while minimizing less important items like nondisclosure statements.

With double-sided printing, you can make right- and left-hand pages identical or make them mirror images. Identical right and left pages simplifies adding or removing pages, reducing production time.

In Western cultures, we read from top to bottom, left to right. Make the top rule heavier than the bottom rule to draw the eye to the top of the page. The rule is the line running across the page from margin to margin.

7 Select a page-column design that balances page limits, production requirements, readability, and graphics size flexibility.

See ELECTRONIC SUBMITTAL for guidelines on proposals that will be viewed and evaluated on-screen.

Good page design encourages reading. In contrast, contracts are often written in long lines of fine, closely spaced print to discourage reading.

Most proposal pages are designed with an underlying grid pattern, most frequently one to four columns. Figure 6 illustrates some of the typical grid arrangements. Note that a four-column design does not necessarily mean there are four columns of text. This *Proposal Guide* predominantly uses a 5-column grid.

Multiple columns offer more flexibility in page layout and make reading easier. Column-width should reflect the size of type within the column. Narrow columns are best filled with small type, wider columns with bigger type. Readability study results suggest limiting lines of text to 40 to 60 characters. For example, a 6-inch line of text in 10-point serif font contains nearly 100 characters. While influenced by font choice and leading or spacing between lines of text, readers tend to lose their place when text lines get too long in proportion to type-size.

Increasing the number of columns appears to waste space due to the gutter (the white space between columns). However, the space lost for the gutter is more than offset by the space gained at the end of paragraphs and between paragraphs. In both cases, the loss is across a single column rather than the entire page. Depending upon the exact layout, converting single- to two-column layout can accommodate up to 18 percent more words per page. As you add columns, the additional words gained per page decreases and page layout effort increases.

Single-Column Format. Typical for cover letters and simple proposals. Easy to do.

Two-Column Grid. Typical for page-limited proposals. Harder to do with word processing than page-layout software.

Three-Column Grid. Often used for proposals where page number is not limited.

Four-Column Grid. Also used for proposals where page number is not limited.

Asymmetrical Single-Column. These designs are based on an underlying three- or four-column grid with text appearing as a single column. This design is recommended for non-page-limited proposals. Although it requires a more sophisticated style sheet or template, this design is actually quite easy to execute in word processing packages. When using word processing packages, begin by establishing a single-column with a wide left margin. Use frames or text blocks to place text or graphics in the left column.

Multiple-Column Grid. Both examples show the flexiblity of a multiple-grid page design. Visuals can be placed across one to four columns as appropriate. Note how the "mountain" graphic was placed incorrectly, potentially confusing readers. A better placement would be at the bottom of grid column two or four to eliminate potential confustion about which text to read next.

Figure 6. Using Underlying Grid Patterns to Design Pages. *Using multiple columns in your page design increases both flexibility and complexity. The leading approaches are a two-column format for page-limited proposals and a one-third/two-thirds style format using a three- or four-column grid for proposals without page limits. Place graphics toward the edges of pages to avoid confusing reading patterns that unnecessarily interrupt columns of text.*

8 — Select complementary font styles, sizes, and leading.

In addition to serif and sans serif fonts, you will see script, symbol, and display fonts. Script fonts look like handwriting. Symbol fonts include characters and shapes not found in traditional alphabets and are used for emphasis, bullet points, and decorations. Display fonts are more distinct and often suggest an era or theme. Excepting bullet points, use all three sparingly in proposals. Use simple circles or squares for bullet points. Complex symbols and shapes are often distracting and thin line weights disappear when projected.

Fonts or typefaces are divided into two broad groups, serif and sans serif (also called *gothic*). Serif is usually more compact, has *feet* or flared ends on the type, and is typically used for body text in documents. Serif is easier to read in mass.

Serif fonts are usually not the best choice for slides. The thinner strokes may break up or disappear when projected. Test slide fonts for legibility from the back of the room, whether serif or sans serif.

Sans serif fonts are usually less compact, have squared ends, and are typically used for headings, labels, and slides. Sans serif is perceived as more authoritative and legible when projected.

Web designers tend to use sans serif fonts for on-screen text. Is reading text on-screen more like reading printed-text or projected-text? The best choice depends upon the resolution of the screen and visual acuity of the reader. When you must submit both paper and electronic proposals, use the same fonts for both versions.

Limit a document to two fonts unless a trained designer recommends otherwise. Instead, exploit the variations of styles within the font, such as narrow, normal, italic, and bold.

Designers can be quite emotional about fonts. The following are only guidelines to help those without design background who do their own proposals:

- Avoid ALL CAPITAL LETTERS. They are harder to read.
- Use **bold text for emphasis** rather than underlining. <u>Underlining is harder to read</u> and looks outdated.
- **Avoid overusing bold or any other emphasis technique. Too much emphasis means no emphasis.**
- Use *italics for lighter emphasis than bold,* but limit use to short pieces of text or quotes. Long passages of italic text are harder to read than normal text.
- Use italics to quote the customer's bid request. Readability is less important, and italic type suggests a quote, which it is.

Type must be large enough to be comfortably read. Fonts are measured in points with 72 points equalling 1 inch. The point measuring system dates from the days of lead type.

Use 10- to 12-point fonts, depending on a number of factors:

Font choice—Fonts differ in width and x-height, x-height being literally the height of an *x* in the font. Ten-point in one font may be nearly as easy to read as 12-point in another font.

Printer and paper quality—Printers with a higher dot per inch capability and coated paper will render clearer print, making smaller letters legible.

Submit PDF files to eliminate potentially awkward font substitutions and page breaks.

Copying—If your printed proposal is photocopied or if your customer is likely to photocopy your proposal, use larger type.

Older readers—Many readers appreciate the readability of larger type.

Line length and leading—The longer the lines of text and the narrower the leading or spacing between lines of type, the larger the font required to maintain readability.

With more customers requiring electronic versions of proposals, select commonly available fonts that are identical across all platforms. Inappropriate font substitutions can ruin the look of your proposal. Embed fonts in the files when submitting electronic proposals.

Generally, a safe choice for the proposal body text is 12-point in a font like Times or 10-point in a serif font with a larger x-height.

If you share your document or presentation with others electronically, stick with standard fonts to avoid display problems. When in doubt, embed the fonts within the file. If you get an error message, replace the fonts and try again. In general, TrueType and OpenType fonts are compatible within Microsoft® Windows-based applications. Safe fonts for both Macintosh® and Windows platforms are: Arial, Courier, New Century, Helvetica, Tahoma, Times, Times New Roman, Trebuchet, and Verdana.

9 Establish a consistent system for headings, themes, action captions, lists, and other page design features.

Proposal headings divide and label content, helping evaluators find answers to their questions. Frequent headings at multiple levels help evaluators quickly find information of interest without having to read large blocks of text. Frustrated and confused evaluators give lower scores.

Where possible, use informative rather than telegraphic headings to convey a more complete message.

As part of your style sheet, establish a consistent system for headings, themes, action captions, and lists that includes font, type style, type size, color, placement, and other emphasis devices, such as borders or shading.

Evaluators may not read all theme statements, but they nearly always read headings. The longer the theme statement and the more theme statements included in a proposal, the less likely they are to be read. Consider replacing theme statements at lower section levels with informative headings. Too many proposal writers use long theme statements, short headings, and short captions. Strive for the opposite.

Be cautious about using screens or shades to emphasize text. As the contrast between the text and the screen diminishes, the text

becomes much harder to read.

Many copiers and some printers print screens differently, either fading out or becoming much darker than intended. Check your printer or copier output. Also consider whether customer copying of your proposal will add to the problem.

Be particularly cautious when using a dark background with reverse print. Dark backgrounds tend to swallow light print, requiring a larger and bolder font and type style.

Another caution is warranted for backgrounds with progressive screens, both in proposals and presentations. Legible type at one side of the screen might become illegible on the other side.

Print on photographs may be hard to read. Both regular and reverse-print become illegible as photograph colors change. Place print on a white background to improve print clarity.

Quality and style criteria for headings, themes, action captions, and lists should extend beyond appearance to include content. Evaluators make negative inferences when emphasized items offer no discriminating content.

10 Choose and place graphics for maximum impact and readability.

See ELECTRONIC SUBMITTAL, ACTION CAPTIONS, HEADINGS, LISTS, THEME STATEMENTS, *and*

Use graphics to help evaluators remember your main points. Size graphics to reflect their intellectual and visual value. A tiny graphic can make a medium-sized graphic appear enormous and even more significant. Color in the graphic and white space around a graphic increase its emphasis.

Select an appropriate type of graphic to support your strategy and key point. Too many proposal writers use a graphic simply because

it is available or because it is the only type of graphic they know how to create.

Consider the following contrasting guidelines:

- Use a chart or graph when emphasizing relationships or trends. Use a table when the absolute values of the numbers are important.

- Use a photograph to show that something is real, that it exists. Use a sketch or line drawing to emphasize

GRAPHICS.

Some complex technical graphics will not meet the 10-second rule. Strive to make technical graphics as clear as possible. Consider adding more information to the captions of complex technical graphics.

To eliminate the possibility of missing or substituted fonts and graphics, create a PDF file of your document for submission. A PDF will contain all the elements of your document in a self-contained file. You can touch up any spacing problems or missing graphics using the complete version of Adobe® Acrobat® software.

See ORGANIZATION.

specific details. Photographs show everything, and often the details of interest are not as easy to see.

- Use display lists for greater emphasis. Use paragraph lists when the items are not as important.

Keep the following suggestions in mind when placing graphics in your proposal:

- Introduce the graphic in body text before it appears in the proposal.
- Orient graphics vertically to the text so that evaluators do not have to rotate the page.
- Integrate the graphic so the evaluator can see the graphic without turning the page.
- Ensure evaluators can get the point you intended by attaching an action caption to every graphic. Captions are the most important text on the page because readers' curiosity is aroused by the graphic.
- Observe the 10-Second Rule: Readers must be able to get your point within 10 seconds. If they cannot, consider dividing the single graphic into several graphics.
- Emphasize the right points. All but the simplest graphics should have a fore-, middle-, and background to make the graphic easy to interpret. Use line widths, color, and shading to differentiate the separate graphic elements.
- Remove anything in your graphic that does not contribute to your point.

- Avoid wrapping text around graphics. Uneven margins are particularly hard to read.
- Place graphics at the top of the page, when possible, or at the bottom of the page. Avoid breaking columns of text with graphics.

In addition to the recommendations offered, consider the following observations gleaned from reviewing hundreds of sales documents:

- Many U.S. federal proposals contain graphics that are too complex.
- Too few proposal graphics have captions; those that do are generally too short.
- Sales professionals who would refuse to make a presentation from slides that contain only text seem perfectly happy to give customers non-proposal sales documents devoid of graphics.
- Proposals other than for large, custom bid requests tend to contain graphics that feature logos and clip art (the only color used), and tables and spreadsheets (the only type of graphic the writer knew how to prepare).
- Organizations should focus more on developing boilerplate graphics and less on developing boilerplate text.
- Boilerplate, both text and graphics, is generally used poorly.

Be sure all graphic files are included when submitting an electronic proposal. Otherwise graphics might display poorly or not at all. Certain programs will not open until the appropriate graphic links are located.

---

11   Avoid overusing emphasis devices.

Too much emphasis is no emphasis. Too many different emphasis devices are confusing and distracting.

White space at the end of a column or page is a desirable emphasis device. Filling white space with relatively unimportant points detracts from key prior points.

Emphasize the points most important to your customers, and tie these points to the most important reasons for them to select your solution and your organization. Avoid emphasizing relatively minor points.

---

12   Use left-justified text.

Using left-justified text is a recommendation, and not a rule. If a senior manager insists on both left and right justification, do not risk your career. The difference is relatively minor.

Use left-justified text rather than full-justified text. Full justification has several undesirable attributes:

- Uneven spacing between words and letters creates more eye fatigue and may distract readers from your message. Readers sometimes pause on a poorly spaced word and think, *That word looks funny. I wonder if it's misspelled?*
- Uniform line endings increase the probability that readers may accidentally skip a line or reread the same line of text.

Both of these problems interfere with the clear flow of information to the customer.

Left-justified text with ragged right line endings offers several advantages:

- Text is more readable.
- Words and letters are spaced more evenly.
- Gutters (space between columns) appear wider.
- Pages of multi-column text are more varied, interesting, and appealing.

Photographs convey realism and authenticity. Readers tend to trust photographs, perhaps based on their own experience taking straightforward pictures with relatively simple cameras.

Skilled photographers have, for years, been taking photographs that distort reality, as was emphasized in the PBS television documentary, American Photography: A Century of Images. Aside from any photographic cleverness, the production discussed how Edward Curtis, a 19th century American photographer, traveled with a large trunk full of Native American clothing to dress Native American subjects who did not *look like Indians*.

Photos are persuasive, but evaluators realize that they can be manipulated. As with writing, present your case positively but honestly. Distortions destroy the customer's trust.

Use a photograph to show what exists. Use a sketch or illustration to show what is possible or to emphasize a specific feature in isolation.

Typically, too few photographs are used in proposals. Photographs can be expensive, but hours of graphic artists' time can be even more expensive. Worse yet, engineers' drawings of marginal quality are even more costly, but none are as costly as lost orders due to boring, dense, text-heavy proposals.

These guidelines suggest ways to use photographs more effectively in sales documents. Techniques to either take or compose photographs are left to other sources.

Photographs

1. Visualize what your customer wants to see; then select images that support that vision.
2. Select photographs that support your overall strategy.
3. Collect photographs throughout the entire sales process.
4. Use customers' and existing or past clients' photographs.
5. Go digital and use the resolution appropriate to the finished size.
6. Use color to add realism, add information, and increase interest.
7. Establish the size, scale, and orientation of objects in the photograph.
8. Develop a searchable and retrievable boilerplate photographic and graphics library.

1 Visualize what your customer wants to see; then select images that support that vision.

See GRAPHICS for a further discussion of how benefits are visualized.

Visualize the benefits your solution offers. Then plan or select photographs that make the benefits seem real. The reality of a photograph emotionally reinforces your message and implies a lower risk. Imagine what the customer wants to see after making a purchase, as discussed in these examples:

A customer selecting a design-build contractor for a distribution center wants to see photographs of a similar, complete distribution center with a caption citing success measures.

Parents selecting schools for their children want to see photographs of happy students; clean, bright classrooms; caring teachers; and elated graduates.

When the sales approach extends beyond citing features to stressing benefits, service and product sales are identical. Both products and services enable the customer to do or experience something different and presumably better. Skilled marketers sell benefits. Select photographs for your proposals that do the same.

2 Select photographs that support your overall strategy.

See DISCRIMINATORS and PROPOSAL STRATEGY.

Customers make or justify their selection decisions by identifying differences in offers that relate directly to their issues.

Portray these differences, your discriminators, and directly tie them to the customers' issues. State these differences and issues, using customers' words.

For example, if a customer is worried about whether you can do what you say, then your strategy could be to emphasize your experience. A visual showing you doing what you propose for another organization would emphasize your experience. A quote from the satisfied client would bolster your claim.

Figure 1 offers an extended example of using photographs to support a bidder's strategy. The competition was to prequalify only two organizations to provide $500 million annually in construction services. The customer listed three hot buttons in its bid request:

- Reduce capital cost
- Reduce cycle time from inception to production
- Streamline project planning

The winning two-page executive summary included two small photographs to support the first and third hot buttons. The photographs and quotes have been slightly altered to protect confidentiality.

Note how the first hot button, *reduce capital cost,* is directly supported at the end of the Drugs-R-Us quote, . . . *and significantly under budget.* The third hot button, . . . *streamline project planning,* is supported by the statement,

In 6 months your team is 2 months ahead of schedule . . . Both photos showed the completed facility, shots that are commonly available to constructors.

Sometimes you may not be able to get a photo of the actual object. One solution is to create a high-quality graphic or scale model. Then photograph the graphic or model to make the conceptual item look and feel more real to the evaluator.

Scale models or prototypes have been used for demonstrations for years. Including photographs of a prototype in the proposal permits the evaluator to view the prototype that they cannot view live.

Do not misrepresent photographs of graphics or prototypes as real. If the customer feels you are being deceptive, you lose your credibility, the sale, and often subsequent sales.

"In 10 years of doing projects throughout the U.S. and Europe, this has been the best so far. The Global Constructors difference is the people—uniquely qualified, energetic, and team oriented—they consistently exceeded my expectations and completed the project ahead of schedule, with outstanding quality, and significantly under budget."
**Drugs-R-Us
Corporate Headquarters**

"Trying to describe what your Global team has accomplished during the past 6 months is difficult. Words such as astounding and astonishing are insufficient. In 6 months your team is 2 months ahead of schedule, under budget, achieved a perfect safety record, and the quality of construction work is outstanding."

**World Chemicals Health
Division Laboratory**

Figure 1. Using Photographs That Support Your Strategy. *The photographs and client quotes were selected to reinforce the seller's ability to address the customer's issues of reduced capital cost, reduced cycle time, and streamlined project planning.*

3 Collect photographs throughout the entire sales process.

When you have to write the proposal, you seldom have time to go back and take photographs. Collect them throughout the sales process.

Sales and service people, site managers, and project managers should travel with a digital camera or photo-capable phone. Observe customer or client restrictions. Even when the inner facilities are proprietary, you can often take photos of the outside or perhaps the sign at the front gate.

Photos taken during demonstrations or site visits either remind the evaluator of the experience or reinforce that members of their organization have seen proof of your performance.

To broaden your vision of possible photographs, consider these examples:

Photos of stages of facility construction enrich a project schedule.

Photos of implementation enrich a transition plan.

Group photos of proposed individuals support claims of teaming experience.

Adjacent before-and-after photos emphasize change.

Photos of your own facilities emphasize capacity and ready capability.

4 Use customers' and existing or past clients' photographs.

Photos collected from the customer or taken at the customer's facilities demonstrate client focus.

Many photos are directly available from an organization's marketing, public relations, or investor relations departments.

Web sites are another source, although the resolution is usually limited.

Gather copies of customers' and clients' annual reports, marketing brochures, and employee newsletters. Observe restrictions on the rights to reuse or change the photos.

5 Go digital and use the resolution appropriate to the finished size.

Writers without skilled publishing support often insert digital photos but are disappointed with the poor quality. To increase your success, observe the following guidelines:

- Web photos and graphics typically have a 72 dpi (dots per inch) resolution, marginal in a printed document. Use 72 dpi photos at their actual size or smaller.
- The maximum acceptable enlargement for any digital photo is about 20 percent before the print becomes too *grainy*.
- Aim for 150 dpi when printing on typical office laser or ink jet printers. Higher resolutions increase file sizes with minimal increases in print quality.
- The minimum acceptable dpi resolution for offset printing is 300 dpi. Figure 2 compares the various file sizes for a single 3" x 5" scanned photo using different resolutions, file formats, and degrees of compression. Multiple photos create immense files. Printers generally require TIFF , EPS, or PNG file formats.

- Scan in RGB (Red-Green-Blue), the additive visible light spectrum. RGB files are smaller and easier to manipulate in programs like Adobe® Photoshop™.
- When submitting electronic proposals, embed RGB graphics for on-screen viewing.
- When printing proposals, convert the RGB files to CMYK (Cyan-Magenta-Yellow-Black) or scan directly in CMYK for truer color print quality. WYSIWYG (What You See Is What You Get) does not apply to color viewing on screen versus color printing. Print a trial version before full production.
- Observe all copyright restrictions and licensing agreements when using stock photos, scanned photos, or photos off the Internet. Rules vary widely.

Note that PNG files are the most compact file format with excellent quality, and GIF is the poorest quality. See ELECTRONIC SUBMITTAL for a discussion of file formats relating to photographs, line including, text, file size, application, and image quality.

SCANNED RESOLUTION	300 DPI			600 DPI		
File Type	JPG	JPG	TIF	JPG	JPG	TIF
Compression	none	med	none	none	med	none
File Size	2.5MB	370KB	4.1MB	9.5MB	1.3MB	16.5MB

Figure 2. Scanned Files Can Be Large. *A 3" x 5" scanned photo resulted in file sizes of 370KB to 16.5MB. Variables were scanning resolution, degree of compression, and file format.*

6

Make a black and white copy of color art. If you cannot read it, revise your color scheme to increase the contrast between colors.

See COLOR.

Use color to add realism, add information, and increase interest.

The highest-value places to use color are in your executive summary and in emphasizing your discriminators in the proposal.

Too often proposals simply use color where color is convenient for the writer and production people. Typical but poor uses for color are the seller's logo, the customer's logo, and header and footer lines. When these design elements get the greatest emphasis, you de-emphasize your strategy and discriminators.

7

Establish the size, scale, and orientation of objects in the photograph.

When the size, scale, or orientation of a photo or graphic is not obvious, include rulers, a human hand, or common objects. A car key, coin, coffee cup, or a person will establish scale.

Use arrows to establish orientation, linear movement, or rotation.

8

Develop a searchable and, retrievable boilerplate photographic and graphics library.

The greater effectiveness and higher cost of photographs when compared to text suggest that more organizations should develop a boilerplate photographic and graphics library.

For each photograph, collect relevant information and sample action captions. As with other boilerplate materials, assign someone to verify that materials remain valid.

Another best practice is to attach a unique tracking number to each photo or graphic, including the revision number or date when appropriate. As in figure 3, print the tracking number with the photo in the proposal to facilitate rapid retrieval for subsequent proposals.

Figure 3. Assign Graphic Tracking Numbers. *Attach graphic tracking numbers to all photos and graphics to facilitate reuse. To be less obtrusive, print the numbers vertically in a small point type.*

Presenting Cost and Price Data is routinely neglected in different ways in different markets.
Federal government bidders see it as a time-consuming process of completing numerous forms and spreadsheets. Commercial bidders may hide their price in the back of their proposal, thinking that will force the customer to read their proposal and discover their added value.

While the focus of this topic is on presenting cost and price data in a proposal, the guidance applies equally to pre-submittal and post-submittal customer presentations.

Cost and price depend on perspective. Your proposed price is the customer's cost but often not the total cost. Customers take your price and add acquisition management, implementation costs, and risk premiums.

To understand the following guidelines, consider common differences in how government and commercial customers evaluate cost and price data. Many governments have cost disclosure requirements similar to the U.S. federal government.

Because governments make large purchases from a few bidders, they tend to require full disclosure of the bidder's cost and pricing data above defined monetary thresholds. The U.S. government defines cost and pricing data as all facts at the time of agreement on price that can be expected to affect price negotiations significantly.

If cost and pricing data are not disclosed, the government can adjust the price. Price adjustments seldom happen in the contractor's favor.

Often, governments get so much cost and pricing data that no one but specialist cost analysts look at it. This creates an opportunity for bidders to gain a competitive advantage by presenting their cost and pricing data clearly and concisely in a cost volume summary.

In commercial markets, 90 percent of the bidders think that their price is higher than their competitors, so they try to hide their price. Instead, disclose your price early in the executive summary. To limit the customer's ability to negotiate, include detailed price breakdowns only when required.

Presenting Cost and Price Data

1. Include pricing in the executive summary, unless prohibited.

2. Explain and quantify, where possible, your added-value components instead of just claiming to offer added value.

3. Present cost and price data graphically to engage senior management, promote rapid understanding, and establish perspective.

4. Substantiate cost or pricing with past performance data.

5. Present relative cost comparisons in the technical proposal when actual cost data is not permitted.

6. Prepare a cost volume summary for markets where costs are prohibited in the technical proposal.

1

Include pricing in the executive summary, unless prohibited.

If you wonder whether price is important, consider how your account executives spend their time when the proposal is being prepared. Do they spend more time seeking a price cut or reviewing the proposal?

Sales professionals who get the opportunity to present their proposal to their customer usually say they keep the customer's attention for about 5 minutes, then the customer begins turning through the proposal, looking for the price.

Keep the customer's attention by putting your price in the executive summary, unless prohibited.

Seldom will a sales professional say that price is not important. Even when price is not the most important factor, price invariably falls into the customer's top four hot buttons.

Even if price is a minor selection factor, everyone has a budget. Price is a rapid screening factor as long as several bidders are within the customer's budget. Consider the following examples:

A company was bidding an IT support contract to a large city, priced at approximately $1 million. The price was placed on the front page of the executive summary in bold type larger than the text. The seller's comment, "We offered excellent value for money. Why hide our price?" The customer's comment, "We appreciated having the price on the first page. Everyone else hid theirs."

A buyer of a retail store computer system valued at $50,000 made the following comment, "I had 15 proposals and little time to evaluate. One cover caught my attention, and I remembered that the account representative for that organization was competent. I opened their executive summary and found the price was within my budget. I gave them the contract. I had no requirement to open the other 14 proposals."

2

Explain and quantify, where possible, your added-value components instead of just claiming to offer added value.

Your capture manager or sales lead should collaborate with the customer to develop a comprehensive value proposition. Only customers can accord value. *See* VALUE PROPOSITION, *Capture Guide.*

Most sellers claim to offer added value. Many government bid requests cite *best value* as an award criterion. Yet few sellers explain or attempt to quantify their added value.

Added value is essentially quantified cost-benefit selling. Figure 1 illustrates the concept.

Price to the seller is simply the cost plus profit, assuming the sale is profitable. However, the customer sees the price as the cost. These terms change as the perspective changes.

Added value to the customer is the difference between the value of the benefits of the solution less the customer's costs. The customer's costs include both the purchase cost and potential implementation costs.

Customers trying to obtain maximum added value must determine the difference between the value of each seller's solution and the total cost to the customer of each seller's solution.

Added Value

A's added value = (16-10) = 6
B's added value = (11-8) = 3

For one unit of added cost, the buyer gets three additional units of added value. Providing that A is within the buyer's budget, A offers the greatest added value.

Figure 1. Understanding the Concept of Added Value. *Most proposals claim to offer greater added value but never attempt to explain or justify their claim. Credible explanations require an intimate understanding of the customer's business and collaboration to understand the customer's cost and value structure.*

3

Present cost and price data graphically to engage senior management, promote rapid understanding, and establish perspective.

Graphic presentation of cost and pricing data elevates the analysis to the level where best value decisions can be made. Examine your proposed costs or prices from the point of view of the customer's senior management.

Senior managers are interested in the following cost or price-specific items:

- How is the cost spread among products and services?
- What are the major cost drivers?

- What is the spending pattern over time both in total and by major cost category?
- Which costs are at risk, and what is being done to manage that risk?
- Which items are subcontracted?
- Who are the major subcontractors, and where are they located?

Potential ways of presenting different cost elements are listed in figure 2. Review the mocked-up cost volume summary in figures 3 through 14 for more examples.

TYPE OF COST DATA	POTENTIAL PRESENTATION METHODS
Cost distribution among cost elements	Pie or bar chart
Major cost drivers	Table, pie, or bar chart
Spending pattern or profile	Line chart over time, one line for each category. (Sum can be additive.)
Higher risk cost elements	Line chart showing standard deviation; tables citing the category, amount at risk, and risk management approach
Subcontracted vs. in-house sourced	Pie or bar chart
Subcontractors by location	Combination map and pie chart, perhaps accompanied by a table insert

Figure 2. Present Costs and Pricing Graphically. *Succinct, graphical presentations of costs are more likely to influence decision makers. Place similar graphics in your executive summary and cost volume or pricing summary.*

4

See **RELEVANT EXPERIENCE/PAST PERFORMANCE.**

Vendor quotes, cited by many estimators as the most reliable, are negotiated and purchased at a lower price. Analysts apply a negotiation decrement to vendor quotes.

Substantiate cost or pricing with past performance data.

When costs or prices have to be justified, cite past performance data. Enhance credibility by citing how this data has been adjusted for future conditions.

Understanding how government cost analysts evaluate cost proposals will help proposal writers in all markets. Cost analysts begin with two primary assumptions:

1. **Nothing is new. Everything has been done before.**

   Even if the overall task has never been done, the subtasks, when sufficiently segmented and defined, have all been done before.

2. **The accuracy of cost estimates is directly related to the basis of the estimate.**

   Cost analysts rank the following bases of cost estimates from most accurate and credible to least accurate and credible:

   a. Firm negotiated price by future delivery date

   b. Actual past price paid, escalated for future delivery based on an accepted cost index

   c. Vendor quote

   d. Engineering judgment

On seeing *engineering judgment* as the basis of estimate, one cost analyst said, "I offer them 25 to 50 percent of their quoted price and see what they can do to justify any amount above that figure."

5

Present relative cost comparisons in the technical proposal when actual cost data is not permitted.

Relative cost comparisons in the technical proposal help justify your approach compared to alternative solutions when direct cost figures are not allowed.

Evaluators are trying to compare approaches and want to know that a bidder considered all feasible alternatives. Many technical people complete an exhaustive analysis of alternatives, select one, then describe only the selected approach in their proposal. Evaluators get the impression that only one approach was considered.

When costs cannot be included in the technical proposal, present relative cost comparisons:

1. Cite your selection criteria.

2. List the alternative considered.

3. Cite cost differences in relative terms.

4. Justify your selected approach.

5. Explain why others were not selected.

6. Note potential changes in your selection if the selection factors change or the importance of the selection factors change.

6

See **EXECUTIVE SUMMARY.**

Prepare a cost volume summary for markets where costs are prohibited in the technical proposal.

Beginning the cost volume with a summary is a best practice in federal proposals. This means going beyond preparing a Standard Form 1411 or the equivalent, the top-level cost summary form for U.S. government proposals.

Evaluators of the cost volume rarely make the selection decision, and decision makers rarely look at the cost volume because it is too difficult to quickly understand. A good cost volume summary can be read and understood by the decision makers and senior influencers and positively sets up the cost analysts' evaluation of the cost volume.

A cost volume summary uses the graphical presentation methods outlined in guideline 3 in this section to present a clear, easily read summary of your costs for the customer's senior management and decision makers.

Federal cost analysts must prepare a summary document, a Price Analysis Report, to summarize their evaluation. Think of the cost volume summary as the draft of the report you would like the cost analyst to present to the source selection authority or decision maker.

Place a copy of your executive summary in the front of the cost volume—directly in the binder or in the pocket in the binder cover. Make it available to every cost analyst.

Prepare a cost volume summary that meets as many of the following objectives as possible:

• Projects overall proposal themes

• Overviews your approach

• Discusses total prices or costs in graphics and words

• Discusses price and cost implications of your approach while ghosting alternative approaches

- Emphasizes how costs are fair and reasonable
- Summarizes exceptions taken to the RFP
- Summarizes your estimating approach
- Summarizes how costs are accurately tracked and controlled
- Demonstrates sound logic
- Indicates your cost system has been audited and approved by the appropriate agencies
- Contains approximately 50 percent graphics and 50 percent text
- Comprises no more than 12 pages

An open mock-up of a cost volume summary for a large, multiphase systems program is shown in thumbnail version in figures 3 through 14. As shown in figure 14, the cost volume comprised eight chapters, all in separate binders.

Evaluators look favorably at proposals that are easy to evaluate, giving them higher scores. The last portion of the cost volume summary, figures 12 and 13, sets up the evaluation, telling cost analysts how the cost volume is organized. A 40-year veteran of cost proposal evaluation made the following comment:

A well-organized cost proposal is traceable. I should be able to open the cost volume at random, page backward or forward to the beginning of any subsection, and directly see where it ties to other sections. I can see where these costs are supported in greater detail and where they roll up to the next cost level.

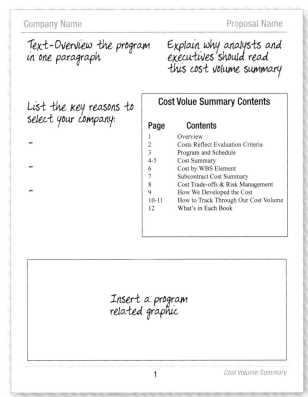

Figure 3. Summary Page. *Overview the entire program in one paragraph followed by the key reasons to select your organization. Insert a graphic that summarizes the overall program. Explain how this cost volume summary will aid cost analysts, then preview how the cost volume summary is organized.*

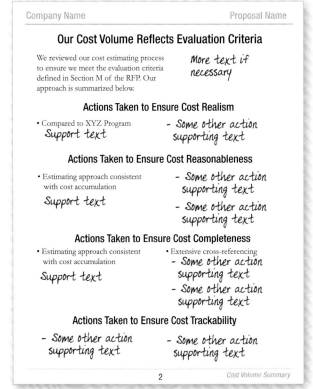

Figure 4. Reflect the Cost Evaluation Criteria. *Summarize how your costing approach reflects the customer's bid request cost evaluation criteria. Stress responsiveness as well as compliance. You are essentially presenting your costing strategy, drafting a justification that the cost analyst can later use to help justify supporting your approach.*

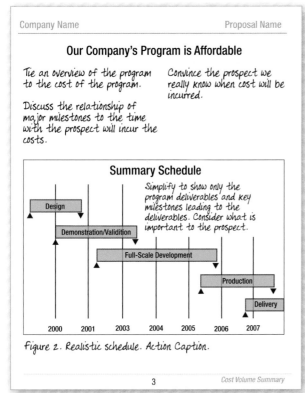

Figure 5. Stress Affordability Tied to Your Schedule. *Use this page to present an overview of the program schedule, the first opportunity for the cost analyst to see the relative costs of different parts of the program over time.*

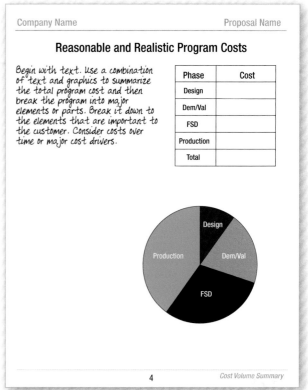

Figure 6. Stress Your Cost Reasonableness and Realism. *This page gives each reader some perspective on the major cost drivers, whether by component, task, or program phase.*

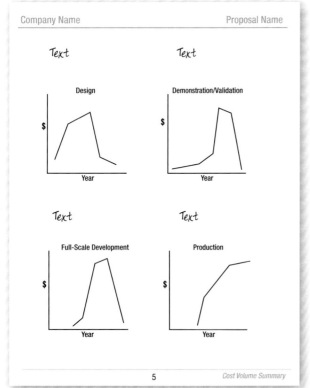

Figure 7. Cost by Phase Over Time. *Present your cost profile, so the cost analyst can easily compare it to the funding profile. The funding for complex programs often comes from different sources with different restrictions. For example, maintenance money may have to be spent within a fiscal year, while capital expenditures are usually allocated for longer periods.*

Figure 8. Cost Summary by Element. *This is the most detailed presentation of costs in the cost volume summary. Present costs by phase, cost element, Work Breakdown Structure (WBS) tracking number, Statement of Work (SOW) task, and year.*

The following tables appear in Figure 8:

DESIGN

Cost Element	WBS	SOW	Year					Total
	1000							
	2000							
	3000							
	4000							
	5000							
Total	0000							

DEM/VAL

Cost Element	WBS	SOW	Year					Total
	1000							
	2000							
	3000							
	4000							
	5000							
Total	0000							

FSD

Cost Element	WBS	SOW	Year					Total
	1000							
	2000							
	3000							
	4000							
	5000							
Total	0000							

PRODUCTION

Cost Element	WBS	SOW	Year					Total
	1000							
	2000							
	3000							
	4000							
	5000							
Total	0000							

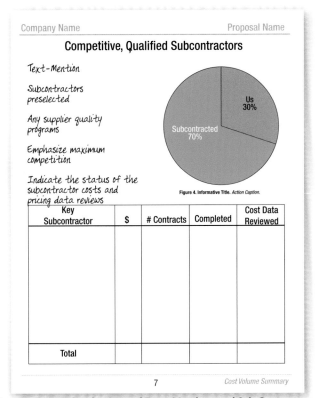

Figure 9. Summarize the Costs of Team Members and Sub-Contractors. *Who is doing what work and where they will do the work are important to cost analysts and their managers. Funding sources want to make sure that they get their share of work. For example, congressional representatives want work in their state, and export customers want a fair share of the work in their country under co-production agreements.*

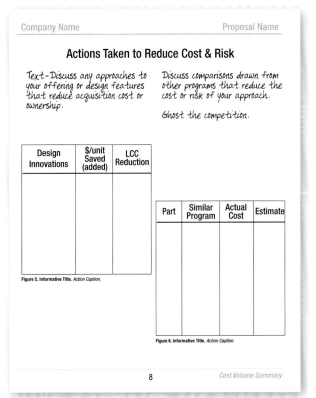

Figure 10. Reflect Strategies that Reduce Cost and Risk. *Technical proposals are full of claims of superior approaches. Summarize the actual cost impact of each of these claims, cross referencing the cost analyst to the appropriate pages in your technical proposal.*

Figure 11. Summarize Your Costing Approach. *Use both text and a graphic to summarize your costing approach. Summarize and justify any changes in your approach. If you have calculated new labor standards, justify why. For example, one cost volume manager justified a high engineering cost per hour by noting that all drafting and computer support costs were wrapped into the engineering overhead rate.*

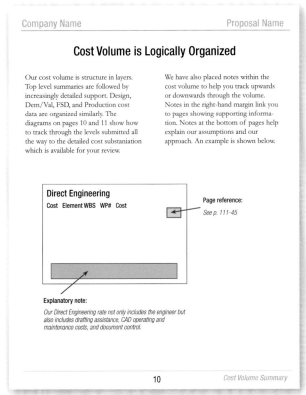

Figure 12. Explain Your Cost Volume Organization. *Cost analysts are often forced to spend a lot of time just trying to figure out how cost volumes are organized. Eliminate this wasted time and improve cost analysts' evaluation perspective by clearly explaining your approach.*

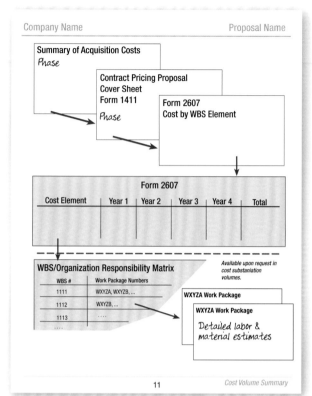

Figure 13. Graphically Show the Organization of Your Cost Volume. *Emphasize the traceability of costs through the cost volume, emphasizing the relationship between the various forms either required in the bid request or used by your organization.*

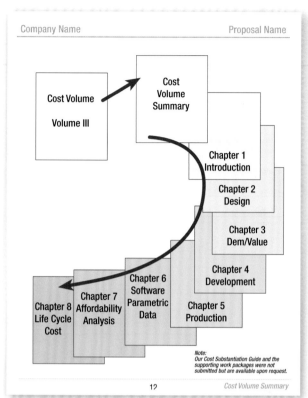

Figure 14. Overview Major Elements of Your Cost Volume. *Until you see the boxes of paper submitted with some major government procurements, few individuals would understand the value of the last four pages suggested. While numbers are objective, the credibility of numbers is pretty subjective. Cost analysts tend to believe bidders that make their jobs easier.*

Process is defined as a systematic series of actions or steps directed toward a specific end. Consistently successful proposal managers repeatedly follow defined and documented processes based on best-practices.

Organizations with effective business development processes gain the following benefits:

- Reduced costs
- Increased productivity
- Improved forecasting
- Increased management visibility and control

Defining, building, and sustaining an effective business development process require management focus and continuous effort. Barriers include corporate inertia, individual resistance to change, and constantly changing priorities that blur focus and erode commitment.

For a broader focus on the capture process, see PROCESS, *Capture Guide.*

The impetus to reengineer an organization's business development process often stems from one of the following situations:

- Merged or reorganized organizations
- Changes in management
- Failure to meet sales or win-rate goals
- Staffing fluctuations
- Sale of the organization
- Analysts' concerns affecting stock price
- Maturing markets
- Loss of key customers or contracts

The following guidelines focus on proposal development components within the overall business development process.

Process

1. Commit to a single, flexible, tailorable, scalable business development process based on industry best practices and championed at the executive level.

2. Define process phases broadly, delineated by clear milestones with verifiable inputs and outputs.

3. Use document-based reviews at each milestone to control and add value to the process.

4. Adapt your proposal process to individual opportunities by using flexible support tools.

5. Define business and proposal development roles, responsibilities, and levels of authority, including thresholds by type of opportunities.

6. Align your proposal development process with corporate policies, strategies, practices, and other processes.

7. Document your proposal development process to make it consistent and repeatable.

8. Train participants to give them the understanding and skills to follow the process.

9. Designate a process owner to collect metrics, foster continuous improvement, and maintain tools and infrastructure.

1

Commit to a single, flexible, tailorable, and scalable business development process based on industry best practices and championed at the executive level.

Organizations with a **single** process can conduct business more efficiently and effectively. Every opportunity falls within the single process—no exceptions. Individuals assigned to proposal teams can immediately focus on the opportunity rather than determining or justifying what needs to be done.

A **flexible** process works for you, not against you, by including best practices based on the type of opportunity. Categorize two-to-four types of opportunities.

A **tailorable** process implies that phases, Decision Gate reviews, and color team reviews are included based on the category of opportunity. Milestones might be mandatory, recommended, optional, or not applicable.

A **scalable** process can be adapted to the size, delivery deadline, and available resources. For example, a mandatory kickoff meeting might be shortened, conducted virtually, and include fewer participants. A color team review might be serial and virtual rather than a co-located, single event.

Determine industry best practice by regularly comparing your process to other organizations, by participating in industry forums and professional associations, and by engaging professionals who specialize in business development best practice reviews and business development process re-engineering.

A champion at the executive level will help your organization realize the benefits of committing to a single, flexible, tailorable, and scalable business development process. Two examples illustrate how such a champion can influence the adoption of improved proposal practices through both small and large actions:

After sitting through 4 days of business development training, the managing director of a large organization was asked to approve an executive summary. He returned the executive summary with the following: *You have attended the training. This is no longer acceptable.* Word of the incident spread quickly and everyone adopted the new standards and approach.

To improve business capture effectiveness, an executive vice president of business development wanted to establish a single process with global standards for business development. After actively participating in the development and documentation of a single business development process, he commissioned custom training for all process participants. He attended the entire first workshop with all of his direct reports.

At the next 10 workshops, he personally introduced the workshop, reviewed participants' work, and concluded the workshop. All subsequent workshops were introduced and concluded by one of his direct reports. Within 3 years, this organization improved from second to first in global market share.

2   Define process phases broadly, delineated by clear mandatory milestones with verifiable inputs and outputs.

Define business development phases broadly to include the wide variety of opportunities your organization may pursue. Narrower definitions encourage participants to work outside the process.

Phases are separated by decision gates, where executives determine whether or not to allocate resources to continue new business pursuits. The business development lifecycle shown in Figure 1 is divided into seven phases. Phase 0 and Phase 1 are cyclical and customer focused. Phases 2 through 6 are oportunity specific and project oriented.

1. **Phase 0: Market Segmentation.** Marketing teams are formed by senior management to explore potential markets or to target market segements most likely to buy whatever your organization wants to sell them.
2. **Phase 1: Long-Term Positioning.** Campaign plans are executed to establish your organization's presence with specific customers, all aimed at identifying leads or opportunities.
3. **Phase 2: Opportunity Assessment.** Newly identified opportunities are assessed to determine your organization's interest and whether they are winnable.
4. **Phase 3: Capture Planning.** Individuals in customers' organizations are influenced to prefer your organization and solution set.
5. **Phase 4: Proposal Planning.** The proposal effort is planned while your organization's capture efforts continue and while the customer is preparing the bid request.
6. **Phase 5: Proposal Development.** Your proposal is prepared, approved, and submitted.
7. **Phase 6: Post-Submittal.** Customers' questions are answered, hopefully leading to negotiations and contract award.

Defining clear, mandatory milestones with verifiable inputs and outputs establishes a solid business development process for opportunities, large or small. Predefined quality checks and business case justifications at each milestone minimize wasted proposal development efforts and increase win rates. All opportunities benefit from a few, well-conceived management milestone reviews. Each phase ends with a specific decision gate:

- **Gate 0: Marketing/Campaign Decision.** Management decides whether the pursuit of a potential market or segment fits your organization's long-term strategic goals.
- **Gate 1: Interest Decision.** Management verfies whether the pursuit of a specific customer seems to fit your organization's mid-range direction and justifies investment in sales activities.
- **Gate 2: Pursuit Decision.** Management assesses the opportunity, the customer, and the competition to decide whether to invest in business capture activities.
- **Gate 3: Preliminary Bid Decision.** Management evaluates your opportunity-specific capture pursuits, including win strategy, competitive position, technical/management solution, and price-to-win, determining whether to plan a proposal.
- **Gate 4: Bid Validation Decision.** Management confirms your tentative plan to prepare a proposal after reviewing the customer's bid request. If approved, proposal development begins immediately.

- **Gate 5: Proposal Submittal Decision.** Management determines whether your completed proposal presents your organization and offer acceptably and whether the potential programmatic risks are justified by the probable financial reward.

- **Gate 6: Final Offer Decision.** If changes have occurred since your original offer was submitted, this is management's last opportunity to accept or reject the deal.

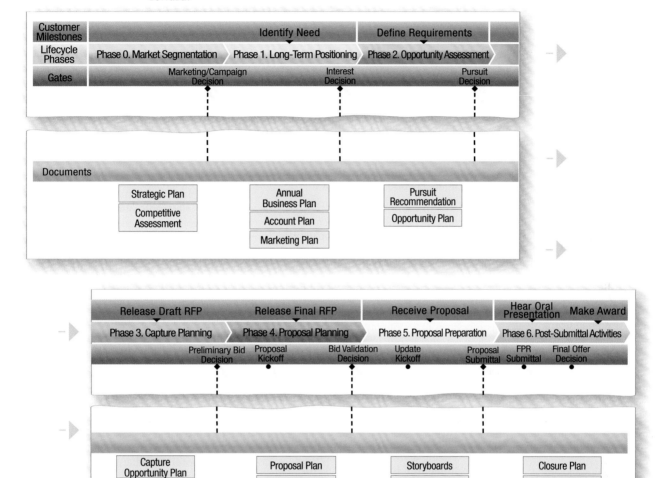

Figure 1. Sample Process Framework for New Business Capture. *This framework process is aligned with the customer's buying cycle. Management milestone reviews apply to every opportunity. Key documents are shown along the bottom of the chart.*

3 Use document-based reviews at each milestone to control and add value to the process.

Documents are the only evidence that an intellectual task has been completed. Without documents, you cannot control and manage intellectual work. The quality of a business development review document reflects the quality of the work done to research, develop the lead, and collaborate with the customer. Each review should incorporate standard documentation requirements, appropriately tailored for the type and size of the opportunity.

Manage to your standards. Do not omit reviews or compromise your standards. Figure 1 suggests documents for each milestone review. These may need to be adapted to reflect the requirements of your organization. The availability and quality of these documents at the review are indicators of your readiness to advance to the next phase. Poor documentation should raise serious doubt about continuing to spend resources.

4

See PROPOSAL PREPARATION TOOLS.

Adapt your proposal process to individual opportunities by using flexible support tools.

No single process is right for every business organization and every opportunity. The one shown in figure 1 is widely useful, but might not be right for your products, services, or market. The tasks completed during each phase may need to be adjusted based on the following considerations:

- Value of bid, both in absolute terms and in comparison to other business you have
- Knowledge of customer, especially relating to prior working relationships
- Time projected to be available during each phase of the business development cycle
- Similarity of new business to other work your organization has performed
- Knowledge of other competitors
- Expectations in the marketplace concerning sophistication of proposals and other aspects of business development process

See BID DECISIONS; *and* DECISION GATE REVIEWS *and* COLOR TEAM REVIEWS, *Capture Guide.*

Likewise, the information required to support the milestone reviews may be different. For example, in a commodity market, knowledge of competitors may not play a large role in deciding whether to bid; instead, information about price will be more significant in each phase.

Regardless of the tasks that are right for your organization, or the information needed for decision-making, a consistent process will help you spend more of your business development resources pursuing better opportunities. You will typically submit fewer bids, but will improve your win rate and total dollars won.

High-level process definition provides structure, but you need flexible tools to respond to shifting market demands. Otherwise, the temptation to abandon your process—and give up its benefits—will be strong.

Tools need to support both knowledge and process management. Knowledge management includes boilerplate development, retrieval, and maintenance. It also supports collaborative solution development by giving access to previous work and products. Process management tools direct the user, save time, and improve effectiveness.

Potential tools come in many forms, from paper templates and forms to fully integrated web-based, electronic systems. To be broadly accepted, your process must do more than give direction—it must help users do their jobs effectively and efficiently. Tools that save time and improve effectiveness help users and promote acceptance and adherence to your process.

The best business development tools are adaptable to a broad range of opportunities and proposals. They help collect, organize, and analyze information so better decisions can be made. Ultimately, they help your organization prepare winning proposals.

Not all tools are created equal. Some tools speed the activity cycle, permitting a user to produce more proposals. But if the effectiveness of the proposal is unchanged, the cost of the tool may exceed the benefits. The best tools empower the user to be better organized, more customer-focused, and more responsive to the specific requirements of each business opportunity.

5

When business development staff circumvent your process, your process may no longer fit your circumstances. Processes can be changed, but should not be modified without good reason.

See APPENDIX A: TEAM ROLES AND RESPONSIBILITIES, *Business Development Lifecycle Guide.*

Define business and proposal development roles, responsibilities, and levels of authority, including thresholds by types of opportunities.

Roles are customary functions of a person in business development, such as capture manager, proposal manager, proposal specialist, writer, and estimator. A single person can fill multiple roles. In some organizations, a person in the account manager position might assume sales, proposal manager, proposal writer, estimator, and reviewer roles.

Responsibilities are tasks that people are accountable for, whether they complete the task themselves or assign the task to another. In business development, people in roles are assigned specific responsibilities. Traditionally, an individual in the proposal manager role is responsible for the preparation of the proposal document to a defined standard.

Levels of authority delimit the power of a person to command, direct, or decide. Levels of authority establish whether the person can make a decision and the limits of the decision. For example, the level of authority to make pursuit, bid, and bid submittal decisions usually varies with the size and risk of the opportunity.

Proposal development processes are more flexible and scalable when roles, responsibilities, and levels of authority are clearly defined.

Proposal contributors need to know the following:

- What do you want me to do?
- When is it due?

- What is my budget & charge code?
- What are your quality standards or expectations?

---

6 Align your proposal development process with corporate policies, strategies, practices, and other processes.

Alignment is critical in all areas. A corporate strategy to be the technology leader is more compatible with a sales approach that emphasizes added value than one that stresses low price. For each opportunity, align your sales strategy, proposal strategy, boilerplate, and solution.

Align performance metrics, incentives, and proposal development processes:

- Share sales or capture team information with the proposal team.
- Streamline the proposal review process to support a short sales and proposal delivery schedule.
- Balance reviewers' rewards for preventing risk with the potential cost of lost sales.

---

7 Document your proposal development process to make it consistent and repeatable.

Document your proposal development process as part of your business development process. Documenting only your proposal process is less effective.

To avoid losing proposal contributors in complexity, consider developing small, compact or on-line proposal process *guides*. Alternatively, embed your process in your tools, making much of the process transparent.

Finally, consider contributor turnover. Mix experienced and inexperienced contributors, if possible.

Follow your defined process and use your tools. Contributors follow what you do, not what you say.

---

8 Train participants to give them the understanding and skills to follow the process.

Even users who understand and accept the process need the skills to execute and adapt it appropriately. The same applies to support tools. Users must be able to locate, acquire, and use tools properly.

An initial and ongoing investment in training is critical. To achieve maximum return, training must be process specific and role specific. Otherwise, people will not understand the reasons for their assigned tasks.

Business development process and tool training cannot consist of lectures and one-time demonstrations. Participants must practice the expected skills during the training and receive immediate feedback to improve their performance. Without practice, participants usually return to their pre-training approach.

---

9 Designate a process owner to collect metrics, foster continuous improvement, and maintain tools and infrastructure.

Processes erode quickly without an owner. Turnover, loss of learning, and even active resistance to process discipline reduce process effectiveness. Consider these all too common occurrences:

- A simple template with an outdated logo is used, creating an inconsistent brand image.
- An electronic template incompatible with an upgraded operating system is abandoned, forcing business development staff back to inaccurate, inefficient, manual techniques.

- Boilerplate graphics and text describing obsolete products and services prompt a customer to select another source.
- Inadequate reviews lead to unacceptable risk or low profit margins.
- Contract disputes arise because the bidder is not fully aware of the content of a proposal.

Assigning an owner to implement, monitor, and improve the process keeps the benefits alive.

Metrics are a basis for continuous improvement—we manage what we measure. Define metrics to monitor sales support costs, cycle times, and proposal quality. All are usually related to higher win rates.

Metrics help process owners understand which elements of their processes work well and which need to be changed. Accurate and credible metrics are the only valid way to justify requests for additional resources, to resist reductions in current resources, or to measure the value of enabling technologies and tools.

Consider the following questions when determining what metrics to collect:

- **How will you use this metric?** If you cannot anticipate its use, do not track it. For example, tracking turnaround time from different outside printing vendors could help you decide which printer has earned more of your business. The same statistic from an internal department that is giving good service is less useful.

- **Can the metric be collected with minimum impact to staff and clients?** Try to capture metrics as by-products of your normal process. For example, collect labor hours from time sheets. Determine page counts from printing records.

- **Does the potential value of the data exceed the cost of collection?** A relatively expensive program to obtain customers' feedback on wins and losses is often justified. Conversely, one process owner decided not to compute a cost per page even though it could be calculated from available data. Central expenses were minimal, proposal teams worked virtually from home offices, so travel costs were eliminated, and internal printing costs were annually allocated to business units on a revenue basis. Neither the process owner nor the responsible mangers could think of a use for the cost-per-page metric.

- **Does the metric broaden your potential understanding of a process that you own or can influence?** Keeping metrics on organizations or individuals outside your control and influence may only lead to conflict. If you have no control over your field sales force, why track data on account executives? Leave that to sales management.

Avoid tracking metrics that overlap unless you are trying to determine which metric is most representative. For example, overlapping metrics might be kept on desktop publishing (DTP). You could track pages per day of combined graphics and text, or separate measures of pages per day of text and graphics per day. The appropriate measure might depend on whether your DTP professional also does the graphics and whether the ratio of graphics per page is expected to change. Figure 3 lists potential business development process metrics.

COMMONLY COLLECTED PROPOSAL METRICS
Proposal Quality
Duration (start to finish)
Staff hours expended
Hours by resource
Proposal Won/Lost
Dollars Won/Lost
Number of copies
Page count
Number of graphics
Percent new vs. existing graphics

Figure 3. Potential Business Proposal Metrics. *Proposal process owners track many of the listed metrics but never track all of them. Balance the number of metrics collected and the collection cost against the potential value of the metric.*

Production

Production is the step that turns all of your hard work into the product that represents the quality of your products and services. Customers assume that if you cannot organize a team well enough to produce a quality document, then you probably cannot deliver quality products and services.

Customers may require offerors to submit both a paper "original" and an electronic "copy" of all proposal documents. *See* ELECTRONIC SUBMITTAL.

Make the quality of your proposal consistent. Poorly prepared or differently presented or appended materials suggest uneven quality.

Decide early how the proposal will be produced as the process will affect schedules, timelines, and how the proposal is written. Decisions on layout, software, graphics, and color can significantly affect production.

Production personnel frequently are under-appreciated, misunderstood, involved too late in the process, and repeatedly abused. However, some production managers forget that they manage a service organization.

Excellent production support throughout the proposal preparation process is essential to consistently win competitive business. While having a dedicated proposal production support group is ideal for control purposes, three extremes are possible:

1. Production is done by the sales support staff or the proposal team. Both may lack the time, skills, and resources required.
2. Production is done by a company organization that also supports product manuals, newsletters, brochures, technical reports, and marketing presentations.
3. Production is outsourced to an organization that specializes in high-volume printing, binding, and delivery of varied documents for multiple clients.

Publications groups may have conflicting, prior commitments; limited familiarity with customer-directed documents; and a *First In First Out* approach. Carefully plan all aspects of production and delivery.

Production

1. Establish a clear vision of what the customer expects to be delivered.
2. Identify and assign the production management role and include that person in your core team planning.
3. Set clear ground rules in a written proposal production plan to minimize rework.
4. Determine precisely what will be produced for each color team review.
5. Test systems prior to production.
6. Determine how the proposal will be *packaged* and delivered while section writers are planning and preparing initial drafts.
7. Maintain a secure master book of hard-copy files backed by electronic files.
8. Ruthlessly enforce version control on a section-by-section basis.
9. Increase your quality checks and production time if proposal production is remote.

---

1   Establish a clear vision of what the customer expects to be delivered.

Understand the customer's expectations. Imagine getting a 1,000-page proposal when you expected 100 pages. Imagine the opposite.

See COMPLIANCE AND RESPONSIVENESS *and* OUTLINING.

When the customer establishes clear document preparation and delivery requirements in the bid request, follow them. When these requirements are unclear or unstated in the bid request, or when preparing an unsolicited proposal, explicitly discuss proposal requirements with the customer.

Guide the customer toward a proposal that is both easier to evaluate and easier to prepare, usually a shorter proposal. Be careful about what you suggest; you may get it, as these examples illustrate:

> An account executive asked if the customer would like to see a video submitted with the proposal.

When the customer said, "Yes," the account executive's organization had limited time and resources to produce anything that looked better than an amateur, home movie.

An account executive asked the customer if they would like to see a concise proposal that simply focused on what they planned to do on the immediate project. The customer agreed. Unfortunately, the account executive's support group was only equipped to do a Search and Replace for the customer's name and print 250 pages of boilerplate.

A multimillion dollar, multiple-volume proposal was completed by an aircraft manufacturer for a large federal bid. The plane was waiting at the local airport to deliver the proposal. Unfortunately, the small aircraft could not take off when they discovered the packaged documents weighed more than 3,000 pounds.

2 Identify and assign the production management role and include that person in your core team planning.

The production management lead supervises the publication process, including word processing and graphic support, desktop publishing to integrate text and graphics, overall document design, and printing.

The complexity of the proposal influences whether the production lead role is assigned to the proposal coordinator, the proposal manager, or to a separate full-time position. Early involvement reduces the cost of proposal rework far more than the cost of the production lead's time.

Involve the production lead early to foster a commitment to do what is needed to win. Ideally, the production lead, graphic artists, and editors are directly assigned to support individual proposal teams.

Proposal managers on larger proposals do not have to be production experts, but they do

need to know what to discuss with the person who is assigned the production management role. The proposal lead, the proposal coordinator, or the production manager should prepare the following items:

- **Presubmission Checklist:** Lists all items required by the customer
- **Printing and Delivery Checklist:** Lists all items that must be selected or prepared, and all tasks that must be completed that are relevant to printing, document assembly, packaging, and shipment
- **Print Mock-up:** Tells the printer how to correctly assemble the proposal

A sample presubmission checklist, a printing and delivery checklist, and a print mock-up are shown in figures 1, 2, and 3, respectively. When you show these examples to most production managers, they will nearly always understand and complete the checklists for your proposal.

Presubmission Checklist

ITEM	NOTES
☐ Cover	
☐ Cover Letter	
☐ Proprietary/Nondisclosure Notice	
☐ Signature Papers	
☐ Bid Bond	
☐ Performance Bond	
☐ Small or Disadvantaged Business Qualification	
☐ All Certifications of Compliance	
☐ Table of Contents	
☐ Compliance Matrix/Cross-Reference Matrix	
☐ List of Figures	
☐ Acronyms/Glossary/Definitions	
☐ Executive Summary	
☐ Technical Volume	
☐ Management Volume	
☐ Support Volume	
☐ Relevant Experience/Past Performance Volume	
☐ Cost Volume	
☐ WBS/WBS Dictionary	
☐ Index	
☐ Appendices	
☐ Exceptions	
☐ Brochures, Data Sheets, Reports	
☐ List of Sources of Supporting Materials	
☐ Supplementary Technical Data or Reports	

Figure 1. Prepare a Presubmission Checklist. *Prepare a presubmission checklist to help you identify, prepare, and assemble all required materials. Limit submissions to only the materials requested by the customer. Inclusion of an item in this figure does not mean that item should be included in your proposal.*

Printing and Delivery Checklist

ITEM	NOTES
☐ Printer selected	
☐ Delivery method determined	
☐ Back-up delivery determined (if needed)	
☐ Cover sent to printer	
☐ Tabs identified, named, and sent to printer	
☐ Paper for cover, tabs, text identified and ordered	
☐ Paper received by printer	
☐ One- or two-sided printing	
☐ Binder determined and ordered	
☐ Final art complete	
☐ Final text complete	
☐ All inserts to printer	
☐ Art and text integrated	
☐ Final print mock-up prepared	
☐ Electronic files to printer	
☐ Electronic submittal prepared (usually burned on CD-ROM)	
☐ Printing complete	
☐ Documents assembled with all inserts	
☐ Final turn-through (all copies)	
☐ Materials packaged for shipment	
☐ Shipment	
☐ Delivery verified	

Figure 2. Prepare a Printing and Delivery Checklist. *Using this checklist as an example, ask your production lead to prepare a specific list for your proposal. Checklist items will vary with proposal complexity. Portions of this list will be repeated for each internal review cycle. Experienced managers of large proposal efforts often plan on three production passes or cycles before Red Team and three more production passes from Red Team to submittal.*

The thumbnail print mock-up, or print dummy, is used to show the printer the number of pages in each section, where to insert tabs, photos, foldouts, or any other nonstandard items. The print mock-up is particularly important when you print double-sided and assembly is done by an organization separated from the proposal team.

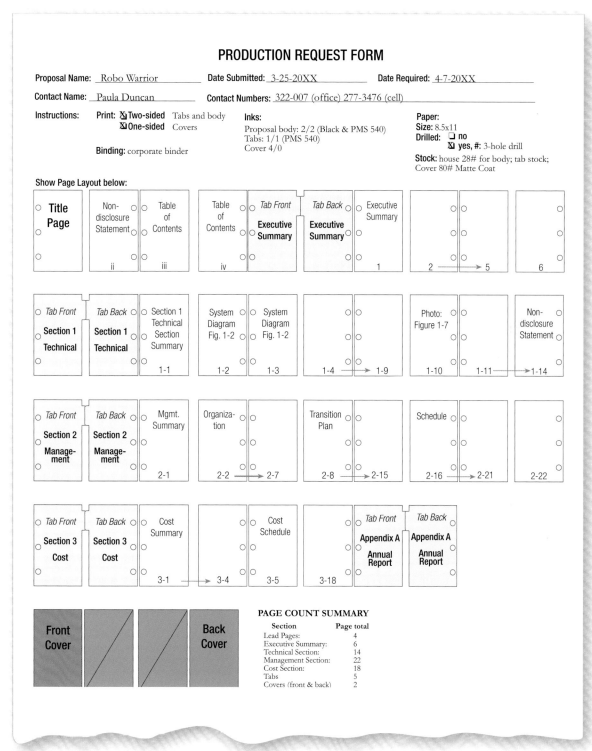

Figure 3. **Reduce Production Errors by Preparing a Print Mock-up.** *Print mock-ups tell the printer where major sections begin and end. Indicate all tabs and major graphic items, especially those placed as low-resolution or FPOs (For Placement Only) that will need to be manually inserted or replaced with the high-resolution scan or image by the printer.*

3

Set clear ground rules in a written proposal production plan to minimize rework.

Set ground rules to control how the proposal is processed through each draft. Include ground rules in the writers' packages distributed at the kickoff meeting.

See PROPOSAL MANAGEMENT PLAN.

Set ground rules to manage the flow and style (such as spacing, boxing, or shading) for the following items:

- Storyboards
- Mock-ups
- Graphics
- Section drafts
- Time and material estimates

Flow procedures define how the drafts are processed and usually include deadlines. Style procedures set standards for each document, both form and content.

Style procedures for writers should be kept as simple as possible to both save writers' time and to simplify production. Extra formatting by writers must be removed by production before imposing a standard style sheet. Eliminate this wasted effort.

Configuration control ensures the most current version of each proposal section is safely stored and available on an as-needed basis to other members of the proposal team.

Insist on a written production plan, which is the only clear proof that you have that the plan is complete and correct.

Your written proposal production plan should address both process and production issues.

Process issues

- How documents are prepared, reviewed, and printed
- How hard and soft files are managed, named, stored, and backed up
- How various proposal tools, templates, and forms are obtained, used, submitted, displayed, and reviewed
- Who will be given access to files and materials, and the degree of access permitted

Production issues

- How the proposal will appear, including a detailed electronic style sheet that establishes both interim and final page layout, headers, footers, font choice and size, etc.
- What materials will be used, including paper, tabs, and binders
- What types of headings, captions, jargon, acronyms, titles, and naming conventions will be used
- What, how, and who will prepare other required items, such as the cover letter, table of contents, compliance or cross reference matrix, lists of figures, acronym list, glossary or index, transmittal letter, tabs, and special forms or certifications
- How the proposal will be produced, including the number of copies and volumes; printing schedule; printer, backup printer; special print needs such as oversize documents, pockets, or tabs; and color photographs or pages
- How security will be maintained on all materials from the kickoff through final production and archiving

4

Determine precisely what will be produced for each color team review.

Interim reviews create a production dilemma. Senior reviewers give a more thorough review to material that looks more professional. Yet more professional material increases production support costs.

Compromise by reviewing for the right things at the right time.

See COLOR TEAM REVIEWS, *Capture Guide.*

At the Blue Team, review your competitive position, strategy, and baseline solution. Prepare copies of the first draft of the executive summary, the Bidder Comparison Matrix, the Integrated Customer Solution Worksheet, other competitive assessment products, strategy statements assembled into a strategy white paper, and prospective win themes. None require extensive production assistance.

Make reference materials available for each evaluator, such as a draft or final bid request, and relevant marketing intelligence.

Limit the Pink Team review to the storyboards and mock-ups. Some organizations include the first draft of the proposal, and others have multiple Pink Teams, reviewing each additional draft.

Few organizations pursuing non-federal business have time for more than one Pink Team review. Assuming storyboards and mockups are reviewed on the walls, displayed on tables, or posted on a secure web site, then production assistance is limited to preparing reference materials and comment forms for each reviewer.

Most reviewers expect a near-final document for the Red Team. You can reduce your production cost and perhaps facilitate revisions if management will agree to the following simplifications:

- Print all review copies on paper with pre-punched holes and insert them in ring binders. Copying on one side simplifies production moderately, but reviewers will not see opposing pages.

See Scheduling.

- Start each section on a new page to facilitate dividing the proposal for different reviewers and distributing pages with reviewers' comments to the people making revisions.

- If reviewers are given electronic files, consider the form and planned review process. Does the file type support comments? Do reviewers have access to and are they comfortable using this software for a review? How easy is it to consolidate reviewers' comments?

The Gold Team reviews the fully completed proposal, including all cover letters and introductory materials, all files and folders, all attachments and appendices, and any other documentation or signatures required by the customer. This final "book check" verifies that all modifications approved by the Red Team and Green Team were accomplished. Changes should be minimal and only if absolutely necessary.

Identify production support needs early. Estimate how many times each page will be produced both before and after the Red Team. Figure 4 offers some production time estimates that you can use until you develop more accurate estimates for your organization.

TASK	TIME
Simple graphic	1-3 hours each
Complex graphic	2-6 hours each
Retouch photo	1-3 hours
Complex illustration	1+ days
Desktop publishing (DTP) with clean text import	30-60 pages/day
DTP with graphics development	10-20 pages/day

Figure 4. Estimate and Identify Production Support. *Obtain the necessary production support. Without adequate support, writers with limited production skills are forced to prepare their own graphics and design pages. Proposal quality drops, and the total cost increases.*

---

5 Test systems prior to production.

If systems are not checked, something may go wrong. Proposal managers frequently see one of the following problems:

See Electronic Submittal.

- Screened or shaded effects will fade on one copier and increase in intensity on another, obscuring the text.

- Word-processed proposals will print differently depending on the printer, the printer driver, and the precise supplier of the selected font. Fonts with the same name from different vendors might print differently.

- When sending electronic proposals, the only way to ensure the document will print exactly as intended is to send it in PDF format.

- Contributors are likely to be using different software or different releases of the same software, especially if they develop their own graphics.

- When files are sent via e-mail, files can be corrupted by different ISPs (Internet Service Providers), firewalls, and mail encoders and decoders (plug-ins).

Check everything, especially when you have remote contributors or teaming partners.

6

See ELECTRONIC SUBMITTAL, INTERNATIONAL PROPOSALS, ORAL PROPOSALS, *and* PAGE AND DOCUMENT DESIGN.

Determine how the proposal will be *packaged* and delivered while section writers are planning and preparing initial drafts.

Packaging includes determining the binding method, the size and number of binders required, and cover art. More than a few proposal managers have been surprised by proposals that outgrew the binders that were ordered.

Cover art can get your proposal read in a commercial competition. Good covers both attract readers and project the bidder's win strategy. If you develop custom covers, develop and approve the art early as color printing on custom stock often requires more time.

On smaller proposals, prepare a custom cover in one of the following inexpensive ways:

- Cut a page from one of your marketing brochures, then overprint the proposal title text.
- Consider using some of the customer's materials for the cover, especially if you can directly connect those materials to your offer.
- Create your own cover, print on heavier stock, then laminate.

Use quality binders. Economizing on binders is false economy and high risk.

Consider how proposals with multiple volumes will be packaged for shipment.

Consider individually wrapping each binder to reduce damage and to prevent binders from opening during shipment.

If being late means automatic disqualification, plan a backup delivery system. International proposals increase delivery problems. While reducing delivery problems, in-country production can lead to other potentially greater problems:

- Skilled editors and proofers may not be available.
- Content can be altered.
- Expenses increase if final reviewers must work in-country.
- Security may be compromised.

Consider requirements for electronic submittal, CD, or some combination of paper documents, CD, electronic submittal, and an oral proposal. Regardless of the medium and submittal procedure, adapt the design to the medium while aligning the message and content. Inconsistencies interject doubt, distrust, and reduce your win probability.

7

Maintain a secure master book of hard-copy files backed by electronic files.

Maintain a master book containing copies of all material in the latest, approved version. All contributors must accept that none of their work is complete until it is inserted in the master book.

The master book can take several forms. Most are kept in ring binders by the proposal specialist, production manager, or proposal manager. When material is revised, the new material is inserted in the binder; the previous version is placed in a backup file ordered by section and date.

Insist on getting electronic files with all hard copy submittals. Store them on a server that is frequently backed up. Ensure that all contributors insert their name, section number and name, date, time, and page number in the footer of every page.

The master book is also used to check the printed copies. Turn through each printed page to confirm pages are not missing or printed blank.

8

Use the electronic version control features of different software applications. Features vary and are not discussed in this *Guide.*

Ruthlessly enforce version control on a section-by-section basis.

Enforce version control to prevent more than one person from making changes on the same material in different files. Writers inadvertently lose files. The potential for problems with multiple versions of files increases with the number of contributors on the proposal team.

Assign version control to one person on a section-by-section basis. Normally, writers have version control through the initial reviews of their content. Once version control is passed to the proposal or production coordinator, insist that all suggested changes be made on hard copy, or hard copy backed by electronic insertions.

9

See ELECTRONIC
SUBMITTAL *and*
INTERNATIONAL
PROPOSALS.

Increase your quality checks and production time if proposal production is remote.

Remote production could mean in another building, another city, or another country. Each presents different challenges.

Have one person from the proposal team present at the print location during heavy production to answer questions and detect errors early.

Front load production by printing components or sections early. Components that can be printed early include covers, tabs, inserts, foldouts, and appended materials.

Print individual sections as they are approved. Early print options include resumes, past performance, management, and the executive summary.

International production invites special problems:

- Software, hardware, printers, keyboards, spell checkers, and paper quality may vary.
- Paper size may be A4 versus 8.5 x 11 inches.
- Ring binders change in number and size.
- Translation can create further delays and the need for an additional review.
- Language dialects vary.

Printers do have equipment breakdowns, so identify a backup printer.

Electronic submittals invite additional production problems, far more than are discussed here, so be forewarned.

Proposal Management Plans (PMP) document the roles, responsibilities, tasks, and deadlines before writers start developing proposal sections, volumes, and ultimately the complete proposal.

While a PMP is described as a single document, most PMPs are a series of documents or files that are prepared, posted, shared, and repeatedly updated on a secure web site. Use this virtual, shared-document approach, especially when team members are virtual and not co-located.

Establish direction, then velocity. Too many proposal managers start holding too many meetings with writers and managers before planning is complete. The result is wasted effort, conflicts, and loss of commitment to a quality effort.

Save time by extracting and adapting content from the capture plan and account plan with direction from the account executive. Insert boilerplate PMP descriptions of roles and procedures.

Proposal Management Plan

1. Always prepare a Proposal Management Plan.

2. Complete and review the PMP prior to the kickoff meeting.

3. Distribute the PMP at the kickoff meeting.

4. Keep the PMP current, but manage to the plan.

5. Develop a PMP template for your organization.

---

1   Always prepare a Proposal Management Plan.

Preparing a Proposal Management Plan (PMP) is a proven best practice that leads to improved win rates and higher quality proposals produced with less frustration and cost. When you do not have time to prepare multiple drafts, always prepare the fundamental elements of a PMP.

Many commercial sector proposal plans begin in a conference call termed the proposal kickoff, which is at best a loosely organized planning meeting. At a minimum, develop a strawman PMP before the conference call.

---

2   Complete and review the PMP prior to the kickoff meeting.

See EXECUTIVE SUMMARY, KICKOFF MEETINGS, *and* PROCESS for a discussion of the other tools, events, and milestones.

Core team preparation, the planning activity between the Bid and Proposal Kickoff milestones, requires developing three documents:

1. Proposal Management Plan
2. Draft Executive Summary
3. Proposal Kickoff Package

Review the PMP with management to get their buy-in and endorsement. If they are not willing to support the effort as outlined, you must change the plan or review your bid decision.

If you must call a kickoff meeting prior to completing the PMP, advise contributors that they will be given clear assignments later. Set the date for the meeting, and ask contributors to clear their schedules.

---

3   Distribute the PMP at the kickoff meeting.

The PMP is your plan for the entire effort. Distributing the PMP clarifies everyone's tasks and engenders confidence that their efforts are well-managed and supported by management. A well-conceived PMP suggests that you are not wasting contributors' time.

If your PMP comprises files posted on a secure web site, then *distribution* entails communicating and confirming that contributors can access that site. Then, confirm that they do access that site.

Your complete kickoff meeting package includes five items:

- PMP
- Storyboard forms
- Writing template
- Cross-reference matrix
- Draft executive summary

4

Keep the PMP current, but manage to the plan.

Reflect changes in the RFP, dates, and contributors by updating the PMP. Absent external changes, avoid sliding completion dates. Manage to the plan.

Whether your PMP is a physical or electronic document or series of documents, post the most recent version on the team web site. Instruct contributors to set up automatic notifications to alert them when documents are modified and new files are posted.

5

Develop a PMP template for your organization.

Adapt the format and contents of a PMP to the complexity of the proposal, the size of the proposal team, the value of the proposal, and the experience and skills of the managers and contributors.

The contents of a PMP are summarized in figure 1. A template for a PMP is presented in thumbnail form beginning on this page and continuing on the following three pages, figures 2 through 12.

PMP CONTENTS	ATTACHMENTS
1. Proposal Project Summary	A. Proposal Schedule
2. Customer Profile	B. Proposal Outline
3. Competitive Analysis	C. Writers' Information
4. Proposal Strategies and Themes	D. Proposal Strategy
5. Staffing Roles and Responsibilities	E. Executive Summary
6. Proposal Operations	F. Work Breakdown Structure (WBS) and WBS Dictionary

Figure 1. PMP Contents. *Include these topics in your PMP in the detail appropriate to each proposal effort. Post all PMP documents and files on a secure web site that is accessible to the proposal team.*

1.0 PROPOSAL PROJECT SUMMARY

General Information
- Customer
- Contract Name
- Solicitation Identification
- Type of Contract
- Terms of Contract
- Estimated Contract Value
- Duration of Contract
- RFP Release Date
- Proposal Due Date
- Customer Procurement Office

PMP-1

1.0 PROPOSAL PROJECT SUMMARY

Project Focal Points
- Program Manager
- Marketing Manager
- Teammates
- Capture Plan
- Capture Team Head

Project Scope and Deliverables
- Scope of Work
- Primary Tasks
- Deliverables
- Proposal Organization

PMP-2

Figure 2. PMP Proposal Project Summary. *Written primarily for upper management, reviewers, and the proposal team, this section of the PMP summarizes the customer's program needs, key program information, key program personnel, overall scope, and deliverables.*

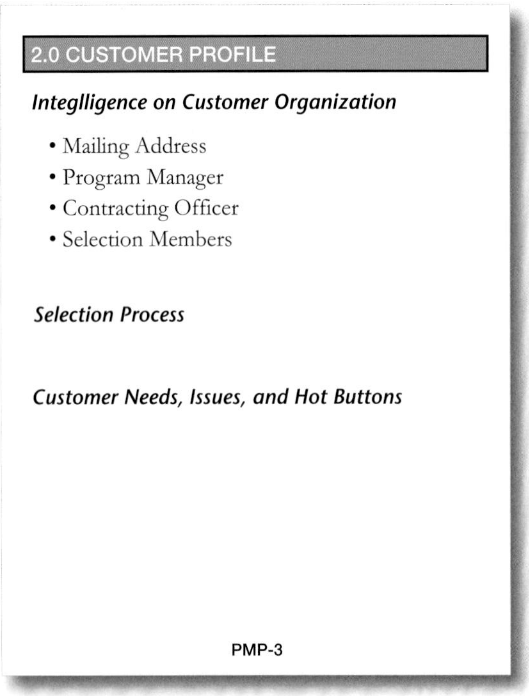

2.0 CUSTOMER PROFILE

Integlligence on Customer Organization

- Mailing Address
- Program Manager
- Contracting Officer
- Selection Members

Selection Process

Customer Needs, Issues, and Hot Buttons

PMP-3

Figure 3. PMP Customer Profile. *This section identifies key members of the customer organization, then summarizes the selection process and the customer's perception of your organization.*

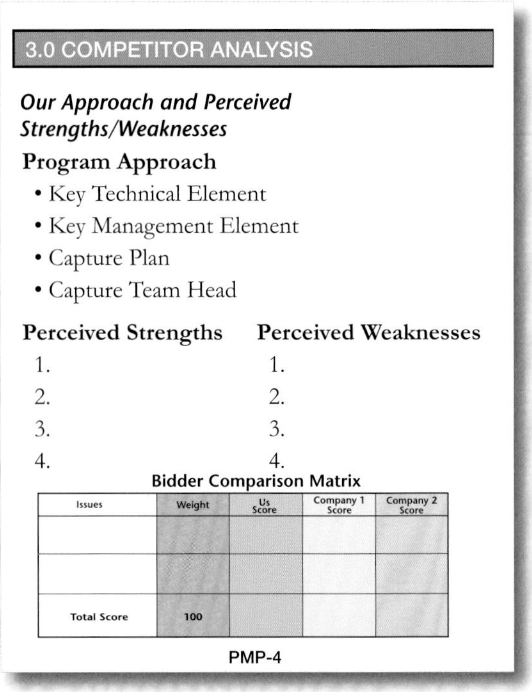

3.0 COMPETITOR ANALYSIS

Our Approach and Perceived Strengths/Weaknesses

Program Approach
- Key Technical Element
- Key Management Element
- Capture Plan
- Capture Team Head

Perceived Strengths   **Perceived Weaknesses**
1.   1.
2.   2.
3.   3.
4.   4.

Bidder Comparison Matrix

Issues	Weight	Us Score	Company 1 Score	Company 2 Score
Total Score	100			

PMP-4

Figure 4. PMP Competitive Analysis. *This section summarizes the key elements of your approach and the customer's perceptions of your competitive position.*

See DISCRIMINATORS, PROPOSAL STRATEGY, TEAM SELECTION AND MANAGEMENT, *and* THEME STATEMENTS.

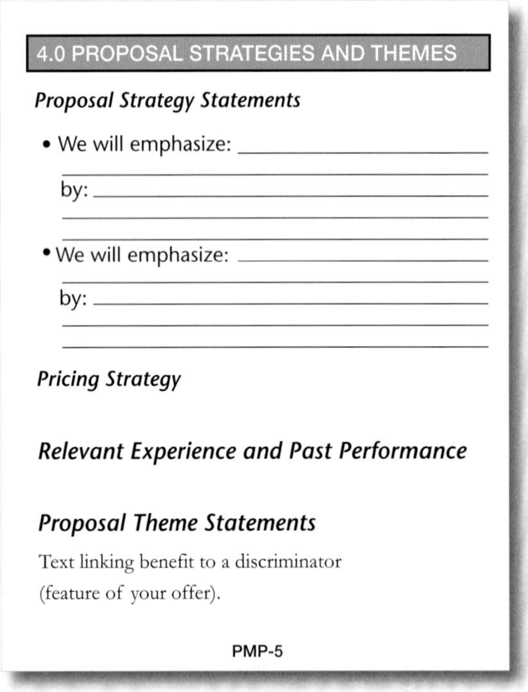

4.0 PROPOSAL STRATEGIES AND THEMES

Proposal Strategy Statements

- We will emphasize: _____
  by: _____

- We will emphasize: _____
  by: _____

Pricing Strategy

Relevant Experience and Past Performance

Proposal Theme Statements

Text linking benefit to a discriminator (feature of your offer).

PMP-5

Figure 5. PMP Proposal Strategies and Themes. *The strategy statements indicate what you plan to include in your proposal to support your major claims. Themes are actual statements that will be printed in your proposal.*

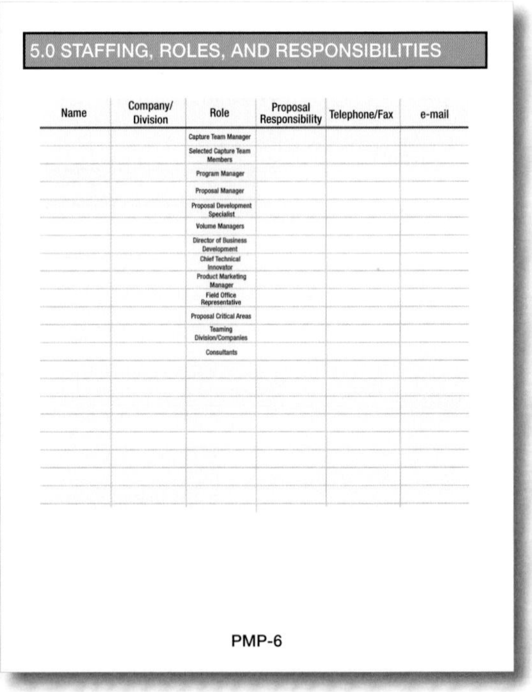

5.0 STAFFING, ROLES, AND RESPONSIBILITIES

Name	Company/ Division	Role	Proposal Responsibility	Telephone/Fax	e-mail
		Capture Team Manager			
		Selected Capture Team Members			
		Program Manager			
		Proposal Manager			
		Proposal Development Specialist			
		Volume Managers			
		Director of Business Development			
		Chief Technical Innovator			
		Product Marketing Manager			
		Field Office Representative			
		Proposal Critical Areas			
		Teaming Division/Companies			
		Consultants			

PMP-6

Figure 6. PMP Staffing, Roles, and Responsibilities. *This section is used primarily to improve teamwork and understanding among individuals assigned to the proposal team. Extend the matrix to include additional information as needed. Descriptions of roles and responsibilities can be taken from earlier PMPs.*

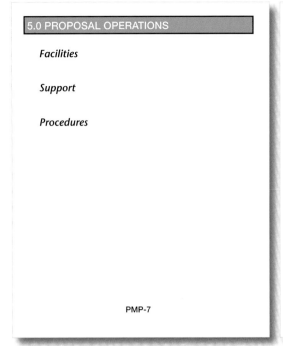

Figure 7. PMP Proposal Operations. *This section indicates the resources available, procedures, and development tools that will be used. Much of this section can be extracted from earlier PMPs.*

Figure 8. PMP Proposal Schedule. *Issue a milestone schedule at the kickoff meeting, then follow up with an "inch-stone" schedule.*

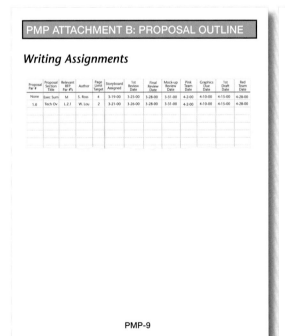

See Scheduling *and* Storyboards and Mockups.

Figure 9. PMP Proposal Outline and Writing Assignments. *Assign a single person with the primary responsibility for each proposal section. Consider integrating the outline, assignments, and completion dates into the same matrix.*

Figure 10. PMP Writers' Information. *Include any information, tools, forms, or references to resources that will help writers complete their assignments correctly and efficiently.*

See EXECUTIVE
SUMMARY.

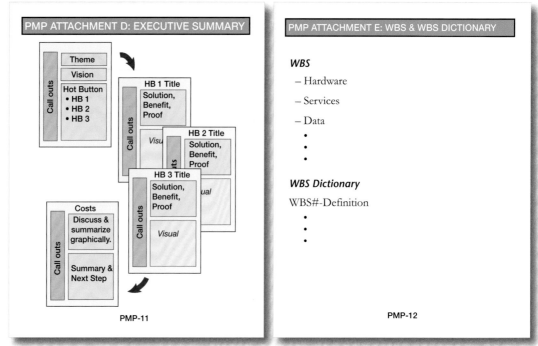

Figure 11. PMP Executive Summary. *Include the most recent version of the proposal executive summary.*

Figure 12. PMP WBS and WBS Dictionary. *This section both defines and separates the seller's proposed work into hardware, services, and data elements. The WBS is essential to describe and cost your proposal tasks.*

Proposal Preparation Tools help you prepare proposals more efficiently and effectively. Using the correct tool to capture, analyze, and manipulate information decreases rework, reduces preparation costs, and increases win rates.

Some tools improve both efficiency and effectiveness. An efficiency tool might incorporate conceptual prompts.

Efficiency tools help you prepare proposals faster. They save time and improve consistency. Typically electronic, efficiency tools include knowledge management, document management, workflow management, collaboration, bid request stripping, estimating, integrated design, and pricing tools.

Effectiveness tools help you prepare proposals with better content. Whether electronic or paper-based, effectiveness tools improve users' conceptual thinking and process consistency resulting in more customer-focused, responsive, and persuasive proposals. Effectiveness tools take time to use but ultimately save time by eliminating unnecessary or iterative tasks. Effectiveness tools include milestone checklists,

decision matrices, capture plans, proposal management plans, bidder comparison matrices, strategy statement templates, Four-Box organizers, storyboards, and oral proposal planners.

Use *both* efficiency and effectiveness tools. Define proposal quality standards, thoroughly train users on both types of tools, and then manage to your standards.

The following guidelines will help you analyze, select, and use the best efficiency and effectiveness tools for your organization. These guidelines do not recommend specific tools because users' needs and tools frequently change.

Many of the tools discussed apply to business development and capture management, not just proposal preparation.

Proposal Preparation Tools

1. Integrate proposal preparation tools into your defined business development process.

2. Manage to meet clearly defined, measurable quality standards.

3. Use both efficiency and effectiveness tools.

4. Train users to think conceptually about the purpose of the tool, and then how to use the tool.

5. Link tool outputs to sequential tool inputs.

6. Reexamine your tools and quality standards if your success metrics do not improve.

7. Designate a process owner to collect metrics, maintain tools, and maintain support infrastructure.

---

1   Integrate proposal preparation tools into your defined business development process.

See Capture Planning, Proposal Management Plan, Process, Page and Document Design, *and* Proposal Strategy.

To use any type of proposal preparation tool effectively, your organization must define and commit to follow a single, flexible, and scalable process. Consider how business development best practices are thwarted by poor use of good tools:

- **Make sound bid decisions.** A tool that helps you rapidly assemble reuse material into proposals is wasted if customers have minimal interest in buying from your organization, or the material is not directly relevant to the services sought.

- **Appoint a champion at the executive level to maintain broad management support.** A tool that helps you prepare

a capture plan is wasted if no one is committed to review, execute, and monitor the strategies and tactics defined in the plan.

- **Focus on the customer's issues throughout the sales process.** A tool that helps writers rapidly identify potentially relevant material is wasted if management and writers do not know how to tailor and link that material to the customer's issues, the competitive situation, and your sales strategy.

When good tools are used poorly and bids are lost, users and management often blame the tool. Instead, define your business development process, including the tools.

---

2   Manage to meet clearly defined, measurable quality standards.

If you define and manage to meet clear, measurable, proposal quality standards, you can determine if a tool is used effectively, misused, or needs to be modified or supplemented. For

example, no matter how well-written, material reused from a previous proposal cannot specifically address *this customer's issues*. The best you can do is address typical issues of typical customers.

See CUSTOMER FOCUS *and* REVIEWS.

Boilerplate proposals are seldom effective because they are not customer focused. Consider this common situation:

Company X purchases proposal preparation software that helps writers identify, select, and insert potentially relevant reuse material into a word processing file. Their template defines styles for theme statements, action captions, headings, summaries, introductions, bullet lists, callouts, success stories, and even reserves a wide left margin for emphasis devices. However, if nothing is placed in the left margin, the customer's

perception is that Company X has nothing worth emphasizing. Alternatively, if the left-margin callouts comprise bland, me-too claims, this reflects adversely on Company X, as well.

Tools can actually reduce proposal quality if the writers do not know your quality standards and management does not understand and enforce these standards. Defining standards is the first step in measuring the contribution of your proposal preparation tools.

3 Use both efficiency and effectiveness tools.

See MODEL DOCUMENTS.

Efficiency tools save time, helping you complete tasks faster. Effectiveness tools help you complete the right tasks better. Organizations that use both effectiveness and efficiency tools gain the most.

Use effectiveness tools to *eliminate wasted effort, reduce rework,* and *improve output quality.* Use the efficiency tools to *save time.* Various tools and tool benefits are listed in figure 1.

EFFICIENCY TOOL	TOOL BENEFITS
Knowledge Management	Label, store, search, identify, and retrieve reusable information
Workflow Management	Identify, define, schedule, and manage project tasks
Collaboration	Help individuals work and contribute productively in virtual teams
Bid Request Stripper	Identify, extract, group, and assign compliance requirements to contributors
Integrated Design & Pricing	Automatically determine individual task price and total solution price at each design step
Estimating	Extend and roll up total solution price; test alternative pricing strategies
EFFECTIVENESS TOOL	TOOL BENEFITS
Milestone Checklists	Improve quality and consistency of milestone decisions
Decision Matrices	Improve quality and consistency of decisions
Capture Plans	Position organization as preferred provider before proposal submittal
Proposal Management Plans	Better organization of information to prepare a better proposal at lower cost
Bidder Comparison Matrices	Better assess competitive position; improve teaming analysis; identify discriminators
Strategy Statement Templates	Improve clarity and implementation of strategy
Four-Box Organizers	Improve customer focus and clarity of written documents and oral presentations
Storyboards	Reduce rewrites and improve proposal quality
Oral Proposal Planners	Improve presentation effectiveness; align presentation with the proposal

Figure 1. Consider Efficiency and Effectiveness Tools. *Both classes of proposal preparation tools offer benefits.*

4 Train users to think conceptually about the purpose of the tool, and then how to use the tool.

Rote manipulation of a tool yields mediocre results. Consider these questions:

- How can capture managers use a capture plan template unless they understand customer issues, motivators, and hot buttons?
- How can proposal managers prepare a proposal strategy without a prior sales or capture strategy?
- How can proposal writers preparing a storyboard draft a section theme

statement without understanding features, advantages, benefits, and theme statement standards?

- How can proposal writers effectively tailor reuse materials without understanding the customer's needs, your strategy, and fundamentals of organization?
- How can account executives use Four-Box Organizers to conceive and mock-up executive summaries if they have never been trained to use them?

Without a conceptual framework, tool users are simply operating a piece of software or completing a form. Garbage in; garbage out.

The most effective training is tailored to the market and organization. Ask participants to use the tool during training, and then offer constructive suggestions for improvement. *Just showing them how it works* is a waste of time, even if it requires less training time. Then reinforce the training with activities based upon your review of their work products.

Avoid these common training errors:

- Call a meeting, position the new tool as the means to solve a problem, have an expert user demonstrate the tool, then give everyone the tool and expect expert use.

- Call a training session, ignore the trainer's recommendations on how to train users because, *Our people are smarter, more skilled than the average user*, and then cut training time in half.

- Assume everyone enters training with the same level of understanding. For example, A tool built in Excel often requires reasonable knowledge of Excel. A scheduling tool that outputs to project planning software requires both the software and how to use that software.

- Assume everyone will *get it* in a single session.

- Fail to train the managers, who will not understand the tool or how to review tool output.

- Experts unfamiliar with the tool and inherent assumptions distrust and do not use the tool.

---

5   Link tool outputs to sequential tool inputs.

Link your tools. Outputs or products of one tool should be the input to another tool in your business development process. No one wants to fill in a box or complete a field just because it exists. Professionals must be convinced that their actions are useful to themselves, or secondarily, to others.

For example:

A global IT services organization developed a comprehensive series of templates to support their sales process. When asked how the output was linked to another template, the tool developer and sales managers admitted: *This data is not used elsewhere, but it is nice to know.* The company's sales executives seldom used any of the templates, and their sales managers never asked to see completed templates. Yet all account executives insisted that they followed their organization's defined sales process but *did not use the forms.*

Linking your proposal preparation tools has three major benefits, in order of importance:

- **Improves coordination and hand-off between sales and sales support groups.** How often does your field sales team complain about the quality of proposals prepared by sales support? How often does sales support say they know little about the customer and the sales strategy?

- **Improves communication of key sales points in the proposal.** How often have you seen vital storyboard data omitted from the section draft? How often is a key sales point omitted from the proposal?

- **Saves time.** Transferring data manually from one field or form to another is nearly as frustrating as entering data that is not used.

---

6   Reexamine your tools and quality standards if your success metrics do not improve.

Valid reasons to use any tool are to improve results and save time. Reexamine your process and quality standards if your success metrics do not improve after adopting a new tool.

Two of the most commonly collected metrics are **win rate** and **capture ratio**.

$$\text{Win Rate} = \frac{\text{\# of bids won}}{\text{\# of bids submitted}}$$

$$\text{Capture ratio} = \frac{\text{\$ value of bids won}}{\text{\$ value of bids submitted}}$$

See PROCESS for more on using process gate reviews to manage capture effectiveness.

Win rates tell you little about whether you are winning the most important opportunities. Capture ratio is a better measure of process and tool effectiveness, because large bids, which are likely to be more competitive, carry a greater weight. When organizations have higher win rates than capture ratios, they are winning more of the small, less competitive competitions. When organizations' capture ratios exceed their win rate, they are usually winning more of the larger competitions.

Comparing win rates and capture ratios between organizations is unreliable because organizations track win rates and capture ratios differently. Consider tracking seven categories of won-lost data: **Won, lost, no-bid, cancelled (by customer), withdrawn (by bidder), pending,** and **unknown.** Then:

$$\text{Win Rates} = \frac{\text{Opportunities Won}}{\left[\begin{array}{c}\text{Total Opportunities Submitted - pending -}\\ \text{withdrawn - cancelled - unknown}\end{array}\right]}$$

The justification for excluding withdrawn, cancelled, and unknown opportunities is that they are not controlled by the bidding organization. The counter argument is that many of these are avoidable if the bidder thoroughly understands the customer and competitive environment. Define your metric and be consistent.

Organizations can broadly assess the effectiveness of their processes and tools by collecting *trailing, diagnostic,* and *leading* metrics. *Trailing* indicators, such as win rates and capture ratio, are the easiest to collect and tell you how you did. *Diagnostic* metrics, such as the customer focus indicators discussed in Customer Focus, indicate process or tool-use deficiencies.

Leading metrics help predict outcomes and guide management decisions. While less precise than "trailing" metrics, they are essential to managing capture effectiveness. Leading metrics, often summarized and

discussed in gate reviews, attempt to measure win probability, price to win, risk, compliance, and responsiveness.

Many purported measures of process and tool effectiveness measure activity but not effectiveness. Consider this example:

Company A invests $X00,000 in knowledge management, boilerplate identification and retrieval, and proposal preparation software. They prepared and submitted 400 proposals this year, up from 200 proposals the prior year, using 20 percent fewer sales support personnel. Company A appears to have reduced their proposal preparation costs more than half and shortened preparation time, achieving the return on investment promised by the software vendor.

But did Company A invest wisely? Did their win rate increase, stay the same, or decrease? What happened to their capture ratio? And even if these measures worsened, the cause could be poor use of the tool in a defective process rather than a poor tool.

If you want to assess the effectiveness of your proposal preparation tools, assess the improvement in your results. While many factors contribute to capture effectiveness, isolated measures of activity, such as person-hours per proposal, tell you little about tool effectiveness.

7

Designate a process owner to collect metrics, foster continuous improvement, maintain tools, and maintain support infrastructure.

See Process.

Processes erode quickly without a process owner. Process owners collect metrics to focus attention on key practices and to quantify improvements in the business development process

To remain effective, your business development processes and tools must be maintained. To keep your processes and support tools synchronized, assign maintenance responsibility to the same person.

Many proposal managers develop effective tools, use them personally, and share them with colleagues. Subsequently, colleagues modify the tool, impair the functionality, and become frustrated. In addition, repeated software and operating system updates impair functionality, and the original developer is unavailable and no one understands the implicit assumptions and operation.

Vendors are increasingly offering proposal development tools on their web sites. Use these tools if you understand the implicit assumptions and can confirm that these assumptions apply to this proposal and your organization.

Establish a tool review interval. Make sure the tool is accurate, adds value, and is being used. Review the accuracy of your boilerplate two to

four times annually. Set an expiration date on each boilerplate item. Either remove expired boilerplate, warn users it might be incorrect, or mark it *Expired.*

Many organizations have invested in tools that promised to save time but did not improve effectiveness. Evaluate the effectiveness of tool output, as illustrated in these examples:

A process owner uses a knowledge management tool to archive and retrieve boilerplate and to measure writers' productivity in pages per day. As a result, writers insert more boilerplate, appearing to increase productivity. Consider adding measures of quality, customer focus, compliance, win rates, or direct customer feedback.

A process owner measures the number of proposals issued to gauge sales force and proposal center productivity. The organization purchased proposal preparation software to improve the productivity of both groups. Subsequently, the number of proposals written and submitted doubled, but sales revenue remained flat as win rates dropped.

While the software may be effective, review the organization's pursuit and bid decision discipline. To win more business, use both effectiveness and efficiency tools in a defined business development process.

Proposal Strategy is a plan to write a persuasive, winning proposal. Proposal strategy is a subset of capture strategy.

To win business most effectively, align your business, market, capture, sales, and proposal strategies and tactics. Misaligned strategies prompt customers to doubt your messages.

This topic section discusses proposal strategy as a subset of the capture strategy. For a full discussion of capture strategy, refer to Strategy in the *Capture Guide.*

Proposal Strategy

1. Distinguish capture strategy and proposal strategy.

2. Define and agree to use common definitions of terms.

3. Identify the economic buyer, the users, and the technical buyers; then list their issues.

4. Use a Power Rating to meld individual buyers' issues into a set of organizational issues.

5. Use an Integrated Solution Worksheet to arrive at a competitive solution that is aligned with the customer's issues and requirements.

6. Prepare a Bidder Comparison Matrix to discern how the customer organization perceives your solution versus competitive solutions.

7. Identify your value proposition and how you will present it in your proposal.

8. Draft specific strategy statements that define both what you will do and how you will implement them.

9. Use trade-offs to validate your approach and ghost the competition.

---

1   Distinguish capture strategy and proposal strategy.

Strategy might be the most misused word in business. *Strategy* might refer to a position, an action, the entire solution, an aspect of the solution, or a favorite catch phrase or slogan.

To craft and present an aligned message, all members of the selling team must agree to use a common process and common definitions:

- Business strategy is an organization's plan to achieve overall business objectives.

- Market strategy is an organization's plan to achieve specific market objectives, typically involving multiple sales.

- Capture strategy is the plan to win a specific, defined opportunity.

- Sales strategy should be identical to a capture strategy; i.e., opportunity specific, but sales strategy has been used so generically that the term was not used in the *Capture Guide* or *Proposal Guide.*

- Proposal strategy is a plan to write a persuasive, winning proposal. The proposal strategy is a subset of the capture strategy. The message is the same; only the tactical aspects of implementation differ.

Win strategy is often used to describe the over-arching actions required to win an opportunity. In reality, capture strategy and win strategy are identical, but some practitioners have opted to limit capture strategy to the specific positioning actions of the capture team.

First, prepare the capture strategy, and then prepare the proposal strategy. If you lack a capture strategy, you are poorly positioned to win and should consider not bidding.

In capture planning, you plan and take actions to convey information that persuades each customer to prefer, or at minimum, favorably regard your organization and solution. Your persuasive actions might comprise white papers, presentations, meetings, site visits, demonstrations, and media buys or events.

In a proposal, you should be conveying identical, aligned information in words, text, and graphics. Hence, the proposal strategy evolves from the capture strategy.

2

Concerns that the seller has about a solution or approach are called gaps, the difference between what the customer wants and what the seller can offer. Issues are owned by the customer, not the seller. Avoid the confusion caused by mingling customer gaps and seller issues.

Define and agree to use common definitions of terms.

Common understanding requires common terms. Three of the most universally used and misunderstood terms relating to strategy are issues, motivators, and hot buttons. The relationship of these three terms is illustrated in figure 1 and defined as follows:

Issues are the customer's concerns. Issues are the worry items that keep the customer awake at night.

Motivators are the objectives that the customer is trying to achieve:

- Improve profits
- Increase sales
- Reduce costs
- Improve safety
- Reduce risk
- Improve quality

Hot buttons are a consolidated set of issues and motivators, preferably two to five items. State hot buttons using the customer's words. Then organize your executive summary around the customer's hot buttons.

All motivators are issues, but not all issues are motivators. For example, training could be an example of a hot button that is an issue but not a motivator. Few customers are motivated to buy because they get to attend training. However, if users were poorly trained on a previous similar purchase, and problems ensued, then training could be a customer's hot button.

Figure 1. The Relationship Among Issues, Motivators, and Hot Buttons. *Hot buttons are mostly motivators but could also include a small number of issues that are not motivators.*

3

Roles may overlap. For example, the president of a small technical company might be both the economic and technical buyer.

Some sales professionals say that there is only one buyer, the individual empowered to make the final purchase decision. All other types of buyers, such as users or technical buyers, are called "influencers."

Identify the economic buyer, the users, and the technical buyers; then list their issues.

Economic buyers are the individuals who give final approval to purchase. They sign the check and retain veto power. Economic buyers tend to be concerned about the trade-off between price and performance. They focus on bottom line impact. While many people may offer input and recommendations, only economic buyers can give final approval.

Users are the people who judge the potential impact on their job performance. Their personal success is impacted by the sale, so their concerns are often emotional and subjective. Users' issues are reliability, support, ease of operation, maintenance, safety, potential impact on morale, and potential impact on their personal success. Because they use or supervise the use of your product or service, they can ruin a good sale.

Technical buyers are gatekeepers. They cannot give final approval, but they can give a final "No." Technical buyers often determine the short list. They tend to focus on the features of a product or service as measured against

objective specifications established to screen offers.

Technical buyers may not be technical in the scientific sense. Purchasing agents, lawyers, contracts people, and licensing or regulatory authorities are technical buyers. Because technical buyers are primarily focused on how well you meet their screening tests, the better you understand their criteria, the better your chances of getting their recommendations.

Another way to examine buyers is according to their source of power. Power could be economic, control (typically users), or technical. Or power could be by level of management, such as executive management, middle management, and operations.

After identifying all the different types of buyers, list the issues of each individual buyer. The most important issues of the entire organization are usually associated with a majority of the buyers.

4

Use a Power Rating to meld individual buyers' issues into a set of organizational issues.

One-on-one selling affords the opportunity to address individuals' issues. However, this is not possible when you are preparing a proposal that will be evaluated by multiple buyers. Combine individuals' issues into a set of organizational issues that can be addressed in a single proposal or presentation.

Use the Power Rating to determine the relative importance of the group's issues. The Power

Rating is the product of the power of the individual buyer, the decision maker and influencers, times the relative importance of that issue to each individual.

Use the template shown in figure 2 to produce a combined, weighted list of issues from the individual buyers' issues. Then use this weighted list as the basis for the Bidder Comparison Matrix, discussed in guideline 6.

NAME	POSITION	POWER	ISSUE	IMPORT-ANCE	POWER RATING
Mrs. Ellis		10	Look and feel	10	100
			Reliability	6	60
			Price	3	30
Mr. Douglas		2	Price	5	10

ISSUE	TOTAL POWER RATING	CUSTOMER'S WEIGHT
Look and feel	100	50
Reliability	60	30
Price	40	20
		100%

Figure 2. Power Rating Calculation Shows Organizational Issues. *Allocate a rating from 1-10 for the 'Power' that each individual buyer has in the buying decision (1 = least influence; 10 = most influence). Then list the issues that concern each buyer and allocate an 'Importance' rating from 1-10 for each of these issues-the rating reflecting how important each issue is to that particular buyer. Then multiply the 'Power' by the 'Importance' to give a 'Power Rating' for each issue, then group the issues together across multiple buyers and total their Power Ratings. Finally, choose the top 6-8 organizational issues and scale their scores so that they total 100.*

5

Use an Integrated Solution Worksheet to arrive at a competitive solution that is aligned with the customer's issues and requirements.

The Integrated Solution Worksheet (ISW) is a powerful analysis tool throughout the capture process. The ISW is first developed as part of the capture plan. The ISW is shown in figure 2.

If your capture plan includes an ISW, confirm that it is current. If not, prepare the ISW.

If the customer already has a solution in mind, as stated in meetings for unsolicited bids or in the bid request as requirements, the ISW helps define the underlying issues driving their requirements, time permitting. Analyze your competitive position, then work to favorably influence the requirements.

Next, extend your analysis to outline your solution, to outline your competition's solution, and to identify discriminators. Then define the strategies and actions required to better position your solution with the customer, discussed in guideline 8. Note that the *Action Required* column comprises specific positioning activities in the capture phase and things that you say or do in the proposal phase.

Item No.	Customer Issues	Customer Requirements	Available Solution	Gap	Competitor Solution	Discriminators	Strategy	Action Required
1	System must be available.	8 hr. response time.	2 hr. response time	1 hr	3 hr. response time	Faster response but more expensive?	Emphasize no additional cost with cellular.	Show current response time. Show photo-service with cell phone.

Figure 2. Integrated Solution Worksheet. *Begin by filling the "Issues" column when you are early in the process. If the customer has identified requirements, fill the "Requirements" column. Then complete each row, relating each item in the row.*

6

Prepare a Bidder Comparison Matrix to discern how the customer organization perceives your solution versus competitive solutions.

See CAPTURE PLANNING *and* EXECUTIVE SUMMARY.

Use the Bidder Comparison Matrix, shown in figure 3, to analyze the customer's current perception of how your solution compares to various competitors. Update it during proposal preparation if the underlying information changes. The Bidder Comparison Matrix can be an excellent customer collaboration tool if you are permitted access to the customer.

ISSUES	WEIGHT	US (SCORE)	COMPANY A	COMPANY B
Specific Experience	30	25	20	15
Low Price	20	5	10	15
Familiarity with Manager Named	20	15	10	10
Ability to Meet Schedule	30	25	21	15
TOTAL SCORE	100	70	61	55

Figure 3. Bidder Comparison Matrix. *First list the customer's issues, then the relative weight of each issue as perceived by the customer. Establish the relative weight of each issue in one of three ways: (1) Use the customer's evaluation criteria, (2) Assign a weight, forcing the total score to equal 100, (3) Assign an arbitrary weight (such as 1-to-5). Then assign a score (perhaps 1-to-10). Complete each row horizontally, indicating your estimate of the customer's perception of each competitor's ability to satisfy that issue. Compare the products of the weight times the score. The absolute value of the numbers assigned is not important. Only the comparative value matters.*

7 — Identify your value proposition and how you will present it in your proposal.

See VALUE PROPOSITION, *Capture Guide.*

See EXECUTIVE SUMMARY.

Total added value is the summation of the benefits minus the purchase cost and implementation cost of the seller's solution.

Best value is cited as an evaluation factor in many U.S. federal and commercial bid requirements. Rather than being forced to adhere to specific and potentially incomplete quantitative criteria, best value preserves room for judgment.

A value proposition is a disciplined way of expressing and substantiating best value, used by many organizations in the business-to-business sector, and conceptually applicable to the government sector. Sales presentations and proposals have always stressed linking the features of your solution to the benefits to the customer. Fundamentally, a value proposition is the summation of the net benefits of your solution.

> *Value proposition = Net Benefits of seller's solution*

Having determined your solution, prepare value propositions for each type of buyer: the economic buyer, the users, and the technical buyers. Good value propositions are detailed, specific, and quantified.

Value propositions establish the value basis for the business relationship. They describe how your solution will improve the customer's business and how that improvement will be measured. Tailor value proposition(s) to each type of buying influence.

Value propositions include the following elements:

- Quantified business improvement
- Timing
- Solution
- Investment cost
- Payback
- Results measurement and tracking

The over-arching value proposition is typically stated in the executive summary. If you state a quantified value proposition in the executive summary, consider organizing the executive summary around components of your value proposition. Essentially, the quantified component values sum to the total value.

Place supporting value propositions targeting the economic buyer, technical buyer, users, and contract managers in the relevant volume summary or major section summary.

8 — Draft specific strategy statements that define both what you will do and how you will implement them.

Section strategy statements appear in Proposal Development Worksheets (PDWs) or storyboards. Some proposal managers develop them from proposal strategy statements, or section writers develop them as they develop storyboards.

See STORYBOARDS AND MOCKUPS.

Strategy can be implemented in four fundamental ways:

1. Emphasize your strengths
2. Mitigate your weaknesses
3. Highlight your competitors' weaknesses
4. Downplay your competitors' strengths

Effective strategy statements incorporate both strategic and tactical aspects. The strategic portion establishes your position. The tactical portion defines how you will implement the strategy, the action steps. Use the worksheet in figure 4 to develop effective strategy statements. Think of the strategic part as *what you will do,* and the tactical part as *how you will do it.*

Strategy statements apply at the capture, proposal, and proposal section level. Capture strategy statements are global. They apply to all aspects of the sales cycle.

Capture strategy example

What:

We will emphasize our perceived ability to complete the design-build of a distribution center on time

By:

- Taking the customer on a plant tour of the XYZ distribution center in Orlando, FL
- Citing three other distribution centers completed on schedule during the past 5 years
- Providing contact names, phone numbers, and quotes verifying our on-time completion of three similar projects

Proposal strategy example

What:

We will emphasize our perceived ability to complete the design-build of a distribution center on time

By:

- Including in our proposal photos of the XYZ distribution center in Orlando, FL

- Citing three other distribution centers in a table in our proposal, all listing the center, place, owner, promised completion date, and actual completion date

- Listing in our proposal the contact names, phone numbers, and quotes verifying our on-time completion of three similar projects

Section strategy statements, while more limited in scope, are essentially the same as proposal strategy statements in form, content, and implementation.

A well-written proposal strategy statement enables the reader to visualize how the strategy will appear on the page. For example:

- *Describe or Discuss* implies text.

- *Show* implies a graphic.

- *Include* implies a sketch, drawing, photo, table, flow chart, or graph.

- *Cite or Quote* implies text set off or emphasized by different formatting or white space.

If you cannot visualize the page, refine the strategy statement.

In terms of implementation, the way you emphasize your strength may be identical to how you highlight a competitor's weakness. Similarly, how you mitigate your weakness may be identical to how you neutralize a competitor's strength, as demonstrated in the following examples:

Proposal strategy example

Your competitor has a reasonable reputation for completing projects within budget. Your organization had a recent cost overrun on the similar ABC project. The strategy statement to mitigate your weakness and downplay the competitor's strength might be the same.

Proposal strategy statement example

We will mitigate our perceived weakness in completing similar projects within budget by:

- Citing the lessons learned from the recent ABC project

- Including a table listing all materials and sub-contract tasks that have been pre-negotiated prior to submittal.

We will downplay our competitor's perceived strength in completing similar projects within budget by:

- Citing the lessons learned from the recent ABC project

- Including a table listing all materials and sub-contract tasks that have been pre-negotiated prior to submittal.

STRATEGY STATEMENT WORKSHEET

- We will emphasize our perceived strengths in <issue>: _
  _____
  as a result of <discriminator> by: _____
  _____
  _____
  _____

- We will mitigate our perceived weaknesses in <issue>: _
  as a result of <discriminator>_____
  by: _____
  _____
  _____
  _____

- We will highlight our competitors' perceived weaknesses in
  <issue>: _____
  as a result of <discriminator> by: _____
  _____
  _____
  _____

- We will downplay our competitors' perceived strengths in
  <issue>: _____
  as a result of <discriminator> by: _____
  _____
  _____
  _____

Copyright Shipley Associates.

Figure 4. Strategy Statement Worksheet. *Using either the Integrated Solution Worksheet (figure 2) or the Bidder Comparison Matrix (figure 3), identify your relative position versus each of your competitors. Then draft one strategy statement for each issue or requirement. Treat the "How" portion as possibilities, implementing those that you can support with facts or resources. Collect all of your strategy statements and distribute them to the entire capture team and proposal team.*

9   Use trade-offs to validate your approach and ghost the competition.

Trade-offs show you have considered alternatives and have selected the best solution for the customer. Instead of just selecting the first item available or your usual approach, you considered the customer's needs, risks, and budget, and offered the solution that maximizes benefits and minimizes risks.

Ghosting is simply offering a trade-off when one of the alternatives you rejected is being offered by the competition. You ghost the competition when you raise the specter of competitors' weakness.

The primary way to downplay competitors' strengths and highlight their weaknesses is through ghosting. Never mention competitors by name. Instead, reject their approaches.

One of the advantages of ghosting is that you do not have to fully justify your position. You only create doubt, as shown in the following examples:

> We first thought a full design-build approach would be ideal, as it could shorten the time to completion by 3 months. However, with the lack of reliable data on the stability of the soil at the site and the potential for hazardous materials, we have proposed a full site characterization and analysis prior to design. Our conservative approach reduces the risk of construction interruptions and potentially more costly site remediation.

> We considered using the recently developed new glue to assemble the supersonic aircraft at a reduced cost, but rejected glue as being potentially higher risk in long-term use versus the long-proven rivet approach.

Figure 5 offers some additional ghosting approaches. Use ghosting judiciously. Overuse can turn off the customer.

COMPETITOR'S WEAKNESS	YOU STRESS
Safety problems	Cite your strong safety record. Offer industry averages for comparison.
Labor unrest	Emphasize the importance of a reliable workforce. Note that avoiding the cost of a strike justifies higher hourly wages.
High design cost	Emphasize low overheads and specific industry focus.
Poor reliability	Stress redundant design costs less than lost revenues from poor availability.
Extended downtime	Emphasize your local service center and built-in diagnostics.
Cost overruns	Cite the extra care taken in estimating, material selection, and purchasing.

Figure 5. Use Ghosting to Validate Your Approach. *Plan your ghosts carefully at the capture or proposal manager level. Determine what ghosts will be introduced and where they will be inserted in your proposal. Trade-off analyses are appropriate in every proposal section where realistic alternatives are available.*

Question/Response Proposals are responses to bid requests that consist of a series of questions. Bidders are asked to answer the questions in order.

See EXECUTIVE SUMMARY.

MODEL DOCUMENT 12 is an excerpt from a question/response proposal.

Bid requests largely composed of questions are common in telecommunications, professional services, health care management, and many international sectors. Question/response proposals are rare in U.S. government proposals.

Many question/response bid requests are created by consultants hired by customers' organizations because they lack the internal expertise or time to prepare the bid requests themselves. Consultants compete for this business by selling a more thorough approach, often resulting in more questions, longer responses, and more evaluation time.

Increase your win rate by concentrating on two activities:

1. Place additional emphasis on your executive summary, the only part of your proposal the customer is likely to read.

2. Develop a response strategy to enable you to concentrate your effort on the most important questions.

The second activity requires taking a modified storyboard-like approach. Allocate your time, plan your response, review your planned response, then draft your response.

Question/Response Proposals

1. Review all questions and identify critical ones.

2. Allocate more time to investigate and space to answer critical questions.

3. Use more boilerplate on less-critical questions.

4. Quickly outline each response and review with management before drafting.

5. Identify where graphics can be used to cut text.

6. Answer the question.

7. Insert section summaries to provide perspective and to gain a competitive advantage.

---

1 Review all questions and identify critical ones.

Review all the questions on an 80-20 basis. Identify the 20 percent that are of equal or greater importance than the remaining 80 percent. Look for questions with the following characteristics:

- Involve the customer's major issues
- Offer an opportunity to discriminate your offer
- Create a gap between the requirement and your immediately available solution

Depending on the size of the proposal and the time available, the proposal manager, the writer, or both can review the questions.

---

2 Allocate more time to investigate and space to answer critical questions.

Giving each person the same number of questions to answer usually results in an uneven work load. Ask writers to split their time between the two groups of questions but to devote more time to the 20 percent that are critical.

---

3 Use more boilerplate on less-critical questions.

See ORGANIZATION.

Offer short, concise answers to the simpler, less-critical questions. If a more extensive answer is needed, draft a short introduction; then support your answer with boilerplate.

---

4 Quickly outline each response and review with management before drafting.

Ask writers to outline their answers to the critical questions first, brainstorm their response to the most difficult ones, then review their answers with the core team. If more research is needed to answer a question, decide who will do it and move on to the next question.

Your goal is to be 100 percent compliant and 80 to 90 percent correct with your first answer to all questions.

Answer every question in the first sentence of your answer. Use the remaining text and graphics to support your answer.

5 Identify where graphics can be used to cut text.

Think *graphics first*.

Most question/answer proposals are deadly boring. Given the same answer to the same question, the question answered with a graphic and minimal text will nearly always outscore a competitor's response answered with text alone.

If you insert a graphic with an action caption, you will have much less text to write. If the graphic lacks a caption, add one. If it has a caption, tailor it to the proposal.

6 Answer the question.

Proposal writers can err by failing to answer a question or by overanswering a question.

As noted in guideline 4, answer each question in the first sentence, then support your answer with boilerplate. Writers tend to insert the boilerplate first, then answer the question.

Overly elaborate answers can create more questions. Lawyers coach witnesses to limit their answers. Follow the same *keep it simple* approach.

In the following example, the poor response offers extensive information without directly answering the question. The last two sentences seem to conflict with the first sentences. The better response directly answers the questions in the order asked, omits potentially confusing details, and does not mingle the discussion of maintenance costs and upgrade costs.

Poor response

Is software maintenance available? If yes, is the price included in the price of the software?

Operating system (OS) and database management software (DMS) maintenance is regularly applied at no additional cost. Also FLOORS software, database access software, utilities, and all other system software utilized by the Master Control system will require no maintenance fees. Any maintenance or upgrade can be done by your technicians or ours. Our maintenance is supplied on a time-and-materials basis at $600/day.

Better response

Is software maintenance available?

Yes. ISI provides regular software maintenance on all system software used by the Master Control System.

If yes, is the price included in the price of the software?

Yes. Software maintenance is included in the price of the software. You would incur NO additional costs for software maintenance.

7 Insert section summaries to provide perspective and to gain a competitive advantage.

With question/response proposals, evaluators may read your answers but still have no clear perspective or general understanding of your approach.

Insert a short section summary before answering individual questions on a common topic. Enhance it with a summary graphic when appropriate. Evaluators will appreciate the added perspective and often give higher scores as long as the summary is concise. The helpful tone of your approach suggests that your organization is easy to work with.

See ORGANIZATION.

Do not insert section summaries or graphics if doing so violates bid request instructions.

Few organizations submitting question/response proposals bother to include summaries other than the executive summary, so a series of concise major topic summaries gives you a competitive advantage. Make each summary more persuasive by stressing the overall benefits to the customer at the beginning. End the summary by noting that each question from the customer's bid request is answered in the order listed in the bid request.

Good example of a proposal section summary.

4.0 SOFTWARE MAINTENANCE

ISI offers Acme comprehensive, trouble-free software maintenance at no additional cost for 10 years following software installation.

All of Acme's needs for convenient, low-cost, system availability are met by our software maintenance plan. Our Client Services Organization was commended by Software Research, Inc. as, ... *one of the premier service organizations in the information services industry.* We deliver 24-hour-a-day, 7-day-a-week support, and are able to resolve 99 percent of all problems within 1.57 hours.

Below are our responses to the specific questions in your bid request regarding software maintenance.

Redundant Words or phrases unnecessarily qualify other words or phrases. Eliminate unnecessary words.

Redundant words reduce the persuasiveness of your sales documents, unless used for emphasis. Like any other emphasis device, overuse reduces the effectiveness.

The *qualified expert* that you propose is redundant because any expert is by definition more than just qualified. Your new, innovative approach is redundant because it must be new to be innovative.

Redundant words and deliberate repetition are different. To make a proposal more persuasive, memorable, and clear, good writers deliberately repeat key words throughout the proposal.

Deliberately repeat memorable sales messages in the executive summary, section summaries, theme statements, section headings, and action captions. Repeated items are more likely to be remembered.

Good writers avoid confusion by using the same word for the same concept. Inexperienced proposal writers mistakenly change words referring to the same item or concept because they think it makes their writing more interesting or impactful. Throw out your thesaurus. Use words consistently through the sales cycle.

Redundant Words

1. Eliminate redundant words unless used occasionally for emphasis.

---

1   Eliminate redundant words unless used occasionally for emphasis.

Eliminate unnecessary words. Most redundant words are unnecessary. If the meaning is the same after removing a word, do it.

Do not say that you offer desirable benefits, since all benefits are desirable by definition. While employing a licensed electrician might be absolutely essential, nothing is more important than essential. Absolutely essential does suggest urgency by exaggerating , but too much exaggeration prompts customers to discount your ideas.

Past experience is redundant because any experience was in the past. Similarly, *past performance* is redundant because all performance was in the past.

Use redundant words to match the wording in bid requests. For example, when asked for a *Past Performance* section, call it *Past Performance.*

Use redundant words in proposals in two circumstances:

1. To emphasize a point.
Planning is absolutely essential to meet every milestone.

2. To mirror the bid request.
Every bidder must include a chapter on past performance.

Call the chapter Past Performance, even if the words are redundant.

The impact of using redundant words for emphasis diminishes rapidly. Readers see it as hype and you lose credibility.

Additional examples of redundant words and preferred alternatives are listed in figure 1.

REDUNDANT WORDS

a.c. current *(a.c. = alternating current)* absolutely complete *(complete)* absolutely essential *(essential)* actual experience *(experience)* after very careful consideration *(after considering)* along the lines of *(like)* arrive on the scene *(arrive)* as a matter of fact *(in fact)* as a result of *(because)* ask the question *(ask)* at all times *(always)* attach together *(attach)* at this point in time *(now)* at which time *(when)* **B**asic fundamentals *(basics)* be cognizant of *(know)* black in color *(black)* by virtue of the fact *(because)*	**C**heck up on *(check)* close proximity *(proximity, near)* combine together *(combine)* come to a decision as to *(decide)* completely opposite *(opposite)* consensus of opinion *(consensus)* continue to remain *(remain)* contributing factor *(factor)* **D**esirable benefits *(benefits)* **E**nd product *(product)* end result *(result) (benefits)* **F**ew in number *(few)* final conclusion *(conclusion)* for the purpose of *(for)* for the reason that *(because)* foreign imports *(imports)* free up *(free)* **G**ather together *(gather)* give consideration to *(consider)*	**H**eat up *(heat)* have the ability to *(can, be able to)* **I**mportant essentials *(important)* in order to *(to)* in spite of the fact that *(although, though)* in the event that *(if)* in the final analysis *(finally)* in the nature of *(like)* is now employed *(works)* it is often the case that *(often)* **J**oin together *(join)* joint cooperation *(cooperation)* joint partnership *(partnership)* **L**arge in size *(large)* large sized *(large)* lift up *(lift, raise)*	**M**ain essentials *(essentials)* make mention of *(mention)* make use of *(use)* mix together *(mix)* more preferable *(preferable)* **N**ew innovation *(innovation)* **O**ne and the same *(the same)* one specific case *(one case)* on account of the fact *(because)* on or about *(near)* on the grounds that *(because)* owing to the fact that *(because)* **P**ast experience *(experience)* period of time *(period) (experience)* period of time *(period)* plan ahead *(plan)* plan in advance *(plan)* postponed until later *(postponed)* pre-planning *(planning)*	**Q**ualified expert *(expert)* **R**epeat again *(repeat)* **S**ame identical *(identical)* shuttle back and forth *(shuttle)* single unit *(unit)* specific example *(example)* still remains *(remains)* subsequent to *(after)* surround on all sides *(surround)* **T**rue fact *(true)* this is a subject that *(this subject)* throughout the entire *(throughout)* **U**ltimate end *(end)* unsolved problem *(problem)* until such time as *(until)* **V**isit with *(visit)* **W**ays and means *(ways/means)* with the exception of *(except)*

Figure 1. **Examples of Common Redundant Words and Phrases.** *If you can eliminate a word without changing the meaning, do it.*

Relevant Experience and Past Performance are directly solicited sections in many bid requests and are vital content for all proposals. Both are frequently cited in evaluation criteria. Both are also redundant words, but the customer is always right.

Relevant experience and past performance are quite different but directly related.

Relevant experience includes past, similar experience of the offeror. Relevant experience applies to the organization as a whole, the specific actions being performed, or the experience of the individuals contributing to the services proposed.

Past performance indicates how well you did similar work: the results, impact, or process changes resulting from performing the work. However, some bid requests exclude similar work performed by proposed individuals when they were not part of your organization.

Without proof of experience and performance, proposals are a collection of *trust me* claims. The fatal error for many proposals is to relegate experience and performance data to a separate section or attachment.

Integrate relevant experience and performance data into the body of the proposal adjacent to your claims.

Even when separate relevant experience and performance sections are requested, include both within other proposal sections to support your claims. Different evaluators reviewing different sections seldom link your proposed approach to proof in a separate section.

Relevant Experience/Past Performance

1. Include relevant experience and past performance data in your proposal in the exact location the bid request requires.
2. Integrate support examples when making experience and performance claims.
3. Emphasize experience and performance graphically.
4. Use a *success story* template to tell a consistent, complete story.
5. Address all weaknesses known or potentially known by the customer.
6. Emphasize lessons learned personally over lessons learned from others.

---

1 Include relevant experience and past performance data in your proposal in the exact location the bid request requires.

See COMPLIANCE AND RESPONSIVENESS *and* OUTLINING.

Directions in the RFP can be quite detailed. Follow them explicitly.

Customers view past performance as one of the best indicators of future performance. As proof, U.S. acquisition regulations require past performance as one of two mandatory evaluation factors, along with price or cost.

The Office of Federal Procurement Policy requires the following performance areas be considered:

- Quality of product or services
- Timeliness of performance
- Cost control
- Business practices
- Customer (end user) satisfaction
- Key personnel past performance

---

2 Integrate support examples when making experience and performance claims.

Much like the guidelines for introducing and integrating graphics with text, integrate your support of claims on the same or a facing page. Evaluators should not have to turn the page to find support.

Support and scientific proof are not the same. If a customer is concerned about completing a task on schedule, one example of completing a task on schedule supports your claim. Proof might be completing the same task on schedule 99 percent of the time.

Too many proposal writers, concerned about poor past performance, offer no support of their claims. Cite the following as proof of performance:

- Bonuses or awards paid
- Complimentary customer statements, letters, or client newsletter excerpts
- Performance ratings
- Exceptional aspects or quantifiable benefits

3

See Graphics *and* Photographs.

Emphasize experience and performance graphically.

Graphics draw evaluators' attention and persuade emotionally as well as logically. Seeing a photograph of a task being performed adds credibility.

Visualize and emphasize the benefit whenever possible over raw data. A table of Mean Time Between Failures (MTBF) data is not nearly as interesting or as emotionally charged as seeing people enjoying the service.

Consider combining the graphic and the data. Cover either half of figure 1 to see the difference.

#	Accepted	Refused	Percent
23	22	1	95.6
25	25	0	100.0
⋮	⋮	⋮	⋮
500	*495*	*5*	*98.0*

World-Wide Acceptance. *With acceptance in 234 countries, our SmarT™ Card makes your travel more convenient and safe. Independent surveys show a 98 percent acceptance rate.*

Figure 1. Visualize Benefits Over Features. *While many writers can build tables, numbers presented on their own are not as effective as a visual alone or a visual with the numbers. Note the difference by covering either half of figure 1.*

4

Examples cited to support the seller's claims are often referred to as "success stories." Look for relevant success stories in your organization's marketing materials, news releases, employee newsletters, and web pages.

See Action Captions.

Use a *success story* template to tell a consistent, complete story.

Templates help proposal writers support claims consistently and credibly. Follow the steps listed below and illustrated in figure 2:

1. Select and insert a graphic. The graphic does not have to prove the claim. Rather it enhances credibility and commands attention.

2. Indicate the customer's need.

3. Indicate the basis or reason for selecting your organization.

4. Indicate the solution you delivered and the resulting benefit, quantified when possible.

Early Completion Earns $200,000 Award Bonus. *Global Manufacturing needed to complete a critical plant expansion on a fast-track basis under difficult winter conditions. After a careful evaluation of six design-build contractors, Global awarded the contract to Shipley Constructors. We completed the expansion 23 days ahead of schedule, on budget, and earned a $200,000 bonus.*

Figure 2. Use Graphics to Support Claims. *Write your caption in a customer-focused style. Include the customer need, the reason you were selected, and the result. Make the caption long enough to tell the complete story.*

5

See PROPOSAL STRATEGY.

Address all weaknesses known or potentially known by the customer.

If you lack directly relevant experience, break the proposed tasks into subtasks, each of which you have done.

A company with no PC manufacturing experience might emphasize its ability to design similar electronic components, source standard subassemblies and components, test their design, and assemble components reliably.

A laboratory researching a cure for cancer might emphasize its ability to review existing literature, attract experienced cancer researchers, conduct specific tests, and produce clear reports.

If performance was not as good as you would like, develop a risk mitigation and avoidance strategy:

- Cite the lessons learned.
- Cite the changes you have already made in your approach, and emphasize the positive results attained, if any.

- Cite your decision to team with another organization or hire a proven individual with a record of performance in the area.

Never over apologize. Admit the facts and move on. Relevant experience and performance relate to the customer's risk, so emphasize the benefits of lower risk.

A common way to emphasize either the experience of individuals or the task experience of your organization is with a *meatball chart* like the one in figure 3.

Another method is to develop a matrix that relates the tasks anticipated, relevant experience, technologies required, potential problems, and your proposed solution. Shown in figure 4, this type of graphic is a powerful way to demonstrate your technical understanding.

List the tasks required on one axis. On the other axis, list either the experience, technologies, regulations, organizations, or licenses that are needed to perform the tasks requested.

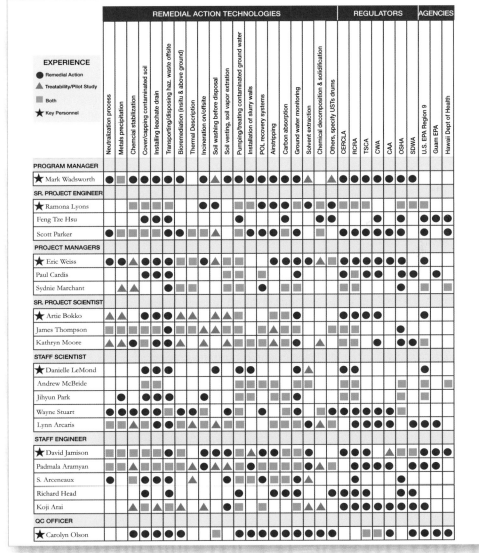

Figure 3. Use Meatball Charts to Emphasize Experience. *While often complex, the complexity supports the message that, "We have ample experience and capability." Use smaller versions to support discussions of an individual's experience.*

While violating recommendations to keep graphics simple and uncluttered, casual readers are impressed that everything seems to be covered. Detailed readers like these charts because they reduce the time needed to review and summarize resumes, relevant experience, and past performance charts.

TASKS ANTICIPATED	TEAM EXPERIENCE EXAMPLES	REMEDIAL TECHNOLOGIES APPLIED	PROBLEM AREAS	RESOLUTION COST SCHEDULE IMPACT
Leaking fuel tanks and pipelines	Confidential Client (#14)	• Ex situ bioremediation • Tank demolition	• Site characterization underestimated amount of contaminated soil by factor of 4 • Limited space for bioremediation	• Bioremediation in sequential lifts allowed original scheudle to be met • Used remediated soil for backfill. (Over 2 million yd)
	Mystic River Petroleum Storage Area (#33)	• Groundwater treatment • Soil venting • Covering/capping of contaminated soils	• POL recovery • POL contaminated soil • PCB contaminated soil • Metal contaminated soil • UST removal	• Removed 9,000 gals. liquid hazardous waste • Met budget and schedule • Closed six USTs • Closed RCRA disposal facility • Removed over 3,600 chemical drums
Lined and unlined landfills	Moab Superfund Site (#22)	• Groundwater monitoring • Soil vapor extraction • Pump and treat	• Unlined quarry used as hazardous waste disposal site • Groundwater contamination under residential area	• Groundwater monitoring • Soil vapor extraction • Pump and treat
	Red Sands Superfund Site (#29)	• Neutralization • Chemical stabilization • Cap & cover • Leachate drains • Incineration • Groundwater monitoring: pump & treat • Carbon absorption	• Acidic tarry waste in floodplain • Benzene emissions	• Solidified material, placed in new landfill out of floodplain • Reduced cost by more than 50 percent over incineration alternative

Relevant Experience Reduces Risk. *The ECO Team's experience is directly relevant to environmental issues in your bid request, significantly reducing performance risk.*

Figure 4. Use Matrices to Relate Experience to Technical Understanding. *When examples of experience must be placed in another section, matrices like this one tie relevant experience directly to your technical discussion in the body of the proposal. Even if evaluators do not check each one, they get the strong impression that you have relevant experience.*

Emphasize lessons learned personally over lessons learned from others.

Too many incumbents with performance problems fail to understand and present their lessons learned as strongly as they could. Reading how to juggle does not make a person a juggler.

Reading studies about how and why a component failed or a service was inadequate is inferior to having done the study. Some items or facts, often intangible, are omitted from published studies.

The following example illustrates how an incumbent used direct, personal experience to win a 5-year contract renewal:

A company that operated a government facility under contract for three consecutive, 5-year terms was competing for another 5-year renewal. To avoid the appearance of favoritism, the government intentionally limited the size of the solicited proposals to negate the incumbent's advantage.

The incumbent's overall strategy was to stress the complexity of the tasks it performed to frighten the evaluators from changing contractors. The proposal strategy was to present the proposed tasks and lessons learned in a series of detailed tables, charts, diagrams, and lists to emphasize the complexity of those tasks.

The incumbent won. A comment in the debrief was, "We did not realize that the support you provided was so complex."

Resumes in a proposal are critical to selling what is often your most important discriminator—the individuals you propose.

See ORGANIZATION.

Resumes, like other documents, should be organized according to the readers' needs. However, resumes are evaluated differently when individuals are being hired versus when teams are being hired for a proposal.

People filling individual positions screen resumes to eliminate unsuitable applicants before reading in depth to determine who to invite for interviews. Individuals' resumes usually begin with an employment objective, then present a logical progression in their experience, skills, and training.

Evaluators who screen resumes in proposals face a more complicated task; multiple positions and tasks are involved and the subsequent personal interviews, if any, are limited. Proposal resume evaluators are trying to assess four aspects of each team:

1. Understanding of the customer's needs
2. Degree of commitment
3. Match between position requirements and the individuals proposed
4. Team coverage of all requirements

Sellers lose when they only demonstrate adequate resources. Resumes in best-in-class proposals address all four aspects:

1. Clearly define the requirements of each key position
2. Name and commit individuals for all key positions
3. Include tailored resumes to precisely match position requirements and individuals' specific experience
4. Use matrices to demonstrate all requirements are covered

Resumes

1. Always name the individuals recommended in your proposal.
2. Tailor the resumes for key positions in every proposal.
3. Identify who will be proposed and prepare their resumes before the heavy writing and production effort begin.
4. Arrange your tailored resumes in a functional requirement and/or accomplishment format.
5. Include abbreviated or summary resumes of individuals proposed for key positions in the body of your proposal.
6. Assemble a resume database that is searchable, current, and easily tailored.
7. Keep resumes brief, clear, and error free.
8. Use capability and skill matrices to emphasize the total capabilities of large teams.
9. Avoid adding photos of the people proposed unless it supports your strategy.

---

1 Always name the individuals recommended in your proposal.

If you want to win, overcome resistance to naming people in your proposal. A clear, best practice when selling services is to name specific individuals who will do the work.

Resistance to using specific names is usually because the bidding organization cannot be certain that the individuals recommended in the proposal will be available when the project is awarded.

Do your best to be realistic. Do not intentionally propose a *bait and switch,* proposing one person when you plan to use a different person. In the long run, you lose your credibility. If you fear a competitor might propose its most experienced people with no intention of using them, ghost them as shown in the following examples:

We could follow common practice and propose using only our most experienced people to provide this service. Instead, we have done our best to identify and propose the most experienced people we expect to be available at the anticipated start date. Should any individual proposed not be available, we will give you the right to review and approve all changes.

If you doubt the importance of naming individuals, consider how some service bid requests read:

Indicate by name the individuals who will provide services. Indicate whether they will serve a primary or secondary role. All individuals with primary roles must be full time. For individuals with secondary roles, indicate the percentage of their time already committed to other projects, name those projects, and indicate the percentage of time that will be available for this project.

2 Tailor the resumes for key positions in every proposal.

If you do not have time to tailor the resume for key positions, you should not be bidding. Tailor each resume to emphasize the fit between the requirements of the position and the experience of the individual proposed.

Clearly identify key positions. In one debrief, a losing bidder was told:

Your failure to recognize the Software Development Manager as a key position indicated your lack of understanding of the requirements.

Your identification and justification of the key positions should be part of your strategy and solution.

3 Identify who will be proposed and prepare their resumes before the heavy writing and production effort begin.

Teams that wait to name individuals for key positions until the end run out of time to tailor resumes. Force an early decision and get the resumes tailored.

If necessary, tailor the resumes of several individuals for the same position. Then insert the correct one at the end.

4 Arrange your tailored resumes in a functional requirement and/or accomplishment format.

Resumes are usually ordered in one of the following ways:

- Reverse chronology
- Functional requirement
- Accomplishment
- Narrative

The reverse-chronology resume lists experience and education from latest to earliest.

The functional-requirement resume organizes work experience by job function, disregarding chronology.

The accomplishment resume features positive achievements and emphasizes results over chronology.

The narrative resume is written in first or second person, telling a story about the person, presenting data in complete sentences.

Functional and accomplishment resumes are best for proposals. Evaluators try to minimize risk, hence their concern that the bidder understands the requirements of the position, and the named individual has performed the same task well in the past.

The easiest proposal resumes to evaluate are the ones that directly match the functional position requirements to the accomplishments, like the one shown in figure 1. Resumes like this can be quite compact, permitting two or three to be placed on a single page. Develop this type of resume in the following manner:

1. List the name of the person and the position you are proposing them to fill at the top.
2. Develop a list of the primary functional requirements of the position. List them on the left side, most important ones first.
3. Directly adjacent, list where the person has performed the same duties, stating their accomplishments or results achieved.
4. List the years they performed the job, if appropriate, making it easy to total their years of similar experience.
5. List any other relevant data about the person in the column to the right.

The width of the columns can vary, depending on the amount of information required. This type of resume can be rapidly assembled from standard, searchable resumes kept in a resume database.

Name, Position

RESPONSIBILITIES	YEARS	RELEVANT EXPERIENCE	PROFESSIONAL
• Major responsibility	3	Describe what they accomplished.	List degrees, additional training, licenses, patents, certifications, professional associations, awards, etc. List the most important ones first, as space permits.
	2	Describe what they accomplished.	
• Major responsibility	1	Describe what they accomplished.	
	2	Describe what they accomplished.	
• Major responsibility	3	Describe what they accomplished.	
	4	Describe what they accomplished.	
	15	Years	

Figure 1. Develop a Functional Requirement /Accomplishment Resume Template for Your Proposals. *This design visually emphasizes the direct relationship between responsibilities and relevant experience.*

5 Include abbreviated or summary resumes of individuals proposed for key positions in the body of your proposal.

Abbreviated resumes inserted in the body text are an easy way to answer the questions in the bid request and to make evaluation easy.

Examples are shown in figure 2, with a slightly different design.

COSMOS PROGRAM

Manager Requirements

- Licensed Professional Engineer
- 6 years experience with space imaging projects
- 4 years experience as senior project engineer

Aye C. Klearly

Qualifications

- Professional Mechanical Engineer, B.S. Mechanical Engineering
- Business Management Certificate
- 8 years experience with NASA projects
- 13 years as a project manager; 8 years as a senior project engineer

COSMOS PROGRAM

Superintendent Requirements

- 5 years construction management experience
- 1 year of experience on NASA construction projects

Izzy D. Bosse

Qualifications

- 18 years construction management, including 5 years on Mt. Olympus observatory update
- 4 years managing NASA construction projects

Figure 2. Insert Summary Resumes Within Body Text. *The two examples, designed for a balanced, two-column proposal page design, directly match the requirements. Position requirements are either established in the bid request or by the proposing organization as it develops its management approach.*

6 Assemble a resume database that is searchable, current, and easily tailored.

Develop a standard, searchable resume database. Numerous database software products are available.

Consider some of the proposal preparation software products. While many of these products are of questionable value for preparing customer-focused proposals, some offer excellent ways to retrieve and match position requirements to personnel capabilities using internet-like search engines.

Assign a person to regularly update resumes, not just to build the initial set. Many organizations routinely insert long resumes that are more than 5 years old and contain obviously irrelevant information.

Place an expiration date on each resume, just like your boilerplate. Automatically flag expired resumes for updates at set intervals. If no update is received within 3 months, then remove the resume from your database.

7 Keep resumes brief, clear, and error free.

All of the resumes included in your proposal must meet the clear and brief criteria. Keeping them error free is critical when evaluators are looking for reasons to eliminate bidders. Mistakes imply poor quality and are valid grounds for elimination.

Do not expect to hear poor quality cited as a reason for elimination in debriefs, but it is cited in private.

Some bid requests include forms that must be completed for named positions. However, the forms are often poorly designed, difficult to read, and waste space.

When faced with a typed, lined form, recreate the form in the exact order given, as shown in figure 3. Group the information and summarize it to make the resume easier to read. While some might consider this risky, evaluators have given positive feedback to this effort. Seek the customer's approval if possible.

Place the following note at the beginning of the resume section:

All the following resumes are arranged in the order requested and contain all information in the order requested on the forms in your bid request. To make them easier to read, we have reentered them to facilitate your evaluation and to maintain a consistent appearance.

Bid request excerpt:

All personnel proposed for key positions must meet the following minimum requirements:

- Project Manager—Two years of management experience and 5 years of applications development

- Application Development, Lead Programmer/Analyst—5 years of programming experience

- Common Code Development— . . . (text omitted)

For each position, also complete the Resume Data Forms.

Resume Data Form

Position _____   Name _____

Education _____

_____

Hardware _____

Software _____

Experience _____

_____

PROJECT MANAGER

Noah Lott

Education	Hardware	Experience	
M.S. Computer Science, University of Iowa, 1987	IBM 3400 & 370, Digital Alpha servers, Cisco Systems routers, PC and Apple networks	**Years**	**Assignment**
MBA, UCLA, 1992		1	Managed major application development project for IS under a contract awarded by General Motors. Supervised a team that grew from 5 to 30 professionals during 3 months. Completed project 2 weeks ahead of schedule and within budget.
		1	Project leader for Y2K update for major petrochemical producer. Tested, re-coded, debugged, and replaced major legacy systems. Supervised a team of 12. Project completed on schedule. Achieved a 20 percent annual cost reduction and experienced no Y2K service interruptions.
	Software	**2**	**Total Management Experience**
	OS/MVS, DOS/VSE, VM/CMS, ISPF, COBAL, C++, NOVELL, DR DOS, MAC OS 8 through OS X, Microsoft Windows DOS through Windows 7	4	Developed numerous utilities programs for a major consulting engineering company. Applications included security, CAD/CAM, general ledger reporting, estimating, and project management. Based on the savings generated, the client awarded two one-year contract extensions for additional work.
		3	Developed applications software for the US Census Bureau to operate on IBM 370 series computers. Involved structuring, storage, and retrieval of large data bases.
		1	Developed and maintained home delivery contract and data collection systems for large publishing company on Windows NT network.
		8	**Total Years of Applications Development**

Figure 3. Design Resumes that Do Not Have to be Read. *Given the bid request requirements, evaluators can easily see if the person meets their requirements without having to read the resume. Many evaluators check a few, then accept the rest as accurate.*

8   Use capability and skill matrices to emphasize the total capabilities of large teams.

See Graphics.

Reviewing resumes has to be one of the dullest tasks for an evaluator. Simplify this review by offering capability and skill matrices like the one shown in figure 4.

The graphic works on two levels, although it violates the guideline to keep graphics simple and uncluttered. For the senior evaluator, the graphic gives the impression that the requirements for people with a wide range of skills are both covered and backed up.

For the detailed resume evaluator, the matrix offers a way to summarize capabilities, yet perhaps not read all the resumes. The detailed evaluator will likely check a few for accuracy, then accept the matrix as accurate. Make sure that it is accurate.

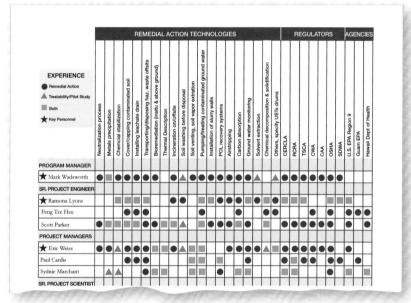

Figure 4. Use Capability and Skill Matrices to Emphasize Your Total Team's Capability.
List the positions and people on one axis and some combination of their skills and experience on the other axis. The example uses shapes to differentiate the types of experience and the role of each individual. While complex, it does serve both senior evaluators and detailed evaluators.

9   Avoid adding photos of the people proposed unless it supports your strategy.

See Photographs.

In general, more things can go wrong when inserting photos with resumes than can go right:

- Is the photo current? Outdated photos get the same reaction from evaluators as you have when looking at old school yearbooks.
- Do all the photos look alike? Dissimilar appearance, backgrounds, dress, or lighting detract from your claims of having an integrated team.
- Are you positive that all evaluators are free of prejudice? Appearance has no bearing on a person's ability to perform. What if someone objects to a person's gender, age, youth, race, hair color, hair length, facial hair, height, or weight?

- Do you have the time to take photos? Are the people available? Do you have the systems to incorporate and print quality photos?

Use photos if they support your strategy. For example, if the customer organization knows and likes the people proposed, the photo reinforces that relationship. If you have been building the relationship between the people proposed and the customer during the capture process, use photos.

The most effective use of photos in a proposal is to emphasize teaming experience with group photos and to emphasize applications experience with site photos.

Risk Management is the seller's strategy for managing or containing the risks inherent in a proposed approach or offer. The underlying assumptions are that every offer entails risk and that risk can be contained or reduced with appropriate management.

Some sellers prefer to avoid any discussion of risk. They correctly see risk as negative but incorrectly avoid discussing risk because it is a negative topic.

Customers know every offer entails risk; the best practice is to explicitly discuss how the risk in your offer will be managed. Government buyers of complicated systems are well aware of risk and require risk management plans in proposals. As a result, risk management practices, including formal discussions of risk in proposals, are more advanced in government market sectors than the nongovernment sectors.

Risk is normally associated with cost and schedule, but risk permeates every aspect of a program, including program management, technical performance, quality, service support, and security. Proposal teams often struggle to demonstrate that their solution offers the least risk. However, most customers recognize that superior value justifies increased risk. The key is to understand what degree of risk is acceptable to each customer.

Company risks are internal concerns or gaps and are not relevant unless they affect proposal or performance risk.

Risk Management

1. Recognize all aspects of risk.

2. Develop a risk management strategy.

3. Consider placing a risk management paragraph in your executive summary.

4. Analyze and discuss risk and risk management similarly in each proposal section.

5. Reduce risk premiums by explicitly costing anticipated risk management actions.

---

1   Recognize all aspects of risk.

Evaluators normally focus on risk in two evaluation criteria items: proposal risk and performance risk.

Proposal risk is the risk associated with a seller's proposed approach to meeting the bid request requirements. Proposal risk includes both your technical and management approach.

Performance risk involves evaluating the seller's ability to perform based on relevant present and past performance. Evaluators consider the data included in your proposal and data gathered independently. Evaluators assess several factors:

1. Is the experience you cite relevant?
2. What was the result?
3. What did you learn that reduces risk on this contract?

Risk is not limited to the prime contractor. Performance evaluations include all proposed members of your team, including partners, other corporate divisions, subcontractors, and vendors.

In the U.S., the Office of Federal Procurement Policy (OFPP) has increasingly emphasized performance risk. Other sophisticated buyers are doing the same.

Buyers realize that minor savings in the purchase price are often lost when they select a higher risk contractor. To better identify positive or negative patterns in contractors' performance records, OFPP has taken several initiatives to standardize the evaluation of performance risk:

1. Evaluate corporate performance rather than just experience. (What if the result of the experience was poor?)
2. Check references of past customers.
3. Develop standard questionnaires to improve both quality and comparability.
4. Encourage contractors to complete customer satisfaction surveys every 6 months.

Seeing what sophisticated buyers are evaluating begins to suggest what should be in your proposal.

2

Develop a risk management strategy.

Assume customers will learn about your past performance, either on their own or through your competitors. Most customers develop a good information network within their industry.

Developing a risk management strategy is a key part of your overall strategy development. Use the same strategic approach:

1. Emphasize your strengths.
2. Mitigate your weaknesses.
3. Neutralize your competitors' strengths.
4. Highlight your competitors' weaknesses.

And do all this without mentioning your competitors by name.

Risks are both managed and mitigated, but rarely eliminated.

See PROPOSAL STRATEGY.

Where you have demonstrated strong performance, tell the customer why you are the low risk choice. Include testimonials, quotations from performance reviews, award fee ratings, published data, and data that you have collected to support your claims. What others say about you is more credible than what you say about yourself.

Where your performance was weak, emphasize what you learned and what changes you have made. If you try to hide your weaknesses, customers assume nothing has changed.

Neutralize competitors' strengths by discussing the lessons learned from studying industry best practices or by hiring people with similar performance experience.

Highlight competitors' weaknesses by citing trade-off analyses of different approaches. Or cite your early failures or known industry failures, then contrast them with your recent successful performance.

3

Consider placing a risk management paragraph in your executive summary.

Risk is often a discriminator and can be an effective way to ghost competitors. Decision makers and senior influencers are more likely to worry about risk, what could go wrong, than about relatively minor price or technical differences.

Identify the top two or three areas of greatest risk, then briefly discuss your risk management approach in the executive summary. If competitors do not discuss risk, evaluators may assume they do not understand the problem. Your discussion must be credible and real, or it could backfire.

See EXECUTIVE SUMMARY.

Discuss risk management in one or two short paragraphs as shown in the following example:

> Software development projects have been notoriously difficult to estimate correctly and to deliver on schedule. Acme Software has developed sophisticated and detailed metrics from all of our software development projects since 1989, enabling us to significantly reduce performance risk. Our specific management approach is discussed in detail in the section 3.2 Software Project Management.

Another best practice is to support your risk management with a chart similar to the example in figure 1.

Risk Area	Risk Assessment	Impact With Our Proposed Management Approach	Summary Of Our Approach	Discussed In Proposal Section
Key personnel not available	Medium	Low	All positions filled & backups identified	4.5
Limited construction area on site	High	Low	Use modular design, construct modules offsite, then assemble on site	2.3

Figure 2-3. Major Risks Mitigated. *The two biggest risks to on-time completion have been addressed in our risk management plan.*

Figure 1. Place a Risk Management Matrix in the Executive Summary. *Consider supporting a short risk management discussion with a matrix that summarizes the major risks and assesses the risk both with and without your mitigation approach. If space permits, add columns like the two on the right that summarize your approach and indicate where your approach is discussed in the proposal.*

4

See ORGANIZATION and THEME STATEMENTS.

Analyze and discuss risk and risk management similarly in each proposal section.

Top-level discussions of risk must be supported where relevant in each proposal section. Evaluators look for an established, proven risk management process to identify, assess, track, and manage/mitigate risk.

Increase the credibility of risk discussions and cut writing time by following a consistent process to both analyze risk and draft your response.

Risk Analysis Procedure

1. Identify all risk areas.
2. Assess the risks (low, moderate, or high), on a defined scale.
3. Prioritize each risk according to its potential impact on the solution, schedule, or cost.
4. Determine and analyze the causes, not the symptoms, of the risks.
5. Develop alternative, backup, or parallel procedures to track, manage, reduce, or eliminate the risks.
6. Assess the modified risk with your proposed risk management approach, considering how the changes could impact other aspects of your solution.

Draft your risk management story in a similar style in each major proposal section.

Writing Procedure

1. Introduce each risk management section with a theme statement, a section summary, and a preview or introduction.
2. Consider including a more detailed form of the risk management matrix illustrated in figure 1.
3. Identify and define all relevant risks. Be complete and honest but not alarmist.
4. Follow each defined risk with an explanation of how the risk will be managed. Cite clear decision points tied to your proposed alternative, backup, or parallel approach. Demonstrate your ability to manage this risk by citing experience, independent research, or trade studies.

5

Reduce risk premiums by explicitly costing anticipated risk management actions.

Senior managers often add risk premiums as a percentage of total cost or price. However, such premiums are based on historical perspectives that may have little to do with risks associated with a specific offer.

Most people contributing to cost estimates have compelling incentives to add risk premiums but few reasons to reduce them. So layer upon layer of premiums accumulate during estimating and reviewing processes with little or no documentation or acknowledgement:

- Estimators add "cushions" for unknown factors.
- Supervisors inflate estimates to cover mistakes and rework.
- Department heads elevate the base, because they are rewarded for delivering under estimates and penalized for exceeding them.

By the time a total cost estimate reaches senior management for approval, the risk premium already incorporated is poorly understood and usually already too high. But with their fiduciary responsibilities to owners, senior managers find it all too easy to tack on a little more. Sales professionals are the

only group with a sales-commission incentive that strongly motivates them to minimize risk premiums, minimize the bid price, and maximize win probability.

Counter the tendency to overprice risk. Extend the risk management approach outlined in figure 1 by explicitly costing planned risk mitigation/recovery activities:

1. Develop a *risk register*, a tabular listing of potential risks.
2. Estimate the probability of occurrence for every risk.
3. Describe your risk mitigation/recovery tasks for each listed risk.
4. Cost each risk mitigation/recovery task.
5. Multiply each cost by the applicable probability and sum the total.
6. Disclose your analysis and risk premium in your proposal.

Most bidders who explicitly cost risk find their management-approved premiums significantly lower than when based on a percentage of bid cost or price. Thorough documentation of premiums in a proposal will also bolster credibility with the customer and simplify contract negotiations.

Scheduling your proposal is essential to visualize the task ahead and monitor progress. Even a one-person, single-day proposal benefits from having a schedule.

Common scheduling principles apply equally to proposals. Preparing a realistic schedule requires a clear understanding of each task and the capability of the individuals assigned. The task of developing a schedule clarifies your understanding of the proposal preparation project.

The complexity of the schedule depends on the size of the proposal and the number, expertise, and location of contributors.

One of the most common mistakes in proposal management is poor scheduling. Tasks originally regarded as optional become mandatory. The time lost to nonproposal preparation activities at the beginning and end leaves surprisingly little time for writing.

See COLOR TEAM REVIEWS, *Capture Guide.*

Something goes wrong on every proposal. Expect and prepare to cope with changes. The following broad guidelines will improve your overall scheduling effectiveness:

1. Consider the total time available, then deduct 10 percent for a reserve to handle unanticipated tasks and problems. Then schedule proposal activities in the remaining 90 percent of the available time.

2. Build a list of events that have to be scheduled. A generic list of potential proposal preparation tasks is given in figure 1. Schedule the major events first, then add the finer details or granularity later.

3. Complete the major milestone schedule prior to the kickoff meeting.

4. After the kickoff meeting, build an *inch-stone* schedule, planning events to the day and hour (see guideline 6).

Scheduling

1. Develop a proposal schedule backwards from the drop-dead date.

2. Schedule a proposal as you would any other project, using the same scheduling tools.

3. Minimize sequential tasks. Maximize parallel tasks.

4. Realistically estimate the time required for specific tasks based on your own standards.

5. Assign a person to each task with start-and-end dates. Avoid assigning people indefinitely to the proposal.

6. Divide major tasks into smaller, discrete tasks.

7. Avoid scheduling weekends and holidays.

8. Know and plan proposal production time.

9. Schedule time for all planned reviews, allowing time to implement valid recommendations.

10. Lock down the project scope early to enable contributors to work efficiently in parallel.

11. Schedule the time to prepare the essentials of the Proposal Management Plan (requirements checklist, outline, strategy, response matrix, and style sheet).

12. Maintain a continuous focus on meeting every schedule date.

1 Develop a proposal schedule backwards from the drop-dead date.

Begin at the drop-dead or due date because late proposals are usually eliminated.

Schedule time to deliver the proposal. Electronic delivery may be faster but can increase production time.

Then consider print time and electronic check time. Outside printing often takes longer than in-house because printers try to keep their facilities producing at capacity. Your job deadline may be affected by the printing vendor's entire workload. Schedule time for a page-turn after printing to check each copy. Verify that every file in your submission opens and displays correctly.

Consider time for the final senior management buy-off, perhaps a final Gold Team. Then schedule time to prepare for the Gold Team.

When you begin to lose perspective, examine the proposal events or tasks from the beginning. How much time was lost getting the bid request to the proposal manager? In a 28-day schedule, time lost at the beginning waiting for the bid request and at the end for reviewing and production leaves perhaps 14 days to actually develop the proposal.

Activity	Start Date	End Date
Set budget and scope		
Receive approval to start		
Determine review cycles		
Develop baseline solution		
Draft Proposal Management Plan (PMP)		
Mock up executive summary		
Train proposal contributors		
Bid request release		
Receive bid request in-house		
Analyze bid request		
Prepare compliance matrix		
Update strategy & PMP		
Review solution, strategy, and PMP		
Prepare & conduct kickoff meeting		
Freeze design		
Initiate detailed costing		
Develop storyboards		
Pink Team review (of storyboards)		
Create first draft		
Final graphics cutoff		
Receive & review costs		
Prepare & conduct Red Team		
Revise draft		
Finalize costs		
Final review of draft		
Final executive summary to production		
Final text revisions & editing		
Desktop publishing		
Gold Team		
Final production & assembly		
Page turn		
Packaging		
Delivery time		
Due date		

Figure 1. Prepare the Proposal Schedule Backwards. *Add or delete items as appropriate, then develop your proposal schedule backwards from the delivery date. Tasks are listed in an approximate chronological order. Start dates and end dates will overlap with parallel task scheduling.*

---

2 Schedule a proposal as you would any other project, using the same scheduling tools.

Simple timeline charts are adequate for simple proposals. Full critical path software tools are more appropriate for complex proposals.

Using the scheduling software tool that you know is often more constructive than trying to select the best package.

---

3 Minimize sequential tasks. Maximize parallel tasks.

Clear task descriptions, quality standards, and start-and-end dates enable contributors to work in parallel without conflicts. Fast-track construction managers plan parallel tasks to radically shorten total construction time. Do the same on your proposal.

If you hear contributors saying that they are waiting on someone else to finish his or her task before they start, you have sequential tasks and are probably in trouble.

---

4 Realistically estimate the time required for specific tasks based on your own standards.

Too few organizations have developed time standards or metrics for specific proposal tasks. They simply do what they can in the time available.

However, many organizations have been estimating document production time for years. Begin by adopting similar standards for similar proposal development tasks until you develop your own standards.

Meaningful productivity standards must be accompanied by complexity and quality standards. Standards are most useful to show trends in your organization and much less useful to compare different organizations.

For example, bidders on complex, custom systems will have more design costs incorporated in their proposal writing standards than bidders of relatively similar

See PRODUCTION.

Citing reliable, meaningful proposal preparation productivity standards across market sectors and organizations is mostly meaningless. Develop your own standards.

products and services. A one-page-per-day standard for proposal preparation in one organization may be more difficult to attain than an eight-page-per-day standard in another.

Extensive use of proposal boilerplate and search and retrieval software can radically increase the pages per day a writer can produce, but what is the effect on the quality and win rate? Without a clearly implemented strategy and a clearly organized document, you may simply be rearranging the deck chairs on the Titanic; you are still going to lose.

Figure 2 offers some metrics to estimate writing time per page depending on the availability, relevance, and quality of boilerplate available.

TASK	TIME
Writing: New material	4 pages/day
Writing: Extensive revision	8-10 pages/day
Writing: Minimal revision	20-25 pages/day
Simple graphic	1-2 hours each
Complex graphic	2-6 hours
Retouch photo	1-2 hours
Complex illustration	1+ days
Red Teaming (new)	40 pages/day
Red Teaming (with extensive boilerplate)	80 pages/day
DTP (clean input)	30-60 pages/day
DTP with graphics development	5-10 pages/day

Figure 2. Estimate Time Standards by Task. *Use these time standards as a start until you develop more appropriate standards for your organization. Requiring less time in your organization is not necessarily excellent performance nor is taking more time a sign of poor performance.*

5 Assign a person to each task with start-and-end dates. Avoid assigning people indefinitely to the proposal.

While once common, too many organizations continue to assign people to participate on proposal teams from the kickoff to submittal. Get them on the team; then get them off. While your scheduling is more detailed and complex, you will have fewer individuals to manage at any single time and will cut preparation costs.

Assign one person primary responsibility for each scheduled task, even if multiple people contribute. In some cases that person might not be the primary writer or content expert.

Consider the time to complete each task, determine the time available per day, then set the start-and-end dates. Pay for the task, not show-up time.

6 Divide major tasks into smaller, discrete tasks.

Assigning major tasks with relatively long completion times increases your risk. If the contributor stalls early, you find out too late to respond.

See DAILY TEAM MANAGEMENT.

Contrast the following two approaches to section writing assignments. Assume that the assignment is made on the first Monday, and the completed section is due on the second Friday.

Approach 1 *(General and poor)*

Take the bid request, identify and answer all of the implementation and management questions, and complete a responsive management section in 2 weeks. (Actual elapsed time is 10 days, excluding the weekend, or 12 days, including the weekend.)

Approach 2 *(Specific and recommended)*

You have 10 days to complete a reviewed and approved management section. Weekends are not scheduled. Each task is due at the date and time indicated on the following table.

Schedule due times rather than due dates to smooth work flow, as shown in figure 3. Setting due times conveys a more disciplined tone for proposal development tasks.

DAY	TIME	TASK
1	2 pm	Review bid request response requirements and complete section outline. Identify potential omitted or misaligned tasks and recommend appropriate reassignments.
2	9 am	Draft all section themes to follow first-and second-level headings. Write on transparencies and come prepared to review them with the team.
3+	time	(Additional tasks not listed here)
⋮	⋮	⋮
10	2 pm	Submit completed draft as both electronic file and hard copy, reviewed and approved by your volume manager.

Figure 3. Schedule Due Times for Tasks. *Smooth work flow by setting both due dates and due times for proposal development tasks.*

7 Avoid scheduling weekends and holidays.

You may have to work on weekends and holidays, but do not plan to. Contributors find it negative from the beginning and lose commitment to a winning effort. Many feel abused. Contributors feel that if management considers winning competitive new business important, they should assign additional resources.

When you do ask contributors to work weekends, management must be visible, both as a morale booster and to encourage continued commitment to quality work.

When contributors routinely work more than 10 hours per day and 6 days per week, productivity tends to drop to little better than what could be done in a 40-hour work week.

8 Know and plan proposal production time.

See PRODUCTION.

Production people tend to be the most routinely abused individuals on a proposal team. They inherit the consequences of all the scheduling and management mistakes. After they work extended days and weekends to complete a proposal on time, management tends to view that performance as standard.

Consider adding 50 percent to your production estimate to cope with potential time delays. Use any extra time to polish the proposal. Do a thorough page-turn to identify and correct small errors and improve overall production quality.

9 Schedule time for all planned reviews, allowing time to implement valid recommendations.

See COLOR TEAM REVIEWS, *Capture Guide.*

Delaying scheduled reviews results in the following common problems:

- Individuals completing their sections on time are delayed.
- Reviewers have conflicts, forcing a change of reviewer who has less time to prepare.
- Reviewers are rushed, reducing the quality of the review.

- You lose time to respond to reviewers' recommendations.

One reviewer can do a quality review on approximately 40 pages per day. If the proposal uses extensive boilerplate and has had previous reviews by the assigned and other evaluators, you can increase this to 80 pages per day but review quality will drop.

10 Lock down the project scope early to enable contributors to work efficiently in parallel.

The project schedule should be distributed at the kickoff meeting. Avoid schedule changes except those prompted by external events, such as changes in the bid request.

Major changes indicate poor management. Frequent minor changes, 99 percent of them

delays, suggest a lack of discipline or that proposal managers are not honest with their teams. Contributors begin to expect delays and are less disciplined about completing tasks on time.

11 Schedule the time to prepare the essentials of the Proposal Management Plan (requirements checklist, outline, strategy, response matrix, and style sheet).

See PROPOSAL MANAGEMENT PLAN.

Pressure from management or impending deadlines prompts proposal managers to schedule kickoff meetings before the essential elements of the PMP are complete. Contributors then commence work that is loosely defined, requiring more extensive revisions or even starting over.

Avoid rework by doing things right the first time. Clearly define each task assignment, including clear quality standards. Contributors seldom meet a proposal manager's expectations when they do not understand their tasks.

While planning seems to delay initial work, planning actually saves more time than it takes.

12 Maintain a continuous focus on meeting every schedule date.

See DAILY TEAM MANAGEMENT.

Hold a daily stand-up meeting to keep contributors focused on meeting every schedule date. Remind them what must be accomplished and the impact of slipped dates.

Planning smaller tasks also helps maintain schedule focus. Improve schedule focus by using one of the following approaches:

- Send short, concise, daily e-mails or text messages to each contributor, especially if the team is dispersed.

- Post an enlarged schedule on the proposal room wall. Contributors see it daily. Refer to the schedule in every morning stand-up.

Some proposal managers schedule two stand-up meetings each working day. They quickly review progress and expectations for the day in a morning meeting. They use a mid- to late-afternoon meeting to review inch-stone progress and unresolved issues.

Service Proposals

Service Proposals and product proposals are more alike than many proposal managers and writers think, especially when used in complex sales. In complex sales, winners are selected based on the benefits that buyers believe will be delivered. Few buyers select systems, services, or products based on appearance.

Certainly products are tangible and services are intangible. However, thinking products are easier to sell than services, reflects an immature or incomplete view of the sales process.

Successful sellers of both products and services help their customers build a vivid vision of how customers' processes will improve after selecting their solution.

While customers may feel more comfortable paying for a physical product than an intangible service, the product only promises to deliver something that is intangible, just like the service.

Customers have the difficult task of selecting services without knowing the quality of the services to be delivered, so they rely on indicators:

- Experience with the seller
- Promptness, clarity, and courtesy of responses to inquiries
- Relationship with the sales team
- Quality of presentations and demonstrations made
- Relevant experience and performance of the selling organization and the individuals proposed
- Customer testimonials
- Quality of the proposal submitted
- Price, whether high or low

Your success with these indicators will help demonstrate your understanding of the services needed.

Service Proposals

1. Create a vision for the customer of what life will be like after you deliver your solution.

2. Visualize your solution with graphics and good writing.

3. Discriminate services using people.

4. Discriminate services with clear descriptions of what will be done.

5. Present service processes graphically.

6. Exploit or attack incumbency, as relevant.

7. Cut costs, not margins.

---

1 Create a vision for the customer of what life will be like after you deliver your solution.

Every sale of a service or product impacts the buyer's processes:

- Reduces operating or capital cost
- Improves quality
- Improves service level
- Reduces cycle time
- Improves profitability

The vision you create for your customer must cover three areas:

1. What and how services and products will be delivered

2. How people and processes in the customer's organization will be impacted

3. How individuals and the customer's organization will benefit, both tangibly and intangibly

---

2 Visualize your solution with graphics and good writing.

See GRAPHICS *and* PHOTOGRAPHS.

Both graphics and text are essential for visualizing your solution and making it memorable.

Consider how images are used in advertising to indicate customer satisfaction. Advertisers present images of happy people using the product or experiencing or recalling the service to convey feelings of satisfaction.

Novelists use words to evoke such vivid personal images of events, places, and emotions that many people are disappointed when they

see the movie. Or recall how people viewing images of an event often remark, "You had to be there."

To improve your proposals, consider the following methods to convey a service or product vision in each of the three areas listed under guideline 1:

1. What and how services and products will be delivered

   - Use graphics such as sequential sketches, photos, or icons with short subcaptions.

- Use text to present lists of sequential tasks or actions that will be taken.

1. How people and processes in the customer's organization will be impacted
   - Use graphics such as sequential sketches or photos to show what their employees will do or see.
   - Use screen prints of the images operators will see on their operations console.
   - Use photos of other customers using the same products or experiencing the same or similar services.
   - Use text to describe the impact of a product or service, as in the following emotional proposal excerpt for a cancer detection device:

   Imagine, doctors operating on a patient can point a RxT laser at live tissue, analyze the reflected light through a spectroscope and PC, and immediately determine if the tissue is malignant or benign. Further imagine that this can be real within 16 months if you fund this program.

   The following example was used to sell a design contract:

   A proposal for a traffic management system for a major northern European city used 2-1/2 pages to describe how the system would cope with a typical winter morning commute. The scenario described minute-by-minute how traffic was rerouted to cope with snowfall, accidents, and temporary tie-ups.

2. How individuals and the customer's organization will benefit, both tangibly and intangibly
   - Use graphics such as individuals appearing relaxed, happy, satisfied, and more energetic, whether using the product or experiencing the service.
   - Combine before-and-after images. An architectural firm took photos of a proposed site, then superimposed images of the proposed or a similar facility.
   - Use familiar icons such as images of stacks of coins, bills, or gold bars to represent monetary benefits or smaller trash bins or fewer trash bins to represent reduced waste.
   - Use text to help evaluators visualize the impact of not having an item or service, like the cancer detection device discussed earlier in item 2:

   Imagine the consequences when a surgeon removes too little tissue. Further imagine the impact when a surgeon removes too much tissue.

   Contrast real-time cancer detection with the alternative biopsy method. Doctors send patients through recovery while waiting for test results. Patients and their loved ones are subjected to a painful, higher-risk, and anxiety-filled recovery, perhaps followed by further surgery.

---

3 Discriminate services using people.

People are potentially the most powerful discriminator when selling services. To be a discriminator, two conditions must be met:

1. The feature cited must be unique; clearly, no two people's abilities are identical.
2. The customer must care about the uniqueness of the person or people, a condition often created during the sales process.

See Discriminators *and* Resumes.

Use the following methods to discriminate your people:

- Name the people you propose to fill key positions. Correctly identifying which positions are key also demonstrates your understanding of the tasks required.
- Consider naming the people proposed for additional positions.
- Indicate the percentage of their time to be devoted to this project and the percentage of time already committed to other projects.

- Introduce the key people to the customer organization's influencers and decision maker during the capture process, prior to submitting your proposal.
- Consider ghosting typical bait-and-switch tactics to emphasize your honest, realistic approach.
- Tailor all resumes. Place abbreviated resumes in the body of your proposal.
- Include individual photos of the people proposed only if you have previously introduced them to the customer organization.
- Include photos of groups or teams containing individuals proposed if they show previous teaming experience or specific performance experience.
- Use matrices to summarize the directly relevant skills and experience of individuals on your team.

---

4 Discriminate services with clear descriptions of what will be done.

Take a hint from some of the most experienced and sophisticated purchasers of complex services. U.S. Government agencies often require an Integrated Master Plan (IMP) and an Integrated Master Schedule (IMS). Prepare and include task descriptions with clearly defined and measurable completion criteria, directly tied to your project schedule.

Generalized, boilerplate descriptions of tasks and generic schedules will win only if your competition is equally incompetent or lazy.

5

See GRAPHICS *for examples. See also* RELEVANT EXPERIENCE/ PAST PERFORMANCE *and* RESUMES.

Present service processes graphically.

When described in text, most service processes appear hopelessly complex. When presented graphically, they appear clear and straight forward, increasing an evaluator's confidence in the seller.

Consider some of the following ideas for service graphics:

- Include a series of small icon-like sketches to illustrate each service step.
- Present an excerpt of a service procedure from your service manual.
- Insert a sequenced, numbered checklist.

- Insert actual screen shots or graphics from your on-line service manual.
- Show a flow chart.
- Use a collage of photos or sketches to illustrate the variety of services available.
- Emphasize quality results by inserting a service report, service rating, or positive quotes from customers.
- Insert summary resumes that emphasize relevant experience.
- Insert photos showing the proposed people performing identical or similar tasks.

6

Exploit or attack incumbency, as relevant.

Incumbents win approximately 80 percent of all re-competes. Surveys of why incumbents lose cite poor service as the overwhelming reason.

Exploit incumbency by correcting service problems before the bid. If you are too late, stress the specific corrections planned and the complexity of the required service. Fear of change is a powerful incentive to retain the incumbent.

When attacking incumbents, stress the specific steps you will take to improve service. While incumbents can be replaced on price, many winners regret the losses resulting from a low-ball win.

7

See COSTING, *Capture Guide.*

Customer satisfaction is subjective. Customers must be continuously sold and resold before, during, and after the service is sold. Seamlessly, flawlessly delivered services are often forgotten.

Service deliverers must repeatedly reinforce the value of their services or risk being replaced or eliminated. The more customized and tailored the service, the harder the incumbent is to replace.

See TEAMING, *Capture Guide.*

Cut costs, not margins.

The cost differences among the top bidders in service competitions are often a fraction of a percent. Develop a more competitive price by focusing on cutting costs out of your bid rather than simply reducing margins.

Bidders that uniformly pare time and materials estimates by a uniform amount over the entire bid are effectively reducing margins. A cost evaluator with more than 30 years of experience called this the *peanut butter approach.* If you must resort to this method of cost cutting, he recommended simply reducing the total cost, calling it a management contribution.

Make your bid more competitive by looking for ways to improve delivery efficiency. To improve your cost competitiveness, consider the following methods:

- Increase the span of control of managers, effectively reducing head-count in your most costly labor categories.
- Reduce the levels of management.
- Adjust the placement of individuals in required labor categories. When customers mandate labor categories and rates, they typically cite midpoints in each category. You may not have to propose at the midpoint.
- Establish a new cost center for each major bid to prevent including overhead allocations irrelevant to that bid.
- Identify and incorporate physical assets within your organization that have been fully depreciated. This reduces corporate overhead allocations based on asset values.

- Subcontract tasks which can be delivered more economically by others.
- Recalculate existing cost standards. Existing standards may not be based on the same assumptions. For example, a military depot had been repairing aircraft landing gear. The practice was to upgrade all landing gear to the latest standards whenever any maintenance was performed. The result was that relatively minor repairs had historically high standard costs.

   This depot's practice was similar to requesting a tune-up and getting a complete engine rebuild and upgrade to the latest standards. By developing new standards for each required maintenance action, the depot won a major contract.
- Review task descriptions to prevent tasks from being overspecified. Identify which tasks could be performed by a lower cost labor category.
- Review delivery processes for potential productivity improvements through skill improvement, tooling improvement, or additional technology.
- Reduce reporting cost by proposing at the minimal level required in the bid request.
- Search for opportunities to cut overhead and increase business through automated order entry, billing, and payment, perhaps using the internet.
- Actively manage the account post sale to identify additional sales that you can deliver cost effectively with the existing or an augmented team.

Storyboards and Mockups are planning tools used to develop and review new content before writing text. Like any tool, they should save time and improve quality to justify their use.

Storyboards and mockups are closely related but distinctly different. Both are used to help writers plan, develop, and review key concepts before drafting text.

Storyboards have a one-to-one relationship with major sections of the proposal pertaining to a common topic, while mockup pages relate directly to proposal pages. For example, a single storyboard may apply to a 10-page proposal section. The mockup for the same section would contain a full 10 pages.

The motivation to storyboard, whether in movies or proposals, was always the same—to cut costs. In early movie making, silver-coated film was the most expensive element. Now film is inexpensive and the actors, sets, and support crews are expensive. Similarly, proposal professionals use storyboards to reduce preparation time and costs.

Storyboards use words and graphics to outline a concept. When someone builds a house, the storyboard equivalent is a plan book that shows a sketch of the home accompanied by a short description, as shown in figure 1.

Extending the house analogy, the mockup is equivalent to the floor plan, showing the allocation of space and the relationship of key elements to scale, also shown in figure 1.

One problem among proposal managers and writers is inconsistent definitions. Keep the following definitions in mind:

Outlines are a sequential list of topics to be discussed.

Annotated outlines are outlines with annotations or comments about the contents of the topics. For proposals, annotated outlines may include references to the source of requirements, the author assigned, section length or page allocation, approximate number of visuals desired, and various dates materials are due. When annotated to this degree, the annotated outline becomes the proposal responsibility matrix.

Storyboards are conceptual planning tools used to help writers plan each section before drafting text. They contain assignments, bid request requirements, strategies, preliminary visuals, and content.

Storyboards are frequently misunderstood, misused, and have poor reputations with many proposal writers. Shipley Associates' storyboard form, the Proposal Development Worksheet (PDW), is shown in figure 3.

Mockups are page-for-page representations of the actual pages in the finished proposal. Mockups contain the same elements as the draft, namely, headings, themes, visuals, action captions, and text. Mockups transition writers from the storyboard to drafting.

Like eating the elephant one bite at a time, mockups permit writers to draft any section in any order while maintaining the planned organization. Mockups help writers appropriately allocate the space devoted to each point.

Anyone who has worked with advertising agencies on brochures has probably encountered mockups. Mockups are similar in function to prototypes, scale models, floor plans, and general arrangement drawings.

Storyboards and mockups aid managers as well as writers. Proposal managers use them to review and improve the writer's plan before wasting time and money on text that cannot be used.

Storyboards were invented by movie directors, with early use attributed to D. W. Griffith, who directed *Birth of a Nation.* Alfred Hitchcock is reputed to have been the best user of storyboards, while Charlie Chaplin was the worst. Hitchcock planned his shooting to fractions of a second while Chaplin set up the cameras and improvised.

The Proposal Development Worksheet (PDW) was developed to lessen the initial reluctance of many writers to use storyboards. Writers often completed their PDWs before they knew they had used a storyboard. Most importantly, writers learned how much easier and faster they could draft quality proposal sections when using storyboards.

See OUTLINING.

A sample storyboard is included in MODEL DOCUMENTS.

Storyboards and Mockups

1. Use storyboards to develop and review new material.

2. Focus on the storyboarding process more than the tool selected.

3. Use the core team to prepare the assignment; use the writers to develop the content.

4. Make the storyboard a key management tool.

5. Use mockups to allocate space and simplify the writing task.

6. Storyboard sequentially; mock up interactively.

7. Train writers to storyboard and mock up.

8. Manage the difficult transition from storyboarding to the first draft.

Storyboard

Mockup

VENEZIA SPECIFICATIONS

Announcing the "Venezia," our newest 2-story design with 4 bedrooms, 2.5 bathrooms, and 4,664 total square feet (3,025 finished.) This spacious design features a large family room, laundry room, den, and 9 ft. ceilings on the main level. The upstairs has 3 bedrooms and a large master suite with walk-in closet and grand bath. The basement can be finished to include up to 3 more bedrooms and 1 bathroom.

Total Sq. Ft.: 4,664
Finished Sq. Ft.: 3,025
Unfinished Sq. Ft.: 1,639
Width: 52'-9"
Depth: 51'-0"
Bedrooms: 4
Bathrooms: 2 1/2

©2001 Ivory Homes.

Figure 1. Home Builders Use Storyboards and Mockups. *The combination of text and graphics on the left is like a storyboard. Yet few people would proceed on the basis of the graphic and text without first seeing the floor plan. Like a mockup, the floor plan allocates space and shows the relationships of major design elements. Of course, if money and time were not limited, you could build the house first, then make changes. Early paper changes are both easier and less expensive. The planning takes time and delays the start, but later changes take even more time. (Images courtesy of Ivory Homes, Salt Lake City, Utah.)*

1 Use storyboards to develop and review new material.

See QUESTION/RESPONSE PROPOSALS.

Storyboards and mockups are most valuable when developing new material. They are less valuable and often should not be used when proposing essentially the same products and services to similar customers. When you have previously written material (boilerplate) available, focus on tailoring your sales message, adjusting the details and length.

Many proposal efforts do not warrant using storyboards and mockups for every section. Storyboards should save more time than they take. For similar informally solicited proposals, use a single storyboard to plan the entire proposal. Then mock up the executive summary, which should be written for every proposal.

For Question/Response bid requests, use a modified storyboard approach to outline and review your responses before drafting. Identify the more important or more difficult questions, then plan and review your response before drafting text.

2 Focus on the storyboarding process more than the tool selected.

The overall process of making clear assignments, then planning, reviewing, and approving each writer's approach before drafting is more important than what information is selected to be on the storyboard form.

While some practitioners say their storyboards are proprietary and give them special names, most storyboards are not that different. Adapting the storyboard form to fit the effort warranted and the time available is more important than the form's detailed design.

Most storyboards have been developed for large, competitive systems proposals to governments. These detailed storyboards are often not directly applicable to small, 2-week, commercial responses.

For example, the topics contained in a detailed Shipley PDW are listed in figure 2 beside a shortened version that might be used for a rapid, commercial response.

The Shipley Sales Proposal Planner is a storyboard-like tool used to plan an entire small proposal. The contents of the Planner are also listed in figure 2.

PROPOSAL DEVELOPMENT WORKSHEET	SHORTENED STORYBOARD	SALES PROPOSAL PLANNER
1. Writers Information: Relevant Proposal Information Relevant RFP Locations Section Compliance Checklist Section Outline (Based on Requirements of RFP) Relevant Proposal/Volume Strategy **2. Defining Your Solution:** Major Issues Approach(es) to Requirements and Issues Features and Benefits of Your Solution **3. Developing Your Section Message:** Section Discriminators Risk Management Relevant Experience Past Performance Section Messages Section Theme Statement **4. Creating Key Visuals:** Graphic or Table Action Caption	**1. Understanding the Task:** Section Assignment **2. Analyzing the Bid Request:** Compliance Requirements **3. Defining Your Offer:** Major Issues Approach (Technical/Management) Features & Benefits Support of Claims **4. Developing Your Strategy:** Section Discriminators Section Theme Statement **5. Creating Key Visuals:** Figure Number Figure Title Action Caption	**1. Positioning the Proposal** Identify Decision Makers, Influencers, and their Issues Build a Bidder Comparison Matrix Draft Proposal Strategy **2. Planning the Proposal:** Allocate Your Time Define Your Baseline Solution Define Your Price to Win Develop a Proposal Outline and Requirements Checklist Extend Sales Strategy into Proposal Strategy Design Your Proposal—Develop a Style Sheet **3. Writing the Proposal:** Implement Your Proposal Strategy What's Next?

Figure 2. Tailor Storyboards to the Opportunity. *The first column lists the contents of a detailed Proposal Development Worksheet (PDW) appropriate for large, competitive efforts. The second column lists the contents for a shortened version. The third lists contents of the Commercial Proposal Planner used to plan rapid response commercial proposals where the services and products being sold are similar for different competitions. Note that this figure merely lists potential contents and is not an actual storyboard.*

3 **Use the core team to prepare the assignment; use the writers to develop the content.**

On larger efforts, the proposal core team consisting of the proposal manager, volume managers or content leads, and the proposal specialist should develop clear, concise assignments for each contributor prior to the proposal kickoff. At the kickoff meeting, contributors are given their assignments.

A generic storyboard, called a PDW, is shown in figure 3. PDWs are used to prepare both major government and commercial proposals.

The portions on *Understanding the Task* and *Analyzing the Bid Request* should be completed by the proposal manager or proposal core team and given to the writers at the kickoff meeting.

If writers develop their own compliance checklists, you will have *orphans* (unanswered items) and repeats (items answered by more than one writer). With repeats, answers often vary and may be costed twice.

Writers need to develop the content in the storyboard to prepare them to write. If their thinking is unclear, their writing will be unclear.

Some proposal professionals advocate using a small, select, trained group to prepare the storyboards completely, then giving storyboards to the writers to save time. This approach usually backfires. Writers tend to ignore storyboards done by others, and they draft text with little forethought.

Most writers can write well if they can develop a clear concept prior to writing. The process of storyboarding leads to a clearer concept, reducing the rework for everyone involved, and improving document quality and win probability.

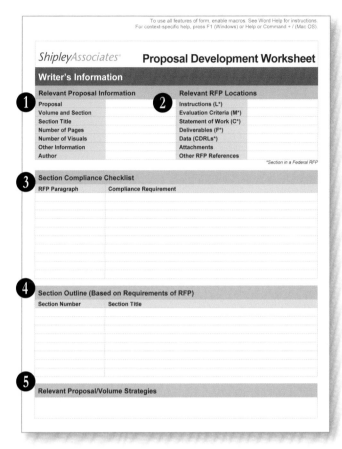

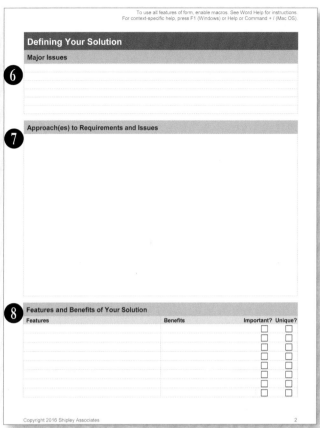

1 The Proposal or Volume Manager should provide the information required in this section. If you do not have it, ask for it, especially for the number of pages allocated.

2 The Proposal or Volume Manager should provide information on relevant bid request pages and paragraph numbers. If you do not have it, ask for it.

3 The Proposal or Volume Manager should complete this section by *stripping* requirements from appropriate bid request sections. Use the compliance checklist to ensure responsiveness and compliance.

4 The Proposal or Volume Manager should provide an outline breaking down the section as required by the bid request and inserting any other subtopics needed to address additional requirements or evaluation criteria. Check with the Proposal Manager to see if further subdivision is allowed before adding lower level topics.

5 The Proposal or Volume Manager should indicate any top level proposal or volume strategies this section should support. Not every proposal or volume strategy can be supported in every section, but it is critical that important win strategies be explicitly supported at appropriate points in the proposal.

6 Major issues or hot buttons are what keep the customer up at night:

- Worry items
- Core needs
- Reasons behind the requirements
- Hidden agendas

7 Identify your approach(es) to meeting section compliance requirements and addressing major issues. Document what you are proposing, but do not be concerned at this stage with how to sell it.

8 Develop the features and corresponding benefits of your offer or solution for this section. Be sure to include benefits that address the major issues identified above. Features and benefits should be developed in pairs, not as unconnected lists.

Check boxes to indicate benefits important to the customer and unique among competitors. This knowledge will help identify discriminators, which are important elements of proposal strategy. Only important benefits can turn unique features into discriminators.

Figure 3. Completing the Proposal Development Worksheet (PDW). *Follow the instructions for each portion of the PDW.*

9 Discriminators are features of an offer that are important to the customer and unique from competitors'. Your discriminators should be the foundation of your section's messages. Your competitors will probably emphasize their own, which you must offset.

Check boxes to indicate competitors' discriminators that are candidates for ghosting. Ghosting raises doubt about a competitor's approach without naming the competitor.

10 Enter risk factors in technical, cost, schedule, or other appropriate areas. These are risks to your customer, not to your company. Identify the most likely risks and biggest impacts. For every risk, identify a management approach. Do not conceal or ignore risks. Demonstrate your value by proactively reducing the customer's risk.

11 Identify your company's relevant experience and past performance. Relevant experience is what you did; past performance is how well you did it. Tie past performance to the benefits to this customer on this program.

12 Summarize your section messages. Reflect all important elements and information on the PDW. Address all requirements. Focus on discriminating features that produce important benefits. Cite supporting arguments. But do not write the section yet.

13 Your theme statement should be your strongest message:

- Link a benefit to a discriminating feature
- Quantify the benefit
- Include a *proof statement* to increase credibility
- Answer the question, Why choose this offer?

Think of your theme statement as a *silver bullet* the evaluator can use to justify giving you a high score.

14 Develop visuals for this section in the area provided (and on additional sheets as necessary) before drafting text. Visuals should:

- Be simple and uncluttered
- Be vertically oriented
- Be independent of text—able to stand alone
- Be discussed in the text prior to introduction
- Have action captions

Don't try to make them pretty. Just create rough sketches.

15 Develop an *action caption* to tell evaluators what you want them to understand about this visual. Use two or three sentences if needed. Ask:

- What is the purpose of this visual?
- What is this visual supposed to communicate?
- What conclusion do I want evaluators to reach?
- What is the selling point?
- Are features tied to benefits?

Use the section number, followed by consecutive numbers for each visual, *e. g.*, Figure 3.2-1. Provide an informative figure title.

4 Make the storyboard a key management tool.

With storyboards, managers can see what writers are thinking before they write, thus reducing expensive rewriting. To ensure that writers treat storyboards seriously, managers must review all storyboards thoroughly and frequently.

Do not wait to review storyboards until they are complete. Review sections incrementally to get writers on track faster.

One way to speed storyboard preparation is to facilitate the work in a workshop-like manner. Follow these steps:

1. Explain each task, establishing clear quality standards.
2. Ask each writer to complete that task in a relatively short time.
3. Circulate, answering any questions.
4. Review individual storyboard sections as a group, encouraging collaborative, constructive information sharing and suggestions for improvement. Repeat as warranted.
5. Advance to the next storyboard section.

Keep a copy of the latest version of each storyboard mounted on the wall in the proposal war room or its equivalent. Walk the walls daily, and encourage team members to do the same. If storyboards are posted and maintained electronically on a secure web site, establish common procedures to control versions, reviews, approvals, and revisions. Most tools offer features that parallel traditional manual processes, but they are specific to the software and not discussed in this *Guide*.

Post all suggestions for improvement on the storyboards with the reviewer's name and phone number.

Remove unsigned comments. Remove comments that are vague and require further discussion. Anonymous comments are often negative and hurt the team environment. If a comment is valid, sign it and assume ownership.

Comment on storyboard progress in a daily stand-up meeting. Praise the better examples.

Maintain either the original or a first copy in the proposal master book in case any storyboards are lost.

Storyboards can be done by hand or electronically. Both have advantages and disadvantages. Make sure the tool does not encumber the process. For example:

A proposal manager asked an untrained organization to complete storyboards. The group met and decided that they would have to draft their sections to complete the storyboards. They worked all weekend on their drafts, primarily by pasting in boilerplate. Then they electronically pasted text from their drafts into the storyboard forms. After all, they wanted them to be legible.

The result was terrible. The proposal manager required all subsequent storyboards to be handwritten to encourage thinking before writing.

Their process was essentially the same as constructing the building or apparatus, then preparing the as-built drawings.

Electronic storyboards offer advantages when used and managed properly. Major advantages are (1) storyboard material can evolve into a draft and (2) managers can more easily manage a geographically dispersed team.

Resist the impulse to cut and paste boilerplate into electronic storyboards.

See DAILY TEAM MANAGEMENT.

5 Use mockups to allocate space and simplify the writing task.

Mockups are an intermediate step between the storyboard and drafting the text. The act of constructing a mockup forces writers to consider the relative importance of topics to the customer and to the offer. After mockups are complete, writers can work on any section without losing direction or momentum.

Mockups should be done quickly. Neatness does not count. A 5-page section should be mocked up in less than 2 hours; a 20-page section in less than one-half day. Experienced writers can mock up a 10- to 15-page executive summary in about an hour.

Many writers construct thumbnail mockups first. Using thumbnails, they can see the entire document at once, making it easier to allocate topics and content over the available pages. Then they sketch full-scale mockups if they need greater detail before drafting. The entire mockup development process is shown in figure 4 in thumbnail sketches.

Mockups should be hand sketched. Constructing pretty mockups on the computer wastes time and interferes with the creative process.

Construct a mockup in the following steps:

1. Establish the overall page layout from the proposal style sheet, such as single- or double-column.
2. Estimate the number of pages for the entire section, including text and integrated graphics.
3. Allocate the pages available to the topics to be discussed according to their importance to evaluators, tempered by their complexity. Then place section subheadings to reserve the space allocated. In formally solicited proposals, top-level topics reflect compliance requirements.
4. Place and label boxes to reserve space for major visual elements like themes, summaries and introductions, and visuals.

1. Go back and begin to flesh out the mockup. Insert the following items, in the approximate order listed:

- Insert the top-level theme statement from the storyboard.
- Identify each graphic and identify it in the reserved space.
- List the key points to be made.
- Draft complete three-part action captions for each visual.

- Draft every planned theme statement.
- Draft the section summary and introduction.
- Begin drafting text. Start where you feel most prepared or comfortable.
- Do not worry about how many iterations are required to do a mockup.

STEPS

1 Establish the overall page layout.

2 Obtain or estimate the number of formatted blank pages available for your section. Example at right is a page bogey of three pages using double columns.

3 Overlay your section outline (located on the bottom of page 1 of the PDW) on the pages, drawing boxes for the assigned space for each topic. Base the allocation of space on your best judgment of how much space will be required for each outline topic. Identify adequate space for your section introduction and summary, as shown at right.

4 Draw boxes to show the location for the graphics you developed on page 4 of the PDW in the locations within the space you designated for each outline item. Describe or sketch the graphic in those boxes, and enter the appropriate figure number, title, and action caption. Identify the location for themes by drawing boxes and entering your section theme(s) from the bottom of page 3 of the PDW.

5 In each outline space, identify the content that will be discussed under that topic by using key words. Show the estimated space that will be devoted to that topic by the juxtaposition of the key words.

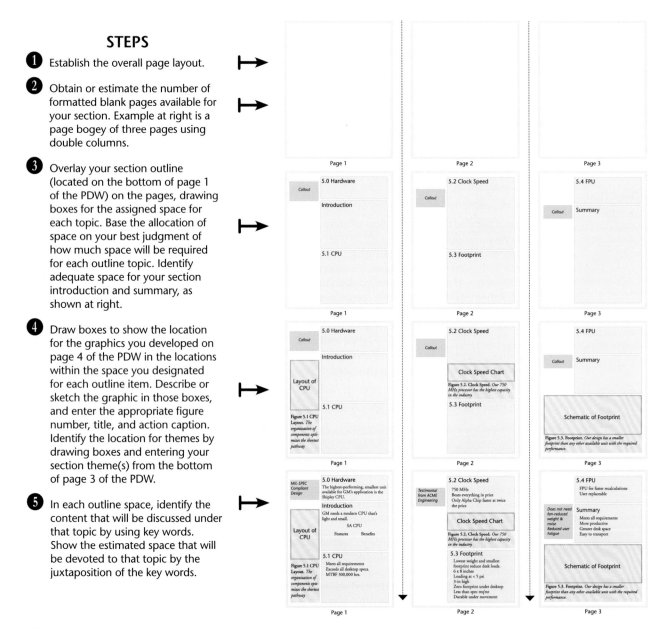

Figure 4. Mockup Development Process. *Mockups evolve from top-level concepts to specific details. After constructing the reduced-size "thumbnail" pages shown, most writers proceed to a first draft. Construct a full-scale mockup only if the document is particularly important or expensive to produce. While shown here in print form for clarity, most mockups are and should be handwritten.*

6 Storyboard sequentially; mock up interactively.

When you prepare storyboards, each portion builds on previous portions, so they must be constructed sequentially. For example, a writer must know a customer's requirements and major issues before determining benefits.

When you develop mockups, use a top-down process, from the general to the specific. Mockups constructed sequentially usually cram so much into a small space that they are unrealistic. After review, visuals and tables are often the size of a postage stamp and the space for text is inadequate.

7 Train writers to storyboard and mock up.

Developing storyboards and preparing mockups is not intuitive to many writers. Writers need training and must experience how these tools save more time than they take.

When writers are told they will be developing storyboards and mockups, they often make comments like the following:

Why waste time filling out forms? I could be writing.

———————————

Boy, am I glad that storyboard is done because I have my section already written. Translation: I've already done a *search and replace* on the available boilerplate.

———————————

So you want us to draw pretty pictures.

———————————

You are turning the proposal into a comic book.

Few writers are convinced storyboards and mockups work until they build them. Then they see how much easier it is to draft their section. Here are some of the comments from the converted:

Having everyone throw rocks at my themes and captions in all of their iterations was brutal. But I learned how others were thinking and the improvement was huge.

———————————

After you finally let us write our drafts, the section practically wrote itself.

———————————

I was asked to join a proposal team that had been working for 2 solid weeks. I remembered what I was taught in the workshop. We had 5 days until the first Red Team. Despite the proposal manager's pressure to see my draft, I completed my storyboard, reviewed it with the volume manager, constructed a thumbnail mockup, and drafted my section. My section was the only one to pass the Red Team. I went home while the others started over.

8 Manage the difficult transition from storyboarding to the first draft.

Many writers have difficulty transitioning from storyboards, to mockups, then to their first draft. They seem to forget everything they went through, sit down at a blank screen, and start writing about themselves, their products and services, and their organization.

To ease your writers' transition from storyboards and mockups to their first draft, consider the following techniques:

1. Take the writers' storyboards, in electronic form, and sequentially paste them into a word processing file for the writers.

2. Personally check with each writer within 1 day of when the writer will begin drafting the text. Waiting longer allows their frustration level to get too high.

3. Demonstrate how to move text from a storyboard into a first draft in a group training session; then check with each writer.

4. Ask experienced writers to mentor less-experienced writers.

5. Tape the completed storyboard to a flip chart page or white board. Then draw arrows to show where each item can be moved onto a mockup page.

6. Remind writers to leave labeled boxes to reserve space for content not yet available.

Style is the sum of the choices that writers make; tone is the impact on the reader. Style choices heavily influence whether your sales documents help you win competitive business.

Presenters and writers make numerous style choices. Some choices apply to both presentations and documents. Some are unique, but all should convey a business-like tone. The choices listed are representative, not exhaustive.

Presentation style choices:

- Appearance
- Length & timing
- Organization
- Room set-up
- Timing
- Visual aids
- Voice tone & inflection
- Word choice

Document style choices:

- Graphics
- Length
- Medium
- Organization
- Page and document design
- Sentence structure
- Word choice

Desirable business document tone:

- Accessible
- Clear
- Courteous
- Customer focused
- Friendly
- Helpful
- Honest
- Informative
- Personal
- Persuasive
- Polite
- Sincere

Style and tone are often confused. Style is the cause, and tone is the effect.

Writers' and speakers' style choices are implicit, whether intentional or accidental, conscious or unconscious. Your style choices include the type of document or presentation planned; medium; word choice; sentence, paragraph, and document length and organization; page and document design; emphatic devices; use and type of graphics; and the environment where the presentation is made or the document read.

Tone reflects your attitude towards the customer. Tone refers to the feeling or impression that is conveyed by the speaker or writer. Tone is a product of style.

Document and presentation styles are often categorized as formal and informal. Formal documents and presentations, such as technical reports, technical presentations, and contracts, are primarily written to inform, to objectively convey information. Typically the writer neither has nor anticipates a personal relationship with the reader. Therefore, humor or familiarity are inappropriate and might cloud the message.

Informal documents and presentations, such as email, personal letters, trip reports, and most memos, are generally written for people that the writer knows or feels comfortable with. Informal documents are often informative, friendly, subjective, casual, and personal.

The distinction between formal and informal styles is blurred in sales communications that are meant to persuade. While sales presentations need to be logical, factual, informative, and deliberate (formal characteristics), they also need to be positive, informative, non-threatening, and supportive (informal characteristics). While a seller seeks to convey an objective tone, customers rarely expect sellers to be objective.

The acceptability of text messages, *tweets*, and other informal social media depends upon the receiver and is rapidly evolving. One customer might find them insulting and too public while another might see them as efficient, direct and more credible than messages via more conventional mediums.

Never excuse or confuse bad writing with style. In the end, good sales communications are clear, persuasive, informative, supportive, well-organized, and concise. Poor sales communications are vague, confusing, unconvincing, chaotic, and wordy.

Consider the tone of a brochure, regional newspaper, national newspaper, fashion magazine, scientific journal, maintenance manual, audit report, legal document, poem, situation comedy, or network news. Each seeks acceptance by a specific audience. Each makes specific style choices to connect with its audience and achieve its objectives. Each typically defines its style choices in its own style *guide*.

Style and Tone

1. Match the tone of each document to your objective.

2. Organize sales documents as the customer directs, then follow the Four-Box organizational style.

3. Adapt sentence length and structure to each sales communication.

4. Use abbreviations and jargon only when you are sure readers understand them.

5. Adopt a customer-focused writing style.

6. Choose correct words.

7. Eliminate cliches, false subjects, gobbledygook, and redundant words.

8. Choose a page and document design appropriate for this customer and opportunity.

---

1 **Match the tone of each document to your objective.**

The tone of each document should support your objective and intended effect on the reader. A writer's objective for most documents is a combination of *to do, to know,* and *to feel.* The emphasis on each varies. Turn to guideline

6 in the Organization section to see how the *to do, to know,* and *to feel* are mapped into the four-box organizational style.

The relationship between style and tone puzzles many business professionals. They scan thousands of documents in their

See PERSUASION, *Capture Guide.* Guidelines 2 through 8 summarize key style choices for persuasive sales documents.

professional, educational, and personal lives and are confused by the differences. Figure 1 summarizes six types of documents by tone, intended effect, and example.

Many organizations document their style choices in a style *guide* and software templates.

Marketing or public relations departments set and maintain organizational style guidelines to support branding and positioning objectives. However, if corporate style guidelines conflict with bid request instructions, comply with bid request instructions.

The most effective styles are context specific. Because your relationship and position with each customer change by competition, adapt your style guidelines to the situation and your sales strategy.

Individual writers on proposal teams have different writing styles. Smooth the roughest, most obvious differences, but avoid the temptation to make all writing exactly alike. The added expense and off-putting effect on the writers are seldom justified by the minimal improvement in win rates.

TONE	INTENDED EFFECT	EXAMPLE DOCUMENTS
Persuasive	Changes perception, accepts, believes	Proposal, brochure
Motivational	Changes intentions, plans to . . ., willing to . . .	Advertisement
Informative	Factual knowledge, knows that . . .	News report, e-mail, text message, *tweet*
Supporting assessment	Make decision	Test report
Instructive	Know what and how to do	Workshop manual, how-to book
Affective	Feel, amuse, offend, entertain	Joke, novel, apology letter , e-mail, text message, or *tweet*

Figure 1. Tone Is Driven by the Intended Effect. *Writers tend to adopt writing styles similar to the types of documents they were trained to write. Hence, scientists tend to adopt a scientific style that is less effective in sales documents.*

2 Organize sales documents as the customer directs, then follow the Four-Box organizational style.

Organization is one of the most important style choices for all types of business documents, including proposals. A well-conceived organization simplifies the writing, especially for writers with limited confidence in their writing skills. Nothing can save a poorly organized sales document.

The over-riding principle is to organize every document according to the reader's interests. Apply this principle to proposals by following customer instructions, then placing the most important items to the reader first.

Adapt the Four-Box organizational structure to, executive summaries, entire proposals, individual proposal sections, reports, e-mail, phone calls, text messages, and virtually any type of business document.

In the simplest form, the four organizational boxes are:

1. Summary
2. Introduction
3. Body
4. Review

For expanded examples of the Four-Box Template, *see* COMPLIANCE AND RESPONSIVENESS, EXECUTIVE SUMMARY, ORGANIZATION; PRESENTATIONS TO CUSTOMERS, *and* SALES LETTERS, *Capture Guide.*

For example, when drafting a response to a bid request question, you might eliminate the *Box 4-Review* if you feel the customer will quit reading as soon as they find the answer. Conversely when making a sales presentation, you might opt to summarize between each key point in the *Box 3-Body* to help the audience reconnect. When preparing a short e-mail, you

might opt to place a short, concise message entirely in an informative subject line and eliminate Boxes 1-4. (Unless you consider the subject line as part of Box 1.)

The Four-Box organization has been used in *Proposal Guide* Model Documents 1-11 and 13-17. Refer to these model documents to see how the Four-Box organization can be adapted to your documents. Refer to the referenced topic sections for more specific explanations.

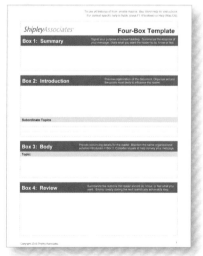

Figure 2. Four-Box Template. *This template helps writers create an organized message for each sales document. Annotated examples can be found throughout the Guide.*

3

See ACTIVE/PASSIVE VOICE.

See LISTS *and* THEME STATEMENTS.

Adapt sentence length and structure to each sales communication.

Sentence length and structure are key style choices. Keep the average sentence length under 20 words. The average length of sentences is more indicative of style than individual sentence length.

Vary sentence length to make your writing more interesting. Readers notice extremely short and long sentences. Occasional short sentences, perhaps in a single-sentence paragraph, are excellent emphasis devices. Long sentences are more difficult to write well and punctuate correctly, but are not incorrect simply because they are long.

If you lack confidence in your writing, punctuating, and spelling skills, write short sentences using the simplest, yet most accurate words possible. If you maintain a subject-verb-object construction, you need only limited punctuation and spelling skills.

Sentence structure includes the grammatical structure, such as active or passive voice, the sequence of ideas, and word patterns.

Grammatical structure includes selecting active or passive voice and parallel construction. The sequence of ideas relates to placing ideas or points in either a logical order, usually for clarity, or order of importance, for emphasis.

Consider two, similar sentences:

> If you place your order before June 30, we can complete construction by November 30.
>
> ────────────
>
> We can complete construction by November 30 if you place your order before June 30.

The first emphasizes placing the order; the second sentence emphasizes completing the construction. The best choice depends upon your situation. Generally, your tone will be positive and forceful if you state your claim and then qualify it.

The sequence of ideas in a sentence impacts theme statements. Most theme statements will be stronger if the benefit is placed before the feature.

You have many ways to structure a single sentence. Your choices increase exponentially when you put multiple sentences together.

A series of oddly structured sentences, perhaps broken into multiple phrases, slows the reader and conveys a stuffy, formal tone that might seem cold, unfriendly, or arrogant. A string of short, direct sentences is efficient and can sound clean and brisk, or jarring and abrupt, depending on the context.

4

See ABBREVIATIONS, JARGON, *and* LISTS.

Use abbreviations and jargon only when you are sure readers understand them.

Using words that customers do not understand projects an arrogant tone. Eliminate unnecessary abbreviations and jargon. Define acronyms, initialisms, other potentially unfamiliar abbreviations, and jargon the first time you use them in each major section of your proposal.

Insert a list of abbreviations with definitions in proposals exceeding 25 pages. Define unfamiliar jargon when you first use it, but you do not need to define jargon in the list of abbreviations.

5

See CUSTOMER FOCUS.

Adopt a customer-focused writing style.

Customer focus is an aspect of tone. While most sellers claim to have a customer focus, few make the style choices to project a customer-focused tone.

Increase the customer-focus of your proposals by making these style choices:

- Cite the customer organization's vision.
- Link the customer's vision directly to the immediate purchase.
- Cite the customer's hot buttons.
- Make customer ownership of the hot buttons explicit.
- Address each hot button in the order listed.
- Name the customer before the seller in paragraphs and sentences.
- Name the customer as many or more times than the seller.
- Cite benefits before features.

6

See CHOOSING CORRECT WORDS.

Choose correct words.

Choosing correct words makes sales documents more persuasive, effective, and easier to read. Recognize and eliminate common word problems:

- Simplify or replace wordy phrases.
- Use the correct word in context.
- Revise words or phrases that could have more than one meaning.

7

See CLICHES, FALSE SUBJECTS, GOBBLEDYGOOK, JARGON, *and* REDUNDANT WORDS.

Eliminate cliches, false subjects, gobbledygook, and redundant words.

Cliches are worn-out phrases that are no longer effective. Avoid cliches. Regular use indicates lack of thought and effort.

Cliches are tempting when the writer is struggling to express an idea. However, cliches reduce the persuasiveness of sales documents. If the cliche is noticeable, reword the phrase.

False subjects are words like *it* and *there* that refer to nothing. *It is* and *there are* at the beginning of sentences are false subjects. False subjects displace the true subject of a sentence, waste readers' time, and obscure meaning.

Eliminate false subjects whenever possible to make your writing clearer and more concise.

Occasionally, false subjects are necessary, as in: It is raining.

Gobbledygook is the use of abstract or pompous words and long, convoluted sentences. The meaning is often unintelligible. Gobbledygook, like cliches and false subjects, reduces the persuasiveness of sales documents and should be eliminated.

Redundant words unnecessarily qualify other words or phrases, unless used occasionally for emphasis. Overuse often projects a pompous tone that is tiresome. Most redundant words should be eliminated.

8

See PAGE AND DOCUMENT DESIGN.

Choose a page and document design appropriate for this customer and opportunity.

Page and document design impact whether your document is read, how it is read, whether it is understood, whether it is persuasive, and whether it is remembered. The physical design of your document and individual pages emphasizes or de-emphasizes your messages, much like body language, word dynamics, and facial expression in conversation.

Well-designed sales documents project an accessible, engaging, and customer-focused tone. A good design promotes clear, persuasive communication even though readers may not be conscious of the techniques used. Well-

designed documents attract readers, and then help them locate, comprehend, and remember key information.

While individuals' personal preferences differ, design guidelines are supported by scientific research. These guidelines, summarized in PAGE AND DOCUMENT DESIGN, are broadly reflected in public media, such as newspapers, magazines, journals, and books. Page design principles apply equally to web communications such as e-mail and text messages. Short words, sentences, and paragraphs; font and color changes; and lists are page design elements.

Task Order Proposals are typically awarded within a governing master contract. Gain a competitive edge by developing processes and systems that support quality, rapid, specific responses.

Master contracts and task order proposals are increasingly used in many market sectors and countries by governmental and private organizations. Most contracts are for services, but products can be included. Master contracts are also called blanket contracts, period contracts, panel contracts, Indefinite Delivery/Indefinite Quantity (IDIQ) contracts, task order agreements, basic ordering agreements, and Government Wide Acquisition Contracts (GWACs).

Customers use master contracts and task order proposals for three primary reasons:

- **Reduce contracting time.** Customers give pre-qualified bidders 5 to 10 days to respond to a task order bid request, and then award the task within 10 to 30 days. Occasionally, the entire process is completed in less than 5 days. Some task orders require immediate starts, but set work limits until terms and conditions are finalized.

- **Increase flexibility.** Customers cannot accurately predict the types of services or products that could be required.

- **Support a purchasing organization.** A purchasing or contracting organization establishes a broad, flexible, contract vehicle with a high purchase limit. Virtually any buyer can use the master contract to quickly purchase services by transferring their funds and purchasing authority to the organization that issued the master contract. In return, the purchasing organization collects a surcharge on the purchase that supports their organization.

Winning most task order proposals requires two steps:

1. Win a master contract to pre-qualify to compete for specific types of work.
2. Compete for individual task orders under the terms of the master contract.

Competing for master contracts is similar to competing for a large services contract. Competing for each task order is similar to competing in rapid-response, narrowly focused, business-to-business competitions.

Task orders might include performance-based tasks. If so, see PERFORMANCE-BASED ACQUISITION, *Capture Guide.*

Task Order Proposals
1. Regard master contracts as a license to hunt.
2. Market your organization proactively to gain a competitive advantage, influence requirements, and win sole source contracts.
3. Prepare to respond quickly by developing and maintaining a searchable database with experience examples, proof of performance examples, and key-person resumes.
4. Follow bid request instructions explicitly.
5. Focus on the task, not on re-qualifying to bid.
6. Use graphics to rapidly and clearly describe your processes.
7. Match experience and proof of performance examples with each specified task.
8. Integrate success stories within technical task, process, and management descriptions.
9. Limit management discussions to this task.
10. Tailor resumes for each key position.

1 Regard master contracts as a license to hunt.

Master contract bid requests might also include task orders, which are addressed in guidelines 2-10.

Master contracts pre-qualify vendors to compete for subsequent task orders. The master contract value is a ceiling on the total value of task orders that can be awarded under the contract. You can win a billion-dollar master contract but not have any work. Winning a master contract simply gives you a license to compete for subsequent task orders.

Compete for master contracts much like other diverse services contracts; win by addressing the customer's issues.

The primary issues for an organization seeking pre-qualified vendors for anticipated work are:

- **Qualifications** to do the work
- **Capability** to perform

See RELEVANT
EXPERIENCE/PAST
PERFORMANCE, RESUMES,
SERVICE PROPOSALS;
and TEAMING, *Capture
Guide.*

- **Responsiveness**, including both the ability to quickly respond to task order requests and the ability to solve problems
- **Best value**

The primary issues for an organization seeking pre-qualified vendors to fund their purchasing organization are:

- Ability to market their services
- Ability to persuade other organizations to purchase under the master contracts

Qualifications, capability, responsiveness, and value are also important in this scenario because vendors lacking these qualities will not be selected for task order work.

Purchasing organizations desiring to cover their costs often issue broad contract vehicles, qualify numerous bidders, and set high contract ceilings. A recent bid request stated they wanted to award contracts to 14 to 16 vendors.

---

2   Market your organization proactively to gain a competitive advantage, influence requirements, and win sole source contracts.

Be proactive in marketing your services under the blanket contract. Identify customer needs, suggest solutions, and influence the requirements. Submit brief white papers outlining potential task descriptions or statements of work. Busy customers often convert these into task order bid requests.

When customers' needs are urgent, they often request 5- to 10-day responses. Some task order requests require a 24-hour response.

Vendors with advance notice have a distinct advantage, especially if they helped draft the task description.

Many vendors win sole source task orders because they were the only vendor that either understood the requirements or responded within the deadlines. One veteran program manager noted that he spent 60 percent of his time drafting sole source task order descriptions and justifications. Of course, they were called *white papers*.

---

3   Prepare to respond quickly by developing and maintaining a searchable database with experience examples, proof of performance examples, and key-person resumes.

Database software
is not required.
Searchable paper or
electronic files are
sufficient.

When multiple vendors are pre-qualified, the ability to quickly prepare a quality response might be your most significant discriminator. Organizations accustomed to 30- to 60-day response periods struggle to prepare quality task order proposals in short time frames.

Prepare to respond quickly by developing and maintaining a searchable database. Many organizations archive their old proposals, but these boilerplate libraries often are filled with vague, seller-focused, dated, inconsistent, and incorrect material. Figure 1 lists the types of material needed to quickly prepare focused, persuasive, task order proposals.

MATERIAL	SEARCHABLE BY:
Work experience and performance	Type of work, client and agency, industry, period of performance, award value, budget versus actual cost, actual performance, number of people, key people by position, reference contact, performance assessments, customer issues, key decision maker, key influencers, customer values, site photos, lessons learned
Resumes	Names, projects, responsibilities by project, dates, performance results, client comments and references, education, licenses and certifications
Process/product descriptions	Graphical depictions, action captions, text descriptions, site and product photos, test results, performance data

Figure 1. Recommended Database/Boilerplate Materials. *Organizations that develop and maintain searchable databases can prepare persuasive, winning task order proposals more efficiently, effectively, and quickly than their competitors.*

---

4   Follow bid request instructions explicitly.

See COMPLIANCE
AND RESPONSIVENESS,
OUTLINING, *and*
QUESTION/RESPONSE
PROPOSALS.

Follow bid request instructions explicitly, especially when the time to respond is short. Follow the prescribed format. Answer questions immediately after the question, and then support your answers with boilerplate as needed.

While this guideline might seem obvious to most readers, task order evaluators say that failing to follow instructions is the most frequent vendor mistake and a common reason bids are disqualified. Evaluators often need specific information in a prescribed format to obtain internal approvals to award a task order contract.

5 Focus on the task, not on re-qualifying to bid.

Focus your task order proposal on the task, not on re-qualifying your organization. You qualified under the master contract.

Figure 2 lists and describes the primary issues of task order evaluators.

ISSUE	DESCRIPTION
People:	Who will fill the key positions, by name? Are they available during the time required? What is their specific, relevant experience? (Not a chronological list of all experiences.) Do the people proposed understand this customer's issues, needs, and organization?
Approach:	Can you simply and clearly describe exactly how you will complete this particular task? (Not a description of how you generally approach similar tasks.)
Performance:	What past performance is relevant to this task order? When bidding for the master contract, you likely cited large projects that covered many aspects of the work described in the RFP. That work might have been delivered by another part of your organization and might not be relevant to this task. Past performance examples need to be of similar size and scope; offer similar people; and offer a similar, local management team.
Schedule:	Do you know exactly when each task element will be started and completed?
Cost:	Do you know what the cost will be, based upon a nearly identical previously completed task? Are the conditions sufficiently similar to trust your estimate?
Management:	Exactly who will manage this task and how? Secondarily, where does this person report in your organization? (Not how is your organization managed, or what is your management philosophy.)
Risk:	Exactly what risks do you anticipate? How serious are these risks, both in impact and probability, and specifically how will you manage these risks?

Figure 2. Key Task Order Evaluator Issues. *Task order evaluators are most interested in these issues. Address each one clearly and succinctly in your response.*

6 Use graphics to rapidly and clearly describe your processes.

See ACTION CAPTIONS *and* GRAPHICS.

Graphics are the single, easiest way to describe your processes. Clear graphical depictions of processes inspire confidence that the bidder knows what they will do. Text descriptions often appear complex, suggesting to many evaluators that the process is complex, risky, and perhaps not well understood.

When using graphical process descriptions, make them specific to the task. Avoid generic, conceptual graphics. Placing words in ovals, and then drawing lines between the ovals, does not mean that they are connected.

Avoid generic text and graphic process descriptions that suggest you will figure out what to do after contract award. You probably will not get the award. The major advantage of a graphical task description is that you can quickly tailor it in the action caption and labels. Text descriptions are more time consuming to modify, so they are often not tailored.

7 Precisely match experience and proof of performance examples to each task.

See RELEVANT EXPERIENCE/ PAST PERFORMANCE, RESUMES, *and* SERVICE PROPOSALS.

Buyers prefer vendors that have successfully completed identical tasks and employed the same people under identical conditions, in the same industry. Prove that you satisfy those preferences by citing experience and performance examples that match the requirements of each proposed task.

Match this customer's issues with a prior customer's issues. For example, if the customer is concerned about on-time completion, describe a similar task that you completed on time. If the need is to solve a complex design problem, then cite where you solved a difficult design problem.

The quality or degree of the issue/example match is more important than having numerous examples. Additionally, the relevance of the individual members' professional experience to the issues is more important than the organizational experience of the vendor.

8

See RELEVANT EXPERIENCE/PAST PERFORMANCE.

Integrate success stories within technical task, process, and management descriptions.

If the bid request asks for a Past Performance section, include it. If the bid request limits past performance to a specific number of contracts, follow the instructions. Select a range of projects that addresses each of this customer's issues rather than multiple examples addressing the same issue.

Add further emphasis, interest, and credibility to the experience of your key personnel and organization by integrating success stories in your process descriptions. Few evaluators will take the initiative to explicitly link the Past Performance section to task descriptions. Make the link for them. Also link the proposed personnel to the past performance citations, if possible.

Keep success stories short, following the four-step process summarized in *Relevant Experience/ Past Performance,* guideline 4.

Integrating success stories offers two additional advantages:

- Bidders can cite more experience examples than permitted in the Past Performance section. Past performance examples are usually limited in the bid request.
- Bidders can directly link cited Past-Performance-section examples to specific contract tasks. Repetition increases memory retention.

9

Limit management discussions to this task.

Evaluators want to know how tasks will be managed, how the personnel will be managed, and how the manager will address typical risk issues such as employee behavior, turnover, absences, and training. They are not interested in broad descriptions of how your organization is managed. Address the task manager's level of authority and the resources controlled by or available to the task manager.

In some instances, evaluators might reduce management discussions for subsequent task order awards under the same master contract.

For example, they may know that you report progress on all active task orders weekly using a specific format and submittal process. You might not need to sell them on the quality of this process or explain the report structure and format.

When bidding on successive task orders, ask customers to clarify what they want. When in doubt or if the customer is not available, follow the bid request instructions.

10

Avoid deliberate *bait and switch* tactics. Evaluators either know that the named person is already committed to another contract, or they learn to distrust your word. *Ghost* competitors that use *bait and switch* tactics. To prevent "bait and switch" the RFP may state that those filling key positions will be required to support the task for a minimum of 6 months unless there is a compelling reason not to, e.g., quitting the company, serious illness, death.

See RESUMES.

Tailor resumes for each key position.

The single, most important discriminator in task order proposals in a services environment is the people that you propose to complete the task. No matter how short the response time, tailor the resumes for every key position. Typical or representative resumes for non-key positions are usually acceptable.

Your ability to correctly state which positions are key is an important indicator of your understanding of the task and the customer. Many bidders fail because they do not identify key positions or they identify key positions incorrectly.

Name all people who will fill key positions. *Generic* individuals are never as appealing as named individuals. Evaluators often interpret unnamed positions as lack of qualified resources or poor planning. Better to ask permission to change a person than to not name anyone to fill the position.

Organize resumes according to the evaluators' needs and interests. Evaluators prefer functional requirement and accomplishment resumes. They seek to understand precisely how the proposed person's accomplishments, knowledge, and experience match the requirements of the position. Create an *executive summary* at the beginning of the resume showing the relevance of the person's qualifications to the task order effort.

Team Selection and Management are a matter of roles rather than positions. Proposal efforts range from a single person to dedicated teams comprising hundreds. Selecting proposal team members and managing them vary widely by organization, market sector, and even culture. Most aspects of project team management apply equally to proposal teams.

Team Selection and Management

1. Establish a proposal management structure with defined roles and responsibilities.
2. Tailor your approach to each proposal by adjusting role assignments.
3. Document your approach in a Proposal Management Plan (PMP).
4. Select the right types of people for each role.
5. Differentiate process and content responsibilities.
6. Scope proposal preparation tasks based on a clear vision of the document to be delivered and realistic time standards.
7. Manage the proposal like other corporate strategic projects.
8. Reward good performance.

---

1 Establish a proposal management structure with defined roles and responsibilities.

See Process.

Certain roles must be filled on every proposal team. If you vary the role to suit the people available, proposal quality will suffer.

The following roles are required on proposal teams of all sizes.

The **capture manager** must win the order and is responsible for customer contact before, during, and after the proposal is submitted, conforming to the customer's rules. The capture manager owns the capture strategy.

The **proposal manager** leads the team and is responsible for resources, planning, scheduling, development, and production. The primary focus of proposal management must be to produce a winning proposal document. The proposal manager owns the proposal strategy, derived from the capture strategy.

The **project manager** develops a winning solution that complies with the organization's objectives. Generally the project manager (sometimes called a "solution architect") is responsible to the strategic business unit manager for profitability and risk management.

The **volume leader** (or "book boss") develops a specific volume for the proposal manager. Volume managers are directly responsible for input into their volume.

The **proposal coordinator** or specialist helps the proposal manager control the proposal development process. Typical tasks include helping develop and update plans, schedules, materials, and files; coordinating with other process specialists; and helping with reviews.

The **production lead** supervises production, including word processing, graphics, desktop publishing, and production.

The **editor** ensures that materials, both text and graphics, meet the organization's style standards.

The **proposal writers** obtain whatever information is required to draft and deliver a compliant, responsive, clear, and persuasive proposal section to proposal management when scheduled.

The **time and materials estimators** prepare supportable task descriptions, time and material estimates, and estimating rationale when required, that precisely match the tasks described by the corresponding writers.

The **pricing staff** roll time and material estimates into a final price that meets customer and seller standards.

The focus of each of these roles changes as you progress through the six-phase business development cycle: (1) Positioning, (2) Pursuit, (3) Capture, (4) Proposal Planning, (5) Proposal Development and Production, (6) Post Submittal Negotiation and Closure.

2   Tailor your approach to each proposal by adjusting role assignments.

The roles described in guideline 1 must be assumed on all proposals. Ignore any of them, and the quality of your proposal will drop.

On small proposals, combine roles in a single individual. On large proposals, several people may share a single role. Worry more about having the role covered than about how you assign the roles among the individuals available.

3   Document your approach in a Proposal Management Plan (PMP).

See PROPOSAL
MANAGEMENT PLAN.

Any plan worth doing must be written. Even on a one-person effort, develop and document a minimum plan, then work to the plan.

Define the structure and content required in your organization's proposal management plans as part of your business development process definition and documentation. If you happen to be assigned the proposal manager's role in one of the many organizations that lack a defined process, tailor your organization's project management process to the proposal project.

4   Select the right types of people for each role.

Different skills are required for the different roles. Some people are suited to multiple roles, some are not. Figure 1 summarizes some of the skills that help individuals fill specific roles more effectively.

ROLES	SKILLS AND EXPERIENCE
Capture Manager	Big picture; customer focused; marketing savvy; has senior management access and respect; understands proposal development; guides solution development, teaming, competitive assessment, price to win, and strategy development; knows competitors' products, services, people, and reputation
Proposal Manager	Disciplined project manager; leads as well as manages; knows and drives the process; has senior management access, respect, and a sponsor; generalist who can focus on details; can delegate content issues to focus on process
Volume Manager	Can maintain the respect of writers (content specialists) while managing the process to standards and schedules; disciplinarian; excellent trainer, coach, and communicator; content generalist with some detailed knowledge; allergic to jargon, platitudes, unsupported claims, and fluff
Proposal Specialist	Believes the process works; understands and often prepares compliance checklists, outlines, cross-references matrices, WBS, WBS dictionaries, and schedules; can help writers with hardware, software, and storyboards; knows where to find relevant reuse materials; pleasant, professional nag; knows where to go or who to talk to for information and action; obsessed with meeting the details of schedule, compliance, and quality; functions well without sleep; thrives on adrenaline; works well with production staff
Section Writer	Technically knowledgeable; knows where to get needed information and willing to do it; clear, logical thinker; understands customer's view; understands pros and cons of alternative approaches; computer literate and competent writer; can follow directions and listen

Figure 1. Select the Best Person for the Role. *Consider the skills and experience listed as desirable for the role listed.*

5   Differentiate process and content responsibilities.

Proposal managers, proposal specialists, and production leads tend to have process responsibilities. When in a process role, remember that many contributors are primarily concerned about content. People in content roles will only concern themselves with process if they are convinced that the process will save them time and embarrassment while letting them focus on content.

Those in capture management, sales, program or product management, estimating, and pricing are primarily interested in content. When their content interests conflict, they all see process issues as an irritant that forces them to compromise the content.

Embed process in tools, making the process transparent to the user. For example, a structured tool that prompts users focuses individuals using the tool on the task and content; users forget that they are following a defined process.

Volume managers tend to have split roles: they have been selected to manage a process, producing a winning volume, but they usually have a content background relevant to their assigned volume. They often find the content issues more interesting and fail to manage the process to the schedule.

6 Scope proposal preparation tasks based on a clear vision of the document to be delivered and realistic time standards.

See SCHEDULING.

Any person using a parametric approach to estimating knows that accurate estimates rely on the assumption that the content and process are the same. Similarly, a 1,000-page proposal will require more writing time than a 100-page proposal, assuming similar tasks and processes. Develop a clear vision of the product you will deliver, then specify the tasks required to produce that product.

If you have a consistent process and clearly defined tasks, you can accurately scope your proposal based on standards collected from earlier proposals. The flaw is that too few organizations collect the data required to develop proposal management standards.

Proposal professionals tend to look to someone else to suggest the correct standard, but with inconsistent processes, products, management, resources, and skills among organizations, standards transfer poorly.

Develop your own proposal preparation metrics and quality standards.

7 Manage the proposal like other corporate strategic projects.

Best practice reviews show that organizations that are most effective at winning business view winning new business in a competitive environment to be one of their most strategic and important activities. Organizations that effectively capture new business possess many of the following characteristics:

- They assign their best people to proposals, not whoever is available.
- Management requires individuals seeking to advance to senior management to demonstrate an ability to contribute to and manage teams that capture new business.
- They define and document their business development process.
- They train the participants and provide the resources required.
- They regularly review capture and proposal projects like all other strategic projects.

8 Reward good performance.

Good performers must be rewarded and encouraged at all phases of a proposal project. Commend good performance in the daily meetings. Recognition is often more effective than prizes or monetary rewards.

Sell your approach and process. People who understand why they are doing something are more willing and likely to exceed your expectations.

Hold a victory party immediately after submittal, win or lose. If you win, hold a 2nd victory party. At minimum, notify every contributor, win or lose. Too many participants never hear if you have won or lost.

Many contributors to proposals are temporarily assigned, pulled from their regular position.

Their managers tend to be inconvenienced by the loss and may remember it negatively at the next performance review. Thank good performers in writing, sending a written note to their managers. Some proposal managers ask the best performers to tell them when their salary review is due, then they personally talk to these performers' managers to support a better review.

The best proposal managers seem to be able to make the effort fun. Most proposal managers will be managing a future proposal development project and would like the best individuals to be willing to help again.

Theme Statements

Theme Statements in proposals link a customer benefit to the discriminating features of your offer. Themes tell readers why they should select you. The most powerful themes contain the most important and unique discriminators, something the customer wants that no one else offers.

Win themes or major themes apply to the entire proposal. They usually tie a single, unique discriminator to a critical customer need:

> Development risk and cost are eliminated by selecting the only transport aircraft in this class that is in current production.

Theme statements are not sales slogans, like the catchy phrases most commonly seen in consumer marketing:

Have it your way™

Where's the beef?™

Just do it™

It's the economy, stupid.

Be all you can be™

We try harder™

When it absolutely, positively has to be there overnight™

See Proposal Strategy.

Section, topic, or paragraph themes are specific statements that appear in a consistent place and style within a proposal. Section themes are the primary focus of this section.

Business capture teams sometimes confuse strategies and theme statements. **Strategies =** *things to do*. **Themes =** *things to say.* Effective strategies have two parts:

- **Strategic:** The position you will take
- **Tactical:** The specific actions you will take to attain the desired position

Inserting theme statements in a proposal is one tactical way to implement a strategy.

Experienced business development professionals often use the terms *theme* and *strategy* interchangeably, confusing both their customers and their sales support teams.

Theme Statements

1. Use a logical process to brainstorm theme statements.
2. Use theme statements consistently.
3. Link benefits to features, trying to state benefits first.
4. Quantify benefits if possible.
5. Draft concise theme statements, preferably in a single complete sentence.
6. Differentiate section theme statements and section summaries.
7. Ensure benefits go beyond advantages.
8. Tailor your theme structure and approach to the evaluation process.
9. Use the Theme Litmus Test to enhance the impact of your theme statements.

---

1 Use a logical process to brainstorm theme statements.

Following a logical process enables you to develop meaningful theme statements more consistently and rapidly. Use the following theme statement brainstorming checklist to help you determine the key point you want the customer to remember:

- What is the point of this section?
- Why should the customer be impressed with what you're proposing?
- What aspect of your offer or approach makes it worth buying?
- What do you offer that is different from competitors' approaches?
- What makes your offer unique, desirable, or beneficial?
- What does your offer do for the customer?
- Why should the customer prefer your offer and organization over the competition?

- Does your offer answer the question, *So what?*

Brainstorming theme statement contents sparks creative input from the entire team.

You may prefer to develop theme statements more logically. Proposal theme statements should flow from the capture and proposal strategy. If you have neither, follow the process outlined below:

1. List the customer's issues.
2. List a feature of your solution that addresses each issue.
3. Define the issue as specifically and uniquely as possible.
4. Identify a similar success story. Try to quantify the benefit.
5. Draft a theme statement linking the feature and the quantified benefit to a customer issue and substantiate the claim in the proposal.

See DISCRIMINATORS *and* FEATURES, ADVANTAGES, AND BENEFITS.

While helpful, you do not need to substantiate your claim in the theme statement, but you must substantiate your claim in the proposal.

Review the following examples to see how these five steps would work:

1. A customer in the travel clothing and accessory business is concerned about increasing telemarketing sales revenue.
2. You sell IT support services, including supplying and supporting Point-of-Sale software and terminals for e-commerce and catalog sales.
3. Individual sales clerks often do not know the customer's purchase history, interests, or which related items they could recommend.
4. You helped a client achieve a 35 percent increase in dollars per order in a similar situation with a bicycle component and accessory telemarketing retailer.
5. Incorporate the previous information into a theme statement: *If Expedition Clothing sees gains similar to Saddle Sores Bike Company, your typical $100 per order sale would increase to $135, for a total annual revenue increase of $3.5 million, after installing Sales Aide™ software and terminals.*

2

Use theme statements consistently.

See PAGE AND DOCUMENT DESIGN.

Place theme statements consistently throughout the proposal at the beginning of every major section, subsection, or summary. If you use theme statements in the first- and second-level sections, (section 3 and section 3.1, for instance), use them for all first- and second-level sections. If you insert theme statements at other points in the proposal, do it consistently.

Give theme statements an identical appearance. Most theme statements are visually emphasized to differentiate them from body text, as illustrated in figure 1. The amount of emphasis can vary from the minimal emphasis of a single-sentence opening paragraph in standard body text font to a large, bold, colored font surrounded by white space, borders, shading, or other emphasis devices.

Writers forced to create theme statements to fill the space assigned when they have no discriminating features will often draft poor, ineffective theme statements. When too many theme statements are included, no matter where they are placed, evaluators have said, "We knew that was the marketing hype, so we ignored them."

1. Top and bottom rules

2.0 TITLE

Our team of 47 software engineers has a combined total of over 600 years of experience designing, testing, and installing conversion software on time and within budget.

2. Second color contrasting font

2.0 TITLE

Our team of 47 software engineers has a combined total of over 600 years of experience designing, testing, and installing conversion software on time and within budget.

3. Shaded box, drop cap, second color, two-column format

2.0 TITLE

Our team of 47 software engineers has a combined total of over 600 years of experience designing, testing, and installing conversion software on time and within budget.

Unified Network Management provides integrated end-to-end control of all your physical network resources. The result is direct, dedicated, quality service . . .

Figure 1. Give Theme Statements a Consistent, Appropriate Emphasis. *Different styles are appropriate for different customers and markets. Select a tasteful, appropriate style for your customer and use it consistently throughout each proposal.*

3

Do not *fall on your sword* over whether benefits appear before features. If benefits and features are clearly linked and the features are discriminators, then you have an effective theme statement.

See CUSTOMER FOCUS.

Link benefits to features, trying to state benefits first.

Evaluators must see a clear, logical link between the benefit and the feature included in each theme statement. While every benefit could plausibly be linked to lower cost, you do not have to take them all that far.

The following story illustrates the *plausible trail* concept:

> An account executive had been traveling for 3 weeks. Immediately after takeoff, he pulled a crumpled pile of receipts from his briefcase, placed them next to his expense form on the seat tray, and said, "And now to create a plausible trail."

The customer must see the *plausible trail*, the link between the feature and the benefit.

Poor example

> Our Easy Link™ software will reduce your cost.

Better example

> The intuitive, graphical user interface of our Easy Link™ software can reduce your training time from 4 hours to 1 hour.

Customers buy benefits, not features. Improve the customer focus of your theme statements by stating the benefit before the feature. The impact is subtle but makes the theme statement more persuasive.

Best example

> Reduce your training time from 4 hours to 1 hour due to the intuitive, graphical user interface of our Easy Link™ software.

4

Quantify benefits if possible.

Theme statements that include quantified benefits tend to be more credible.

Theme statement—benefit not quantified

> Reduce order entry cost by installing e-Entry™ order entry software.

Theme statement—benefit quantified

> Reduce order handling cost 30 percent by installing e-Entry™ order entry software.

Quantified benefits must be supportable. If you cannot support your claims, change your theme statement. Support your claims in the proposal shortly after making the claim.

Whenever possible, quantify the benefits collaboratively with the customer. Customers who help determine the potential benefits of your solution are more likely to continue to believe the calculation is correct.

State the quantified benefit realistically and precisely. Broad generalizations are perceived

broadly; overly precise numbers will not be believed. For example, the 30 percent savings in the previous theme statement will be interpreted as plus or minus 5 to 10 percent:

Theme statement—benefit more precisely quantified

> Reduce order handling cost 33 percent by installing e-Entry™ order entry software.

Depending on how the calculations were completed, the following theme statement borders on being too precise:

Theme statement—benefit more precisely quantified

> Reduce order handling cost 33.4 percent by installing e-Entry™ order entry software.

The following theme statement is too precise to be credible:

Theme statement—benefit too precisely quantified

> Reduce order handling cost 33.37 percent by installing e-Entry™ order entry software.

5

Draft concise theme statements, preferably in a single complete sentence.

The longer the theme statement, the more likely the evaluator will not read it. Writing short, concise, discriminating theme statements is difficult.

If you can remove any words in your theme statements without changing the meaning, do it. If you can use a shorter but still accurate word, do it. If you can use a short, active verb instead of jargon, do it.

Note how following these recommendations improves the following theme statement:

Poor example

> Our integrated design process, incorporating the lessons learned on all earlier generation aircraft engines, has resulted in an engine that uses four common fastening systems for engine assembly, offering maximum maintainability.

Too many features confuse the reader. Which ones are most unique? Most sellers would claim to have an integrated design process and to incorporate lessons learned.

Better example

Our engine uses four common fastening systems for maximum maintainability.

Now cut the jargon. Fastening systems are bolts; maximum maintainability means easy to fix.

Better example

With only four common bolts used for assembly, our engine is easy to fix.

Then put the benefit first.

Our engine is easy to fix because only four common bolts are used for assembly.

Save the proof for the section graphics and text. Do not try to incorporate complete proof in the theme statement.

Evaluators tire from reading long theme statements. High-impact theme statements resemble sound bites. If evaluators had to justify why you should be selected, what should they say? Draft selection justification statements for the evaluators in your theme statements.

Many adults recall an English teacher who said, "A complete sentence reflects a complete thought." With theme statements, a complete sentence is more likely to contain both features and benefits. Theme statements that are incomplete sentences too frequently contain only features or only benefits. Good theme statements enable the reader to answer both questions: "So what?" and "How so?"

One way to test your theme statements is to read them aloud. Most theme statements that sound good are good. We can actually tolerate reading longer theme statements than we can tolerate hearing them. If you have to take a breath when reading your theme statement, it is too long. Focus your thoughts, and shorten your theme statements.

6 Differentiate section theme statements and section summaries.

Writers often create long theme statements that incorporate all of the key features and benefits discussed in the section. These long theme statements make better section summaries. Use them as the first paragraph in the section, then write a concise, focused theme statement.

Note how the following section summary is converted into a concise, specific, and focused theme statement.

Section Summary

All environmental waste cleanup services will be conducted by our 75-person team, centrally located in Omaha, Nebraska. Ima Green has successfully managed this team for 3 years, completing 22 cleanup actions on schedule and at or under budget. Team members are licensed to perform all action requested in the bid request.

Section Theme Statement

Ima Green's team has completed 22 cleanup actions for your organization during the past 3 years. All cleanup actions were on schedule and at or under budget

To illustrate the difference between a section theme and a section summary, try the following two-part exercise:

1. Consider the place where you live. When you were looking for your current apartment or house, you probably saw several places at the same price. Jot down the specific feature that prompted you to select the one where you live. Typical answers are *location, space, the fireplace, large garage, fenced yard, it was bright and airy,* or *it just felt good.*
2. Now write a one- or two-sentence description of the place where you live. Typical descriptions read like a real estate agent's description:

   The home is a 2,000 sq. ft. brick rambler with 3 bed-rooms, 2 full baths, a full basement, located on a .25-acre lot near neighborhood schools.

Form a theme statement by linking discriminating features identified in part one to a benefit. The second statement is a summary. Emulate this in section themes.

7 Ensure benefits go beyond advantages.

See FEATURES, ADVANTAGES, AND BENEFITS.

Benefits are something that customers have acknowledged they want and value. Benefits are owned by customers. Advantages are potential benefits. Advantages sound good, but customers may not actually want them. In some instances, customers might value the advantage, turning it into a benefit, once they understand how it helps them.

Proposal writers cannot draft effective themes if they do not know what customers value.

Consider the following examples:

You can economically commute to work with this new hybrid gasoline-electric auto, rated at 65 miles per gallon.

What if the customer is looking for an auto to race in weekend road rallies?

Your fitness will improve rapidly when you use the Pro Star programmable treadmill for only 20 minutes, 4 days per week.

What if the customer detests walking or running, lacks space to place a treadmill, lacks the initiative to workout alone, or simply does not care about personal fitness? Then the treadmill offers this customer no benefit.

Organizations that use boilerplate extensively often have ineffective themes in their proposals. The benefits, while desirable, are often generic rather than specific and are not in the customer's terms.

Consider a proposal to provide a telephone system to a business. A typical proposal includes a list of 50 features of the phone system linked to the benefit of each feature. Many customers see no need for 80 percent of the features, so the system appears over-specified, complex, and more expensive than necessary. Many of the remaining 20 percent of the features are linked to benefits that are not particularly appealing or useful to the customer.

In an attempt to cover all aspects of their system, sellers unintentionally turn off customers.

---

8   Tailor your theme structure and approach to the evaluation process.

Proposal professionals advocate distinctly different standards for theme statements, usually because a particular approach has worked well in a specific market. All of the following approaches are used:

1. Place a single theme statement only at the beginning of sections, typically at a uniform indenture level.
2. Place a theme statement anywhere a significant discriminator is discussed.
3. Place a series of theme statements at the beginning of major sections in a single box.
4. Place a single theme statement at the top of every page.

Each approach has potential advantages and disadvantages, depending on how the proposal will be evaluated. Remember that having focused, persuasive content is much more important than the number of theme statements and the placement of those theme statements in your proposal.

The **first two approaches** are more effective in the less-disciplined, more-casual approach to evaluation common in many nongovernment market sectors. Short, concise theme statements are more likely to be read and remembered when the winner is being selected in a group discussion. The telling comment from an evaluator is likely to be something like the following: "I think we should go with Company A because they were the only one that . . . " The evaluator's justification usually mirrors a particularly effective, persuasive, and memorable theme statement.

The **first three approaches** effectively capture the attention of *skimmers*. Skimmers are usually senior managers who play a major role in the selection decision but are not assigned a formal evaluation role. Skimmers read only the parts that capture their interest.

Placing a single theme statement at the beginning of the section requires a writer to identify the single most important discriminator in the section and incorporate it into the theme statement. The concept is correct, but the implementation is more difficult.

Placing theme statements anywhere a significant discriminator is discussed suggests the seller has numerous discriminators. If a theme statement directly answers a specific bid request question or requirement, the highly visible theme statement makes evaluation easy.

The risk in requiring theme statements at set points in a proposal is that writers might lack a discriminating feature, writers must draft more theme statements, and often these theme statements are not as focused and persuasive. Evaluators reading numerous theme statements are less likely to remember your major discriminators.

The **third approach**, placing a collection of themes in a single box at the beginning of a section, has advantages in complex, formally solicited proposals with a detailed, disciplined evaluation process. The example in figure 2 demonstrates this process.

Summarizing your response to the compliance requirements in a single place makes evaluation easy, potentially increasing your score. However, individual evaluators at the item level have minimal influence over the final selection. Evaluators with decision making power tend to skim proposals and are less likely to remember anything said in a collection of themes. They are more likely to remember a single, concise statement.

The **fourth approach**, placing themes at the top of every page, is the least-effective choice. Evaluators tend to perceive themes at the top of the page as headers and ignore them. Writers forced to draft a theme for every page tend to draft ineffective, general, and less-persuasive theme statements.

The only difference between *pull quotes* and *margin themes* is whether the statement is identical to what is said in body text.

See ACTION CAPTIONS; FEATURES, ADVANTAGES, AND BENEFITS; *and* HEADINGS.

Theme statements are things you say in the proposal to support your strategy. Writers have alternative devices to theme statements to emphasize their strategy in a proposal, specifically, informative headings, action captions, pull quotes, and margin theme statements. Each emphasis device is explained below:

- *Informative headings* are similar to themes, even if they do not incorporate both features and benefits.
- *Action captions* include features and benefits, but they can be longer than themes. The graphic seems to prompt people to eagerly read long captions when they refuse to read long themes.

- *Pull quotes*, often found in magazine articles, resemble themes. Pull quotes are literally quotes pulled from the text and displayed in a larger point size, often in the margin or with body text wrapped around them. Readers tend to remember items that are repeated and emphasized.
- *Margin theme statements* are often placed in page margins adjacent to where the point is supported, anywhere in a proposal section. Margin quotes are effective. Consider using them in all proposals.

Compliance requirement	*Theme statement*
INDICATE YOUR APPROACH TO SITE REMEDIATION	**THE KLEAN TEAM WILL REMEDIATE EACH SITE IN A RAPID, COST EFFECTIVE MANNER BY:**
Discuss cost-effective practices, ... job site safety, ... team structure, ... and how you will use subcontractors, if relevant.	• Eliminating double handling of material • Loading trucks with identical material to eliminate decontamination • Limiting team size by assigning individuals qualified to handle several jobs • Using specialized subcontractors wherever they are available, qualified, and cost competitive

Figure 2. Limit Grouped Themes to Formally Evaluated and Solicited Proposals. *Grouped themes reflect individual section compliance requirements. In this example, compliance requirements are listed on the left. The corresponding group theme is shown on the right. Grouped themes are typically placed at the beginning of a proposal section. A similar alternative is to place a benefit-feature matrix at the beginning of each proposal section that reflects the compliance requirements.*

9   Use the Theme Litmus Test to enhance the impact of your theme statements.

Chemists use litmus paper to quickly discriminate acidic and basic solutions. Writers can use the theme litmus test to quickly discriminate effective and ineffective theme statements.

Can you honestly answer "No," then "Yes" to both of the following questions?

1. Could the competition plausibly make the same claim?
2. Could an evaluator cut-and-paste this theme statement into an evaluation form to justify giving you the highest rating for a factor or subfactor?

If not, then refine your theme statement. Try to make your feature more specific until it is unique. Then try to make the benefits more precise. Try to quantify the benefits.

While not foolproof, these questions can help you detect themes that require improvement. Eliminate jargon, slogans, and platitudes from your theme statements. Consider the following examples:

Poor

Elbonia Telephone has committed to partnering with the Elbonian Navy to assure success.

Improved

The Elbonian Navy can eliminate the cost of purchasing their own communications satellite by leasing encrypted and secure channels from the Elbonia Telephone satellite network.

Poor

Master Constructors is uniquely qualified to manage your project.

Improved

As the only company to ever construct a bridge of this type and length, we will assign the same project manager and construction superintendent to better ensure completion on time and within budget.

Virtual Proposal Teams are both increasingly common and necessary. Proposal managers must complete the same tasks in a virtual environment that are required when managing a co-located team.

Organizations are increasingly using virtual teams to prepare large, complex bids that were once exclusively prepared by co-located teams.

Teams are small groups of people with complementary skills who are committed to a common goal. Virtual teams are small groups of people who primarily interact electronically and may occasionally meet face-to-face to accomplish a common goal. Whether virtual or co-located, proposal teams have the same goal, preparing a winning proposal.

Organizations are driven by several factors to increasingly deploy virtual teams to complete a variety of tasks, including crafting proposals. The primary enablers and drivers are:

- Increase in broadband web connectivity and web collaboration tools

- Increase in travel costs

- Increase in employees working from home or remote locations

- Expansion of multinational organizations

- Expansion of services that do not require a central production site

- Access to lower labor costs in emerging markets or unique personnel in remote locations

Research on high-performance teams and virtual team management is extensive and active. Here are some trends in how organizations use virtual teams:

- Larger proposal teams are less likely to be virtual, although some contributors might be virtual. Virtual proposal teams tend to be smaller (3 to 10 members).

- Virtual proposal teams often have shorter response deadlines (5-10 days).

- Virtual proposal teams tend to be concentrated in the non-government and multinational market sectors.

- Virtual proposal teams tend to sell relatively similar, modular services and products, and use more boilerplate in the proposal.

- Co-located proposal teams predominantly serve organizations that sell larger, more complex, higher-risk systems.

- More organizations are using virtual proposal teams for large, complex bids that were once prepared exclusively by co-located teams.

- Most proposal teams have virtual contributors, and most contributors operate virtually to some extent.

Virtual teams do sometimes fail. Senior management and virtual team managers will sometimes need to shift to a partially or fully co-located team.

The following guidelines focus on aspects of virtual team management that differ or require greater emphasis than when managing a co-located team.

Virtual Team Management

1. Exploit the advantages and compensate for the challenges of virtual teams.

2. Establish and maintain a *high-trust* environment.

3. Define and assign key virtual team roles clearly.

4. Establish clearly defined, discrete tasks.

5. Select task-appropriate, easy-to-use technology.

6. Over communicate.

7. Distinguish team management, leadership, and member motivation.

8. Establish virtual meeting ground rules.

9. Establish a rigorous review structure.

1 Exploit the advantages and compensate for the challenges of virtual teams.

Many organizations, business development managers, and proposal managers prefer co-locating their entire team, but have little choice; they must increasingly use virtual proposal teams to offset the challenges shown in figure 1.

Virtual proposal team managers face social and technology challenges. The social challenges require managing, motivating, and coaching team members. The technology challenges require tools to monitor tasks, schedules, and performance quality and are usually easier to address. Technical challenges are addressed in guideline 5.

Common social challenges are low individual commitment, role overload, role ambiguity, absenteeism, social loafing, and limited and/or conflicting management priorities. Consider these social challenges:

- Team members in different time zones resent inconveniently scheduled meetings.

- Critical decisions are delayed because key people cannot find common meeting times.

- E-mail or off-hand teleconference comments are misconstrued, causing confusion and distrust.

- Time and resources are wasted because multiple team members unknowingly work on the same task.

- Isolated team members feel left out and are minimally committed to the team objective.

- Managers who do not benefit from team success direct team members to work on other tasks.

- Team members can hide poor performance and then blame technology, management, lack of information, or other team members.

The recommendations in subsequent guidelines will help virtual proposal managers overcome these challenges.

ISSUE	ADVANTAGES	CHALLENGES
Flexibility	Rapidly form, execute, and disband teams.	Cumbersome to manage and motivate people over time and distance.
Resources	Assign the best talent available across time, space, and cultures.	Loss of effectiveness due to low individual commitment to team goal. Time, distance, and cultural differences can lead to miscommunication and conflict.
Cost	Reduce by eliminating travel, housing, per diem; and assigning lowest cost resource.	Possible increase due to more complex management, technology, and training.
Response Time	Reduce travel delays and time spent waiting for resources.	Possible increased time for re-work, delays, inconsistencies, conflict, and mistrust due to miscommunication.

Figure 1. Advantages and Challenges of Virtual Proposal Teams. *Virtual teams offer a number of advantages and challenges.*

2 Establish and maintain a *high-trust* environment.

Researchers overwhelmingly agree that trust is the key prerequisite for an effective team. However, trust develops differently in co-located and virtual teams. Trusting team members exhibit these characteristics:

- Admit weaknesses and mistakes to each other.

- Request help and assist members outside their area of responsibility.

- Accept questions and suggestions openly without defensiveness.

- Give others the benefit of the doubt.

- Risk offering constructive feedback.

- Disclose their agendas and motivations.

- Offer and accept apologies without reservation.

- Look forward to meetings and team interaction.

- Seek to understand others' viewpoints and perspectives.

- Share responsibility for overall project success.

- Avoid dysfunctional behaviors, such as blaming, attacking, rescuing, or playing the victim.

Managers face a number of obstacles to developing trust within a virtual proposal team. Members bring expectations and potential fears from prior virtual experiences. They must learn to trust team management and other members in spite of the risk factors inherent in time, distance, and cultural separation.

In addition, tight deadlines leave little time to build trust. Because team members may be less willing to participate in a high-risk, low-trust situation, managers must mitigate risks and build trust to enable full team participation.

Virtual proposal managers can rapidly build and maintain trust by adapting their communication techniques to convey a clear sense of action, support, and constructive feedback.

Begin by defining the objective, member roles, individual tasks, and expectations. Trust erodes quickly if objectives, roles, tasks, and expectations are blurred, unclear, or fluid.

Balance pre-kickoff strategy and solution development activities. Target 75 percent completion of strategy and solution development pre-kickoff, especially when

submittal deadlines are one week or less. This compromise supports an earlier kickoff and fosters members' input, buy-in, acceptance, and identification with the team. Begin with a face-to-face kickoff meeting, if you can afford the expense and travel time.

Team members that sense clear, decisive, management and member action remain confident the team will manage the uncertainty and risk inherent in preparing winning proposals. Use the communication techniques summarized in figure 2 to establish high levels of trust early and maintain trust as you prepare the proposal.

TECHNIQUES TO BUILD TRUST EARLY	TECHNIQUES TO MAINTAIN TRUST
Encourage non-task, social communication. Foster comments on hobbies, activities, families, etc. and integrate with other exchanges. Set up an online, shared-space where team members can post their pictures, bios, and other social items. However, do not allow social communication to substitute for progress on tasks.	**Communicate predictably.** Set and maintain all meeting times, balancing the demands on members in different time zones. Explain every change or absence in advance. Avoid irregular, inequitable, and unpredictable communication. During a crisis, maintain near-real-time communication. Maintain a consistent style and tone in all communication.
Communicate optimistically and enthusiastically. Promote team as a virtual family. Use *we*. Encourage positive comments among members. Discourage negative remarks.	**Develop schemes to deal with technical and task uncertainty.** Have three or more ways to connect with team members (e-mail addresses, both home and work; phone numbers for work, cell, spouse's cell, team buddy, manager(s), and key co-worker(s); instant messaging; and perhaps, social media links)
Develop schemes to handle task and technology uncertainty. Number and date the messages and meeting notes consecutively so members can place them in context and detect missing items. Confront and promptly handle vague statements, allegations, and complaints. Publicize members' activity and inactivity. Encourage exchanges that clarify and develop consensus.	**Encourage proactive action.** Reward and praise individual and sub-team commitment and accomplishment. Communicate positively, concisely, and specifically. Avoid weak, vague, or equivocal statements. Weak: *Complete in 4 or 5 days.* Stronger: *Submit before 3:30 PM on Thursday.*
State exactly how you will manage. First impressions are critical. Emphasize performance, not behavior-. State how you will manage missed deadlines. Members tend to respond similarly to how they are initially treated.	**Respond promptly, explicitly, and predictably to all messages.** Low-trust teams characteristically get little feedback from managers or members.
Clarify roles, procedures, and quality standards. Be unequivocal. Then transition from procedural to task focus.	**Assign task leadership based upon skill, ability, interest, and enthusiasm.**
Focus on, praise, and reward on-time completion of initial tasks. Say what you mean, and mean what you say. Laud good performance; praise in public.	**Use peer pressure constructively. Continue to praise good performance.** Note impacts of substandard performance; scold in private; escalate repeated poor performance; eliminate non-performers.

Figure 2. Team Communications Strategies Establish and Maintain High Trust. *Your communication with your virtual proposal team and members' communication among themselves are the only means that you have to develop and maintain the member trust needed to prepare a winning proposal.*

3 Define and assign key virtual team roles clearly.

See TEAM SELECTION AND MANAGEMENT for descriptions of traditional proposal team roles.

Roles for virtual proposal teams are subtly different than typical proposal team roles. The same tasks must be completed, but the roles shift. Key virtual proposal teams roles and descriptions follow.

Manager/Facilitator: Encompasses the traditional proposal manager role and often some of the proposal coordinator role. As with the proposal manager role, the primary

responsibility is to prepare a compliant, responsive, winning proposal. Assign others to develop the solution and pricing. The primary tasks are to facilitate team meetings and manage participants.

Participants: As with co-located proposal teams, participants are contributors. Their primary responsibility is to produce a compliant responsive proposal section and/or other assigned, scheduled tasks.

Knowing when to ask Champions for help is difficult, especially with short deadlines. In general, make specific requests for action. Avoid presenting vaguely formulated problems. Take *advice* question to a *coach* or mentor, someone that you can talk to openly and constructively.

Technologist: Similar in many respects to the proposal coordinator role, the technologist sets up virtual meetings and workspaces. The technologist also handles security and access issues, and coaches/trains participants to use the technology correctly. Ideally, the technologist supports multiple proposals in a consistent manner so that participants who contributed to prior virtual proposals can use the same tools and procedures as before, reducing training costs and start-up delays.

Owners: Whether a single person or multiple people, owners sponsor and pay for the proposal. Owners are usually not the sales lead, but have overall responsibility to win the opportunity.

Board of Champions: The ideal Champion is two or three levels above the participant and not the immediate supervisor. Champions have the authority and big-picture vision to replace participants, free participants from conflicting direct management assignments, and offer additional direct support. Immediate supervisors often have split or conflicting interests in that they must oversee members' regular responsibilities while members are contributing to the proposal. Dual or split assignments exacerbate the problems.

4 Establish clearly defined, discrete tasks.

See SCHEDULING, guideline 6.

While this recommendation applies to any team, it is vital for virtual team success. In a face-to-face environment, team members are more likely to ask questions, and managers can more easily view work products. In a virtual environment, participants tend to overstate their progress and misunderstand instructions.

In co-located team environments, proposal managers can establish major tasks and milestones to quickly get the team started, and then prepare inch-stone tasks and completion dates to more precisely track progress.

In a virtual environment, begin with more task granularity. If you do not, team members tend to think that their task assignments are being changed mid-course, and they lose commitment to the project. With virtual teams, inch-stone tasks help you identify late tasks before they threaten your schedule.

Use these questions to determine if your tasks are clearly defined:

- **Is the task sized?** For example, 2 pages, 4 hrs. of engineering time, or limited to work at the Erie facility.
- **Is the due date precise?** For example, 10:00 AM EST, Tuesday, February 4, 20XX.
- **Is the person responsible named?** Naming **a position or group is seldom sufficient.**
- **Are quality standards defined or referenced?** For example: Sections must have theme statements and all figures must have action captions. Sections must be spell checked before submitting.
- **How will you verify task completion?** Normally you verify when you receive a file, or when something that you can see, hear, or touch is delivered.
- **How will you escalate responsibility if this task deadline is missed?** Disclose the quantified impact on subsequent milestones, and possibly name the person you will escalate responsibility to.

5 Select task-appropriate, easy-to-use technology.

Match technology to task complexity. Small virtual teams can be managed using e-mail, scheduling, and word processing tools. Larger, more complex teams require more sophisticated tools. Advice on tool selection is well beyond the purpose of this *Guide*, and these tools are evolving rapidly.

Virtual teams work in an on-line, collaborative workspace. Participants' work should be open and available to managers to monitor progress. Managers often need to control team members' ability to view and modify files. Typically, team members check out files, modify those files, and then re-save modified files in the shared workspace. While some tools support team members' simultaneous access to the same file, many proposals are too large for this approach.

The easier the technology is to use, the better. Participants must be comfortable with the technology before they can focus on completing assigned tasks. Give participants hands-on tool training, not just a demonstration of the tool being used by an expert user.

Here are a few suggestions on using virtual team management tools:

- Use familiar technology as much as possible. For example, if you routinely use specific e-mail, scheduling, and net-meeting technology, use the same technology for the proposal.

- Establish 24/7 technical support. When participants in multiple locations and time zones lose access to files and shared workspaces, they begin working off-line and use lost access to justify late deliverables. Integrate live and on-line support. Even when the technologist is on-duty, every team member cannot be helped simultaneously.

- Automatically back up files daily. Time-stamp files in case you need to return to prior versions.

- Be clear and decisive about technology issues. Do not tolerate member resistance on technology and tools. Even if member suggestions are valid, you lack time for discussion and adaptation. Members perceive indecision as a weakness in proposal management.

- Establish and maintain consistent procedures. Use identical passwords, call numbers, call times, agendas, and forms.

- Consider interoperability issues. Prime contractors, subcontractors, and teaming partners need to be able to work together compatibly while protecting proprietary and limited-access data. Address these issues before they impact your proposal.

6 Over communicate.

One of the surest ways to lose member trust is to communicate infrequently or sporadically. One veteran virtual proposal manager reports that she routinely uses three modes for every message: text-message, voice mail, and e-mail. The greater the urgency, the greater the need to use more communication modes.

- Adapt your communication style to your corporate and team members' local culture, and within reason, to the preferred style of the participant. Some members resent messages that clog their e-mail accounts, especially when sent to both home and work accounts. Members in some cultures object to messages sent to their homes, preferring to distinctly separate work from private life. However, most team members see communication as a sign that the proposal is important, their assigned task is important, and their team leader cares. They will realize that team and organizational needs often outweigh personal preferences.

- Keep your messages short and to the point. Use informative subject lines containing signal words. State the essence of your message in the e-mail subject line.

- Keep voice mail messages under 2 minutes.

- Leave your return phone number at the beginning and end of your message. A good practice is to prompt the listener to prepare to write down your number by saying, "I will repeat my phone number at the end of this message." Improve the callback rate by saying your phone number clearly, slowly, and then repeat your number. Do not assume that the listener will or can use the voicemail playback feature, or that the caller ID will display your number.

- Limit web conferences to 30 minutes and never exceed 50 minutes. If you need more time, take a break and resume or schedule another meeting.

- Consider establishing a secure proposal team blog where participants can post questions and share information. Otherwise, every question is unaddressed until the next meeting, directed through a management chain, or ignored.

7 Distinguish team management, leadership, and member motivation.

Proposals are not managed by group consensus; the proposal manager is in control. However, control is complicated in temporary, task-focused teams when the manager/facilitator is not the direct manager of team members.

To compensate for a tenuous control position, effective virtual proposal managers must lead as well as manage. Managers control, but leaders inspire and motivate. Managers get people to do what the managers want; leaders get people to want what the leaders want.

Management entails clearly defining tasks, quality standards, schedules, and key roles. Managers then assign the best available people and train members when necessary. Both sponsors and champions must understand team members' roles, responsibilities, and schedules.

Effective virtual proposal mangers lead, as noted in guideline 2, by fostering early trust among the group, and by maintaining member trust until tasks are completed. Effective leaders emphasize the common objectives of winning the deal; being successful; contributing to their organization, team, and industry; and serving the customer. Effective leaders also recognize and adapt their communication style to team members' unique interests, motivations, circumstances, and cultures.

8 Establish virtual meeting ground rules.

Virtual meetings present additional challenges. Face-to-face communication integrates visual, vocal, and verbal elements such as body language, gestures, movement, posture, and appearance. Vocal elements are **how words are said, pronounced, and emphasized**. Verbal elements are **composition, word choice** and **order**.

In teleconference meetings, all visual elements and cues are eliminated. Participants are limited to vocal and verbal elements, which are often degraded by poor transmission quality. Simultaneous comments are difficult to hear in live meetings but are completely lost in teleconferences.

In videoconference meetings, the quality of visual elements is degraded as well. People can step out of camera range or turn the camera off. Video quality is often compromised, especially with lower fidelity web conferencing equipment. Images can be small, jerky, and low-resolution. Some people are uncomfortable seeing themselves on video, which can negatively affect their contributions.

Virtual proposal team managers can partially compensate for these challenges by establishing virtual meeting ground rules similar to those found in figure 3.

Effectively managing virtual proposal teams may be challenging but is well worth the effort when the result is a winning proposal.

PRE-MEETING	DURING MEETING	POST-MEETING

• Make attendance mandatory. Anyone not able to attend must appoint a replacement and notify the meeting facilitator. Announce replacements when the meeting begins.
 	
• Define in writing all roles and the authority and responsibility of each role. These role definitions can be used from proposal to proposal. Participants represent and make decisions for their groups. Participants cannot go back to their organizations for approval.
 	
• Have an agenda for all meetings. Distribute a detailed, written agenda to participants before major meetings, allowing participants reasonable time to prepare for the meeting. Informal meetings can be effective with a verbal agenda.
 	
• Ask your technologist to be available for every meeting until you are confident that all participants can enter the meeting and use the chosen meeting tools. If the technology or team is new, test all systems before the meeting.
	• Enforce a culture of on-time call-ins, verbal identification of participants and purposes, and announcements of early departures.
	  —Virtual meetings must be as professional as regular meetings. Insist that participants focus on the meeting rather than completing other work, checking and answering e-mail, or babysitting.
	• Begin by summarizing the agenda items, meeting ground rules, and schedule. Seek acceptance, and then keep your word.
	• Appoint a note-taker to keep meeting minutes. Facilitators cannot effectively facilitate and take notes.
	• Appoint a timekeeper. The timekeeper can be the note-taker or any participant except the facilitator.
	• Poll participants for acceptance after each agenda item. Obtain closure and summarize each agenda item before going to the next item, even if your decision is to postpone discussion or to take the discussion to a different group.
	• When assigning tasks, ask the assignee to restate their understanding and acceptance of the tasks.
	  —Note that the assignee is responsible for completing the task, either by themselves or through others. Emphasize that task owners need not be the expert or the doer, just that they must get the task done.
	• Remain positive, proactive, and precise. Commend good performance. Note marginal performance by addressing the team rather than blaming individuals. For example, if pricing input is late, do not say: Why is your pricing late? When will you submit the pricing? Instead, say: Is the pricing team having any particular difficulty developing the price? Is there anything that I can do to help your team complete the pricing?
	  —Note that you will address repeated poor performance off-line. Team members should not get the impression that poor performance is tolerated.
	• Close the meeting on time, noting that you did so. If you can close early, note it and point out that participants have x minutes of additional time.
	• Close each meeting by reviewing agreements, tasks, completion times, and responsible individuals.
		• Distribute minutes immediately after the meeting, documenting agreements, tasks, completion times, and responsible individuals.
		
		• Immediately address poor performance off-line with the assignee. If you must escalate to the relevant Board Champion, tell them what you are doing, and then do it. Team members learn about empty threats. When deadlines are short, you often cannot afford second chances, and never third chances.

Figure 3. Potential Virtual Meeting Ground Rules. *Adapt these virtual meeting ground rules to your organization, management authority, situation, and personnel. Ground rules that are overbearing in one situation are lax in another.*

9

See DECISION GATE REVIEWS *and* COLOR TEAM REVIEWS, *Capture Guide.*

Establish a rigorous review schedule.

Co-located and virtual proposal teams require the same Decision Gate and color team reviews for proposals of similar type, size, and risk. Blue, Black, Pink, Red, Gold, and Lessons-Learned reviews are described in COLOR TEAM REVIEWS, *Capture Guide.*

However, you need to adopt a different approach to reviewing the daily work progress of team members in a virtual environment. Figure 4 compares daily review techniques for co-located and virtual proposal teams.

CO-LOCATED TEAM PROGRESS REVIEW	VIRTUAL TEAM PROGRESS REVIEW
Daily standup meeting	Daily conference call
Review posted drafts on proposal room walls	Open and review individual work files in shared work space
Check sign-in and sign-out logs	Check when files were checked out and in (resaved). Many systems offer automatic notification
Managing by wandering about	Instant message logs, discussion threads in collaboration tool or e-mail
Schedule one-on-one reviews	Schedule one-on-one telephone calls

Figure 4. Reviewing Daily Team Progress. *Co-located and virtual teams managers must use different techniques to monitor team progress. These techniques are increasingly used in blended team management environments.*

229

The Model Documents in this section illustrate best practices in business development and current business English.

Model documents illustrate the guidelines discussed in the *Proposal Guide* as closely as possible, subject to the unique aspect of the specific competition.

Most of the model documents were slightly altered from the original to disguise the seller and the customer. Some documents were written specifically for this *Proposal Guide*.

To reduce the space required, some of the longer documents have been shortened. Vertical dots indicate document breaks. The initial summary and introductory portions of major document sections are included.

The following suggestions will help you use these models to improve your own sales documents.

1. Rely on the overall organization and design rather than exact words and phrases. Most of the time the circumstances of each competition differ.

2. Chose words and phrases that sound like you. Words taken from other documents often appear unnatural to the reader and prompt them to doubt your message.

3. Read the notes at the side and bottom of the documents carefully and refer to the reference sections. Remember that guidelines are not rules. Use sound judgment to tailor your documents for each competition.

4. Begin your own collection of model documents. Collect documents and excerpts from documents that seem appropriate for your industry and organization but also consider outside documents to identify new best practices.

5. Refine and polish every new document that you prepare, regardless of the source. Win more business and improve your persuasiveness by following the principles discussed and illustrated in this *Proposal Guide*.

(1) The informative subject line begins with the signal word labeling the letter as a *request*. A feature is linked to two benefits.

See FEATURES, ADVANTAGES, AND BENEFITS *and* HEADINGS.

(2) The request begins with the benefit to the customer, the only reason for the customer to agree to the request. The setup, a reference to the customer's RFP, is delayed until after the benefit. Every request in every sentence is linked to a benefit.

See FEATURES, ADVANTAGES, AND BENEFITS.

(3) This sentence introduces the structure of the letter.

See ORGANIZATION *and* PAGE AND DOCUMENT DESIGN.

(4) Each request for modification begins with the customer benefit, then states the current RFP language. Then the change is justified in detail from the customer's perspective.

See FEATURES, ADVANTAGES, AND BENEFITS *and* ORGANIZATION.

(5) The seller has made the change easy for the customer by including complete text for the change.

(6) Labels in the left margin make the letter easy to follow. The clear page design enables the reader to more easily focus on the content.

See PAGE AND DOCUMENT DESIGN.

IT Partners, Inc.
1000 Derby Road
Chicago, IL 50501
312.333.3000

January 15, 20XX

Art A. Quire
Purchasing Manager
Big Corporation
Winston Street
San Diego, CA

(1) **Subject: Request to modify Big Corporation's IT outsourcing RFP to reduce cost and enhance flexibility**

Dear Art:

(2) To better meet Big Corporation's IT outsourcing objectives of reduced cost and enhanced flexibility, we recommend two changes in your RFP dated December 15, 20XX. Our recommended changes will help Big Corporation meet its objectives while obtaining more competitive bids. To ensure our proposal is fully compliant and responsive, a prompt decision is critical.

(3) For each recommended modification, we have quoted your RFP, explained our reasoning, and offered a draft RFP text replacement. We request two modifications.

1. To reduce your cost and improve flexibility, eliminate the 10-year firm fixed price provision.

(4)

Current provision:	*All bidders must quote firm fixed prices for each and every year of the 10-year contract.*
Comments:	The uncertainty of inflation in out-years will force all bidders to increase prices to cover inflation risk. Any increase or decrease in the type or level of services required will limit Big Corporation's flexibility to adjust. You could be locked into old technologies and unable to quickly respond to your customers.

(5)

Recommended change:	*All bidders must quote firm, fixed prices on each task, with the annual cost being the simple sum of the cost of all tasks. All required tasks and task pricing will be reviewed annually.*

2. To improve flexibility by easing the restriction on any change in *key positions*.

(6)

Current provision:	*All bidders must name all persons proposed for all key positions, and no substitutions are permitted.*
Comments:	As written, the provision could be interpreted to apply from the proposal stage through the entire 10-year term of the contract. Big Corporation's requirements likely will change, requiring different skills in key positions. Individuals also may change jobs or even choose to retire. Allowing changes with your approval will permit both organizations to employ the best person available to meet the current need.
Recommended change:	*All bidders must name all persons proposed for all key positions. Substitutions are permitted only after review and approval by Big Corporation's designated contract administrator.*

7 The summary restates the benefit and the requested action.

See ORGANIZATION.

8 The seller proactively offers to follow up and leaves a contact number.

See SALES LETTERS, *Capture Guide.*

9 The attached electronic file reduces the effort required for the customer to make the requested changes.

Big Corporation IT RFP
January 15, 20XX
Page 2

7 I hope you agree that the two RFP changes recommended will help Big Corporation reduce cost and improve flexibility. We look forward to receiving an addendum to your RFP so that we can prepare a fully compliant and responsive proposal.

8 I will call you on Tuesday to clarify any details, or you can reach me at 801-333-3000.

Sincerely,

Daniel Miller

Daniel Miller

Proposal Manager

9 Attachment: 1 PC computer disc with electronic file in MSWord® and text-only formats

❶ Executive summaries usually carry an unambiguous telegraphic heading for instant recognition.

See EXECUTIVE SUMMARY *and* HEADINGS.

❷ This customer-focused theme opens by naming the customer, stating a benefit, and then linking the benefit to a discriminator. The word *partner* was used because the customer requested a partner.

See CUSTOMER FOCUS; FEATURES, ADVANTAGES, AND BENEFITS; *and* THEME STATEMENTS.

❸ This paragraph demonstrates the seller's understanding of the customer organization's vision.

See EXECUTIVE SUMMARY.

❹ This *linking statement* demonstrates the alignment between the customer's organizational vision and the objective of the immediate buying group within the customer organization.

See EXECUTIVE SUMMARY.

❺ This sentence incorporates both a short setup and a summary of what the customer has requested in meetings. Setups in executive summaries are occasionally dropped because the reader is assumed to understand, or delayed because other information is more important to the reader.

See EXECUTIVE SUMMARY *and* ORGANIZATION.

❻ The needs or issues are clearly *owned* by the customer, and the list of needs is named immediately before the list. Quote customers directly, even if the items are not parallel.

See CUSTOMER FOCUS *and* LISTS.

❼ A reference quote substantiates the seller's experience and performance.

See RELEVANT EXPERIENCE/PAST PERFORMANCE.

❄ Cascadia Timber

❶ Executive Summary

---

❷ Cascadia Timber can reduce the cost of forest management in remote, roadless areas by selecting a partner to supply 20 versatile ultralight aircraft and proven long-term support.

---

❸ Cascadia Timber is ranked as the No. 1 company in the world by Forester's Monthly for low cost, innovative forest management. Cascadia Timber Chairman Woody X. Pine set the following strategic direction:

> *We have to do everything better, more efficiently from a cost point of view, more effectively from an impact point of view.*
>
> —Cascadia Timber Annual Report, 1996

Cascadia Timber's Forest Management Division helps improve efficiency and **❹** effectiveness by adopting innovative forest management practices.

In support of Cascadia Timber's strategic direction, the Forest Management Division verbally requested proposals for 20 ultralight aircraft to be used as a **❺** forest management tool. In our meetings with Forest Management and purchasing, individuals cited four primary needs: **❻**

1. Affordable, portable, and easily transportable
2. All-conditions observation and communication platform
3. Safe and easy to fly
4. Easy to assemble and maintain in the field

Cascadia Timber can purchase 20 Endeavor ultralights from Jenair for $9,500 each, less than one-half the cost of 3/4-ton 4-wheel drive trucks. The Endeavor offers a unique combination of features:

- For portability, the wings, tail assembly, fuselage, and down tubes are oriented along a slim axis and secured in a rugged transport case.
- Transportable by three people by design, not modification. Two carry the 196-lb. fuselage crate, one carries the 45-lb. engine crate.

❼ "In 10 years of flying the Endeavor for Special Forces, we have been impressed with the durability and portability of the aircraft after successive airdrops in difficult terrain.

Jenair's enthusiastic support was superb."

—Major Buck Rogers

❽ Affordable, portable, easily transportable

❾

❿ Figure 1. Proven in Use. *While no forest management group currently uses any type of ultralight, the Endeavor has been proven in similar operations with Special Forces personnel since 1984.*

–1–

Jenair Sports, Inc.
1400 Airport Road
Boulder, CO 80150
970.359.1000
970.359.1431 (FAX)
www.jenair.com

8 The four primary customer needs are addressed in the order introduced. The wording of each is identical to the numbered list to eliminate possible confusion by the reader.

See ORGANIZATION.

9 The graphic and caption support the seller's claims. The use of a photograph suggests the aircraft is real.

See ACTION CAPTION *and* GRAPHICS.

10 The two-part action engages the reader with the informative heading then seeks to suggest a minimal-risk alternative.

11 Note how most paragraphs open with benefits, the most important aspect to the customer.

See CUSTOMER FOCUS; *and* FEATURES, ADVANTAGES, AND BENEFITS.

12 The Benefit-Feature table also lists benefits first. Most writers tend to think *features* before *benefits*.

13 Here, the seller both summarizes the offer, states they can do the job, and softly asks for the order.

See EXECUTIVE SUMMARY.

14 The seller restates the most significant discriminator in a single-sentence paragraph.

See EXECUTIVE SUMMARY, *and* PAGE AND DOCUMENT DESIGN.

15 The high-level proposal outline in the left margin previews how the seller's proposal is organized. If the executive summary has captured readers' interests, they can easily turn to the information that is the most interesting.

See ORGANIZATION.

16 The final paragraph indicates compliance and flexibility. Note how the tone shifts if *enhancements* becomes *changes*.

See CHOOSING CORRECT WORDS *and* STYLE AND TONE.

 Cascadia Timber

8 All-conditions observation and communication platform

8 Safe and easy to fly

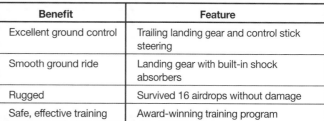

Jenair Pilot Training Named Industry's Best.

The Ultralight Pilots' Association selects Jenair's pilot training program as "Best" in their annual competition.

—Small Aircraft News, July 10, 1995

8 Easy to assemble and maintain in the field

15

PROPOSAL OUTLINE

1. Executive Summary
2. Aircraft Description
3. Program Overview
4. Management Approach

---

11 To ensure accurate and safe observation in all conditions, the Endeavor offers positive stability, the ideal control response. During level flight, the pilot can concentrate on observation, knowing the aircraft tends to fly itself. For stable observation during turns, the aircraft maintains the uniform attitude the pilot commands, instead of seeking to return to a flat attitude.

For versatility, the Endeavor can be equipped to land on land, water, and snow.

Air-to-ground communication is improved by the rear engine, which minimizes pilot noise when compared with front engine models.

Safe and easy operation requires good design and excellent pilot training. Endeavor's design offers clear benefits:

Benefit	Feature
Excellent ground control	Trailing landing gear and control stick steering
Smooth ground ride	Landing gear with built-in shock absorbers
Rugged	Survived 16 airdrops without damage
Safe, effective training	Award-winning training program

12

Cascadia foresters can focus on forest management because the Endeavor is easily maintained. Routine checks of cables, snap-lock bolts, fittings, and simple preflight tests are sufficient for safe operation. Weekly checks of engine fluids, landing gear, and the prop are required. Annual engine overhauls and in-depth checks of the prop are required and can be done at Cascadia's convenience by Jenair personnel.

Reliable, rugged flight instruments, proven in 10 years of use, require only annual calibration.

To ensure fast, accurate assembly, nondestructible instructions are permanently attached beneath the instrument panel. To ensure assembly tools are always available, they are also connected by a steel cable and attached to the aircraft.

Special Forces tests demonstrated assembly in 10 minutes. Inexperienced personnel complete a first assembly/disassembly in 40 minutes.

13 Cascadia Timber has kept on the leading edge of innovative forest management techniques. Jenair Sports welcomes the opportunity to supply 20 Endeavor aircraft, flight and maintenance training, and long-term maintenance and inspection support.

While many ultralights are used for recreation, the Endeavor's unique 10-year use by Special Forces personnel over similar terrain and more difficult conditions reduces the risk of use in continuous operation. **14**

Our proposal mirrors the issues discussed in our meetings. Should your requirements change, we welcome the opportunity to discuss further enhancements. **16**

–2–

Points explained in Model Document 2 are not repeated. Annotations focus on the adjustments made to summarize and substantiate the value proposition basis for this purchase.

1 The over-arching quantified value proposition is stated as the opening theme statement.

2 The executive summary is organized around the components of the value proposition instead of the hot button issues.

3 Explains part 1, the $500,000 savings.

Executive Summary

1 Cascadia Timber can reduce forest management costs $1 million annually by purchasing 20 versatile Jenair ultralight aircraft for $190,000, a 500% percent ROI and 70-day payback period.

Cascadia Timber is ranked as the No. 1 company in the world by Forester's Monthly for low cost, innovative forest management. Cascadia Timber Chairman Woody X. Pine set the following strategic direction:

> *We have to do everything better, more efficiently from a cost point of view, more effectively from an impact point of view.*
>
> *Cascadia Timber Annual Report, 1996*

Cascadia Timber's Forest Management Division helps improve efficiency and effectiveness by adopting innovative forest management practices.

In support of Cascadia Timber's strategic direction, the Forest Management Division verbally requested proposals for 20 ultralight aircraft to be used as a forest management tool. <u>In our meetings with Forest Management and purchasing, we agreed</u> that Cascadia could anticipate the following added values:

2
1. Reduced road construction and maintenance of $500,000 annually
2. Reduced fire losses of $250,000 annually
3. Reduced fire fighting costs of $250,000 annually

Reduced road construction and maintenance of $500,000 annually

3 Cascadia Timber budgets $5 million annually for road construction and maintenance to permit access for both harvesting and forest management. We agreed that a 10 percent reduction in road maintenance costs, $500,000, was reasonable if foresters could monitor forest conditions from the air.

To ensure accurate and safe observation in all conditions, the Endeavor offers positive stability, the ideal control response. During level flight, the pilot can concentrate on observation. For stable observation during turns, the aircraft maintains a uniform attitude instead of seeking to return to a flat attitude. The versatile Endeavor can be equipped to land on land, water, and snow.

> In 10 years of flying the Endeavor for Special Forces, we have been impressed with the durability and portability of the aircraft after successive airdrops in difficult terrain. Jenairs enthusiastic support was superb.
>
> -Maj. Buck Rodgers

Figure 1. Proven In Use. *While no forest management group currently uses any type of ultralight, the Endeavor has been proven in similar operations with Special Forces personnel since 1984.*

④ Explains part 2, the $250,000 savings.

⑤ Explains part 3, the second $250,000 savings.

⑥ Summarizes the total savings of $1 million.

Reduced fire losses of $250,000 annually

Reduced fire fighting costs of $250,000 annually

Jenair Pilot Training Named Industry's Best

The Ultralight pilots' Association selects Jenair's pilot training program as "Best" in their annual competition.

Small Aircraft News
July 10, 1995

Proposal Outline

1. Executive Summary
2. Aircraft Description
3. Program Overview
4. Management Approach

④ Cascadia Timber's Fire Management Director, Mr. N. O. Sparks, estimated that rapid, in-air fire management could cut average losses by half. With 50 fires annually, average losses of 500 acres, and timber losses of $1000 per acre, the annual loss avoidance is $250,000.

While many ultralights are used for recreation, the Endeavor's unique 10-year use by Special Forces personnel over similar terrain and more difficult conditions reduces risks in fire management support operations.

⑤ Mr. Sparks further noted that early detection would cut fire fighting cost per incident by $50,000. With 50 incidents, the annual savings is $250,000.

Capital is Available

Cascadia Timber can purchase 20 Endeavor ultralights from Jenair for $9,500 each, less than one-half the cost of 3/4 ton 4-wheel drive trucks. With these trucks estimated to cost $27,000 each, reducing the annual number purchased by 7 will free budgeted capital dollars for this ultralight aircraft purchase.

Safe and Easy to Operate and Manage

Safe and easy operation requires good design and excellent pilot training. Endeavor's design offers clear benefits:

Benefit	Feature
Excellent ground control	Trailing landing gear and control stick steering
Smooth ground ride	Landing gear with built-in shock absorbers
Rugged	Survived sixteen airdrops without damage
Safe, effective training	Award-winning training program

Cascadia foresters can focus on forest management because the Endeavor is easily maintained. Routine checks of cables, snap-lock bolts, fittings, and simple preflight tests are sufficient for safe operation. Weekly checks of engine fluids, landing gear, and the prop are required. Annual engine overhauls and in-depth prop checks are required and can be done at Cascadia's convenience by Jenair service personnel.

Reliable, rugged flight instruments, proven in 10 years of use, require only annual calibration.

⑥ Cascadia Timber has kept on the leading edge of innovative forest management techniques. Jenair Sports welcomes the opportunity to contribute $1 million in added value to Cascadia Timber's bottom line by supplying 20 Endeavor aircraft, flight and maintenance training, and long-term maintenance and inspection support.

Our proposal mirrors the issues discussed in our meetings. Should your requirements change, we welcome the opportunity to discuss further enhancements.

① Theme statement names the customer first, then cites a benefit linked to the seller's key discriminator.

See CUSTOMER FOCUS *and* THEME STATEMENTS.

② The first two paragraphs demonstrate the seller's understanding of the customer's needs. The customer is commended for excellent achievement. The seller's role in the customer's success is subtly implied but deemphasized.

See EXECUTIVE SUMMARY.

③ This short paragraph states the need or pain.

See EXECUTIVE SUMMARY.

④ The pain is stated positively, and additional immediate needs are linked to the overall organizational need. The unusually long, four-paragraph setup was used to forcefully discriminate the incumbent's deep understanding of the customer's needs to Western's senior managers.

See EXECUTIVE SUMMARY *and* PROPOSAL STRATEGY.

⑤ The term *bid management* rather than *proposal management* is used to reflect the customer's terminology.

⑥ The customer's evaluation criteria are listed precisely as stated in a meeting with the buyer. The list is named immediately prior to the list.

See LISTS.

⑦ The incumbent seller's strongest discriminator is substantiated by proof from the customer's organization.

See RELEVANT EXPERIENCE/PAST PERFORMANCE.

⑧ This sentence says the seller can meet the customer's needs. Note that the customer's spelling of *summarised* has been used.

See EXECUTIVE SUMMARY *and* INTERNATIONAL PROPOSALS.

Executive Summary

① Western Hovercraft can increase its ability to win key contracts by selecting a proven business development partner.

⑦ *7th April 20XX*

Please find enclosed the results of the Western Proposal Training Survey . . .

- *85% have directly contributed to proposals*
- *50% saved time*
- *40% reduced cost*
- *85% improved proposal quality*
- *85% used the skills to prepare other documents...*

. . . we have seen a visible improvement in our proposal quality since we commenced training courses last year.

—Bob Westfield
Regional Business Manager
Western Hovercraft

② Western Hovercraft is at a crucial stage of capturing business—one of opportunity and risk. Western has invested significant time, energy, and resources in establishing its proposal development process. That investment has had positive results, including the recent MOD Attack Hovercraft win and an improved win rate on Export Sales bids. Western's £3 billion order book is the envy of larger competitors.

Today, MOD agencies and many Export Sales customers respect the professionalism and quality of Western's proposals. Government contractors on both sides of the Atlantic, both partners and competitors, admire the quality of Western's proposals. The positive customer comments on Western's current proposals are a marked contrast to the comments made less than 4 years ago.

③ However, backlog does not pay current operating expenses. Western must manage expenditures and cash flow to capture additional orders at a minimum cost.

④ Western's managers have identified the need to continue improving their ability to capture business by improving **⑤** bid management. Additionally, Western is pursuing several must-win export orders where process improvements and expert assistance can increase the win probability and reduce capture cost.

⑥ Western has established the following bid management improvement objectives:

- Reduce bid cost
- Improve win rate
- Increase awareness of risk
- Improve control and monitoring of bids
- Start up proposal efforts faster
- Improve flexibility, including consultancy assistance

⑧ Shipley Associates welcomes the opportunity to continue the improvements begun in 1999, with the results summarised in Bob Westfield's 7th April 20XX letter.

1

⑨ The customer's spelling conventions are used to avoid appearing foreign.

See INTERNATIONAL PROPOSALS.

⑩ A table rather than a bulleted list is used to both summarize the seller's offer and preview how the proposal is organized.

See EXECUTIVE SUMMARY, ORGANIZATION, *and* PAGE AND DOCUMENT DESIGN.

⑪ The action caption on the table restates the seller's primary discriminator.

See ACTION CAPTIONS *and* DISCRIMINATORS.

⑫ The customer's hot buttons are all addressed by the service approach requested, so the approach is discussed separately and not aligned to individual hot buttons.

See EXECUTIVE SUMMARY.

⑬ Note how the adjective used in the heading is substantiated when repeated in the text.

See ACTION CAPTIONS.

⑭ The proposal is introduced or previewed in both the text and the visually emphasized table of contents in the left margin.

See PAGE AND DOCUMENT DESIGN, *and* ORGANIZATION.

⑨ Western Hovercraft's objectives can best be met by partnering with Shipley Associates, as <u>summarised</u> in figure 1.

⑩

Western's Objectives	Advantages to Western from Partnering with Shipley
• Reduce bid cost	Western can leverage its previous investment in process improvement and training by refining, not redefining, its bid management process.
• Improve win rate	Western has been winning with a Shipley process tailored to the UK and export markets. Compare market-specific win rates.
• Increase awareness of risk	Western can leverage Shipley's experience with 43 of the top 50 US DoD suppliers, who must manage risk to strict DoD standards.
• Improve control and monitoring of bids	Western can apply Shipley's unique mix of monitoring of bids full-service consulting, training, products, and templates to improve bid management.
• Start up proposal efforts faster	Western can start up proposals faster by having Shipley train and coach others to work as effectively as Linda Hale or by having Shipley supply a proven consultant.
• Improve flexibility, including consultancy assistance	Western will obtain maximum value for money with consultants that do not have to be educated about Western. Both consultants proposed for the Phase 1 study have experience with both Western and numerous aerospace organisations.

⑪ Figure 1. Complete Consultancy, Tailored to Western Hovercraft. *Only Shipley Associates can offer a full range of services and 4 years of success with Western and associated Western organizations.*

⑫ Flexible, two-phased approach

As requested by Sally Barksdale, we propose a two-phased approach:

Phase 1—Study

Phase 2—Execution

⑬ For maximum flexibility, all phases and recommendations will be independent.

⑭ How our proposal is organized

⑭

> **PROPOSAL OUTLINE**
>
> Executive Summary
> 1. Unique Partnering Qualifications
> 2. Responsive Study Approach
> 3. Schedule and Price

Our proposal is structured as shown to the left. To facilitate your evaluation, section 1 matches each Western objective to Shipley's qualifications and proof of results with organisations setting similar objectives. Section 2 describes our study approach, while section 3 suggests a schedule and establishes the price.

2

① The theme names the customer first to increase customer focus. The initial broad benefit is linked to the seller's most unique benefit, the ability to *best respond to ad hoc inquiries*. Often discriminators are not obvious to less knowledgeable readers.

See CUSTOMER FOCUS, DISCRIMINATORS, *and* THEME STATEMENTS.

② The need is extracted from the customer's RFP.

See EXECUTIVE SUMMARY.

③ *The challenge* both summarizes the customer's current position and future need.

See EXECUTIVE SUMMARY.

④ The list of *capabilities* is extracted word for word from the customer's RFP. Use the customer's language when you name the hot button list.

See CUSTOMER FOCUS, EXECUTIVE SUMMARY, LISTS, *and* ORGANIZATION.

⑤ The seller states they can do the job.

See EXECUTIVE SUMMARY.

⑥ Because this executive summary exceeds two or three pages, the organization of the executive summary is announced.

See ORGANIZATION.

⑦ The heading identically reflects the first hot button. The second hot button would be at the top of the next page.

⑧ This three-sentence paragraph summarizes the seller's solution to the first challenge. Expand or condense solution summaries as appropriate.

See EXECUTIVE SUMMARY.

Garden of Eden Department of Human Services

Executive Information System

Executive Summary

① **Eden's DHS can craft reform programs that work by selecting the Executive Information System that best responds to ad hoc queries by delivering the right information clearly, concisely, and when you need it.**

② **The Need**

The Department needs a system that can analyze data encompassing the broad range of human services to help craft reform programs that work.

—EIS RFP, pg. 2.

③ The challenge: The Department of Human Services (DHS) has effectively managed the delivery of public assistance services in the Garden of Eden by efficient administration and innovative cost-control strategies. With program complexity continuing to increase, the DHS's ability to further improve services requires an improved ability to store, access, and analyze massive amounts of complex data efficiently and effectively.

④ The DHS has requested proposals for a systems integrator to develop an Executive Information System (EIS) that gives DHS personnel the following capabilities:

- Easily access information by users with varied backgrounds

- Quickly handle simple and complex queries, both predetermined and ad hoc

- Maintain on-line processing while routinely adding and purging data

- Flexibly accommodate program changes and data exchanges with other State departments and county agencies

- Efficiently manage the EIS implementation and seamlessly transition to State operation in 2 years

⑤ Cosmos Information Systems (Cosmos) welcomes the opportunity to design, implement, and support an EIS tailored to the DHS's current and future needs based on our experience implementing similar systems.

⑥ Our executive summary first summarizes the basis for our system recommendation against the overall DHS capabilities listed above, then summarizes our development approach, project organization, system architecture, and costs by phase as required in your RFP.

⑥ **How Our Executive Summary Is Organized:**

- Capabilities
- Development Approach
- Project Organization
- System Architecture
- Costs by Phase

⑦ **Easily access information by users with varied backgrounds**

⑧ Users easily access information from their personal computers on their desktop. All staff can develop ad hoc queries using point-and-click tools without writing program code using a Windows-based Graphical Query Language (GQL) tool. To avoid excessive run times or massive data dumps on their PC, GQL allows users to determine run time and output size.

. . .

. . .

COSMOS SYSTEMS • 1400 Moab Road, Suite 6, East Canaan, IL 45014 • 303.666.0000 • www.cosmos.com

---

The same organization can be expanded to accommodate executive summaries and letter proposals of different lengths. This is only the first page of a 12-page executive summary for a state government proposal comprising several hundred pages.

❶ Address the letter as specifically and directly as possible, following all customer instructions.

See Cover Letters.

❷ The subject line signals this is a response to an RFP by number.

See Cover Letters.

❸ The opening line first calls attention to the proposal, then establishes context. While the next sentence may seem long or awkward with the enclosed parenthetical sentence, it suggests a personal style while highlighting a discriminator.

See Discriminators *and* Organization.

❹ The customer's needs are stated in a way that seems to merge with the seller's offer.

See Customer Focus.

❺ To keep the cover letter short, the needs are not addressed in the cover letter, but the writer promises to address them in the proposal. Cover letters to decision makers are expected to emphasize the personal commitment and support of a senior manager. The inclusion of the phone number adds support.

See Organization.

❻ The single-sentence closing paragraph is used for emphasis.

See Page and Document Design.

❼ The most senior manager of the selling organization that is plausibly aware of the proposal should sign this type of cover letter.

See Cover Letters.

ShipleyAssociates | 532 North 900 West • Kaysville, Utah 84037 • 888.772.WINS (9467) • www.shipleywins.com

September 18, 20XX

❶ Ms. Macey S. King
Global Procurement
Ace Global Services
6000 Rock Ledge Drive
Bethesda, MD 20817

❷ **Subject: Response to RFP # RSD-WEB-001, Proposal Consulting Services**

Dear Ms. King:

❸ Here is our response to your RFP requesting proposal consulting services for Ace Global Services. With the relationship between our companies off to an excellent start, this procurement is an excellent extension of the relationship between our companies. (We're already serving you with proposal consulting services on three proposals.)

Ace has requested relationships with companies with the following approaches:

❹
- Are willing to operate effectively in the Ace Global Services environment
- Are willing to provide services and rates through the Ace Intranet Web Site
- Have an excellent winning record
- Are flexible in their approach
- Can provide excellent value as demonstrated through competitive rates

❺ As you will see throughout our proposal, Shipley Associates is strong in all areas. As the CEO of Shipley Associates, I offer my personal commitment to providing Ace Global Services the best resources and services available. If you have any need to talk to me at any time, either before or after your selection decision, please call me at my direct number: 801-451-2323.

I am personally committed to helping Ace win business.

❻ Sincerely,

Stephen P. Shipley

Stephen P. Shipley
❼ Chief Executive Officer

SPS:jb

Enclosure

❶ Cultural differences may change your approach. Here the writer used the customer's title taken from the customer's bid request. Beginning the subject line with the signal word *proposal* would have been awkward, reading: *Proposal for Proposal . . .*

See Cover Letters, Headings, International Proposals; *and* Sales Letters, *Capture Guide.*

❷ The setup is in the first line, a reference to the bid request.

See Cover Letters.

❸ The customer's objective opens the second sentence to increase customer focus.

See Customer Focus *and* Cover Letters.

❹ To ensure the customer is named immediately before the list, the customer could not be named prior to the seller. When customers do not state buying criteria, summarize the most important features of your offer. Use the words that you think your customer would use.

See Customer Focus *and* Lists.

❺ The closing paragraph emphasizes the compliant and responsive proposal and offers a contact number. Depending on the customer's evaluation rules, stating a proactive follow-up time could be inappropriate.

See Compliance and Responsiveness.

Shipley Limited
Abbey Manor Business Centre
Preston Road, Yeovil, BA20 2EN
United Kingdom
Office: +44 (0)1935 434333

16 March 20XX

Henry Hoogenboom
Global Consulting
Koningsstraat 445 Rue Royale
1000 Brussels
Belgium

Proposal Centre Knowledge Management and Structure

Dear Henry,

❶ Here is our response to your bid request for the Proposal Centre Knowledge Management and Structure.

❷ To allow you to fulfill your mission and overcome your challenges, we have outlined a three-phase project in our proposal. In this project, we will provide you with the information and the expertise to allow you to reengineer processes and implement the **❸** infrastructure needed to sustain a best-in-class proposal operation. We detail how your challenges will be met and describe a practical approach to implementation.

By selecting Shipley Limited, Global Consulting will gain access to proven capabilities in creating best-in-class proposal environments, including:

❹
- World-standard processes, disciplines, and tools
- Capability growth without *"having to learn the hard way"*
- Access to a company that is known for its customer focus, rather than a *do it our way or else* approach
- Affordability—take advantage of the breadth of Shipley resource to the extent that is economically feasible

For ease of evaluation, the structure of our proposal precisely mirrors your bid request from section 2 onwards. If you require any further information or clarification of any of the elements of our proposal, please call me on +44 1935 825200.

❺ Yours sincerely,

Tony Birch

Tony Birch
Managing Director

WEAPONS-R-US, INC. ◆ Aeronautics Division

95610 South Coast Highway, Newport Beach, CA 92658 ◆ 714.720.9000 ◆ www.weapons.com

August 17, 20XX

Contracts Division V (Code 255)
Naval Weapons Center
China Lake, CA 93555-6001

Attention: Barb Buyer

① Subject: Proposal from Weapons-R-Us for the Anti-Radiation Missile Countermeasures Program

② Reference: Solicitation N60550-01-R-0202 dated November 14, 20XX

Dear Ms. Buyer:

③ In response to the referenced solicitation, Weapons-R-Us, Aeronautics Division, is enclosing our proposal for the Anti-Radiation Missile Countermeasures (ARM/CM) Program.

④ Your RFP evaluation criteria emphasized the desire to select a source offering the best combination of flexibility, technical performance, and cost effectiveness.

⑤ Our proposal reflects an experienced technical team in place at China Lake. This team has extensive experience assisting the Navy with anti-radiation missile development, countermeasures analysis, proof-of-concept development, software simulation development and documentation, and systems simulation analysis. We can provide a uniquely cost-effective ARM/CM because we are the only organization with both an experienced team and existing facilities in place at China Lake.

⑥ Our proposal is submitted in three volumes as requested in your solicitation:

> Volume I – Technical Proposal
>
> Volume II – Management Proposal
>
> Volume III – Cost Proposal

Contractual and administrative items are included in Volume III.

⑦ ARM/CM will be conducted within the Advanced Programs Office of our Aeronautical Division, directed by Dr. Noah Lott, Vice President. Technical or programmatic questions may be addressed to Ms. Ivanna Jobb, our proposal manager, at 619-446-9099. Cost, contractual, or administrative inquiries may be addressed to my attention at 714-720-7535.

Sincerely,

N.O. Bull

N. O. Bull
Contract Administrator
Advanced Programs

---

① The signal word *proposal* is used in the subject line.

See COVER LETTERS, HEADINGS, ORGANIZATION; *and* SALES LETTERS, CAPTURE GUIDE.

② The formal *reference* line with the solicitation number and date simplifies sorting.

See COVER LETTERS.

③ The opening sentence begins with a short setup phrase.

See COVER LETTERS; *and* SALES LETTERS, *Capture Guide.*

④ The customer's evaluation criteria or objectives are stated in the second paragraph to increase the relevance of the third paragraph.

⑤ This is the only selling paragraph. The last sentence states the seller's most unique discriminator.

See COVER LETTERS *and* DISCRIMINATORS.

⑥ This paragraph emphasizes the compliant and responsive proposal and offers contact numbers for different types of inquiries. Stating a proactive follow-up time could be inappropriate if limited by buying regulations.

See COMPLIANCE AND RESPONSIVENESS.

⑦ This paragraph names the key managers and who to contact for specific types of questions about the proposal.

See DISCRIMINATORS, *and* RELEVANT EXPERIENCE/PAST PERFORMANCE.

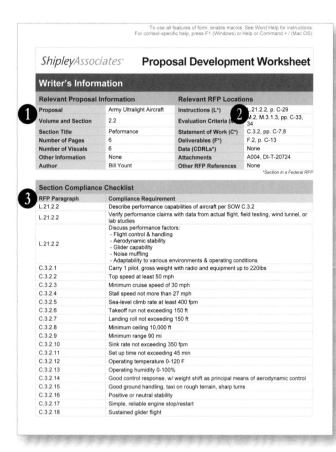

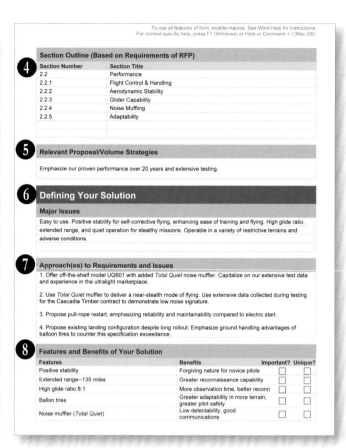

1 The Proposal or Volume Manager should provide the information required in this section. If you do not have it, ask for it, especially for the number of pages allocated.

2 The Proposal or Volume Manager should provide information on relevant bid request pages and paragraph numbers. If you do not have it, ask for it.

3 The Proposal or Volume Manager should complete this section by *stripping* requirements from appropriate bid request sections. Use the compliance checklist to ensure responsiveness and compliance.

4 The Proposal or Volume Manager should provide an outline breaking down the section as required by the bid request and inserting any other subtopics needed to address additional requirements or evaluation criteria. Check with the Proposal Manager to see if further subdivision is allowed before adding lower level topics.

5 The Proposal or Volume Manager should indicate any top level proposal or volume strategies this section should support. Not every proposal or volume strategy can be supported in every section, but it is critical that important win strategies be explicitly supported at appropriate points in the proposal.

6 Major issues or hot buttons are what keep the customer up at night:
- Worry items
- Core needs
- Reasons behind the requirements
- Hidden agendas

7 Identify your approach(es) to meeting section compliance requirements and addressing major issues. Document what you are proposing, but do not be concerned at this stage with how to sell it.

8 Develop the features and corresponding benefits of your offer or solution for this section. Be sure to include benefits that address the major issues identified above. Features and benefits should be developed in pairs, not as unconnected lists.

Check boxes to indicate benefits important to the customer and unique among competitors. This knowledge will help identify discriminators, which are important elements of proposal strategy. Only important benefits can turn unique features into discriminators.

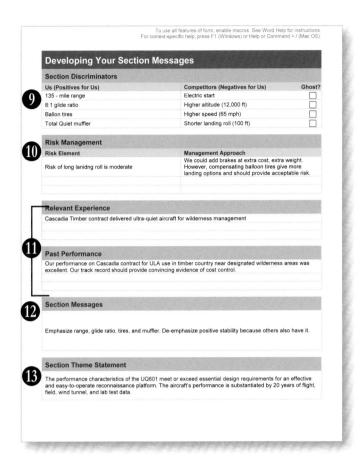

Developing Your Section Messages

Section Discriminators

Us (Positives for Us)	Competitors (Negatives for Us)	Ghost?
135 - mile range	Electric start	☐
8:1 glide ratio	Higher altitude (12,000 ft)	☐
Ballon tires	Higher speed (65 mph)	☐
Total Quiet muffler	Shorter landing roll (100 ft)	☐

⑨

Risk Management

⑩

Risk Element	Management Approach
Risk of long lanidng roll is moderate	We could add brakes at extra cost, extra weight. However, compensating balloon tires give more landing options and should provide acceptable risk.

Relevant Experience

Cascadia Timber contract delivered ultra-quiet aircraft for wilderness management

⑪

Past Performance

Our performance on Cascadia contract for ULA use in timber country near designated wilderness areas was excellent. Our track record should provide convincing evidence of cost control.

⑫

Section Messages

Emphasize range, glide ratio, tires, and muffler. De-emphasize positive stability because others also have it.

⑬

Section Theme Statement

The performance characteristics of the UQ601 meet or exceed essential design requirements for an effective and easy-to-operate reconnaissance platform. The aircraft's performance is substantiated by 20 years of flight, field, wind tunnel, and lab test data.

Creating Key Visuals

To create visual, click in space below and use these options:
- Copy and Paste from another document
- Insert | Picture (choose file or chart) or Object (choose chart, spreadsheet, drawing, slide, picture, file, etc.)
- Select Table | Insert | Table and edit with standard techniques
- Use Drawing Toolbar to add or format graphic elements (unprotect document first and reprotect afterwards)

⑭

Altitude in feet [1/000] — *Guide Ratios for Various Ultralights* — *Range in Miles*

⑮ *Action Caption*

Figure Number	Figure Title
2.2-1	Superior Glide Ratio.

Caption

An 8:1 glide ratio gives the UQ601 longer unpowered range than other commercially available ultralights.

---

⑨ Discriminators are features of an offer that are important to the customer and unique. Base your messages on discriminators, whether positive or negative. Offset negative discriminators with positive discriminators or minimize their importance in this situation.

Check boxes to indicate competitors' discriminators that are candidates for ghosting. Ghosting raises doubt about a competitor's approach without naming the competitor.

⑩ Enter risk factors in technical, cost, schedule, or other appropriate areas. These are risks to your customer, not to your company. Identify the most likely risks and biggest impacts. For every risk, identify a management approach. Do not conceal or ignore risks. Demonstrate your value by proactively reducing the customer's risk.

⑪ Identify your company's relevant experience and past performance. Relevant experience is what you did; past performance is how well you did it. Tie past performance to the benefits to this customer on this program.

⑫ Summarize your section messages. Reflect all important elements and information on the PDW. Address all requirements. Focus on discriminating features that produce important benefits. Cite supporting arguments. But do not write the section yet.

⑬ Your theme statement should be your strongest message:
- Link a benefit to a discriminating feature
- Quantify the benefit
- Include a *proof statement* to increase credibility
- Answer the question, Why choose this offer?

Think of your theme statement as a *silver bullet* the evaluator can use to justify giving you a high score.

⑭ Sketch potential section visuals, adding sheets if needed. Develop visuals before drafting text. Visuals should:
- Be simple and uncluttered
- Be vertically oriented
- Be independent of text—able to stand alone
- Be discussed in the text prior to introduction
- Have action captions

Create rough sketches; refine them later.

⑮ Draft an *action caption* to tell evaluators what you want them to understand about this visual. Use two or three sentences if needed. Ask:
- What is the purpose of this visual?
- What is this visual supposed to communicate?
- What conclusion do I want evaluators to reach?
- What is the selling point?
- Are features tied to benefits?

Use the section number, followed by consecutive numbers for each visual, *e. g.*, Figure 3.2-1. Draft an informative title that is reinforced in the action caption.

① The numbering system and title are dictated by the RFP.

See OUTLINING.

② The theme statement links features and benefits in two sentences. Longer themes can be used on larger proposal sections.

See FEATURES, ADVANTAGES, AND BENEFITS *and* THEME STATEMENTS.

③ The customer's performance needs are summarized.

See ORGANIZATION.

④ The writer introduces the figure in the text, ahead of the figure.

See ACTION CAPTIONS.

⑤ Place figures on the same or a facing page so that the reader does not have to turn the page to see the figure. Occasionally, figures must be placed on the following page.

See GRAPHICS.

⑥ Benefits are introduced before features. The benefit-feature table offers a tempting and easy-to-use summary for the evaluator.

See FEATURES, ADVANTAGES, AND BENEFITS; *and* STORYBOARDS.

⑦ The two-part action caption interprets the table for busy evaluators.

See ACTION CAPTIONS.

⑧ Large proposal sections may include an introduction when space is available in addition to a cross-reference matrix.

Proposal to the U.S. Army

Project Dragonfly

① ## 2.2   Performance

② **The UQ601 meets or exceeds essential design requirements for an effective, low-risk, and easy-to-operate reconnaissance platform. Flight, field, wind-tunnel, and laboratory test data collected over the past 20 years substantiates the UQ601's exceptional performance.**

③ Effective airborne reconnaissance at the small-unit level requires an aircraft that can be flown virtually undetected at low altitudes by personnel with minimal flight training.

④ The UQ601 is a versatile, reliable ultralight that meets the Army's need for a small-unit, low-level, easy-to-fly reconnaissance aircraft. Figure 2.2-1 summarizes the exceptional benefits of Aerodynamics' ultralight—the Army's best value for mission success. The UQ601 meets or exceeds Army requirements for small unit reconnaissance aircraft.

⑤ Figure 2.2-2 on the following page shows the Army requirements aligned with the UQ601 specifications, and Figure 2.2-3 illustrates the durability of the UQ601's major components.

⑥

Benefits	Features
Greater flexibility in photo/radio equipment for increased reconnaissance effectiveness	30 pounds extra payload
Enhanced mission effectiveness because fewer missions can generate necessary information, thus reducing aircraft stress and maintenance	35 miles extra range
Quicker response to mission requirements and less vulnerability for the pilot	20-minute setup time
More forgiving aircraft; less training for pilots	Positive stability
More time for reconnaissance at lower levels	Higher glide ratio
Greater communications capability due to lower detectability; enhanced pilot survivability	Muffled engine noise

⑦ Figure 2.2-1. Overall Best Value. *Aerodynamics' UQ601 meets or exceeds Army requirements for an ultralight aircraft that maximizes mission effectiveness.*

Through years of experience, we have refined the aircraft design to support quick, easy assembly by inexperienced users with minimal tools. Current assembly time is 20 minutes or less, depending on experience. The UQ601 also features a payload capacity of 250 pounds, expanding the aircraft's mission versatility and adaptability.

Aerodynamics' UQ601 aircraft is the most thoroughly tested, reliable, and durable aircraft in the ultralight industry. Our aircraft designs stress simplicity and durability, concepts refined by years of flight, wind-tunnel, and laboratory testing.

Major components have a high MTBF, which demonstrates unsurpassed reliability based on actual flight time. Structural components that last twice as long as the industry average attest to our dedication to safety and durability.

The performance characteristics of Aerodynamic's durable UQ601 closely match the Army's needs for a small-unit reconnaissance platform.

The following major performance factors are discussed in the order requested in the RFP:

⑧

2.2.1	Flight Control and Handling
2.2.2	Aerodynamic Stability
2.2.3	Glider Capability
2.2.4	Noise Muffling
2.2.5	Adaptability

AERODYNAMICS
CORPORATION

–1–

See Organization
and Compliance and
Responsiveness.

❾ The tabular, summary
presentation of
performance
specifications makes
evaluation easy.

See Graphics.

Proposal to the U.S. Army   Project Dragonfly

❾

	Performance Specifications	
Paragraph	**Design Requirement**	**UQ601**
C.3.2.1	Payload capability 220 lbs	250 lb
C.3.2.2	Top speed ≈ 50 mph	50 mph
C.3.2.3	Cruise speed ≥ 30 mph	40–45 mph
C.3.2.4	Stall speed £ 27 mph	26 mph
C.3.2.5	Sea-level climb rate ≈ 400 fpm	420 fpm
C.3.2.6	Takeoff run £ 150 ft	100 ft
C.3.2.7	Landing roll £ 150 ft	200 ft
C.3.2.8	Ceiling ≈ 10,000 ft	10,000 ft
C.3.2.9	Range ≈ 90 miles	125 miles
C.3.2.10	Sink rate £ 350 fpm	400 fpm
C.3.2.11	Setup time £ 45 min	20 min
C.3.2.12	Operating temperature 0–120° F	0-100°F
C.3.2.13	Operate 0-100% humidity	0-100%
C.3.2.14	Good control response	Very good
C.3.2.15	Good ground handling abilities	Very good
C.3.2.16	Positive or neutral stability	Positive
C.3.2.17	Simple engine start/restart	Yes
C.3.2.18	Sustained glider flight	8:1
C.3.2.19	Engine noise muffling system	Muffled
C.3.2.20	Adaptable	Yes

Figure 2.2-2. Performance Specifications. *Positive stability and high glide ratio provide the UQ601 with the best mix of performance characteristics of any aircraft on the market.*

Component	Construction	Years of Use	MTBF (hours)
Frame	Tubular Aluminum	19	8,200
Engine	Zenob G258	8	1,400
Wings/Tail	Dacron	12	1,200
Controls	100% Mechanical three-axis Joystick	6	3,300
Instruments	Gimble Brothers	2	1,700
Landing Gear	Steel Belted Balloon/Tricycle	16	2,200
Ignition	Mechanical Recoil	19	6, 800
Propeller	Laminated Wood	14	7,900

Figure 2.2-3. High Component Reliability. *UQ601 major components are thoroughly flight tested and offer highly reliable service.*

AERODYNAMICS
C O R P O R A T I O N

–2–

⑩ Subsection themes become more detailed but still link features and benefits.

See THEME STATEMENTS.

⑪ Proof of performance must be integrated into the proposal as relevant and not left to a separate, *past performance* section.

See RELEVANT EXPERIENCE/PAST PERFORMANCE.

⑫ The writer offers sufficient background information to both educate an inexperienced evaluator and demonstrate understanding of the requirement. When other offers are equal, this one will appear to be better.

See PROPOSAL STRATEGY.

⑬ Summaries at the end of a section are useful. However, summaries at the beginning are more likely to be read. When time and space are limited, always include summaries at the beginning.

See ORGANIZATION.

⑭ The graphic on the next page is far more dramatic and emphatic than the text description.

2.2.1 Flight Control and Handling

⑩ **Proven three-axis, aerodynamic-control steering provides inexperienced Army pilots with an ultralight reconnaissance aircraft that is exceptionally easy to fly.**

The Army requires an ultralight aircraft that can be easily flown by Army personnel for reconnaissance missions into areas not normally accessible by other means of transport.

The UQ601 has a proven design, enabling pilots with limited experience to confidently fly the ultralight aircraft. The easy-to-operate joystick provides three-axis aerodynamic control. The low stall speed and exceptional handling on rough terrain enable the UQ601 to land anywhere.

Figure 2.2-4 shows the UQ601 control systems.

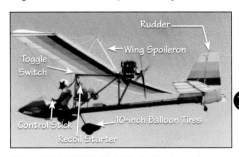

Figure 2.2-4. UQ601 Flight Control System. *The simplicity of flying the UQ601 is directly tied to the forgiving nature of the control and landing gear systems.*

⑪ Inexperienced pilots often have difficulty making coordinated turns flying aircraft that use weight shift as a primary means of steering. The UQ601 control system eliminates this problem entirely because the control stick operates the rudders on a V-tail and automatically coordinates the wing spoilers in turns.

⑫ Extensive studies have proven mechanical engine controls are much more reliable than electrical starters that depend on batteries. Our engine's recoil starter and toggle make the aircraft easy to switch from powered to glider flight.

The shock-absorbing tricycle landing gear and 10-inch balloon wheels allow safe, smooth landings on rough terrain.

⑬ Flight test data prove Aerodynamics' control system and landing gear are easier to learn and fly than any other aircraft on the market. The UQ601's design will fulfill the Army's need for a dependable reconnaissance aircraft.

2.2.2 Aerodynamic Stability

Aerodynamic's UQ601 spoileron control and positive stability free novice pilots to concentrate on their reconnaissance mission without adversely affecting the aircraft's trajectory.

Two tasks confront inexperienced pilots: they must simultaneously control the aircraft and perform reconnaissance. When pilots have to devote less attention to flying the aircraft, they can focus on their primary task—collecting vital information for the battlefield commander.

⑭ The UQ601 is the world's most easily piloted airplane. Extensive flight testing by the Glider Pilots' Association, an independent industry organization, has revealed no unrecoverable pilot error. Any pilot can release the controls for a complete altitude recovery within seconds. Able to fly itself in a straight line due to its inherent positive stability, the UQ601 requires no positive action by the pilot to recover from an erroneously steep dive or too tightly banked turn. Figure 2.2-5 demonstrates this ease of recovery.

AERODYNAMICS
CORPORATION

–3–

See GRAPHICS.

⑮ While technically accurate, the poor use of scale actually deemphasizes the glide capability of the aircraft. The benefit of a superior glide capability is minimized. All of the ultralights look like they would *glide like a rock.*

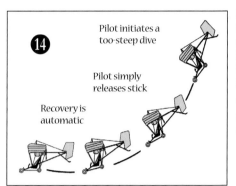

Figure 2.2-5. Positive Stability. *The UQ601's positive stability allows the novice pilot to regain complete control by simply releasing the stick.*

Unlike ultralight aircraft that control bearing through pilot weight shift, spoilerons provide a simple attitude control mechanism that in no way restricts the pilot's freedom of movement. Once pilots are satisfied with their bearing, they have both hands available for taking pictures or accomplishing whatever else the battlefield situation may require.

The UQ601's positive stability and spoileron control give the Army a mistake-proof aircraft that frees the soldier to focus on the reconnaissance mission.

2.2.3 Glider Capability

The UQ601's superior unpowered flight characteristics significantly enhance reconnaissance time by providing the pilot the highest glide ratio and lowest sink rate available on the market today.

The Army needs a reconnaissance platform capable of efficient unpowered and powered flight. In many battlefield situations, engine use may be impractical or even impossible. While powered flight is certainly the primary mode of operation, mission success must not depend on the engine alone.

The UQ601 has the most favorable unpowered flight characteristics available to the Army. An 8:1 glide ratio and a sink rate of 400 feet per minute maximize the pilot's chances of successful mission completion.

Figure 2.2-6 demonstrates the extended range the 8:1 glide ratio affords the pilot. Another benefit is the absolute stealth mode, in which the pilot kills the engine for complete silence. The excellent gliding ability of the UQ601 makes this a viable option for the newly trained pilot.

The UQ601's dual function as a glider and a powered craft will maximize the Army's chances of mission success and greatly expand pilots' in-flight task options.

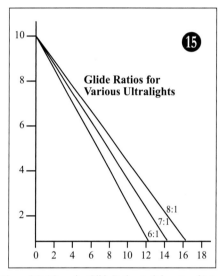

Figure 2.2-6 Superior Glide Ratio. *A glide ratio of 8:1 allows the UQ601 to have higher mission versatility.*

-4-

16 The labels in the graphic effectively use familiar, relative noise-level comparisons.

17 Substantiation is more credible when taken from independent sources.

See RELEVANT EXPERIENCE/PAST PERFORMANCE.

2.2.4 Noise Muffling

Aerodynamics' patented WhisperMuff™ noise suppressor effectively reduces sound emissions to less than 20 decibels, for virtually noise-free reconnaissance.

The Army requires an ultralight aircraft that can fly quietly and safely into enemy territory and effectively gather and communicate reconnaissance information. This requires engine noise muffling that maximizes pilot protection and mission effectiveness.

As figure 2.2-7 demonstrates, the UQ601's noise muffling can greatly decrease the aircraft's vulnerability as an undetectable reconnaissance platform.

Because the WhisperMuff ™ reduces sound emissions to less than 20 db, the UQ601 offers radio communications unhindered by engine noise. Rear-mounted engines sometimes allow adequate radio communication, but when unmuffled, compromise the aircraft's function as an undetected reconnaissance vehicle. The muffled UQ601 provides greater pilot and aircraft survivability while making communications simple and clear.

In a recent test by *Aviation Magazine*, our UQ601 was rated first in minimizing pilot fatigue. Testers cited our WhisperMuff™ as having the lowest noise emission of **17** any ultralight they had tested.

As a result of Aerodynamics' WhisperMuff™ noise suppressor, the Army will have unmatched surveillance capabilities and be able to conduct unhindered reconnaissance missions effectively with enhanced pilot safety.

16

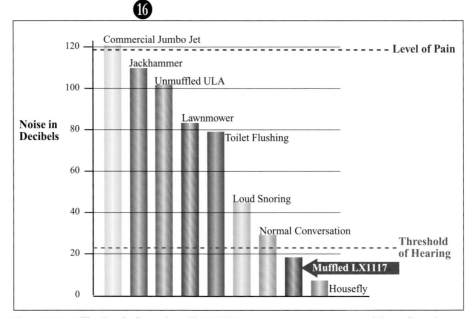

Figure 2.2-7. Muffling Results Comparison. *The UQ601's superior noise suppressing capabilities effectively eliminate engine noise, enhancing reconnaissance effectiveness.*

–5–

(18) The writer is offsetting a weakness in landing roll against a strength in landing safely over rougher terrain.

See PROPOSAL STRATEGY.

(19) Again, the writer offsets a weakness against a strength.

See PROPOSAL STRATEGY.

(20) The section closes with a summary of key benefits and features—a best practice. However, closing summaries are relatively less effective in formally evaluated and scored proposals. Evaluators usually stop reading after they find the answer to each question.

See ORGANIZATION.

2.2.5 Adaptability

Shock-absorbing landing gear and tires, short takeoff and landing distances, and a wide range of operating conditions enable the UQ601 to provide reconnaissance capabilities in a variety of battlefield scenarios.

The Army needs a small-unit, low-level, hard-to-detect reconnaissance aircraft adaptable to a variety of restrictive terrains. The aircraft must be reliable, easy to fly, and readily maintained far from support bases.

The UQ601 is a proven, reliable ultralight aircraft that supports this adaptability requirement. The short takeoff run and landing roll, shock-absorbing tricycle landing gear, and balloon tires ensure exceptional ground-handling capabilities.

(18) Although the 200-foot landing roll exceeds the Army specification of 150 feet, Aerodynamic's investigations indicate that the ability of the UQ601 balloon tires to handle rough terrain means a larger variety of available landing sites.

Figure 2.2-8 shows that the UQ601's range of 125 miles and flight times of over 6 hours can provide Army commanders with more battlefield information than most ultralights with ranges of 80 to 100 miles and flight times of 2 to 3 hours.

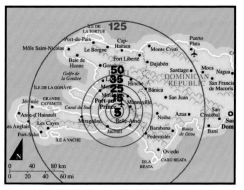

Figure 2.2-8. UQ601 Range. *The UQ601 permits surveillance of more territory due to its extended 125-mile range.*

The Aerodynamic UQ601 has an operational ceiling of 10,000 feet, which is high enough for reconnaissance flights in hilly terrain, but not so high as to endanger the pilot from cold or oxygen deprivation. A humidity range of 0 to 100 percent and an operating temperature range of 0 to 100°F mean the Army can deploy the UQ601 in arctic as well as tropical climates.

(19) The WhisperMuff™ noise reduction system reduces cooling airflow to the engine. This feature maintains the upper temperature range of 100°F, which falls 20°F short of the Army specification (120°F). A trade study conducted by Aerodynamics' test facility showed that the reduction in detectable noise facilitated by the WhisperMuff™ provided more operational capability than the additional 20°F operating range, a relatively rare occurrence.

The UQ601 meets or exceeds all essential Army requirements for small unit reconnaissance aircraft. Based on glide ratio, excellent range, quiet muffled operations, and quick assembly time, the Army can count on an aircraft that offers the following combinations of features and benefits:

(20)
- Reduces detectability for safer operations
- Maximizes time over the reconnaissance target
- Adapts quickly to diverse mission requirements
- Offers a greater range, so fewer missions are required

Other factors, such as control and handling, stability, glider capability, and noise muffling, influence the aircraft's design. Because military operations are global, the aircraft must be readily adaptable to a variety of operating environments.

AERODYNAMICS
CORPORATION

–6–

❶ The customer's logo and colors are placed in the upper-left corner of the page to increase customer focus.

See CUSTOMER FOCUS, *and* PAGE AND DOCUMENT DESIGN.

❷ The customer's RFP name is placed in the header of every page.

See PAGE AND DOCUMENT DESIGN.

❸ The seller's logo and name are placed in the footer.

See CUSTOMER FOCUS, *and* PAGE AND DOCUMENT DESIGN.

❹ A high-level slogan supporting the win theme or slogan was placed in the footer. This slogan emphasizes the seller's primary discriminator and demonstrates the seller's understanding of the customer's hot button issue.

See PROPOSAL STRATEGY *and* THEME STATEMENTS.

❺ The RFP was a casually written five-page letter. The numbering system could not be matched. Requirements were extracted from the RFP and posted in an italic font in the left margin adjacent to the response. This is the only place where the numbering systems match.

See COMPLIANCE AND RESPONSIVENESS, OUTLINING, *and* PAGE AND DOCUMENT DESIGN.

❻ The theme statement links a benefit and a discriminator to the individual proposed.

See THEME STATEMENTS *and* DISCRIMINATORS.

❼ The intentional bolding of key words was designed to attract anyone who scanned the proposal and to make the answer easy to find.

See PAGE AND DOCUMENT DESIGN.

❽ Team roles are listed in the same order as in the RFP.

See COMPLIANCE AND RESPONSIVENESS.

---

❶  **❷** PRE-QUALIFICATION OF STRATEGIC ALLIANCE PARTNERS
Request for Proposal

❺

2. Scope of Work: Identify single company-wide point of contact for all BuzzKola inquiries

2. Project Team

❻ **BuzzKola can streamline project planning by selecting Mr. Lars Nielson of Svensco as your single point of contact for strategic partners with intimate local market knowledge.**

❼ To streamline project planning, Svensco is proposing a single point of contact and a focus on only those countries where we offer unique added value due to our **intimate understanding of the local construction environment.**

Our proposed single point of contact is Mr. Lars Nielson to be located in Sweden or another location of BuzzKola's choice. Mr. Nielson would provide direct support and coordination through the most knowledgeable local support team, whether it is a Svensco company or another BuzzKola strategic partner.

The Svensco development team follows: **❽**

Propose project teams (organization and named individuals) for:
- *Capacity calculations*
- *Conceptual design, schedule, and cost estimate*
- *Site selection*
- *Basic design package*
- *Capital project request*
- *Construction tender package evaluation*
- *Equipment tender package and evaluation*

Team Leader	**❾ Lars Nielson, VP Project Management** Civil Engineer, knowledgeable in 5 languages, 16 years construction process experience—includes Eastern Europe, Middle East, and Russia
Capacity Calculations	**Earl Bouchard, Senior Process Engineer** **❿** Chemical Engineer, 20+ years experience in design and project management—includes the U.S., Puerto Rico, Middle East, Scotland, and South America
Conceptual Design, Schedule, Cost Estimate	**Lars Nielson, Senior Project Manager**
Site Selection	**Nikola Niemi, Project Manager, NIS (Newly Independent States)** Civil Engineer M. Sc. (BS-Econ. and M.S. Operation Mgmt.), knowledgeable in 4 languages, 18 years experience in construction—includes Finland, Russia, and the Middle East
Basic Design Package	**Randall W. Pincher, Design Architect** Architect, knowledgeable in new and renovation process plants facilities, 27 years project experience—includes the U.S., Puerto Rico, and Poland
Capital Project Request	**Dennis MacMahon, Marketing Manager, NIS** Accountant, 17 years experience in construction business and management reporting, 6 years dedicated to NIS
Construction Tender	**Nikola Niemi, Project Manager, NIS**
Package and Evaluation	**Donald Dahlstrom, Operations Manager** Civil Engineer, 20+ years experience in construction project management—including Denmark, Algeria, Tanzania, and Sweden; knowledgeable in 3 languages
Equipment Tender	**Chris Cederwold, Purchasing Manager** Package Evaluation Civil engineer; 30+ years international purchasing experience; Quality Assurance courses & ANSI/ASME certified lead auditor

❸ **❋ SVENSCO**

1

❹ *Local simplicity in a complex world*

See PAGE AND DOCUMENT
DESIGN.

8 Team roles are listed in the same order as in the RFP.

See COMPLIANCE AND
RESPONSIVENESS.

9 To minimize the space required, only relevant information on each person was included in a table format instead of prose. Because some numbers are 10 or above, all numbers are shown as numerals rather than spelled out.

See GRAPHICS.

10 When an individual filled more than one role, the information was not repeated.

11 The theme statement answers the top-level requirement.

See QUESTION/RESPONSE
PROPOSALS.

12 This is the entire RFP design requirement.

13 The informal table of contents roughly matches the RFP excerpt. The subsection headings are previewed along with a short summary sentence.

See COMPLIANCE AND
RESPONSIVENESS.

14 The actual subheading matches the introduction precisely.

See ORGANIZATION.

15 Wherever possible, figures were used to shorten proposal preparation time and emphasize compliance. Figures were easier and faster to prepare due to the diverse international background of the contributors. *(Figure 3-1 is not included here.)*

See GRAPHICS.

BUZZKOLA

PRE-QUALIFICATION OF STRATEGIC ALLIANCE PARTNERS
Request for Proposal

3. Design Approach

11 **An easy-to-use streamlined project planning package will be tailored by Svensco with other strategic partners to develop country-specific estimates within 2 to 5 days.**

Using the design parameters established in the project orientation workshops and proven conceptual design methods, Svensco will team with the other strategic partners selected by BuzzKola to choose a common design package and tailor it for BuzzKola facilities. We have used and tailored different design packages and think the choice should be based on the best fit for all of BuzzKola's partners.

12 *Based on the workshop and your own expertise, you would be required to develop conceptual design methods and (software) tools to turn around typical project inquiries in 2-5 working days for the following warehouse/distribution centers and production plant facilities.*

Our approach to develop the Conceptual Design Package is described in the following order:

3.1 **Conceptual Design Methods**—Project planning accuracy depends on a proven design method and is the basis to structure the project planning package.

13 3.2 **Software and Tools**—A standard package will be tailored for BuzzKola facilities.

3.3 **Schedule**—Describes the tasks anticipated with the minimum and maximum times required to meet the 2- to 5-day target.

3.4 **Design Input and Design Output**—Reviews the level of detail anticipated and how Svensco will compensate if the detail is not available.

14 ### 3.1 Conceptual Design Methods

The accuracy of each design package requires a sound conceptual design process that incorporates the design parameters established in the project orientation workshops. For example, design parameters are used to calculate plant capacity and expansion options from sales volume projections.

15 The *Global Project Delivery Flowchart*, Figure 3-1, the large foldout on the following page, shows the basic process envisioned to estimate and schedule capital projects. To improve estimating accuracy, we pre-define standard steps to adjust for country-specific conditions and variables for each project.

During the *Programming Phase*, some of the variables in the development process include land rights and leases, taxation issues, laws, custom duties, logistic issues, technical-economical study documentation, local construction regulations, local resources, and other unique requirements.

Following a consistent conceptual design process enables Svensco to produce a credible Conceptual Design Package in the 2- to 5-working day range required. . . .

. . .
. . .
. . .

Sections 3.2 through 3.4 were omitted here for brevity.

SVENSCO

Local simplicity in a complex world

2

⓰ This is the entire quoted RFP requirement.

⓱ This preview also summarizes the proposed approach.

See ORGANIZATION.

⓲ The heading matches the introduction.

See ORGANIZATION.

⓳ Success stories are inserted to support claims made in the text.

See RELEVANT EXPERIENCE/PAST PERFORMANCE.

⓴ Figures are used to provide most of the details.

See GRAPHICS.

 BUZZKOLA

PRE-QUALIFICATION OF STRATEGIC ALLIANCE PARTNERS
Request for Proposal

⓰ *Based on the successful completion of the basic design package portion of the prequalification exercise, we will ask you to put together the necessary tools and procedures such that you would be in a position to develop a detailed proposal in the form of a fixed price, turnkey contract for the complete supply of the facility to the agreed schedule.*

4. Turnkey Bid Package

BuzzKola's partners will get a detailed turnkey bid package within 4 weeks based on the conceptual design and modifications using our detailed knowledge of local market conditions.

On confirmation from BuzzKola that the conceptual design package has been completed successfully, we will begin developing the turnkey bid package. In this section, we describe the contents of the turnkey bid package and detail our approach to develop a package that meets BuzzKola's requirements to issue the proposal within 4 weeks.

Our approach to develop the turnkey bid package is described in the following order:

⓱
4.1   Content of the Turnkey Bid Package and Development Tasks
4.2   Additional local input—required to enhance the Conceptual Design Package to meet the local requirements
4.3   Further Value-Added Benefits
4.4   Responsibility and Risk Sharing—will depend on location and completion time required
4.5   Our Approach to Level 2 Countries
4.6   Restrictions and Limitations

⓲ ### 4.1 Content of the Turnkey Bid Package and Development Tasks

Our planning of the Turnkey Bid Package begins with a clear definition of the end product, defining the output or contents of the package. We will then review the input that we would have for each output item and determine what activities we would have to complete. These activities will become our development tasks.

Successful Turnkey Project in a Developing Market. Svensco completed this beverage plant on a turnkey basis, on time and on budget due to careful planning.

⓴ Outputs, inputs, and activities are shown in figure 4-1. The schedule for the development tasks is shown in figure 4-2.

The goal of the development tasks is to enable BuzzKola's strategic partner to prepare a detailed proposal with a firm fixed level of detail for any selected country and location in the world. We plan to have each relevant Svensco location prepare a start-up plan and materials to enable them to meet your 4-week requirement.

Our approach leverages our local knowledge and then specifically relates it to the BuzzKola facilities requirements to save both time and money to the benefit of all parties. As soon as the details are presented from the Project Orientation Workshop, our local project teams will begin the development tasks required for execution of a BuzzKola facility. The development tasks are identified in figure 4-3.

 **❋ SVENSCO**

3

Local simplicity in a complex world

RFP text that did not include requirements was not quoted in the proposal.

See COMPLIANCE AND RESPONSIVENESS.

 This detailed figure is designed to demonstrate the seller's detailed knowledge and to focus on the proposed project. Too many similar proposals describe generic approaches.

See GRAPHICS *and* PROPOSAL STRATEGY.

 The action caption explains the figure and also directs the reader to the associated schedule *(omitted here for brevity).*

See ACTION CAPTIONS.

PRE-QUALIFICATION OF STRATEGIC ALLIANCE PARTNERS
Request for Proposal

 Please describe, together with an activity listing and schedule, your approach to the . . . development tasks.

OUTPUT	INPUT	ACTIVITY
Project Description	Scope of Work, estimate and documentation summary	Present proposal
Price	All information mentioned below	Estimate
Conditions of Contract	Scope of Work	Legal input
Project Organization chart	Scope of Work	Produce Project Organization chart and Technical Descriptions
Master Schedule (Gantt chart)	Start-up date by BuzzKola	Planning
Quality Assurance Plan	Quality Plan form	Adjust Plan to project
General		
• Project Data	Basic Design Package	
• Scope of Work	Basic Design Package	Add local specific items
• Technical Specification	Basic Design Package	Add local specific items
• Room Equipment Specification	Basic Design Package	Add local specific items
• Room Finishing List	Basic Design Package	Add local specific items
• Electrical installations	Basic Design Package	Add local specific items
• Mechanical installations	Basic Design Package	Add local specific items
• Water Quality report	Water Quality Survey Form	Measures to analyze the water quality
Beverage Plant		
• Capacity Calculation Report	BuzzKola input	Capacity Calculations
• Plant Specification	Plant Manufacturer input	Proposal from plant mfging
• Equipment list	Plant Manufacturer input	Proposal from plant mfging
• Utility requirements	Plant Manufacturer input	Proposal from plant mfging
Warehouse		
• Sales Volume Report	BuzzKola input	List of Product type
• Material Flow/Logistics Report	Sales Volume Report	Logistics Analysis
• Equipment List	Logistics report	Market Survey

 Figure 4-1. Contents of the Turnkey Bid Package. *The content of the Turnkey Bid Package is shown together with required input and the activities required to carry out to be able to reach the final result. A schedule showing the sequence of the activities is shown in figure 4-2.*

. . . .

Sections 4.2 through 4.6 were omitted here for brevity.

4

Local simplicity in a complex world

㉔ The single-sentence summary was designed to tie together the diverse items requested in the RFP.

See QUESTION/RESPONSE PROPOSALS.

㉕ Generally limit appendices to requested material. The mention of the *tab* suggests a helpful tone.

See APPENDICES.

㉖ Personnel breakdowns are always difficult. The summary text places a positive spin on overlapping capabilities. The tabular presentation is compact and easy to read.

See GRAPHICS *and* PROPOSAL STRATEGY.

㉗ Success stories are inserted as available and as space permits. Graphics can be placed in either the text or left margin areas. While action captions are placed below most graphics, space restrictions can force alternative placements. Note the structural *success story* organization.

See PAGE AND DOCUMENT DESIGN *and* RELEVANT EXPERIENCE/PAST PERFORMANCE.

BUZZKOLA

5. Backup Data Requirement

㉔ The following backup data supplied to BuzzKola is focused on substantiating Svensco's intimate knowledge of specific local markets and our commitment to a long-term BuzzKola—Svensco partnership.

5.1 Svensco Annual Reports

Annual Reports for last 3 years

㉕ Svensco annual reports for 1998, 1999, and 2000 are included after the *Corporate Reports* tab.

㉖ ### 5.2 Personnel Breakdown

The breakdown of Svensco personnel is shown below. Because of the rapid changes in our business and numerous client projects, employees frequently move between Svensco companies and countries.

Personnel breakdown (numbers excluding support staff). Give total and indicate how many have experience with:
i. manufacturing or warehousing facilities
ii. beverage industry
iii. BuzzKola

Indicate experience in:
• Project Management
• Engineering
• Procurement
• Site supervision

Our policy is to locate and assign the most qualified individual available.

Some of the classifications also overlap. Engineers often serve as project managers or supervise sites.

Svensco Worldwide

Discipline	Manufacturing or Warehouse	Beverage Industry	BuzzKola Facilities
Project Management	330	63	10
Engineer	952	295	6
Procurement	212	44	12
Site Supervision	623	114	8
Total Per Category	2,117	516	43
Total Technical Personnel Worldwide	**5,532**		

Figure 5-1. Beverage Storage and Distribution Center. *Scandia Beverage needed an energy-efficient distribution center to support European markets. Scandia selected Svensco as . . . . . . best value approach. Svensco completed a large underground storage, distribution center, and warehouse in Sweden on time and within budget.*

✳SVENSCO

Local simplicity in a complex world

5

---

① Open a major section with a theme statement, followed by a short section summary to provide perspective for evaluators that primarily are forced to focus on details.

See QUESTION/RESPONSE PROPOSALS.

② This sentence is an introduction designed to reassure evaluators that all questions are answered in the order listed in the bid request.

See QUESTION/RESPONSE PROPOSALS.

③ Each bid request question is repeated in the left margin adjacent to the bidder's answer.

④ Each question is answered directly in the first sentence. All additional text supports or substantiates the initial answer. Placing the answer in bolded text makes the answer easier to spot.

See PAGE AND DOCUMENT DESIGN *and* QUESTION/RESPONSE PROPOSALS.

Proposal to Provide Database Software Development Services for GIBM, Inc.

4.0 SOFTWARE MAINTENANCE

① ISI offers GIBM comprehensive, trouble-free software maintenance at no additional cost for 10 years following software installation.

ISI's Client Services Organization is widely acknowledged as one of the finest service organizations in the information services industry. We provide 24-hour-a-day, 7-day-per-week support and are able to resolve most problems within 1.57 hours. The software maintenance plan we offer meets all of GIBM's needs in a convenient, low-cost manner.

② Below are our responses to your specific questions regarding software maintenance: **④**

③

1. Is software maintenance available?

1. Yes. ISI provides regular software maintenance on all system software used by the Master Control system.

2. If yes, is the price included in the price of the software?

2. Yes. Software maintenance is included in the price of the software. GIBM would incur NO additional costs for maintenance.

3. If priced separately, what is the price and how is it paid?

3. Maintenance costs are not priced separately.

4. How long will the vendor maintain the system?

4. ISI will maintain the system at no cost for 10 years following installation. Following the 10-year maintenance period, GIBM can purchase an ongoing maintenance contract from ISI. Currently, such a contract costs $500/day on a time-and-materials basis.

5. Can a user maintain the software?

5. Yes. Under initial guidance from ISI software engineers and maintenance personnel, GIBM personnel can develop the expertise necessary to maintain system software and install periodic upgrades.

6. How does a user receive a new version of release of the product to which he is licensed?

6. Uncustomized system software is upgraded at least once annually. New software versions or releases are announced 6 to 8 weeks before becoming available. During that period, users can request upgrading for a nominal installation fee. Customized software is upgraded 4 to 12 weeks following release of upgraded uncustomized software. Costs depend on the amount of upgrading and the extent of customization. Upgrading is priced on a case-by-case basis.

7. How long is a user covered by a maintenance contract after a new release/version is available if he does not upgrade?

7. Users are covered by the original maintenance contract for 10 years following installation if software is not upgraded. Each software upgrade extends the maintenance contract to 10 years following installation of the upgrade.

I·S·I Information Systems, Inc. • 8700 South State Street • St. Louis, MO 33701 • 573.222.2222 • 573.222.4747 (fax) • www.infosys.com

---

Document 13 used left-justified text for callouts while right-justified text is used here. Left-justified text is easier to read; however, right-justified text is more easily associated visually with the response. Select a preferred style and be consistent in the same bid.

Index